Nationhood, Providence, and Witness

Nationhood, Providence, and Witness

Israel in Protestant Theology and Social Theory

Carys Moseley

CASCADE *Books* · Eugene, Oregon

NATIONHOOD, PROVIDENCE, AND WITNESS
Israel in Protestant Theology and Social Theory

Cascade Books
An Imprint of Wipf and Stock Publishers
199 W. 8th Ave., Suite 3
Eugene, OR 97401

www.wipfandstock.com

ISBN 13: 978-1-61097-942-9

Cataloguing-in-Publication Data

Moseley, Carys

    Nationhood, providence, and witness : Israel in Protestant theology and social theory / Carys Moseley

    xxxiv + 268 p. ; 23 cm. Including bibliographical references and indexes

    ISBN 13: 978-1-61097-942-9

    1. Church and state—Israel. 2. Israel (Christian theology). 3. Christianity and politics. 4. Niebuhr, Reinhold, 1892–1971. 5. Milbank, John. 6. Williams, Rowan, 1950–. 7. Barth, Karl, 1886–1968.

BR115 C235 2013

Contents

Preface

THE QUESTION OF THE recognition of nations as such, whether or not they have states of their own, is one that has been important in the modern era, and which is associated with forms of nationalism. As such it has been understood to belong to a variety of general theories of political ethics. Rarely has the challenge of recognition been considered within the challenge of the recognition of the modern State of Israel, and of the Jews as a distinct national group. Naturally, there are chronological reasons for this—the State of Israel was founded in 1948, so for most of its history Christian theologians and ethicists could not have considered recognition of nations as part of the set of arguments that arise when considering the State of Israel. It is well-known that many Christian discourses on nationalism have been indebted hermeneutically to re-readings and reinterpretations of the history of Israel in the Old Testament. Such discourses at their best tend to mix aspects of what we would now call liberation theologies with more traditional, deontological ethics and prophetic discourses warning the people of divine judgment, while encouraging them to accept divine grace and mercy for corporate national sins. This mixture has appealed especially to nations that have been subordinated and rendered stateless by other, imperialistic nations. The pairing of Israel and Babylon has been reconfigured across world history many times. In theological terms, it is highly significant that it was Israel that was the chosen nation, a small nation, and one that did not even begin with a state of its own, but issued from a Sumerian commanded to become a nomadic wanderer, at least for a season. Christian theologians and ethicists have often found it difficult to balance these different aspects of biblical discourse on the nation of Israel and, in practice, many have been deeply suspicious of what the Canadian Catholic philosopher Charles Taylor calls the politics of recognition. There is all too often an underlying sense that if Christians who are concerned for a subordinated nation demand proper recognition as nations—challenging the self-designation of the state to which they belong as a "nation-state"—that the bonds of trust within that state will break down, and serious conflict will escalate to unmanageable proportions. The parallels between the cry for recognition by members of subordinate nations and the struggle for recognition in a direct, state formation, as with the history of Israel, is one that often gets neglected by modern English-speaking theologians and ethicists these days. Undoubtedly this is because debates about the State of Israel tend to be stuck around debates about US foreign policy and Israel's relation to the Palestinians. This book is partly an attempt to get beyond this perspective by confronting readers with the necessity of recognition of Israel as part of the Christian necessity for recognition of *all* nations. It does so by pulling the rug from beneath the debates about the USA to look at the British, and therefore European, origins of imperialist discourses on nationhood that tend to put a Gentile imperial nation in the place of Israel in world history. Britain is a very good case to look at for two reasons. First, Britain's was the last empire to rule the Holy Land before 1948. This contrasts with the fact that the USA has never actually governed the Holy Land as part of a territorial empire. Second, the British Empire was the largest empire in world history, and it is precisely at the time of its withdrawal from British Mandate Palestine that it started to disintegrate. Most historians ignore this, because they don't think in Christian terms about the Holy Land being at the center of the world map. The important question then is, when did the British Empire start? I deconstruct this question by looking to its core—English imperialism within the British isles. This leads me back to the English conquest of Wales, which is the nation into which I was born. Thus I inhabit a (partial) perspective within the argument I unfold, looking to the universal horizon provided by the existence of the State of Israel as part of divine providence. This kind of exercise is an important one for the very integrity of Christian theology and ethics precisely because of its very nature; it is best conducted when carried out by as many people from as many countries as possible. It could just as well be conducted by someone uncovering the history of discourses around Ireland, Scotland, Native Americans, or African slaves and their descendants, especially in the West. These connections have, from time to time, been made by historians and cultural theorists, but theologians and ethicists, especially in state institutions, have not really made them.

That said, this book did not only start as a project about the interrelationship of recognition of nations and providence. The questions that ultimately led me to write it were also linked to missiology. There is a popular genre of Christian missionary preaching that tells its audience the reason for the incarnation as follows: God created the world, then human beings turned away from him. Therefore, God formed a people, a nation—Israel—so that they might be faithful to him and be an example of righteousness to the rest of the world. They failed in this task, so God sent his Son to become a man and redeem human beings from their sinful and failure-prone tendencies. This story is told in various ways that are problematic. The problem that came to interest me was that it seemed to imply God formed a nation only to permanently discard it when its people did not live up to his standards. In came the church instead. Preachers who make this argument for the incarnation rarely give evidence of realizing that the very same logic they use to argue that God has discarded the nation of Israel for good could be used to justify discarding the Christian church for good, because it too has such a checkered history. I also began to notice how this kind of preaching effectively means that nations are not taken seriously as part of the divine plan for world history. This struck me as very odd because in the Bible, God is said to have placed people in nations since the time of the sons of Noah. On the ethical side, one worries that the story gave excuses for privatizing the scope of Christian ethics; for limiting it to the church and individuals' lives. The point, it seems, was to be saved *out of* the life-world of nations. Contemporary popular discussions in the West of how Christian should relate to life outside the church never get to this point. They talk about all kinds of other issues—culture, the workplace, etc.—and break down the issues by ethical topic or sphere of life, but never according recognition of the largest population unit permitted in the Bible apart from the church, namely nationhood. Something somewhere has gone very wrong with modern Western Christian ethics, at least in the English-speaking world. Perhaps this is the effect of its being written in English, the language of modern political and cultural imperialism. It is most certainly the effect of decades of chanting the mantra "we dislike nationalism," and of projecting all things to do with nationalism dishonestly onto Nazi Germany, while invoking Karl Barth's work for the confessing church in the process. Most theologians and ethicists who think like this—and there are a lot of them around—are not familiar enough with Barth's writing on nationhood. I have covered that in depth in another book—*Nations and Nationalism in the Theology of Karl Barth* (Oxford University Press, 2013). In the present book, I shall be embarking upon a more adventurous constructive project, albeit one that proceeds via comparative analysis of select theologians and social theorists dealing with both the State of Israel and with Wales and England in relation to Britain. Of course, some readers won't like it. One-nationism dies hard in Britain, especially in troubled times. There are many reasons for this tendency, which I don't explore in this book for reasons of space, as well as because it would take me into the territories of law and constitution, which, while important, wouldn't essentially undo my argument. My hope is that readers may have enough patience with my writing—which, I realize, proceeds down rather intricately woven paths of analytic criticism of several thinkers—to agree that the challenges of recognition lie deeply embedded in broader debates handled in the book. Indeed, recognition is a universal issue, and has become very important in the world post-1948 with the formation of the United Nations, the decline of colonialism, the surge in the number of independent states, anti-racist campaigns, the rise of indigenous people's movements and movements for national and ethnic minorities and linguistic rights. Recognition is in reality a basic requirement of Christian theology and ethics, but many in these disciplines and fields behave as if this were not the case. I live for the day when nobody will be able to be taken seriously, let alone imagine that they could be uttering theological wisdom, when they try to tell me "Wales is not a nation." Until then, what needs to be said is that such refusal of recognition fundamentally goes against the grain of the biblical witness and good missiology and Christian ethics. It will ensure that those who speak in this manner will have no capacity for being taken seriously by any other peoples or stateless minority nations that have endured imperialism and colonialism down the centuries.

Acknowledgments

Bringing this book into being has been a labor stretching over nearly four years of research and writing on my part, though having roots going further back. I held a postdoctoral research fellowship in the subject area of theology and ethics in the School of Divinity, Edinburgh University, between September 2008 and September 2011, funded by the British Academy. This book is the completion of the research and writing project for which I had successfully gained this funding, and so I must express my gratitude to the British Academy for awarding me funding, for all my colleagues in the School of Divinity for their support and encouragement over that time. In particular, thanks are due to Professor John McDowell and Professor David Fergusson for being, successively, my academic mentors during that time, to Professor Larry Hurtado and Professor Stewart Jay Brown as successive heads of school for being supportive line managers, and Professor Jolyon Mitchell for suggesting that I apply for research funding in the first place. The support and library staff of the School of Divinity were unfailingly helpful with the practicalities of the project. Regarding the contents of the book, most of chapters 2 and 5 have previously appeared in peer-reviewed academic journals, though the material has been lightly reworked and supplemented here. I thank Ruth Langer, editor of *Studies in Christian-Jewish Relations*, for permission to reproduce the material from the article in chapter 2. I also thank Patrick Madigan, editor of the *Heythrop Journal*, for permission to reproduce the material from the article in chapter 5. I must also extend my gratitude to the anonymous peer reviewers who gave constructive criticism on these pieces. Regarding questions ranging across the book's subject-matter, whether personally, by email, or at conferences where I presented papers discussing work in progress, I am grateful to conversations and exchanges with David Fergusson, Guido De Graaff, Richard Harvey, Mark Kinzer, Dave Leal, John McDowell, Sophia Magallanes,

Acknowledgments

Esther D. Reed, Stephen Spector, Ruth Tolstoy, David W. Torrance, James Walters, Stephen H. Webb, Berndt Wannenwetsch.

I must also extend my gratitude to Robin Parry, my editor at Cascade Books, for his enthusiasm and support for this project from the beginning, and to all the staff at Cascade for handling the production process. Last, but not least, I must thank my parents for their unfailing support throughout this project. It should go without saying that any errors, omissions, or infelicities outstanding in the text are due to me.

Abbreviations

ASCE	*Annual of the Society for Christian Ethics*
BJS	*British Journal of Sociology*
CC	*Christian Century*
CD	*Church Dogmatics.* Karl Barth. Translated by G. T. Thomson et al. Edinburgh: T. & T. Clark, 1936–1977.
HGS	*Holocaust and Genocide Studies*
JAAR	*Journal of the American Academy of Religion*
JAS	*Journal of American Studies*
JEH	*Journal of Ecclesiastical History*
JES	*Journal of Ecumenical Studies*
JIH	*Journal of Israeli History*
JLR	*Journal of Law and Religion*
JMH	*Journal of Medieval History*
JRE	*Journal of Religious Ethics*
MES	*Middle Eastern Studies*
MQR	*Mennonite Quarterly Review*
NN	*Nations and Nationalism*
PT	*Political Theology*
RHR	*Revue de l'histoire des religions*
RRT	*Reviews in Religion and Theology*
SCE	*Studies in Christian Ethics*
SJT	*Scottish Journal of Theology*
SZ	*Studies in Zionism*
TRHS	*Transactions of the Royal Historical Society*
WACR	*Women: A Cultural Review*

Introduction

NATIONHOOD AND NATIONS LIE at the very heart of the biblical meta-narrative that forms the framework for Christian theology, with the one nation of Israel represented as chosen by God to further his purpose of redemption for the whole world. At the same time, the biblical canon gives us a view of history that denies the division of the world into nations in the beginning and in its consummation. Nations belong to the time "in between." Here surely lies one of the reasons why the topic of nationhood has proven so difficult for theologians. Recognition of nations is an issue that has attracted both positive support and vicious attacks in the modern period. At the heart of this book is a subtle distinction between *nation* and *state*. This distinction lies at the heart of serious discussion of nationhood and nationalism. This book is neither simply "for" nor "against" something called "nationalism." The reason why is very straightforward—there is no one single type of nationalism. It has proven extremely difficult to produce an overarching theory of nationalism, as the liveliness of the field of nationalism studies shows. Many theologians, unfortunately, seem slow to acknowledge this reality, preferring to hide behind generalizations against "nationalism." The second reason why it isn't possible simply to be for or against "nationalism" is that the discourse surrounding the term has moved in the twentieth century, especially since the Second World War, from being about independence to being about recognition. Of course, this is painting matters with a very broad brush indeed. Acknowledging this move on my part does not mean advocating ignoring the political realities. Since the formation of the United Nations and the process of the dismantling of the European empires across the world, more sovereign states ("nation-states") have come into being than at any other time in history. The scholar of nationalism Walker Connor has surveyed the global data and concluded, wisely, that no more than 10 percent of all states in the world can be classified as true nation-states (i.e., states where the overwhelming majority of the population comes from one nation).[1] It is this empirical reality—that most states encompass more than one group that could be historically conceived as nations—that has forced scholars and social and political theorists to face the reality that the idea of the "nation-state" is a modern myth insofar as it attempts to convey a cultural, linguistic, and ethnic homogeneity represented by the state's official name.

If we turn from the empirical realities to Scripture, we also soon discover a dazzlingly complex array of perspectives, and the history of Christianity furnishes plenty of examples of how these have been worked out. It would be easy for the theologian who is not one-sidedly hostile to nationalism to move simply to read the biblical prophets and eschatological texts as being anti-imperial, given that Babylon is the empire constantly opposed to the nation of Israel from Genesis (as Babel) to Revelation. Much historic Protestant exegesis stayed within this mold by recasting Babylon as the Roman Catholic Church and the Holy Roman Empire, later therefore as the Napoleonic project. The late modern example of this is the European Union, yet the undeniable opposition of a world of nations to a global empire is treated in ironic fashion in the Bible, for the Roman Empire is understood as the providential setting for the birth and spread of the Christian faith. Rome becomes a historic type of the "empire of Antichrist," thus furnishing generations of exegetes with material for discerning providential movements of history. The opposition in the New Testament, particularly in Revelation, is ultimately between two cities, not nations and imperialism. In these days of thoughtless anti-nationalism, it is important to recall this—the New Testament authors nowhere deny that the world will continue to be constituted by nations until the end of history. Rather, they affirm that it will be. John of Patmos speaks of the "ten kings" who will "make war" against the Lamb, at the same time attacking Babylon, "the city that rules the whole world." Both the world of nations and that of imperialism are ultimately opposed to the reign of Christ. There is no room here for singling out the idea of a world divided into nations as the unique perpetrator of evil in the world, which is the position that too many Christian scholars are apt to state or imply these days. In addition, as the discourse on Babylon is clearly typological in the sense of not referring to a historical Babylon at the time of writing, exegetes cannot assume a historic global empire is what would transpire at the end of history. Plenty have assumed history will end this way of course, including Abraham Kuyper, whom we will meet later in this book.

---

1. Connor, "Ethnic Nationalism," 91–97.

Defining anti-nationalism is rather difficult, because most people who use the term "nationalism" don't have a clear definition of it to begin with. In strict terms, anti-nationalism can be sub-divided into opposition to subordinated, defeated nations recovering political independence, and opposition to peoples who have never been politically independent becoming so. In more subtle terms, but just as important, there exists a variant of the former case, which constituted opposition to subordinated, defeated nations gaining some form of recognition that falls short of clear political independence (e.g., devolution within the United Kingdom, or regional autonomy within Spain). In the "hard" case, who is being opposed are the defeated breaking free from the rule of their conquerors. In the "soft" case, what is being opposed is the request that the subordinated gain a measure of recognition within the state from the dominant, often historically conquering, national group. Why some Christian theologians have been anti-nationalist is an important question. These theologians tend to stay at the safe level of general theory, rarely venturing out to investigate real case-studies. Most theologians do not really look at the literature in nationalism studies, and in my time as member of the Association for the Study of Ethnicity and Nationalism (ASEN), I have never met another theologian who has also been a member. Yet theologians continue to write a lot about nationalism polemically, though superficially. This is not a happy state of affairs. There are several features of the anti-nationalist discourse among Western Christian theologians. The first is the obvious elitism against popular beliefs. The second is the influence of Marxism on a number of Christian intellectuals who have influenced theologians. Many of these have been Roman Catholic, e.g., Charles Taylor and Alasdair MacIntyre, though John Milbank is Anglican. The third is the provenance of anti-nationalists from the imperial states, or those states that represented the European imperial and colonial projects. The fourth is a tendency for these kinds of thinkers to look back nostalgically to a past golden age of Christian thought, often the medieval period, "before nationalism," though they spell this out in terms of being "before modernity." In reality, what we may be seeing here is a rerun of some of the medieval conflicts between the religious orders, specifically the Dominicans against the Franciscans, the Cistercians and their offshoot the Knights Templar asserting their independence from both church and state, Thomists against Joachimists, and the Thomists, representing the Dominicans, acting as a latter-day intellectual Inquisition bringing to trial those deemed guilty of "heresy," though using philosophical criteria.

Concerning the Thomists opposing the Franciscans, this has contemporary relevance in that the Franciscans championed the notion of subjective natural rights (which were already found in the Decretalists a couple of centuries earlier, much to the dismay of their latter-day critics).[2] Notions of natural rights have often gone hand in hand with modern forms of nationalism. Milbank's attack on John Duns Scotus and William of Ockham fits here, though not quite from an orthodox Thomist angle, more from a "Cistercian" Templarist attempt to appropriate Thomas symbolically. At the same time there is an anti-Joachimist subtext at work. This book does not deal with philosophers, except in passing. To be precise, Taylor and MacIntyre, mentioned above, have dealt with nationalism tangentially, but never really written on nationhood. This is hardly surprising given their background in the neo-Marxist New Left of the postwar period.[3] In saying all this, it is vitally important to acknowledge the timing of these interventions. Anti-nationalism has emerged in the academy partly as a reaction to the Second World War. When viewed in this light, it is easy to see anti-nationalism as the right-thinking approach to political and social theory. At the same time, however, anti-nationalism among European intellectuals has undeniably arisen in reaction to the dismantling of the European empires and the independence of peoples formerly ruled by them, forming new "nation-states." There is undeniably a darker side to anti-nationalism among Western Christian thinkers in this respect that has not truly been acknowledged in scholarship. The most significant form of anti-nationalism in Western thought since the Second World War has undoubtedly been anti-Zionism.

The theological conflicts over recognition of the State of Israel since its foundation in 1948 are conflicts over nationhood as a theological and biblically rooted concept. To be precise, what so many Christian theologians are uneasy about is the idea that theology should be required to give a theological account of the survival of a nation that was deemed cursed and rejected by God for having mostly rejected the view that Jesus is the Messiah. Scattered abroad after the fall of the temple in A.D. 70 and the quashing of the revolt of Shimon Bar Kochba by the Romans in A.D. 135, Jews were divided between a remnant who remained in Palestine and a Diaspora spread across the world. Though the hope of returning home to the land of their ancestors was kept alive down the centuries by many Diaspora Jews, and many successive waves of Jews made their way back at

2. Tierney, *The Idea of Natural Rights.*
3. Smith, *Charles Taylor*, 13; MacIntyre, *Marxism.*

specific points in history, spurred on by apocalyptic prophecies, the practical plan of founding a Jewish state once again (as opposed to imagining how the law might work in a reconstituted Jewish state) belonged to the modern period, the period of modern European nationalisms. Paradoxically, this was also the time of the greatest secularization of Jewry as well as the greatest assimilation, particularly in Germany, the country where Jews would suffer the worst persecution in their history. Mention of Germany brings us to an interesting irony in the never-ending debates over Israel/Palestine, which is that Germany as a nation-state only came into being in 1870, and was split between 1949 and 1989. Yet the *idea* of Germany is a very old one, indeed its very name is found in Tacitus' *Germania*, as that of a people who successfully resisted Roman conquest.[4] Germany is a good example of a nation that pre-existed its state, as an idea formed by language and territory. As such, it is wholly unsurprising that the classic theory of nationalism, that a nation needs to acquire its own state in order to be truly recognized as a nation, should have been articulated by German theologians and philosophers in the Enlightenment, such as Herder and Hegel. The sentiment is sometimes made or implied that the only entities that deserve to be considered nations are those that have ancient roots. Conservative political theorists and theologians of a politically conservative bent often do this, decrying the anticipation of new nations in the form of ideas.[5] Yet by this logic, most of the world's nations shouldn't exist. If those advancing such an argument are Christians, by sheer logic they should only affirm as valid those nations also named in the Bible. Of course, none of them do this, which shows their position to be absurd and arbitrary. There is no objective cut-off point at which a new nation may not be formed. Anti-Zionists, people who oppose the existence of the Jewish State of Israel, sometimes do so on the basis that it was new and disruptive in the Middle East. They seem to ignore the newness of the German state, the Jews' foremost modern opponent. Israel as a state existed in antiquity, unlike Germany. By the same token, Zionists who oppose the possibility of a Palestinian state on the basis that Palestinian national consciousness is a relatively recent phenomenon are incoherent, for they never in practice oppose the existence of existing nation-states of recent provenance. In the same way, those who oppose the formation of a Palestinian nation-state on the basis that it is a nation that has never had a state, and that therefore

4. Tacitus, *Agricola and Germania*.

5. Lockwood O'Donovan, "A Timely Conversation," 377–94; O'Donovan, "A Response to Joan Lockwood O'Donovan," 395–97.

"Palestine" is only "an idea," are obviously inconsistent, for they in practice don't oppose the existing German state simply because before 1870 (i.e., very recently in history) there had never been a unified German state. That a nation has never had its own state is also not a reason that it should never have one in the future. Thus the argument that distinguishing nationhood as an idea from the state as a concrete reality is morally dubious or wrong also falls down.

The conclusion to draw from all this is a discourse, whether theological or not, that is negative and unwilling to recognize the State of Israel has little or nothing genuinely positive to say either about Israel or about Palestine either. This is the central problem underlying the exposition of four Western European mainline Protestant theologians advanced in this book: Reinhold Niebuhr, Rowan Williams, John Milbank, and Karl Barth. Of these, only Karl Barth emerges in a largely favorable light. This is because he distinguishes properly between nationhood and statehood, thus allowing for theological recognition of both nation-states and stateless nations.[6] In plain words, Barth allows for the possibility that the God of the Bible, the God of Israel and the nations, recognizes both nation-states *and* stateless nations as entities in which he has, with the witting or unwitting cooperation of human beings, placed human beings to live in order to seek him (Acts 17, recapitulating Genesis 10). As such, from reading the entire Bible, it should be clear the Bible implies God is ready to judge and pardon not only nation-states but also stateless nations. We see this clearly in the outpouring of the Spirit on Jewish and Gentile members of the nations in Acts 2. Every one of those nations was in fact stateless, not possessing a government of their own, but ruled by the Roman Empire. The descent of the Holy Spirit on all the nations of what was then the known world signaled God's own chosen way of resolving the curse laid on the descendants of Noah when they were scattered at the destruction of the Tower of Babel. It is crucial to realize recognition, while implied in Barth's treatment, is definitely part of a universal missiology. The peoples present at Pentecost typologically represent all the nations in world history, just like in all orthodox Christian exegesis. By contrast, Barth shows no interest in genealogies of nationhood in his work, in stark contrast to the European elites since the Reformation, who attempted to graft their own national legends of origin onto the Table of Nations in Genesis 10–11.[7] In

6. I investigate Barth's developing construction of nationhood at length in my book, *Nations and Nationalism in the Theology of Karl Barth.*

7. Kidd, *British Identities.*

connection to this tradition, Herder and Hegel were the originators of the philosophy of the politics of recognition of nations in the modern period.[8] Heidegger's Nazi commitments, and his refusal to repent of them, were responsible for removing primordialist, ontological conceptualizations of nationhood from respectable intellectual discourse. The German tradition continued to be mined, however, now in a more narrowly self-conscious, pragmatist vein. For this reason we now turn briefly to Charles Taylor, whose own philosophical work on secularity and recognition is deeply indebted to reading Hegel in this fashion.

Charles Taylor is the main modern theorist of the politics of recognition. In his seminal essay "The Politics of Recognition," he argues that the demand for recognition of distinct cultures is pressed due to being considered linked to a cultural group's identity. The underlying view is as follows.

> Our identity is partly shaped by recognition or its absence, often by the misrecognition of others, and so a person or a group of people can suffer real damage, real distortion, if the people or the society around them mirror back to them a confining or demeaning or contemptible picture of themselves. Nonrecognition or misrecognition can inflict harm, can be a form of oppression, imprisoning someone in a false, distorted, and reduced mode of being. . . . Due recognition is not just a courtesy we owe people. It is a vital human need.[9]

It is easy to see here the next step imaginable, namely that recognition of persons or national cultures is a vital human right. The idea of human needs and rights is normally applied to persons. Taylor's two great works on the history of modern ideas of recognition are *Sources of the Self* and *A Secular Age*. Although the former discusses changes in philosophical anthropology, much of what is said is profoundly illuminating for the purpose of understanding the rise of modern nationalist philosophies. This is partly because the same philosophers are involved in both ideological trajectories. Taylor argues that there are key characteristics to the rise of modern Western notions of the self: the focus on inwardness, the affirmation of ordinary life, and harkening to the voice of nature. Regarding the affirmation of ordinary life, he makes the usual, rather tiresome "catholic" charge that Puritanism was to blame for the demise of old conceptions of meaningful order. His treatment of Puritan thought is superficial and deeply misbegotten. For example, he expresses surprise that Puritanism

---

8. Barnard, *Herder's Social and Political Thought*, 55–63.
9. Taylor, "The Politics of Recognition," 26.

specifically, and Calvinism more generally, held a "strong affinity for ancient Israel" as "paradoxical in a faith which starts from a central focus
on the Epistle to the Romans."[10] He seems not to have noticed that Paul
agonizes over the salvation of the nation of Israel at length in Romans,
thus implying a continuity between Israel before Christ and after. Taylor is
only able to comprehend the Puritan focus on Israel as driven by the ex-
trinsic consideration of a felt need to "rectify the disorder in the world," "a
people beleaguered and embattled." Thus Israel is only considered a model
for moral imitation, not the nucleus of the elect people of God to *join* as
in Romans 9–11. Taylor therefore misses the deep connection between
predestination (which he mentions) and election (which he doesn't), thus
falling back on the fake picture of Calvinism that owes so much to Max
Weber. Reading the rise of Calvinist orthodoxy and Puritanism as part
of the history of the Western understanding of nations would put these
traditions in a better light. Taylor devotes a whole chapter to John Locke,
ignoring the fact that Locke was hostile to the Native Americans, unlike
many Calvinists and Puritans, regarding them as lesser breeds before
the law.[11] Taylor also devotes a chapter to the Deist notion of the natural
moral sense, looking at Lord Shaftesbury, Frances Hutcheson, and David
Hume.[12] There is no mention of the polygenetic theory of human origins,
coupled with the theory of original polytheism, and racism, of Hume.[13]
Hume cannot represent a genuine advancement in Western understanding of the origins and recognition of national cultures. What all this tells
us is that Taylor's discussion of the affirmation of ordinary life needs to
be judged in the light of the affirmation of the life of nations as an end
wholly separable from the life of the church. This change is characteristic
of deism. The church at best is an instrument for advancing the natural
religion, but in reality, other religions will do for this task. The turn to
hearkening the voice of nature is one that Taylor investigates via Voltaire,
Hume, Rousseau, Kant, and Herder. Here again, if we look at this theme
insofar as it pertains to understanding the nature, relations, and purpose
of nations in history, we cannot draw such positive conclusions about
these thinkers. In his subsequent work *The Ethics of Authenticity*, Taylor

10. Taylor, *Sources of the Self*, 229.

11. Ibid., 234–47; Ruston, *Human Rights and the Image of God*, 251–66.

12. Taylor, *Sources of the Self*, 248–65.

13. Kidd, *The Forging of Races*, 93–95.

singled out Rousseau, Herder, and Hegel as the originators of the modern idea of recognition, without using that term explicitly.[14]

In *A Secular Age*, Taylor distinguishes three forms of secularity or secularization that have occurred in the West side by side.[15] The first is the privatization of religion in and by common institutions and practices. The second is the shift from trusting religious authority to trusting the internal rationality of spheres of life as the main guide to public and private action. The third is the change in the social conditions of belief. Belief in God used to be inescapable; now it is an option. (This is reminiscent of Peter Berger's theory about the collapse of the sacred canopy and the heretical imperative to be religious in modern society.) *A Secular Age* focuses on the third type of secularity. The key shift that Taylor identifies as responsible for making belief in God optional is the rise of deism.[16] In the Enlightenment Christian belief became optional, but only for the elites. By the late twentieth century it was so for everybody. Taylor's focus is on the rise of modern views of the self, so he is really quite weak on nationhood and politics. The period of secularization is the period of the increasing rejection of the biblical metanarrative about the life of nations. Taylor virtually ignores this, despite pointing out that deism had no time for particular providences regarding nations and individuals. He characterizes eighteenth-century Evangelicalism as a reaction against deism, yet this is one-sided.[17] Evangelicalism was also continuing earlier Puritan traditions, and evangelical preachers such as Jonathan Edwards were self-conscious in developing theologies of divine providence over the history of the world's nations. Indeed, it is an important question as to how vital a role this kind of perspective played in the spread of revivals and missions from the eighteenth century onwards. This is part of the wider problem with Taylor's work, which is its anti-Protestant attitude, seeing the Protestant Reformation as an inevitable way station on the way to deism and atheism. He sides with the currently fashionable theory that Western theology went downhill because of those who supposedly took side with Duns Scotus against Thomas Aquinas (John Milbank, Catherine Pickstock, Fergus Kerr, David Burrell, plus thinkers who aren't metaphysicians, such as Alasdair

---

14. Taylor, *The Ethics of Authenticity*.

15. Taylor, *A Secular Age*, 1–4.

16. Ibid., 221–69.

17. Ibid., 263.

MacIntyre and Stanley Hauerwas, who favor this metanarrative because it seems to defend a Thomistic version of ethics.)[18]

In *The Ethics of Authenticity*, Taylor lists three modern malaises that grip social critics.[19] The first is individualism, or the loss of meaning. The second is the primacy of instrumental reason, the eclipse of ends. The third is the claim that these two together lead to loss of freedom to act in the best way. It is possible to imagine this argument being translated into a critique of nationalism as follows. For "society" substitute "medieval Christendom." Supplement individualism with nationalism. Put instrumental reason in a nationalist context. The result is the claim that nationalism hampers our freedom to act in the best way, for right ends. Self-fulfillment is basic to the ethics of authenticity for individuals. It is easy to imagine a theological critique of nationalism as hampering true human freedom to attain the good. Taylor never gets this far, basically because he isn't explicitly interested in a theological engagement with the politics of recognition. Taylor's prescription for healing the malaise of the culture of authenticity is learning that identities are forged through dialogue with others. Rowan Williams follows him in this respect, though focusing more on the recognition of shared common goods through "conversation."[20] According to Taylor's prescription, more dialogue and more education is needed. Taylor's arguments are hardly original. If we transpose his argument from individuals to nations, it quickly becomes more questionable. The idea that nations are going to avoid conflict thanks to more dialogue depends on a whole host of practical factors. For "dialogue" between nations often means diplomacy and the exchange of intelligence. It is, as such, intimately bound up with surveillance, these days on a global scale. It is worth realizing that in the book of Genesis, God allows nations to be formed by the sons of Noah *after* the Deluge, which was itself a punishment for the fact that human beings had filled the earth with violence, i.e., war and conflict. Nations are now permitted to exist, like languages after Babel, to confound and confuse people, so that mass anarchy becomes near-impossible due to the obstacles and boundaries encountered. We have no prior knowledge of what an unfallen world of national diversity would look like. (Perhaps this is one of the reasons why the cast of mind of many a theologian specializing in politics is more infra-lapsarian than supra-lapsarian.) That dialogue between nations, be they nation-states or stateless nations, is necessary is

18. Ibid., 295.

19. Taylor, *The Ethics of Authenticity*, 10f.

20. Williams, *Lost Icons*, 91–105.

obvious. The problem with a purely philosophical account such as Taylor's is that it appears distant from any authoritative metanarrative. Given that, for Herder, the discourse on recognition of nations was based on reading the Bible, the effacement of the Bible from Taylor's work is a real problem, an obstacle to understanding the purposeful ordering of history.

There is a need for theology to take recognition seriously. The reason is as follows. At the end of Matthew's Gospel, the risen Jesus gives his disciples the Great Commission:

> All authority in heaven and on earth has been given to me. Go therefore and make disciples of all nations, baptizing them in the name of the Father and of the Son and of the Holy Spirit, and teaching them to obey everything that I have commanded you. And remember, I am with you always, to the end of the age. (Matt 28:18b–20)

Because most English speakers only read the New Testament in one version of English, not in *koine* Greek, and because English has become such a loose and, in many instances, sloppy language, the full extent of the meaning of the Great Commission is not always grasped. When Jesus says "make disciples of all nations," he is not vaguely saying "make some disciples *from* each nation." He is saying that all nations as such must obey his authority, and as such the authority of the Father, the God of Israel, which is encapsulated in the Torah and fulfilled in the teaching of Jesus. Read theologically, this must encompass every nation that has ever and will ever exist. The complication, of course, is what counts as a nation. As we have seen, this is highly disputed. All missiology involves communication and reception of the message being communicated in myriad ways. The practical truth of the matter is that a missiology that declines to recognize nations unless they have states of their own is one that declines the difficult challenge of recognition of how identities came to develop as they have done, and as such, will be much less capable of being listened to and respected by its prospective audience. Mission always occurs in particular places among particular peoples. The fact that it obviously transcends these does not absolve it of the ongoing challenge of recognition. Recognition is a very difficult topic in Christian theology because it necessarily lies beneath the surface of explicitly theological and ethical discourse. It cannot simply be an aim in itself, obviously, but it must as a discourse and process of engagement be allowed to permeate theological discourse and be woven into its ethos. In ethical terms, it involves taking seriously the requirement to respect the existence of cultural matrices and settings, rather than dismissing them as obstacles to Christian belief and practice. It requires laying aside imperialisms that hope, openly or covertly, that the subordinated, the defeated, "the natives," the "indigenous," will "come round" to the elite way of seeing the world in order to be considered to have "arrived." It involves acknowledging that by virtue of human beings being continuously "placed," replaced, and displaced from national belonging in the course of history, we all have at least one view from somewhere, even several, and that the perspective of what counts as "good" or "right" theology and ethics is quite often that of the historically imperialist nations. As has often been remarked, the Hebrew Bible has been used both by empires and by subordinated, defeated nations to envision theopolitical discourses and strategies. This is where the second main theme of this book comes in.

If the first theme of the book is that anti-nationalism and anti-Zionism are often two sides of the same coin, and involve taking leave of a serious, providential reading of the Bible as well as a willingness to understand history in broadly providential terms, the second theme is that such an approach tends to also involve a reluctance to recognize subordinated Gentile nations, especially those that have lost independence. I made the argument very briefly that anti-nationalists also have little to say to Palestinian nationalism. That said, I do not pursue the question of Palestine at length in this book. To do so would require a book of its own, as it would involve looking at many different theologians, and indeed at the whole history of the range of Christian approaches to the question. At present, we have no such monograph. Instead, I propose to locate my second theme from the perspective from which I originally became interested in the topic of nationhood, which is the identity of Wales as a stateless nation. This is deliberately in order to enable the reader to understand where I am coming from, and not to get the impression that my argument has come out of an attempt to forge a general discourse about nationhood. This may sound too labored, given that I have already promised discussion of how selected theologians handle the specific nation-State of Israel. However, even then, it is possible for the theologian to talk only about Israel and not to attend closely to the parallels between discourse around Israel and those around Gentile nations closer to home. Precisely because nationalisms differ so much, one must take the plunge and discuss particular examples if one is to say anything meaningful and contribute to a wider discussion. Of the four main theologians selected, only Rowan Williams really speaks about Wales, and he does so within the context of speaking about Britain. His work has affinities with those of John Milbank, who writes specifically about England. Milbank's work is expressly opposed to that of Reinhold Niebuhr, whose manner of handling Israel is connected to how he handles his native America. Other theologians are brought into these discussions as well. In addition, there is a third, subordinate theme to the book, namely how "social theory" or sociology, represented by certain key figures, has handled the same issues. I have attempted to link the so-called social theorists to the theologians to explore their affinities. For example, Niebuhr is paired with Mark Juergensmeyer. Rowan Williams is juxtaposed to the debate between Adrian Hastings and Anthony Smith (the latter could profitably be assimilated to Barth's outlook). The purpose of this is to show an alternative, more concrete way of handling the relationship between theology and social theory than that given by John Milbank. Indeed, the whole question of Israel and nationhood is revealed in chapter 4 to be at the bottom of Milbank's entire approach. It follows, therefore, that the reader may justifiably invert the order of importance of the three themes of the book if they so wish. It would be possible to re-read the book attending primarily to the intersection of theology with social theory, and only then to look at the specific examples of Israel, Wales, and Britain. The reason that the book has been structured as it has been is to give it the broadest concrete horizon, rather than swamping the reader with method. Without further ado, a synopsis of each chapter follows.

PLAN OF THIS BOOK

The book's first chapter opens not with a consideration of nations and nationalism, but with the idea of "religious resurgence" as a recent global threat insofar as it poses a challenge to secularization. The paradoxical claim is advanced that many academics are involved in an alternative religious resurgence of their own against secularism, and that this masks anti-nationalism. At the same time, the anxiety over popular religious resurgence is contrasted with the almost total lack of critique of the "resurgence" of Western esotericism and occultism in society, and at the academic level the adherence of some scholars whom I deem part of the "alternative" resurgence to discourses grounded in some key Western esoteric thinkers such as Hegel. This is the real source of the attack on "religious resurgence" and "fundamentalism"—the long history of attacks on exoteric, confessional Protestant theologies; specifically, reformed, Pietist, and Pentecostal theologies. Naturally, no assumption is made here that there are only two religious discourses involved in late modernity. I am being selective precisely because two of the four main theologians handled in this book, John Milbank and Rowan Williams, have clearly demonstrable affinities with aspects of the Western esoteric tradition that emerged within Western Christendom. The point is that when anxieties are expressed about "religious resurgence," "religious violence," and "religious nationalism," it is religions of revelation that are being criticized. Only after discussions of secularization are recast briefly in this light does the discussion turn to nations and nationalism. Against the contemporary anti-American mood, I propose that the focus can be profitably moved to consider British imperialism. The reason is that anti-Americanism arises today partly as a reaction against the State of Israel, yet it was *Britain*, not the United States, that was the last imperial power to rule over the Holy Land. The remainder of the chapter is occupied with a discussion of the work of Philip Jenkins—a British (Welsh) scholar of religion, largely sociological in his approach, who works in the United States—regarding his handling of religious resurgence and Israel/Palestine. Jenkins is a prolific author whose works are aimed at the more popular end of the academic market and at the popular book market. This is precisely why a consideration of his work matters, for he has made certain global themes visible in a particularly concrete way fitting for such a broad audience. Jenkins embodies what I have called "the religious resurgence of academics" well, thus forming a suitable case-study of a social theorist of religion and theology handling religion and nationalism.

The second chapter turns to Reinhold Niebuhr, the most prominent liberal Protestant theologian to support Zionism in the United States in the mid-twentieth century. Only a minority of theologians, clergy, and laity in the mainline churches ever supported Zionism. Some argue that because Niebuhr's Zionism was not grounded in dogmatic theology and biblical exegesis, it was not transmitted to the next generation of mainline Protestants. Furthermore, the structure of his thought left open the possibility of an anti-Zionist approach. This chapter assesses the tensions between theology and ethics in Niebuhr's Zionism, and links it to his conception of both Israel and America as messianic nations with civilizational missions. First, it assesses Niebuhr's support for a Jewish return to Palestine in relation to Protestant and Jewish relocation of the Promised Land. The second section argues that Niebuhr's Zionism was integral to his Christian realism. The third section probes his shift from viewing Jews as a messianic people to understanding America as a messianic nation, subsuming Israel under America's civilizing mission. The fourth section argues that Niebuhr's natural theology, which was the basis for his understanding of history and divine transcendence, constrained what he could say concerning the "biblical myths" of covenant and election regarding Israel. The fifth section argues that Niebuhr located his Zionism within his reconstruction of natural law and subjected it to his critique of nationalism and religion. As his Zionism was not theologically grounded, his support for Israel could not be persuasive theologically for subsequent generations of mainline Protestants. In the last two sections, I argue that Niebuhr's method had a major influence on American postliberal theology and on Mark Juergensmeyer's sociological assessment of apocalyptic violence as religious resurgence since the end of the Cold War. As Niebuhr's argument for Zionism was kept outside the bounds of theology, it failed to be registered properly by postliberalism, and his denial of the election of Israel opened the door to denial or ignoring by Christians of the implication of Judaism as politics, and therefore of Zionism, in the challenges of modernity. The result is that postliberalism with its heavy focus on narrative, drama, and nonviolence, is powerless to diagnose the ills of anti-Semitism and anti-Zionism that are so prevalent in forms of religious resurgence around the world.

The third chapter steps back from the theme of Israel to look at Wales as a stateless nation, a nation that lost its state due to conquest by England. This furnishes a suitable case for probing the origins of British imperialism because Wales was the first country to be taken over by England, and as such, this moment logically constitutes the true origin of what became British imperialism (with England being represented by "Britain"). The chapter investigates how Rowan Williams handles Wales in relation to Britain. The texts I assess are two pieces on Welsh devolution and British identity, one written in 1979 and the other in 2009. I do so in relation to the paper to which Williams responds at the 1979 colloquium on Welsh devolution, by the distinguished Welsh Reformed theologian and historian R. Tudur Jones. A continuation and modification of Jones' approach is suggested, drawing on Dutch Reformed theologians, Abraham Kuyper and Herman Bavinck. Noting the low priority given to Israel in their work, I turn to analyze critically the debate on nationhood between Hastings and the sociologist Anthony D. Smith, who has argued that ancient Israel in the Bible is a nation analogous to modern nations, and that as such, nationhood is an ancient pre-modern concept, which has been incarnated in new political theories since the Enlightenment.

Chapter 4 mounts an original critique of John Milbank's approach to theology and social theory, building upon and criticizing the existing literature on his work. I argue that his work from *Theology and Social Theory* onwards, which constitutes a concerted attack on the social sciences, is really a theological attack on Protestant and Jewish political discourses flourishing in modernity. This becomes clear in his approach to modern Israel, and in the privileging of a pre-Enlightenment "Christian" Kabbalah and Hermeticism, a theological resourcing from the heart of Western esotericism, one that constitutes a highly idiosyncratic instance of "academic religious resurgence" against certain forms of popular religiosity. The peculiarly English setting of this turn is uncovered, and the problem of the fascination with pagan sources, myths, and legends of British origin that veer close to at least a dubious parallelism, if not in practice a replacement, of ancient Israel's place in the Christian metanarrative. This launches the final part of the chapter, a radical questioning of the much-vaunted "radical orthodoxy" of Milbank's project. This leads onto a similar scrutiny of Rowan Williams' theology.

The fifth chapter explores in more depth the trajectory taken by Rowan Williams in between the 1979 paper on Welsh devolution and the 2009 essay on British identity. Rowan Williams' political thinking is shown to have been secular from his first publication on politics, the 1979 paper. I then analyze critically Williams' reading of Hegel in the three papers he wrote in the 1990s as he climbed the Anglican episcopal ladder. Reading Hegel enables Williams to resacralize his secular political theory. I argue that Williams strives to read Hegel in a non-esoteric style, concealing Hegel's esoteric and pagan roots discussed by Gillian Rose and Andrew Shanks, to whom he is indebted for his reading of Hegel. This challenges Williams' insistence that Hegel's theology is compatible with the construction of Christian doctrine in general, and of a Christian political theology specifically. Williams' Hegelian political theology can be understood as a managerial discourse directed against more "orthodox" Protestant and Catholic theologies. Rowan Williams' Hegelian outlook is framed by an apophatic approach to eschatology and the doctrine of creation "out of nothing." His eschatology is strongly rooted in pneumatology but lacks a strong christological focus. Political projects as the outcome of human transformation are placed in the foreground. The resolution of theological, ethical, and political debates through biblical exegetical debates is deferred eschatologically, which is paradoxical as the *eschaton* is understood apophatically. There are political concerns behind this approach, as there are for Williams' elusive approach to the doctrine of creation "out of nothing." This apophatic approach to the doctrinal limits of history enable both concealment and management of exegetical debates on the beginning and end of history, be they Christian or Islamic. This analysis, along with the analysis provided in the first article submitted, enables a critical analysis of Williams' 2008 lecture on Islamic law in England and Western countries. While his concept of community as applied to Islam shows the influence of J. N. Figgis, it is arguable that his approach is also influenced by Gillian Rose. The lecture demonstrates how Williams' political theology is characterized by viewing Anglicanism as having the right and responsibility to manage other Christian and Islamic discourses. This is relevant to his outlook on Israel/Palestine.

In the penultimate chapter, we start by looking at Williams' Christology in relation to interfaith dialogue with Jews and Muslims, an approach developed explicitly to move Anglican interfaith concerns away from debates about John Hick's soteriological pluralism. His apophatic approach to theology serves both to continue some of the concerns of liberal Protestant "interfaith" approaches to Israel/Palestine, and to draw back from overt soteriological pluralism. Here the managerial apophasis analyzed in the 2008 lecture on Islamic law is revealed as explicitly functioning to hold an ambiguous attitude towards the position held by many Protestant and Roman Catholic Christians, that the future of Israel is underwritten by divine providence understood in prophetic terms. Williams' 2004 proposal for "a liberation theology for the Holy Land" is analyzed in relation to the discussion of his theology thus far. The deeper problem is found, as in 1979, in the reading of the Bible. I argue that Williams' apophatic approach to the Bible needs to be challenged in two ways. First, it needs to be redirected away from his preoccupation with it as cognitive technique to focusing on the Minor Prophets' call to be silent before God in light of the coming Day of the Lord, which I juxtapose with the threefold mystery taught by the New Testament as the revelation of Jesus Christ in history, the salvation of "all Israel," and the final resurrection of the righteous. This contrasts with the mystery cults that have been smuggled into the Christian tradition and left their traces on Hegel's esotericism. The second way in which Williams' apophatic approach to the Bible needs to be challenged is in a move to a more realist view of biblical narrative. I start from George Steiner's consideration that the biblical text is the homeland of the Jewish nation in exile. By analogy, I argue that Rowan Williams' theology has become somewhat exiled from the biblical text, and that this parallels his "apophatic" and "free" approach to poetry, which is exiled from the mainstream metrical Welsh poetic tradition. This parallels the evasive attitude towards nationhood that has been discussed so far. In order to move on from this position, I argue for Petra Herdt's view that realist reading of the Bible has never died out in Israel because of the synchronism of the language and the landscape, which can be inclusive of critical perspectives. Taking this particular sense of place seriously is an ecumenical venture for Christians. This enables a bridge into considering Karl Barth's approach in *Church Dogmatics* III/1, III/3, and IV/2.

Against Williams' view that Israel was formed at the exodus, Barth insists on the election of Abraham, and even goes back to the creation of Adam and Eve in Eden, which medieval Jewish exegetes understood to be a cryptic way of referring to the Holy Land. All of this is included within election by Barth. The formation of modern Israel is understood by Barth to be a secular parable of resurrection. Already this points to an "inclusive" reading of election, as Jesus includes both Jews and Gentiles. The history of Israel is, for Barth, included in the history of Jesus. It is a type of the history of God's dealing with every nation. If Jesus is the New Adam, and the first Adam lived in the Holy Land and was exiled from it to the east, then this transforms our understanding of who may live in the Land. Barth's doctrine of election is one of unconditional grace, which I argue corresponds somewhat on the political level to the Dutch Reformed concept of common grace. For Barth, the modern reunion of Jews in the Land with Jews from the Diaspora constitutes a secular parable of the resurrection and the kingdom of God. At the same time, he argues, as he did before 1945, that any nation intending to destroy the people of Israel will itself forever be frustrated, and that any new state founded with the intention of destroying Israel will never succeed. Barth clearly is arguing on the basis of God's words to Abraham in Genesis 12:1–3, and other passages in the Old Testament. He clearly has Palestinian nationalism in mind. While this reads in a negative light, logically it shows a willingness to consider that a new Palestinian stateless nationhood has come into being and requires proper political expression as a neighbor of Israel and other surrounding nations. Thus while Barth never explicitly advocated the formation of a Palestinian state alongside Israel, he cannot either be said to be categorically opposed to it.

Finally, I show how Barth's approach illuminates approaches discussed in this book. Barth connects back to Anthony D. Smith's concept of nation as close to *ethnos*. He can accept stateless nations and nation-states, nations that have lost their states, and nations that have never had states, because he accepts the fullness of the biblical witness concerning Israel. Similarly, postliberal readings of Barth also confuse Jews as a nation and Judaism due to wanting to espouse a two-covenant theology, thus casting Barth as a supersessionist, which he is not when it comes to the nation of Israel. The church cannot metaphysically replace Israel, because it is a spiritual community of those who are born from above, whereas Israel remains a nation, a community of first birth. In conclusion, Barth's approach is arguably one that can bring conceptual clarity and equal recognition to the national realities of Israel and Palestine, in the Christian reading of the Bible. At the same time, it allows for recognition of nations that have no state of their own.

1

Secularization and Religious Resurgence in Eschatological Perspective

IN THE LAST DECADE, religion and theology have frequently been in the public eye internationally, often being subject to intense yet rather generalizing scrutiny for whether they are apparently going to cause harm to secular Western society, and indeed to civil society around the world. Since 9/11 Christian theologians, ethicists, sociologists of religion, and public policy pundits have rushed to argue over and over again that religion (note, not Christianity) can be a force for good in the world, especially because it can be, and is in its pure form, nonviolent. It is certain Christian pundits within the established or would-be established churches that have led the way, however, in talking in terms of religion, argue that Christians as well as Muslims need a public voice. The implication often drawn is that if they are not allowed this, some of their adherents would drop out and turn violent against the state and civil society. Thus the unspoken foe tends to be a secularist vision of civil society, underwritten by current human rights theory and legislation. To be sure, this kind of discourse was going on before 9/11, but that event provided a massive impetus to make it normative, and to attract funding grants for research and teaching. It provided, in fact, the perfect opportunity for establishment-minded theologians to promote the idea of a "multi-faith establishment."[1] This is more of a cultural idea at present, though it appears to be a creeping legal reality in many places, and as an idea, it has gained sway among university-based theologians and ethicists as a way of continuing to defend the right of Christians to participate in

1. Bretherton, "A New Establishment?," 371–92.

debates in the public sphere by using Christian theological language at the same time as translating their arguments into secular and comparative terms.[2] While I shall not be dealing with ecclesiology in this book, it is worth saying that I am speaking out of a "free church" tradition and perspective. The idea of multi-faith establishment, and related ideas of what constitutes "true religion"—or, by tacit implication, "moderate" and "non-fundamentalist" religion—is not only one that is used in both academic and journalistic discourse; it is one that has had a social effect, and it is designed to have a social and political effect. It has affected how the so-called global resurgence of religion is conceived.

It is the assumption of this chapter, and indeed of this entire book, that this ideal cannot be one to which Christian theologians and scholars in other disciplines can give unqualified and uncritical theological assent. This is because all conceptualizations of which religious discourse is to be dominant, privileged and, in the role of managing other discourses, are rooted in specific historical schools of thought, which in turn are dominant, dissenting, or critically marginal in relation to specific institutions. The motivations for advancing an ideal of multi-faith establishment need to be investigated, for they will have an effect on how theology is ideally conceived and how its norms and preferred practices are aligned in universities, civil society, and public debate. As part of this, orthodox Christians should exercise a theological witness that relearns, indwells, argues for, and accounts for anew the reality of divine providence governing the history of nations and the history of the church, in the light and expectancy of the *parousia*. However, any willingness to do this needs to consider very carefully how theologians handle nations and states, and especially how they handle the paradigmatic nation of the Bible, Israel. This is one challenge, and in the recent past many theologians have responded to the challenges of Old Testament source criticism, with its radical questioning of the historicity of the narrated history of ancient Israel, by attempting to forge a biblical theology. It is interesting that the heyday of biblical theology among Western Protestant theologians coincided with the State of Israel's honeymoon period in the international arena, 1948–67.[3] This then

---

2. For example, it clearly influences the argument made by David Ford for world religions to be taught in confessional mode as forms of theology. This feeds his support for scriptural reasoning conducted by academic Christian, Jewish, and Islamic theologians as a key practice of the modern university department of theology. See Ford, *Christian Wisdom*; Ford, *The Future of Christian Theology*.

3. On the demise of twentieth-century biblical theology, see Hayes and Preussner, *Old Testament Theology*, 241–43.

begs the question of how Western theologians have handled the modern State of Israel, which bears a geographical and historical relation to ancient Israel in important yet highly complicated ways.

This is a book of Christian theology, and not comparative theology across the world religions. It focuses on the State of Israel as the theological mirror for selected theologians and sociologists in their handling of nationhood and nationalism in relation to secularization and religious resurgence. Given this fact, I argue that secularization, as the demise of Christendom, is best understood as having its defining moment in the handling of religious communities within the British Mandate over Palestine. In 1947, Britain handed over the question of Jewish Zionist and Arab relations to the United Nations.[4] The UN drew up a plan to partition the Holy Land between Jews and Arabs, a plan that Britain accepted but refused to implement—clearly cynically, given that it had given up its prior imperial right to rule. This was despite the fact that Britain had mooted a partition plan earlier, in the shape of the Peel Commission's recommendations in 1939.[5] British imperialists and those nostalgic for the Empire typically mourn the partition of British India into the independent nation-states of India and Pakistan, as the loss of "the jewel in the crown" of the Empire. That the partition of British India has had far more symbolism attached to it in British culture since then is a clear sign that a specific type of mapping of the Empire has been acclaimed as the moral norm. This connects with the fact that historians often date the British Empire from the formation of the British East India Company in 1600. This fundamentally connects the British Empire with orientalism and the rise of capitalism. The problem with this emphasis is that it has obscured the fact that if we search for symbols, the partition of Palestine happened at roughly the same time as the partition of British India, so is an equally good candidate for the beginning of the end of the Empire. While both events have religious and theological significance, the decision to partition Palestine, the Holy Land, had a special significance that still matters very deeply on the international level. Interestingly, it might be imagined that given that the Church of England was the established religion of England, the dominant nation of the United Kingdom and the true imperializing nation at the head of the British Empire, that Anglicanism would have been the official religion of the Mandate. In reality, this was not the case.

---

4. Gilbert, *Israel*, 141–52.

5. On the Peel Commission in the context of the history of the British Mandate over Palestine, see Karsh, *Palestine Betrayed*, 8–59.

The Mandate inherited the Ottoman Turkish *millet* system of government, and provided for the religious liberty and autonomy of Muslims in the area, while demoting Islam from its status as privileged and official religion.[6] It is significant that this creation of a level playing-field for the different religions, all of which claim the land as holy, was carried out under British imperial rule, for religious toleration of this kind, apparently not privileging Christianity, originated in the United States not in Britain. This model, in American hands, was a peculiar outgrowth of the debates over religious toleration in Western Christendom, and in practice was pushed by both deist and Trinitarian dissenters. In the British Mandate, matters were very different. Britain had agreed to take over rule of the area with the Allied defeat of the Ottoman Turkish Empire, Europe's long-time Islamic imperial foe, after the First World War. This was not a land to which very many British people flocked to inhabit, unlike the American colonies in the seventeenth and eighteenth centuries. Britain clearly saw its role as one of managing conflict and tensions between Arabs and Zionist Jewish settlers who had come in waves since 1881 (though there had been a long-term Jewish presence in the land for centuries before that). Herbert Samuel in fact conceived of Britain's imperial role in Palestine as manager of the main religious communities. This is very important because it does not fit into the older Anglican model of Christendom that operated in England and Wales during the Tudor and Stuart periods, only to be very gradually eroded by campaigns for religious and political toleration. There is an interesting and neglected parallel with the political theology of John Neville Figgis, the nonconformist-turned-Anglo-Catholic monk of the turn of the twentieth century. Figgis' belief in disestablishing the Church of England, and making the state the manager or policeman of a state-centered "community of communities," has profoundly influenced Rowan Williams, but is also admired to an extent by John Milbank. These influences will be discussed further on in the book.

In light of all this, discussions of religious resurgence by Christian theologians have been too quick to focus (negatively) on the United States and its support for Israel, and ignored the reality of British territorial imperialism that preceded and overlapped with American hegemony.[7] Moving the focus back to British and English imperialism enables discovering the role of Anglican theology in that project. In chapters 5 and

---

6. Tsimhoni, "Continuity and Change in Communal Autonomy," 398.

7. See the contributions in Benson and Hetzel (eds.), *Evangelicals and Empire*. I note that John Milbank, who will be the subject of critical scrutiny later in the present book, contributes a chapter.

6 in particular, I uncover the political theology of Rowan Williams as being the latest mutation of this liberal Anglican Hegelian imperialism, but adapted to be a managerial ideology for the new concept of multi-faith establishment or resistance, as suits the occasion. Moving back to the present chapter, as a more populist sociological counterpart to Williams, who nevertheless diverges from him in some key ways, I look at another Welsh-born Anglican, Philip Jenkins. I deliberately juxtapose Williams, the highly theoretical academic theologian-turned-public figure with Jenkins, a generalist historian of religious movements who has been widely publicized in his interpretation of global Christianity (including global Anglicanism) and the rivalry of Christianity and Islam in Europe today. Jenkins' highly visual approach to religion, paralleling that of Peter L. Berger, anticipates arguments I make later in chapter 6 for transforming Williams' approach to the Bible. At the same time, Jenkins' recollection in this context of Karl Barth's invitation into "the strange new world of the Bible" enables entry into an eschatological perspective on the themes of secularization and resurgent religion. For now we turn to the latter two in historical perspective.

THE GLOBAL RESURGENCE OF RELIGION AND THE MEANING OF SECULARIZATION

When reading academic critiques of religious resurgence, it is important to realize that "religion" is here clearly the category of revealed versus natural religion. In typical post-Kantian fashion, religions of revelation are treated with suspicion.[8] Yet on the part of religious agents themselves, the common enemy tends to be a version of "secularism," and salvation lies either in an intellectual and political reassertion of a neo-traditional vision, or in a thick interreligious discourse in the semi-public sphere. Behind the hostility to secularism lies hostility to nationalism, and behind that lies the age-old political imperialism that has been so important for Christian and Islamic theological traditions. The global resurgence of religion is a category invented by sociologists, and given that sociologists concentrate on what they consider to be religious behavior, it has thrived on the most dramatic manifestations of religion, especially those that have been selected

---

8. Kant's insistence that religion be reasonable necessarily affected his argument that philosophy had the right to criticize theology in the Prussian universities, while being tellingly silent on the possibility of the converse. See Kant, "The Contest of Faculties," 176–90.

for the greatest attention in secular media. Given the increasing role of the media, these dramatic manifestations are being reproduced as "the truth" about religion, thus harboring the potential to act as self-fulfilling prophecies, often of doom. Western Christian responses to fears concerning global resurgence have varied. Christian theologians have been at the forefront of the movement arguing that religion can be a potential for good in the world. This is closely linked to the historic role liberal Christians have played in inter-faith movements, often quietly helping non-Christian religions "modernize." We see this impulse reflected in the work of Mark Juergensmeyer, which will be discussed in the next chapter. Once we realize that resurgence has been partly a dramatic category, which itself has fueled further dramatic religious activity, we are free to face the reality, that religion understood very broadly never really went away, it simply assumed different guises.

The study of religious resurgence has focused heavily on religions of revelation, and not really discussed the rise in esoteric religious thinking and practice in the West, at a much more open level than in the past. Partly, this is because Western esotericism has been classed under "spirituality," suggesting it has been mainly individualist and non-institutionalized.[9] In reality, the evidence suggests that esotericism and occultism in Western societies has taken communal and, at times, institutional forms.[10] If religion is partly defined as shared beliefs that bind groups together, the rise of esoteric beliefs and practices, independent traditions, definitely count as "religious resurgence." This is especially so when we consider that many of the beliefs and practices are a more populist and demotic recycling of beliefs and practices previously confined to elites.[11] For our purposes, it is significant that virtually nobody in the academic study of religion *complains* about the rise of occult groups in Europe. Perhaps the reason is that *violence* has come to be seen as the only real form of sin and evil. Groups such as Wicca may not be interested in international politics, but it represents only one brand of occultism.[12] There is a very long history of men belonging to occultist and esoteric groups closely associated with international espionage and diplomacy—yet no theologian or scholar of religion has yet dared to suggest that their activities constitute a threat to

9. On esoteric and occult movements in the West, see Partridge, *The Re-Enchantment of the West*.

10. Bogdan, *Western Esotericism and Rituals of Initiation*.

11. Hannegraaff, *New Age Religion and Western Culture*.

12. On Wicca and other neo-pagan groups, and their links to nineteenth- and twentieth-century British Anglicanism, see Pearson, *Wicca and the Christian Heritage*.

the peaceful international order conceived by many Christian traditions. One thing we do know is that a number of British occultists from the height of the British Empire had grew up in evangelical homes. Take, for instance, Aleister Crowley, "Britain's most notorious Satanist," who grew up in the Plymouth Brethren then became a Freemason, and eventually joined and headed the *Ordo Templi Orientis,* a powerful German occult group that attracted high-ranking military men and practiced so-called "sex-magick" rituals.[13] Crowley is known to have worked internationally for MI6, and died in 1947, just at the start of the decline of the British Empire. Another occultist who spied for Britain at the height of empire was the Russian spiritual guru G. I. Gurdjeff.[14] Would asking theological questions about the relationship between imperialism, espionage, diplomacy, and esoteric and occult religious beliefs, doctrine, and practices risk bursting the bubble of arrogance that has grown up in criticism of religious violence? Would we start to feel uneasy if we started to investigate the two-way traffic between British and German esoteric and occultist groups before the First and especially the Second World Wars? How would we start thinking of just war theory then? How might we think of the "revolt against the powers"? The questions are potentially endless, yet, esoteric religious groups on the whole are not nearly as open with their archives and libraries as are Christian denominations, colleges, and mission agencies. What would happen if someone were to try to publish a book arguing that the two world wars of the last century were related to the international religious resurgence of occultism? There is a mass of evidence for occult roots to Nazi thinking.[15] Only the fool imagines that no such elements have been present in the thinking of other states. The bottom line is that representatives of Western esoteric movements have taken it upon themselves since the Enlightenment to stigmatize probing questions as well as allegations about their activities as "conspiracy theories." It must be said that in very many cases, they have a point; which is to say, that the targets of their criticism do not really have concrete evidence for their claims, but are only making symbolic connections. Scholars, just like everyone else, are not at liberty to make allegations based on imagination and resentment. In addition, "conspiracy theories" against, for example, Freemasons, all too often tag along with similar talk about Jews. The very idea of a Masonic "conspiracy" is deemed to have started from a thoroughly

13. See the biography by Churton, *Aleister Crowley.*
14. On the claim that Gurdjeff was a spy, see Webb, *The Harmonious Circle.*
15. See Goodricke-Clark, *The Occult Roots of Nazism.*

respectable source, John Robison, member of the Royal Society of Edinburgh, whose pamphlet alleging that the French Revolution was down to a "Masonic conspiracy" ignited the flames of debate.[16] My entire point here is not to support an overarching theory of history that sees it as inexorably driven by esoteric or secretive groups (in the modern world, these two are not necessarily synonymous). Theologically, this would be to capitulate to a secular and negative attitude to history and providence, as well as oddly putting the accent on invisible *people* as opposed to an invisible *God* (and in the process, assuming that history is really governed by fallible creatures). My point is that when one surveys the tone of discourse on religious resurgence and "fundamentalism," and the stream of publications that purport to investigate whether or not "religion causes violence," hardly any of that literature looks at esoteric religious groups, yet there is a respectable body of academic literature that shows that quite a few influential religious esotericists have been spies and soldiers, and indeed that esotericism, espionage, and militarism have always gone hand in hand. Kant's singling out of religions of revelation as alone requiring subordination by philosophy was one-sided at best.

All this prompts further probing as to what the "religion" that is examined for being "resurgent" really is. I said earlier that it is religions of revelation that are under scrutiny, and that varieties of natural religion and esoteric movements are let off the hook, morally speaking. (Indeed, it is an important though neglected question as to the extent to which categories of natural religion can at times be glimpsed underneath the surface of sociological and psychological accounts of religion.) The typical answer given as to what resurgent religion is is that it is "fundamentalist."[17] By now it is apparent how unsatisfactory this answer is, as the term has a protean meaning invariably used as abuse. The term "fundamentalist" was coined by American evangelicals at the turn of the twentieth century to describe an outlook on Christian doctrine that was traditionalist, in the face of serious doctrinal challenges that had built up in the modern era. It found intellectual expression in the multi-volume series *The Fundamentals,* and attracted many of the best minds of American evangelical and Reformed theology and biblical studies.[18] Some of these were associated with Princeton Theological Seminary, and ultimately lost their control

---

16. See Robison, *Proofs of a Conspiracy.*

17. See in particular Marty and Appleby, *The Fundamentalism Project.*

18. The best historical account of the controversy in relation to biblical hermeneutics is Noll, *Between Faith and Scholarship.*

over the seminary to the Modernists so-called, in the 1920s. Thus they also lost control over the Presbyterian Church of the USA, the denomination closely linked to Princeton. Since then, the word "fundamentalist" has acquired a life of its own, used against mainly evangelical Protestants, but increasingly used by sociologists who betray little or no serious knowledge of or interest in the Fundamentalist-Modernist controversy. It has come to be used as a lazy epithet for the equally vague and almost vacuous "extremist," and perhaps in the last ten to fifteen years, of almost anybody who subscribes publicly to an absolute, unwavering truth-claim of any kind. Really, what this means is that it is used in polemics, or attacks upon people, when they show unwillingness to bend to the agenda of their opponents. The corrosive nature of such name-calling should not be lost on us. Nevertheless, if we stick to the original core sense of "fundamentalist" as privileging a religion of revelation in some sense, as opposed to a natural or esoteric religion, we will not go far wrong. The reason is that it is clear that when Kant was allowing philosophy to scrutinize theology in the university, but not vice versa, the real reason for this was to undermine theological claims to authority. Theological speech about divine speech, action, and being were to be considered authoritative in the university, and therefore in the training of ministers in the established churches, only insofar as they did not contradict the supposed authority of philosophy. Philosophy here is clearly *the* secular and authoritative discipline. In this respect, Kant advanced the secularization of theology in the university. Kant was a seminal figure in the history of German Protestant theology for this reason. That he allowed the possibility of belief in revelation beyond reason did not contradict his position. Rather, it relegated theology to the realm of personal, private belief and the voluntary association of the gathered church, but on different grounds than those given by historic, orthodox free church theologians, who did not reduce theology merely to the realm of the interpersonal. In the light of what was said above about the absence of sociological interest in the "resurgence" of esotericism and occultism, it is worth noting that recent scholarship has acknowledged openly that Kant's dualist epistemology of religion was partly motivated by his desire to leave room for the esoteric Christian theology of Emanuel Swedenborg, which held that we can only attain knowledge of God after death.[19] Secularization here meant exchanging orthodox Christianity for esoteric Christianity. The question is, have sociologists of religion

---

19. On Kant and Swedenborg, see Hanegraaff, *Swedenborg. Oetinger. Kant.*

acknowledged that secularization as theory in reality has often constituted a "secular," read esoteric, eschatology?

According to the British sociologist James A. Beckford, debates on secularization tend not to acknowledge that religion is "a product of continuing social construction and disagreement."[20] The result is that they are "a dialogue of the deaf."[21] He points out that the concept of secularization, like many other sociological concepts, "operates at such a high level of abstraction that sociologists do not feel the need to give it up in the face of new and challenging 'social facts' discovered by more empirical research."[22] Beckford resists renaming secularization as "religious change." I wish also to pinpoint José Casanova's thesis that religion has managed to reassert its value and salience in the public sphere since the 1980s, as referring to a form of religious resurgence issuing in more civic forms of belief and behavior than has been the case in many apocalyptic movements.[23] At the same time, he warns that this deprivatization is not inevitable. Deprivatization comes in three forms, according to Casanova: "religious mobilization in defense of traditional life-worlds against forms of colonization by state or markets . . . challenges to the dominance of states and markets, and the maintenance of visions of a common good to offset the prevailing individualism of modern liberalism."[24]

Many types of social thought have contributed to debates about secularization. The first was structural differentiation, the idea that societies evolve in stages, and that religion eventually stops regulating social life and becomes a separate institution that explains and legitimizes the main social form. (This theory could also incorporate the view that religion in modernity intensifies its role as interpreting what goes on.) Beckford lists Saint Simon, Auguste Comte, Herbert Spencer, and Emile Durkheim as proponents of this theory.[25] To these should be added Niklas Luhmann.[26] The second was the scientific approach, which claimed that empiricism was replacing religion due to its superior rationality. David Hume and the French Encyclopedists promoted this view, while also promoting the

---

20. Beckford, *Social Theory and Religion*.

21. Ibid., 68.

22. Ibid., 70.

23. Casanova, *Public Religion in the Modern world*.

24. Ibid., 61–62.

25. Beckford, *Social Theory and Religion*, 35.

26. Luhmann, *Religious Dogmatics and the Evolution of Societies*.

values of empiricism to the public, thus fulfilling their own prophecies.[27] In the light of the first two theories, Beckford cites Colin Campbell's observation that secularization debates typically ignore deliberate campaigns *for* secularization, secularism, atheism, and humanism, in the last three centuries.[28] In fact, apart from Max Weber, a lot of the sociologists debating secularization were active agents of the ideology themselves, helping fulfill its prophecies. The third type of social theory, promoted by Max Weber and Ernst Troeltsch, interests itself in "the inner dynamics of religion."[29] The last three theories are liberalism (in the shape of distinguishing sharply between church and state), Marxism, and Freudianism. Beckford advances the criticism that with the exception of the Weber-Troeltsch approach, none of the other approaches ascribe priority, and therefore agency, to religion or religious decline as a force for social change. Religion is already only a function or epiphenomenon of other instances of change.[30] Clearly this is a doctrine concealing a wish-fulfillment motif, as there is plenty of history showing the influence of religious groups on past societies. The very fact that Durkheim and his colleagues supported the policy of *laïcité* in 1905 demonstrates that they didn't believe what they said they did, i.e., that they actually realized religion (here the Roman Catholic Church) *did* and *could* have influence upon society as an independent agent. Their support for *laïcité* was the promotion of the anti-religion of secularism as a means of influencing the French population.

In fact, standard theories of secularization fail to account for the varieties of religious resurgence in late modernity because what is never properly accounted for is the fact they have been based mostly on Western Christendom as the hermeneutical norm for understanding religion.[31] The particular version of Christendom identified by secularization theory is not easy to identify, because sociologists of religion rarely discuss theology as foundation for particular early modern polities. Whether a given state had a Lutheran, Reformed, Anglican, or Roman Catholic established church varied. The reaction of intellectual and policy-making élites who pushed both theories and policies of secularization varied accordingly. Nevertheless, certain key categories came to be used internationally by

27. Hume, *Dialogues concerning Natural Religion*.

28. Beckford, *Social Theory and Religion*, 36, citing Campbell, *Towards a Sociology of Irreligion*.

29. Weber, *The Sociology of Religion*; Troeltsch, *The Social Teaching of the Christian Churches*.

30. Beckford, *Social Theory and Religion*, 40.

31. Ibid., 33.

sociologists. The "strong" unilinear theory of secularization put forward by many readers of Max Weber, such as Bryan Wilson and Steve Bruce, parallels both the Kantian and the Marxist theory of history in moving in the direction of an atheistic and mechanistic, critical, autonomous, and "progressive" form of secularism.[32] This understanding of history was feared as far back as the late eighteenth century. It provoked the great philosophical theological schemes of the German Idealists. The foremost of these was the massive project of G. W. F. Hegel. Hegel is very important because he appears to stand between the old-fashioned theory that secularization was inevitable and irreversible, and the fragmentation of society and culture into many different religious movements acting somewhat at variance with each other, by forging a large-scale philosophy of history, religion, and politics. I say that Hegel *appears* to stand between the two because Hegel in many ways presented himself as a Christian philosopher and faithful Lutheran theologian, and because his work has been annexed and baptized by many liberal Protestant (and liberal Catholic) theologians. Hegel appeared to offer a philosophy well-suited to the modernization of Christianity in the face of the revolutionary and freethinking movements of the Enlightenment. Although he was active in the late eighteenth and early nineteenth century, it was in the late nineteenth century that he was taken up with great enthusiasm by mainline Protestants in England, Wales, and Scotland.[33] This time his ideas were used to forge a philosophical and political theology that could respond to socialism, liberalism, and Darwinism. Yet the problem of secularization is perpetuated by Hegel. Civil society was effectively more important than the church for him, because he denied that the resurrection, the ascension, Pentecost, and the second coming of Jesus Christ are events that occur external to the personal experience of the believer.[34] Consequently, I argue that both Rowan Williams and John Milbank, pre-eminent liberal Anglican theologians, are misguided to continue using Hegel in their theological enterprises. It is important in this respect to realize that Hegelianism had its heyday in Britain when the British Empire reached its height. Its frankly gnostic and esoteric theology enabled accommodation with the world's religions on the part of many Anglican, Presbyterian, and Congregational theologians, and was undoubtedly part and parcel of the smaller and less dramatic echoes of what blew up as the Fundamentalist-Modernist controversy in

32. Wilson, *Religion in Sociological Perspective*; Bruce, *Secularization*.
33. See Sell, *Philosophical Idealism and Christian Belief.*
34. I deal with this in detail in chapter 5 below.

the United States. We need to bear this in mind, and realize the truth of Gillian Rose's view that Hegel cast a long shadow over subsequent social theory, when considering more recent critiques of American imperialism and evangelicalism, cast as "religious resurgence."[35]

MILLENARIANISM, AMERICA, AND THE FORGETTING OF BRITISH IMPERIALISM

There has been a flurry of populist academic books in recent years on dispensationalist premillennialism in the USA and its impact on US support for Zionism and other aspects of its foreign policy.[36] The problem is that the quality of the discussion varies considerably. A lot of the work is sensationalizing and salacious, choosing to fix on the populist form of dispensationalism that has captures the fantasies of millions of Americans and others worldwide (e.g., the *Left Behind* series).[37]

In his study of American dispensationalist premillennialists' support for interventionism in US foreign policy, Michael Barkun observes that dispensationalists (whom he calls millenarians) are event-sensitive rather than date-sensitive (watching for the signs of the times rather than the second coming).[38] Barkun makes some curious assumptions and inferences about them, e.g.,

> The end of the Cold War in the early 1990s, while it was welcomed by many, was not necessarily welcomed by millennialists, for whom the trumpets of war are often a welcome sound. In this time of seeming millennial doldrums, the concept of the "new world order" suddenly became attractive.[39]

Barkun provides no objective evidence for these claims; claims often made against contemporary dispensationalists. This claim is an inference based on the assumption that because an idea of the Battle of Armageddon

---

35. Gillian Rose set out her view that Hegel furnished a "critique in advance" of sociology in *Hegel contra Sociology*. In chapter 5 especially, but also elsewhere in this book, I explore the significance of her work for understanding John Milbank and Rowan Williams.

36. See Forrester, *Apocalypse Now?*; Clark, *Allies for Armageddon*; Dittmer and Sturm (eds.), *Mapping the End Times*.

37. For a serious sociological study of this phenomenon, see Frykhom, *Rapture Culture*.

38. Barkun, "The 'New World Order' and American Exceptionalism," 119.

39. Ibid., 120–21.

figures in the dispensationalist apocalyptic narrative, therefore an era of relative peace that breaks down the correspondence between contemporary geopolitics and this apocalyptic narrative is unwelcome, because it signals the final battle and the second coming are not imminent after all. This is making the assumption that because a final battle exists in an apocalyptic narrative, therefore believers in this narrative must want to see not only this battle take place, but that this desire must necessarily be based upon a prior warmongering attitude, a blood-thirstiness for battle in general. Thus dispensationalists, taken to stand for all premillennialists and indeed all who attempt to read historical events in the light of prophecy, are effectively demonized as militarists. Ethically, dispensationalists are tacitly deemed to be emotivists, basing their belief in a future final military Armageddon on a *desire for a military battle.* The moral and logical flaw in such an attitude is evident—anybody, dispensationalist or not in their eschatology, who believes there will be such a battle, could respond by arguing that it is those who don't believe such a battle will take place who are emotivists, advancing a pacific eschatology out of their desire not to fight to protect the church and Israel. Thus the charge of warmongering does nothing to advance moral debate.

Barkun writes about the Millerites of nineteenth-century America, seemingly unaware that the reason they were "date-sensitive" was precisely because of their historicist reading of biblical prophecy, shared with many mainstream evangelicals on both sides of the Atlantic.[40] "Historicism" here refers to a tradition of interpreting biblical prophetic writings as being concerned not simply with the very end of history, but with the gradual unfolding of history since the Old Testament. It enjoyed great support in Britain in the modern period. As Timothy P. Weber has argued, the failure of the Millerite and Adventist prophecy of Christ's second coming in 1844 had the effect of discrediting and stigmatizing historicist premillennialism in America much more than in Britain, where it was continued across the churches, most successfully by the sophisticated natural theology and revivalist missiology of Henry Grattan Guinness.[41] Where Barkun is more interesting is in providing the information that contemporary American dispensational premillennialism has provided a place for the United States in its apocalyptic narrative, unlike earlier dispensationalism. He attributes this to the influence of Pat Robertson, from 1991 onwards.[42]

40. Ibid.
41. Weber, *On the Road to Armageddon.*
42. Barkun, "The 'New World Order' and American Exceptionalism."

He also points out that this increased role for America follows the rise of American exceptionalism and interventionism in US foreign policy. Earlier dispensationalism, as formulated by Cyrus I. Schofield in his famous Schofield Bible of 1909, focused on world missions not on America, and coincided with isolationist foreign policy.[43] (It isn't hard to imagine the line of criticism of dispensationalists wedded to isolationism, as being too insular, uninterested in public affairs altogether.) There is an important though neglected parallel between the insertion of the USA into dispensational apocalyptic and the insertion of Britain into premillennial apocalyptic at the height of the British Empire. Unfortunately, contemporary critics of American dispensationalism almost never make parallels with British imperialism and thus demonstrate a rather ahistorical and rather obsessive myopia. There are clear parallels between American dispensational fixation on the European Union as the empire of Antichrist and the British Evangelical fixation on Napoleon in the early nineteenth century, and on the European Union in the late twentieth century.[44] In the latter case, such dispensationalists were openly hostile to Welsh and Scottish devolution as examples of "evil" and "ungodly" nationalism, supposedly disobeying the godly polity of the United Kingdom headed by the Christian Queen Elizabeth II.[45] The United States took over Britain's role as major superpower after the Second World War. Kathleen Burk's magisterial history of British-American relations furnishes plentiful evidence for refuting some contemporary self-righteousness.[46] She dates the turning of the tide from 1871, when Britain was at the height of its imperial power, and the year of the signing of the Treaty of Washington. By the early twentieth century, Britain had the largest empire in history, comprehending over a fifth of the world's surface and a quarter of its population.[47] By the aftermath of the First World War, the Empire was even larger, having acquired mandates for the League of Nations in Palestine (now Israel and the Palestinian National Authority), Jordan, Mesopotamia (now Iraq), as a result of the downfall of the Ottoman Turkish Empire.[48] The Second World War showed all too clearly that Britain wished to retain its

43. Scofield, *The Scofield Reference Bible*.

44. For an example of this, see Thomas, "Defense of the British Parliament," 17–18.

45. George Thomas, Viscount Tonypandy, was of this attitude. For an alternative view, defending the idea of Britain as a state encompassing four nations, see Stein, "Scots wha hae . . . !," 19–20.

46. Burke, *Old World, New World*.

47. Ibid., 380.

48. Ibid., 461.

Empire while America wanted it dismantled.[49] As Burke has observed, right up until the late 1940s, many people did not see Britain's imperial power waning even though they clearly perceived the rise of the USA as a superpower. Burke's observation of the British elites' attitude towards America back then are still apposite for today, especially regarding cultural, if not diplomatic, elites. She comments on the similarities between Britain and America in that both possessed enormous self-righteousness about their superpower status, that their imperialisms were only of benefit to those subjected to it. In a wry passage, she comments that many of the British governing elites in the twentieth century conceived of themselves in relation to rising American superpower status "as the wise guide of a somewhat clumsy and ignorant adolescent."[50] This seems to be the tone used by academic commentators upon American evangelicals, particularly millenarians. Interestingly, this is true of American academics, who often look more to European culture than do ordinary Americans.[51] One American-based academic who has worked across the transatlantic divide is Philip Jenkins. He has contributed significantly to the academic "religious resurgence" and the "new visibility of religion."[52] As such, a consideration of his treatment of religious resurgence is in order.

PHILIP JENKINS ON GLOBAL RELIGION

Philip Jenkins is a historian of contemporary religion who became renowned for his book *The Next Christendom: The Coming of Global Christianity*. He has since expanded this into a trilogy, the second part of which was on *The New Faces of Christianity: Believing the Bible in the Global South*, and the third, *God's Continent: Christianity, Islam, and Europe's Religious Crisis*.[53] Since then he has authored two more popular books on the history of pre-modern Christianity outside Europe.[54] Jenkins not only shares Rowan Williams' Welsh background (and until recently his Anglicanism), he also shares an interest in Christian-Muslim relations today and how they relate to the histories of the religions. Both men can also be

49. Ibid., 504.

50. Ibid., 528.

51. On Anti-Americanism among Europeans as well as American intellectuals, see Markovitz, *Uncouth Nation*.

52. See Hoezl and Ward (eds.), *The New Visibility of Religion*.

53. Jenkins, *The New Faces of Christianity*; Jenkins, *God's Continent*.

54. Jenkins, *The Lost History of Christianity*; Jenkins, *The Jesus Wars*.

characterized as scholars who have a style of synthesizing a wider range of perspectives and concerns in order to bring them into public debate outside of a strictly academic setting. The fact that Williams is a highly philosophical thinker whereas Jenkins writes in a far more sociological style should not obscure this point. Epistemologically, Jenkins is much closer to Peter Berger's approach to the sociology of religion, which combines Weberian and phenomenological perspectives to forge a methodological agnosticism, than he is to Williams' apophaticism. Yet he too sends out "managerial" signals to Christians, Muslims, and secular policy-makers, drawing on scholarly research.

Jenkins' approach opens up the idea that the needs of national communities, and of large communities within nations, are being conceived in religious terms by contemporary adherents of major religions of revelation (primarily Christianity and Islam) precisely by drawing analogies between the biblical witness and contemporary realities. Especially outside the West, the harsh realities of life appear to correspond to biblical apocalyptic narratives about the End of Days, i.e., the time of the church and the time of nations (wars, famines, pestilence, earthquakes), and traditional ways of handling these find more of a fit with the Bible than with secular ways.[55] In Bergerian terms, the overarching biblical story is *plausible* to vastly more non-Westerners than to Westerners, including many Western Christians.[56] Jenkins is saying something that scholars of global Christianity have always known, but which has rarely been taken seriously within Western academic theology, wherein large portions of the biblical narrative have been eclipsed. Jenkins' approach has the straightforward but very important merit of displaying a vast canvas of evidence to readers who might otherwise never become aware of it, unless they happened to come across immigrant churches in Western cities. The internally secularized subculture of both academic theology and the mainline churches means this is unlikely in the case of many of the people who still think they represent Christianity in Western countries. Thus Jenkins' approach uncovers what Grace Davie calls "European exceptionalism," or what Berger terms "Eurosecularity."[57] On the one hand, Jenkins' framework, which I term "biblical plausibility," functions in his own intentions somewhat like Karl Barth's notion that there is "a strange new world within the

---

55. Jenkins, *The New Faces of Christianity*, passim.

56. Berger's idea of a "plausibility structure" for religion was set out in Berger, *The Sacred Canopy*.

57. Jenkins, *God's Continent*, 3.

Bible" that ultimately stems from the God of Israel, and which can never be neatly assimilated to the experiences of its readers or hearers, or to any one particular school of theology. The biblical text disrupts religious consciousness and vision and beckons the hearer and reader to a truer knowledge of divinely-governed reality, and to living more closely according to representations of it.

As there is an elective affinity between Jenkins' style and Berger's method, it is appropriate to sketch out relevant elements of the latter here.[58] Berger views social reality, including religion, as a social construction. In this respect he has been compared to Hegel. Regarding the Hegelian story that modernity is the creature of Protestantism, Berger has three important observations. First, he notes that Christianity has alternatively been blamed for all that is degenerate in modernity, by such as Schopenhauer and Nietzsche (hence the latter's choice of Dionysius against Christ). Second, he suggests that his own view that religion is a human projection may be inverted to produce a viable anthropologically-grounded theology. This constitutes inverting Feuerbach's theory of religion, which inverted and changed the significance of Hegel's dialectic. Berger takes Hegel's dialectic to be about a "conversation" that was ultimately between man and God, while Feuerbach (and Marx and Freud after him) only speak of a dialectical movement between human beings. Third, against Hegel, he argues that Protestantism involved "an immense shrinkage in the scope of the sacred in reality" (he fails to specify that this was more a Lutheran than a Reformed problem), and he celebrates this. Berger's own theology is characterized by himself as classic liberal Protestantism, and he does gesture a number of times towards Rudolf Bultmann.[59] He has a high valuation of the individual, especially the "authentic" individual stripped of social roles. In his early work *The Precarious Vision*, he argues that the fiction of society as a "given" is part of "the burden of Egypt," and that particular individual and group experiences (especially religious ones) remove this veil and reveal that society is precarious and contingent. Sociology presents society as "a structure of dramatic fictions" (similar to Erving Goffman), which can be both determinist and allow human freedom.[60] The "Burden of Zion" is that institutional religion can be the most dangerous social fiction of all, hallowing all others. Hence he takes the view that the critique of

58. Berger, *The Sacred Canopy*, 110–11.

59. On his Bultmannian tendencies, see Berger, *Questions of Faith*.

60. Berger, *The Precarious Vision*.

religion is a step towards freedom. Christianity (as for Bonhoeffer, Barth, Rowan Williams, and countless others) is closer to this critique than to religion so defined. Finally, due to seeing the world under the aspect of redemption, Christianity has a comical view of society, in which human beings are freed of their fictional social roles and the "deadly earnestness" that goes with them. Of course, with the radical secularization of the second half of the twentieth century in the West (mindful nevertheless of the continued vitality of religion in the USA), the very possibility of Christianity's liberating comical role may have declined.[61] Jenkins can also be said to espouse a comic approach, but one that confronts Western scholars of religion with their own parochial wrongheadedness in "knowing" Christianity to be Western. He also confronts hostility and suspicion towards realistic or plausible reading of the Bible, showing that it is often in its traditional forms drawing from this kind of reading that Christianity is improving people's lives. We can see the problem if we take an overview of his trilogy. *The Next Christendom* gave a sobering picture of coming clashes between Christians and Muslims across the world (it was published just after 9/11), at the same time as inviting readers to see Christianity "again for the first time," drawing an analogy between non-Western Christianities and first century movements. In *The New Faces of Christianity*, Jenkins displays how believing the Bible can motivate and issue in comic reversals of old and new, rich and poor, evil and good, and men and women. It can vindicate the persecuted church against the secularized established Christianity of the West. When he turns his gaze to Europe in *God's Continent*, however, Jenkins doesn't advocate the same comic turn. Instead he advances the idea of religion as good for maintaining meaning and adapting to civil society. This is classic American mainline Protestant rhetoric, and we now turn to Berger's analysis of the mainline as it has changed in the twentieth century.

Berger argues that American mainline Protestantism has changed since the 1950s due to class and bureaucracy working themselves out as sociological forces.[62] Mainline Protestantism produced American middle-class culture, and up to the 1950s were "a sort of establishment within it." This was the world in which Reinhold Niebuhr moved. According to

---

61. Berger also published *Redeeming Laughter*. For the view that humor has replaced faith in modern America, Heddendorf, *From Faith to Fun*, relies on Berger's theory; see Robert A. Segal's review in the *Times Higher Education* (8 April, 2010).

62. Berger, "Reflections of an Ecclesiastical Expatriate," 964–69. All quotes are from the online version, hence why I haven't referenced them with page numbers. http://www.religion-online.org/showarticle.asp?title=232.

Berger, the character of American middle-class society has changed due to the split of the middle class into two. The first is "the old middle class, the traditional bourgeoisie, centered in the business community and the old professions." The second is "a new middle class, based on the production and distribution of symbolic knowledge," comprised of people working in education, mass media, therapy, well-being, social justice, and personal lifestyles. Many are paid by public funds, and even when working in the private sector depend on state funding. Following Marx, Berger argues that this "New Class" combines "class interest and class culture." The interests of this class are located on the political left, termed "liberal" in the popular media. The reason for this is that "this class has a vital interest in the maintenance and expansion of those state expenditures on which its social existence depends." This interest is opposed to that of the old middle class, which is invested in the free market. Berger observes that both the values and opinions of the New Class only represent a minority of American culture, yet they exert a disproportionate amount of influence on it. This effect is redoubled by the fact that the old middle class "is culturally passive and inept as it has always been," so has been successfully penetrated by the culture of the New Class. Berger applies this analysis to Protestant denominations, which have been overtaken at the bureaucratic level by the members of the New Class, who see themselves as "a liberal élite." When new radical agendas came along that lay people found uncongenial, they voted with their feet and left, either never to return to church, or to go to evangelical congregations. In more recent years, they have also been converting to Roman Catholicism and Eastern Orthodoxy. Berger argues that "the mainline churches will contribute in a double way to the secularization of America—by legitimating a set of highly secularized values and by contributing to the unchurched population through its emigrants." The New Class will continue to shape the mainline churches, though the precise ideologies that express this class interest will change. This has already happened with the collapse of Communism. I would argue that it has also happened with the switch to an anti-Zionist rhetoric from some quarters. Finally, Berger argues that American evangelicals have not been able to resist the cultural changes effectively because "they lack the institutions and the know-how," and because their political successes bring them into the wider national culture, thus subjecting them to the influence of the New Class.

Berger's analysis of how the splitting of the American middle class affected mainline Protestantism helps us understand Philip Jenkins' work better. Jenkins belongs by virtue of his work to the New Class of opinion-formers and producers of symbolic knowledge. He shot to renown status with his book *The Next Christendom*, and was quickly lauded by American evangelicals among others, who like evangelicals elsewhere have been interested in missions around the world. Jenkins, though based at Penn State University, now also holds a post at Baylor University, an evangelical university in Texas that has in recent years worked to shed its dispensationalist eschatology, and positioned itself as being in dialogue with Islam.[63] Yet Jenkins' sympathetic approach to Islam somewhat crosses the line theologically. For example, in *The Lost History of Christianity*, Jenkins outlined the rise and fall of Christianity in Asia and parts of Africa by 1500, a history of over a millennium barely known to most Westerners. He articulates his argument in terms of the recognition of religious cultures, not in theological terms. Declining what he calls "a lament for a worldwide Christian hegemony that never was," and refusing to criticize Christians in Asia and Africa for not having resisted Islam, he speaks in comparative terms of regretting "the destruction of a once-flourishing culture," analogous to Islamic Spain or Eastern European Jewry.[64] The ultimate loss is one to all "human experience and culture," and the tragedy is that "no religion is safe." Here we have an equivalent to Charles Taylor's Hegelian politics of recognition to world religions and religious cultures as unique expressions of facets of human authenticity. This is a very far cry from how the Old and New Testament authors and characters actually see non-Israelite and non-Christian religions. The likely reason for such an expressivist and subjective approach to the history of Christianity is that Jenkins is very concerned about the US relationship to Israel as jeopardizing Christian-Muslim relations. He contrasts the world's twenty million Jews with its one billion Muslims, a disparity that will grow so that "by 2050, Muslims will outnumber Jews by one hundred to one."[65] Accordingly, he wants US and European policy towards the Middle East to change to be perceived as less anti-Muslim. Jenkins envisages alternative future scenarios. In one, Christians in Africa and Asia are not saddled by guilt about European anti-Semitism, so they might identify much more with the Palestinians than with Israel. This means they could align themselves with Muslims in their localities. Jenkins thinks this is more likely because global churches are founded on "biblical literalism." This is unhelpful

---

63. Philip Jenkins' personal web page can be read here: http://www.personal.psu.edu/faculty/j/p/jpj1/.

64. Jenkins, *The Lost History of Christianity*, 3–4.

65. Jenkins, *The Next Christendom*, 226.

because the definition of "literal" varies enormously between academics and simple believers. Simple believers unschooled in theology and hermeneutics tend to say they read the Bible "literally" when they mean a combination of reading it as real history and at the same time as figurative in the sense of being prophetic. In this sense, there exist plenty of ways for Christians who see themselves as "literalists" to side with either Israel or Palestine. Jenkins has ignored the widespread Zionism among non-Western Evangelicals, e.g., African and Chinese. It is only on strategic, not on biblical hermeneutical grounds, that Jenkins also envisages close alignment of many non-Western Christians with Israel on practical interests. This is because Israel has for a long time allied itself with self-styled Christian groups in non-Western countries who have been in combat with Islamic groups, partly as a strategy against their own Islamic antagonists. Sudan is a case in point.[66] His ultimate concern is that the continued conflict between Israel and its Islamic neighbors could affect Christian-Muslim relations around the world for the worse.

When he turns his gaze onto Europe, Jenkins is forced to acknowledge the reality of Muslim anti-semitic violence against Jews.[67] Unfortunately he ignores the fact that it is linked to widespread Muslim anti-Zionism. He says that European Muslims are more favorable towards Jews than are Muslims in non-European countries.[68] Things changed in the 1980s with the formation of Hamas (1987). There is probably an age discrepancy regarding European Muslims' attitudes towards Jews, with the older being more tolerant. He tactfully doesn't say that this is probably because the older generation was less religious in the first place. Given that our focus on secularization and Israel is linked to ideas of providence, it is of particular interest that Jenkins should argue that Western Muslims' complaint that Western governments operate with a double standard towards Israel and Palestine, and entertain the belief that Israel "dominates" the international policy of those governments, "leads Muslims to be vulnerable to anti-Zionist conspiracy theories."[69] The problem here is moral. People are free to believe conspiracy theories or to repudiate them. Believing in conspiracy theories is a choice, not an illness to which people are vulnerable if they don't inoculate themselves. The reason I introduce the fact of anti-Zionist conspiracy theories here is that they are a type of providential belief

66. Ibid., 227.

67. Jenkins, *God's Continent*, 166–69.

68. Ibid., 166.

69. Ibid., 169.

(and the term "conspiracy theory" itself can at times be used deliberately to discredit any providential, theistic theory of history). There are both Islamic and Christian people who entertain such ideas about Israel (i.e., Jews, dominating world history by pulling the strings behind the scenes). Such beliefs are not rare, especially not among Western Muslims, but nor are they absent from the minds of some theologians either.

While acknowledging the formative power of reading sacred books for Christians and Muslims in the non-Western world, Jenkins later compares adherents of the two religions in terms of key ethical beliefs as registered in surveys of social attitudes. For example, he argues that European Muslims are much like postwar Christians as regards ethical beliefs, e.g., about family and sexual ethics.[70] He uses the fact of Islamic public activism in the West to defend by analogy Christian participation in the public sphere. By putting a positive concept of religion versus secularism into motion, and working from shared moral stances, we can see how Jenkins urges that Christian theologians forge a syncretism with Muslims in accepting Mohammed as a prophet, in order to reach an accommodation with Muslims in Europe, for an unstated reason.[71] This is very unusual. Jenkins seems to be assuming that theological grounds can be found for this, e.g., parallel with two-covenant theology with Judaism in America. He raises the old question of the extent to which Islam is a religion distinct from Christianity.[72] The key idea would here be the idea of God's final prophet prophesied in Deuteronomy 18, which some Jews take to be Ezra, the New Testament takes to be Jesus, and the Qur'an takes to be Muhammad. Much depends here on the figurative reading of Deuteronomy, ideas about its authorship and writing, and on the question of who is the Paraclete promised by Jesus—is it the Holy Spirit who comes after the resurrection, or is it Muhammad? Jenkins' style of argument is one that seems to want to make controversial-sounding points in order to provoke people, but which also wants to be seen to maintain an orthodox Christian line. Yet at the same time Jenkins asks "what alternative is open?" without asking why he wants there to be an alternative. The reason is soon enough supplied—for European Christians to make peace with Muslim claims without completely submitting themselves to them. He never explains openly why he wishes European Christians specifically to accept Muhammad as a prophet, nor does he define what a prophet is in

70. Ibid., 275.

71. Ibid., 267–68.

72. Ibid., 268.

the first place. This is where high-minded, arrogant attempts to manage Christianity and Islam as if they were theological and scriptural equals gets one. It's a case of "oh what a tangled web we weave." He has gotten carried away with a purely comparative epistemological approach to religion. On this view, the Qur'an is equally "plausible" (in Peter Berger's terms) as the Bible—which of course it is, because so much of its narrative is derived from the Bible. The ultimate problem is not which text is more plausible in terms of referring to the sorry course of natural disasters. The narratives in the Qur'an often renarrate biblical narratives (e.g., the story of Noah), as well as introducing an ambiguity as to where exactly the Promised Land was. A key issue here, as should be obvious, is the status of nations in the Qur'an, traditions of Qur'anic exegesis, and Islamic theology. We should read Jenkins as carrying out Peter Berger's wish for an anthropologically-grounded theology, grounded in the West's need to come to terms with Islam and its fear of being terrorized and taken over by Islam. Jenkins' call for positive Christian valuation of Mohammed and the Qur'an is the logical outcome of Berger's call to invert Feuerbach's critique of religion, because that was an inversion of Hegel's theology. What exactly that theology was is a question to which we shall return later on. Given Jenkins' concern for Palestine, however, we need to pick up briefly on the idea of nations in Islam. For if Christian-Muslim relations are important in the conflict, then the concept of nationhood would seem to be one for discussion at the highest intellectual level. The question is, is this the case, or is the concept the elephant in the room?

NATIONHOOD AND NATIONALISM IN ISLAMIC THOUGHT

One crucial concept never written about in the literature recording or engaging interfaith dialogue with Muslims is nationhood. The Western scholarly literature on Islam to which I have access doesn't exactly give the impression that nationhood as a concept has been understood in a theologically affirmative sense within Islam. Anthony Black says that "Muslims have always recognized nationality . . . but until the late nineteenth century, nationhood has never been seen as a basis for statehood."[73] Nation-state as an idea was promoted by some Egyptian and Turkish writers as love of one's homeland or country (*watan*). In the Middle East, the ideology of Arab nationalism complicated and confused things a lot

---

73. For what follows, I am indebted to Black, *The History of Islamic Political Thought*, 344f.

because, as Black and others argue, the prospect of an Arab nation-state was never a realistic one. When we turn to the concept of nationalism, we get into rather alarming territory. Islamic fundamentalists such as Sayyid Qutb demonize nationalism completely, characterizing it as the product of *jahiliyya* (pre-Islamic ignorance), whereas al-Mawdudi describes it as "the satan of racist and nationalist fanaticism."[74] Qutb attacked Arab nationalism, and instead of speaking of the homeland or *watan* as nation, he spoke of the Islamic *umma* as the *watan*.[75] As Black points out, it is wholly unsurprising that it is *Christian* Arabs who took much of the initiative in crafting Arab nationalism. He even goes so far as saying that "the more self-consciously Islamic one becomes, the less inclined one is to endow the nation-state with any moral authority."[76] Thus, the resurgence of Islam in the second half of the twentieth century, in response to modernizing currents that adopted the nation-state ideal, was logically bound to result in different kinds of transnational ideals instead, be it calls for Islamic law to be recognized within Western states, campaigning for the recognition of Islamic financial principles, the intellectual internationalism of scholars, and arguments for economic cooperation between Muslim states, a Muslim world court, and even a new Caliphate. All of this begs the question as to whether what Western intellectuals sympathetic to Islam call "transnational" dimensions and ideals are not in fact variants of imperialism. The very same intellectuals frequently decry "American imperialism," mostly on economic and cultural grounds. Not only is there an obvious hypocrisy here, but by the territorial definition of imperialism, the USA is not an imperial power as England, and later Britain, was. A Muslim world court may or may not be an imperialistic ideal, but a Muslim Caliphate would be, because the Caliphate historically was the body that was alone authorized to call for *jihad* in the Qu'ranic sense of a war against those deemed infidels. The political class and intelligentsia in the Islamic Middle East were more favorable towards nationalism in the aftermath of the First World War than they were in the late twentieth century. Several events provoked this change: the Israeli victory in the Six Day War of 1967, and the Iranian Revolution of 1979. This needs to be compared with Western Christian intellectuals' perspectives. The First World War provoked a surge in anti-nationalism and pro-socialist sympathies among some Christian intellectuals. The Second World War provoked a horror of both nationalism

---

74. Choueiri, *Islamic Fundamentalism*, 132.

75. Enayat, *Modern Islamic Political Thought*, 115.

76. Black, *The History of Islamic Political Thought*, 345.

and anti-semitism. It was not the horrors of the Second World War that provoked anti-nationalism among Muslims. So, after the First World War, Christian intellectuals were becoming wary of nationalism and Muslim intellectuals were embracing it. After the Second World War, Christians became wary. After the Six Day War, Christians became divided, as many supported Israel's right to defend itself. Those who had always been anti-Zionist remained so. What emerged after the First Intifada, however, was that many of those Christians who had supported Israel turned against it. The catalyst for this was their discovery of the Palestinians. What this was was the transferal of paternalism from Jews to Palestinians. This is the pathos of "benign imperialism"; it is the logical opposite of recognition of nationhood. It is also very embarrassingly noticeable how many of those who pity the Palestinians very loudly do not support the two-state solution, but insist on a binational state, currently touted as "the one-state solution."[77] This should not be surprising. Islam from the beginning was supersessionist towards the nation of Israel, and made claims to the Land of Israel. Unless a non-supersessionist approach to the Jewish *nation—not* the Jewish *religion*—can be developed by Muslims which will be accepted by believing Muslims, the prospect for improvement in Muslim theological recognition of both Israel and Palestine is bleak. As for a Christian theological means of recognizing Palestine, the problem is that Christian theologians have not even gotten around to discussing Palestine as a stateless nation, and that is because many have yet to consider the concept.[78]

SECULARIZATION, DESECULARIZATION, AND RELIGIOUS RESURGENCE ONCE AGAIN

When Christian academics do a lot of work on religious resurgence and religious pluralism, they have a tendency to fall quickly from a theological approach to a sociological approach. Superficially this appears to be a move from setting down or acknowledging authoritative norms to developing

77. The available evidence suggests that bi-nationalism, an ideal developed on either side, has been fraught with serious difficulties, but also that it has only seriously appealed to some intellectuals. See Hermann, "The Bi-National Idea in Israel/Palestine," 381–401.

78. Naturally we should not ignore the good arguments made for the view that Middle Eastern nationalisms have in fact been built on antique foundations, and cannot merely be dismissed as the product of colonialism. See Gerber, "The Limits of Constructedness," 251–68. Gerber makes the point that pan-Arabism was partly the result of long-term Ottoman Turkish policy.

merely descriptive accounts of religion. Certain liberal Protestant sociologists of religion, such as David Martin, working in the tradition going back through Max Weber ultimately to Kant, present their sociology as descriptive accounts of religion, admitting that sociology as a discipline is rooted in the Enlightenment, at its more skeptical. Martin believes sociology gives theology a "reality check," especially about power and violence.[79] He acknowledges also Ernst Troeltsch and Reinhold and Richard Niebuhr as kindred souls. As is well-appreciated, and will be discussed briefly later, John Milbank's argument in *Theology and Social Theory* is an attack on this approach within Britain, and without doubt within Anglican circles (Martin is an Anglican priest). Thus Milbank positions himself as an English counterpart to Stanley Hauerwas in the fight against Reinhold Niebuhr's legacy. We will discuss Milbank a little in the next chapter, and more fully in chapter 4. Martin's approach can also be compared to that of Philip Jenkins in some ways, though Martin is less eclectic and has honed his thinking through repeated engagement with the Weberian theory of secularization. Late in his career, he expressed gratitude to Charles Taylor for his work bringing into dialogue philosophical (or history-of-ideas) and sociological work on secularization.[80] This is interesting because in some ways, Martin's work is a sociological form of recognition theory for Christianity in the modern world, in particular for Pentecostalism.[81] Yet Martin's theory is entirely indebted to reading the sociological tradition, and utilizes no theological doctrine of providence at all. Thus Pentecostalism is represented in an extremely selective manner by ignoring the place of Israel in its theology, just as Taylor misrepresents the Puritans likewise. Bringing philosophical and sociological perspectives on secularization has not improved understanding of secularization on a theological level. It could never do this, because fundamentally neither of these scholarly traditions engages in any consistent manner with the biblical hermeneutics and dogmatics of historic groups of Christians. Martin may paint the modern secular world in a more realist and punchy manner than Taylor's rhetoric of conversation about personal authenticity. Yet the two are both working within a modern perspective that pushes considerations of providence to the backstage of history while feeding on theories of history as produced by human action and speech that are, one way or another, invested in the opinion that history—the history of nations included—is

---

79. Martin, *On Secularization*, 11.

80. Ibid., 1–2.

81. Martin, *Pentecostalism*.

a human artifice. Taylor himself explicitly acknowledges that intellectual secularization from the early nineteenth century onwards was facilitated by Romantic aesthetics applied to history.[82] In such a mindset, the survival of the Jews as a stateless nation, a nation that had lost its state and been scattered, was for Hegel a "dark riddle," an enigma that was inexplicable.[83] Not so for the heirs of the Puritans and Pietists.

Here we have an important rift within Western Protestantism, between those who are willing to read world history explicitly in terms of the coordination of concepts of providence and prophecy, and those who tend to read history in naturalist or rationalist terms. Of course, there have been many different attempts to combine elements of both the theological and the naturalist or rationalist accounts, as well as many variants of each. All historic discourses on history have had visions of its end, i.e., eschatologies, as well as discourses concerning how this will be reached. Millenarians have always been deeply concerned to discern the "signs of the times" in history beyond the church, and are thus a very important corrective to the church-centeredness that can sometimes cloy theology. It is a serious error to assume a concern for prophecy as echoed in history has only been the province of premillennialists, and that the belief Jews would return to the Holy Land before the second coming was only a premillennialist belief. The theories about secularization that were discussed earlier all come from the sociology of religion, which has been eagerly embraced by liberal Protestants since Max Weber and Georg Simmel devised them in the late nineteenth century. The argument could be made that secularization theory is to liberal Protestantism what historicist prophecy was for historicist and other evangelicals—a mode of discernment of the meaning of history and religious change. Sociologists and other have argued that dispensationalists have aimed to speed the second coming and bring on Armageddon; in other words, they have been agents of historical change and not only passive observers of it.[84] Yet as we saw above, both things are in fact true of secularization theorists. Moreover, the sociology of religion, which lies at the heart of classical sociology, gained a footing in the state-funded universities at roughly the same time as biblical criticism, in the late nineteenth century. Both denied the prophetic slant

---

82. Taylor, *A Secular Age*, 352–76.

83. On the "dark riddle," see Yovel, *Dark Riddle*.

84. For an overview of the debates, see Spector, *Evangelicals and Israel*.

on providence. These disciplines all formed part of the elite educational ideology of British and German imperialisms and nascent Americanism.

Some scholars have spoken not merely of desecularization but of re-enchantment. In some ways, this is a more helpful term, because it specifies the rise of popular esoteric and occult movements.[85] Desecularization may be too strong a term if it is taken to mean that the public and private spheres are being brought back under theological authority, which they are not really. Religious resurgence has only occurred in certain spheres, and as Casanova argues, it is not inevitable or irreversible. However, I show in this book how it is as much a description of academics and clergy as it is of ordinary people, indeed possibly more so in secularized Europe and increasingly secularized North America. Put bluntly, it is a way for religious scholars to show that they are visible, important, and useful to society. The empiricist nature of the sociology of religion, even more than of the psychology of religion, means that religious resurgence, desecularization, and re-enchantment all rely increasingly on the implied notion of the visibility of religious and spiritual change and activity. It is this empiricism that makes them secular categories that cannot help theologians in our discernment. This focus on visibility is something that we analyzed in the work of Philip Jenkins, who is seen as the foil for Rowan Williams' heavily apophatic approach. What is missing here is the necessary primacy of the Bible as God's Word written as the means for understanding history. Claiming correspondences is not enough. Jenkins wants Christians to accept Mohammed as a prophet. This sort of demand simply cannot be acceded by the churches. For the New Testament clearly understands Deuteronomy 18 to be pointing to Jesus as God's final prophet, and thus to rule out others after him, except those in his body. Islam understands Deuteronomy 18 to refer to Mohammed. Behind this lies the belief that the Qur'an is the verbally inspired gift of God as the true Torah from heaven, correcting the maculated Torah of ancient Judaism and early Christianity. The inevitable corollary is a Christology in both the Qur'an and in Islamic commentary and an apocalyptic that is antithetical to the New Testament and the Christian theological traditions. Christians simply should not go the way Philip Jenkins wants us to go, if we want to remain Christians. Jenkins elsewhere laments, rather naively, that we have no theological account of the decline and disappearance of Christianity in Asia by 1500. There is a possible partial answer from biblical hermeneutics at hand. It is the loss of apocalyptic and perseverance in the faith

---

85. Partridge, *The Re-Enchantment of the West.*

that meant Christians came to see little difference between themselves and their neighbors' beliefs in other religions. In other words, Christians lost their sense of purpose and their "vision of the end." Was biblical illiteracy as much a problem for them as it seems to be in every other age?

The categories of desecularization, re-enchantment, and religious resurgence have only relative value as descriptions of religious change, primarily because of their empiricist and non-theological roots. It would be unwise for Christian theologians to attempt to formulate theological periodizations of history by using them. This does not, however, mean that there should be no discernment of events that are theologically important. The event of the foundation of Israel in 1948 and the non-foundation of a Palestinian nation-state, together with the lack of support by Arab nations for one, is the one under consideration here. Dispensationalists have tended to believe that this either literally heralded or prefigured the End of Days. The rest of us cannot accept this without qualification because the New Testament clearly shows that the End of Days is the entire span of the history of the church since the time of Jesus on earth. However, instead of viewing the dispensational view in an *entirely* negative light, and thus simply operating on the level of exegetical correctness, there is the alternative option of viewing it as an attempt to take seriously a genuinely important world-historical event. Even theological errors can be considered, at times, to show forth important attempts at discernment. In the case of modern attacks on dispensationalism, and on millenarianism more broadly, it should be clear by now that I am not entirely willing to take them seriously. Foremost, what is not being admitted is the sheer annoyance at hermeneutical discourses that dare to proclaim that God still acts behind history. If there were a large amillennialist lobby of Christians declaring that the foundation of Israel was providential, scholars of religion, including sociologists, would still get excited about it. Only because amillennialist theologians tend to be in the mainline churches, and tend to be less populist in their methods of communication, they are much less visible. Indeed, the very existence of such a body of people is not that well-known. Perhaps that is as things should be. Too much publicity can quickly corrupt theologians.

What is important is that theological handling of Israel should not be captive to arguments about dispensationalism, on the one hand, or American foreign policy on the other. They cannot, of course, ignore these things, which is why eschatology was discussed in this chapter, and why in the next we will look at Reinhold Niebuhr. Historically, however, this set of concerns long predates both modern dispensationalism and American globalism. Many critics have real trouble accepting the fact that there have simply always been some Christians, and many Jews, who have hoped for Jewish return to and reunion in the Holy Land, one way or another. In the history of Christianity, anxiety about these beliefs has often been linked to the fear that for Western countries to allow this to happen would be to give ordinary Christians a sign that the second coming is near. At the same time, there was a real fear that the creation of a Jewish state would give a sign that Christendom, the rule of Christians over society and over non-Christians, was coming to an end, and thus, that the "end" was near in the form of the unleashing of the rule of Antichrist. Of course, such fears have not exactly gone away. Indeed they have their secular counterparts insofar as secular anti-Zionism in the West tends all too easily to scapegoat Israel as "the man of sin," as if "dealing with it" would bring secular redemption. The truth is that it is extremely difficult for Christian theology to get away from the difficult patterns of historic thinking about Jews and Israel. The path that I have tried to undertake in this book has been to investigate how selected Western theologians have handled Israel as nation, and in relation to their attitudes to other Gentile nations (their own). The point is that modern Israel functions as a mirror of how we ourselves see our own national identities. Christians are used to the reading of ancient Israel in this way. They are much less comfortable outside premillennialist circles with realizing that this is how we actually approach modern Israel, whether we like it or not. What my concern is, then, is the ethos of theology and its exegesis of the Bible. To what extent a discourse on Israel is theological is an important question, especially for Niebuhr, to whom we now turn.

2

Reinhold Niebuhr and the Postliberals

The Fate of Liberal Protestant American Zionism

REINHOLD NIEBUHR WAS THE most prominent liberal protestant theologian to support Zionism in the United States in the mid-twentieth century. Only a minority of theologians, clergy, and laity in the mainline churches ever supported Zionism. Some argue that because Niebuhr's Zionism was not grounded in dogmatic theology and biblical exegesis, it was not transmitted to the next generation of mainline Protestants. Furthermore, the structure of his thought left open the possibility of an anti-Zionist approach. This chapter assesses the tensions between theology and ethics in Niebuhr's Zionism, and links it to his conception of both Israel and America as messianic nations with civilizational missions. First, it assesses Niebuhr's support for a Jewish return to Palestine in relation to Protestant and Jewish relocation of the promised land. The second section argues that Niebuhr's Zionism was integral to his Christian realism. The third section probes his shift from viewing Jews as a messianic people to understanding America as a messianic nation, subsuming Israel under America's civilizing mission. The fourth section argues that Niebuhr's natural theology, which was the basis for his understanding of history and divine transcendence, constrained what he could say concerning the "biblical myths" of covenant and election regarding Israel. The fifth section argues that Niebuhr located his Zionism within his reconstruction of natural law and subjected it to his critique of nationalism and religion. As his Zionism was not theologically grounded, his support for Israel could not be persuasive theologically for subsequent generations of mainline Protestants. In the last two sections, I argue that Niebuhr's method had a major influence on

American postliberal theology and on Mark Juergensmeyer's sociological assessment of apocalyptic violence as religious resurgence since the end of the Cold War. As Niebuhr's argument for Zionism was kept outside the bounds of theology, it failed to be registered properly by postliberalism; and his denial of the election of Israel opened the door to denial or ignoring by Christians of the implication of Judaism as politics, and therefore of Zionism, in the challenges of modernity. The result is that postliberalism with its heavy focus on narrative, drama, and nonviolence, is powerless to diagnose the ills of anti-Semitism and anti-Zionism that are so prevalent in forms of religious resurgence around the world.

THE PROMISED LAND AS ZION: RELOCATION FROM AMERICA TO PALESTINE

The relocation of the idea of Zion, the promised land, from America to Palestine occurred in the nineteenth century among American Protestants and in the twentieth century among American Jews.[1] Niebuhr's Zionism is located midway between the two. The Congregationalists and Puritans who came to New England in the seventeenth century saw America as Zion.[2] Many American religious people changed from seeing America as the Holy Land to seeing the Land of Israel as the Holy Land. American Congregationalist missionaries in the nineteenth century believed the second coming was imminent, and set off in 1819 to found missions, despite Catholic and Muslim Turkish opposition.[3] Nineteenth-century American Congregationalist missionaries "helped replant the sacred territory of Scripture from America to the Land of Israel, including its eschatological ramifications."[4] This approach was an important source for American evangelical attitudes to Israel. However, liberal Protestants interpreted the issue differently. Gershom Greenberg compares Reinhold Niebuhr's attitude to that of two other prominent liberal Protestant churchmen of the first half of the twentieth century: Adolf A. Berle Sr. and Harry Emerson Fosdick. The distinctions between them—and between Niebuhr and Fosdick in particular—correspond to the subsequent divide among mainline Protestants over Israel.

1. I am indebted to the account of Gershom Greenberg for the basic tenets of this section. See Greenberg, *Holy Land.*

2. Ibid., 15–45; Handy, *A Christian America*, chs.1 and 2.

3. Greenberg, *Holy Land*, 113–41.

4. Ibid., 132.

Berle was an American Congregationalist pastor from Boston, who penned a volume entitled *The World Significance of a Jewish State* in 1918.[5] In it he idealizes Jews and Judaism as superior to Christianity, which had failed both to avert the First World War and mitigate its consequences. He looked for the religious rehabilitation and unification of Jews and the formation of a Jewish state on this basis. He envisioned a Hebrew commonwealth in which the Hebrew language and literature would thrive. This would enable the renewal of ancient Israelite law and national structures. The Jewish state would display its national traditions and idealisms, which had made the politics of the Israelite prophets such an integral part of Christianity. As a result, anti-Semitism would be eliminated. Jewish return to Israel would be the occasion for "world instruction in the religion of Israel, which has never been vouchsafed to any other cult in the history of mankind!"[6] Berle considered Judaism as "the barometer of civilization," a future moral paradigm. In this, he represented a shift away from seeing America as the world's exemplary nation. Placing responsibility upon a future Jewish state for "improving the world" due to disenchantment with Christianity was a significant move, as it opened the door to later liberal Protestant disenchantment with Israel for not being morally perfect.

Harry Emerson Fosdick, a prominent New York Baptist minister, toured Palestine in 1920.[7] Fosdick was disappointed with the land, and disagreed with Theodor Herzl's slogan that it was "a land without a people," given that there were more than half a million Arabs living there. Fosdick, like many American liberals, sympathized with the Arabs' view that they had been betrayed by the British when they were not granted autonomy in return for winning the First World War against the Ottoman Turks. Fosdick sympathized with the Arab fear that Jews would try to rebuild Solomon's temple, thus provoking conflict with Islam. (This was somewhat disingenuous given that he knew most Jews to be secular.) He wanted to restrict the number of Jewish refugees allowed into Palestine, but like Berle, he also wanted Jews to reside in the land in a way that would somehow "benefit mankind." Fosdick spoke about Zionism to staff and students at Union Theological Seminary in New York in 1927. Zionism for him was a form of nationalism and as such, an idol. He would only support a Zionism that was a cultural and educational revival such as that espoused by Rabbi Judah Magnes (1877–1948), then chancellor of the Hebrew

---

5. Berle, *The World Significance of a Jewish State*; Greenberg, *Holy Land*, 281–82.

6. Berle, *World Significance*, as cited in Davis, *America and the Holy Land*, 64, fn. 5.

7. Greenberg, *Holy Land*, 282–84.

University of Jerusalem. This influenced subsequent mainline Protestant attitudes, for Magnes and other intellectuals at Hebrew University were convinced anti-Zionists, favoring the idea of a binational Jewish-Arab state. The most important proponent of this view was Martin Buber, who advanced the concept of the "true Zionism" of the soul.[8]

From the time of his critique of liberalism onwards, Niebuhr differed from both Berle and Fosdick in placing fewer moral expectations upon Jews to redeem the human race. He eschewed moralism, mounting a sharp critique in the early 1930s of the liberal Social Gospel movement and its perceived optimism concerning human perfectibility and the gradual progression of history. Niebuhr saw Palestine as a home for the Jews, not as a project that was supposed to "benefit mankind" (Fosdick) or "improve the world" (Berle). Thus he did not tend to hold Jews and Israel to a higher standard than other nations. He definitely did not want to see ancient Israelite law revived, and was almost paranoid about Israel's becoming a theocracy. Israel for Niebuhr was neither a displacement of Christian hopes for worldly redemption and progress onto Jews, nor a displacement of Christian hopes for religious resurgence. His secularized Zionism was an alternative to more evangelical forms of Christian support for Zionism.

Niebuhr would grasp the "creational" aspects of Zionism, as opposed to its soteriological and eschatological aspects. In this respect, his thinking was closer structurally and substantially to that of Reform and secular Jews than to that of fellow Protestants. Louis Brandeis' case for Jewish assimilation in the United States along with the founding of a Jewish state influenced Niebuhr, as both men shared a commitment to the United States as a liberal democracy.[9] Brandeis' argument was that nations have right and duties to develop and promote the higher goals of civilization, because they are just as "individual" as persons. Niebuhr also agreed with his friend Justice Felix Frankfurter that Palestine would rescue Jewish national identity.[10] Frankfurter had been recruited to American Jewish Zionism by Brandeis even before Woodrow Wilson led America into the First World War.[11] His unofficial diplomacy would prove to be both significant on the Jewish side and supportive of Niebuhr's efforts.[12]

---

8. Buber, *A Land of Two Peoples*, 220–24. For strong Zionist criticism of Buber's role in Israel, see Hazony, *The Jewish State*, 181–93, 267–83.

9. Niebuhr, "Jews after the War: Parts I and II," 133–34, 138–39.

10. Greenberg, *Holy Land*, 341.

11. Merkley, *The Politics of Christian Zionism*, 87–88.

12. Rice, "Felix Frankfurter and Reinhold Niebuhr, 1940–1964," 325–426.

NIEBUHR'S ZIONISM EXPRESSED AS CHRISTIAN REALISM

Early in his career Niebuhr encountered American Jews. His friendships with them nourished a belief that Judaism's sense of social justice was superior to that of contemporary American Protestantism. Also as a result he became a convinced Zionist, expressing this conviction through his method of "Christian realism." The Israeli political theorist Eyal Naveh has recently argued that Niebuhr's support for Zionism formed part of a "non-utopian liberalism":

> As one who always opposed any simple identification between historical events and the divine cosmic structure, Niebuhr refused to give any religious meaning and redemptive significance to the destiny of the Jews. He considered Zionism as a legitimate political movement; a possible, not necessarily inevitable solution; one, not necessarily exclusive remedy, for the Jewish problem in the twentieth century. He admitted, however, that "the ideal of a political homeland for the Jews is so intriguing that I am almost willing to sacrifice my conviction for the sake of it."[13]

Niebuhr's Zionism was central to his Christian realism, which itself was deeply rooted in his favoring what he considered to be the Hebraic moral aspect of the Western Christian tradition over its Hellenic metaphysical aspect. The development of Niebuhr's Zionism reflects the continued coordination of Christian realism's three components: political, moral, and theological.[14] *Political realism* involves taking into account all the different kinds of forces involved in making political decisions. Accordingly, the human condition is too complicated to allow pure moral idealism to affect such decisions, as it risks disempowering political agents through lack of worldly wisdom. Niebuhr's subtlety on this matter has been overlooked, both by critics and supporters. John Howard Yoder accuses Niebuhr of introducing into Christian ethics extraneous concepts that found his political realism upon national self-interest rather than on any Christian moral considerations.[15] The influential International Relations theorist Hans Morgenthau, on the other hand, read Niebuhr in a reductionist fashion, as if he were denying the importance of moral values

13. Naveh, *Reinhold Niebuhr and Non-Utopian Liberalism*, 83, citing Niebuhr, "Judah Magnes and the Zionists," 16.

14. For this categorization, see Lovin, *Reinhold Niebuhr and Christian Realism*, 3–24.

15. Yoder, "Reinhold Niebuhr and Christian Pacifism," 101–17.

for politics, and implying that they are reducible to self-interest.[16] This matters because Niebuhr was committed to an underlying *moral realism*, a conviction that moral statements are true or false independent of the individual or community that espouses them. This rules out ethics solely guided by self-interest as well as moral relativism. Niebuhr formulated his version of moral realism by reconstructing Protestant natural law theory along the lines of "ethical naturalism." This will receive further attention below in section 5. For now it is enough to say that a proper understanding of human nature is necessary to make right action possible. Niebuhr's *theological realism* is intertwined with the morally realist pursuit of justice. This rests on a belief that God is love, and that this love requires justice of human beings. Deflecting fears of moral authoritarianism whereby all theological realists would be required in advance to know or agree on the content of ethics, Niebuhr implies that, due to God's transcendence over creatures, no one has complete knowledge of the divine will and purpose on any particular issue. This feeds his critique of religion in relation to nationalism, which will also be considered below in section 5.

Niebuhr's key writings on Zionism demonstrate his application of this threefold realism. He started speaking and writing publicly in support of American Jewish Zionism in the 1930s, as he realized that the situation of Jews in Europe was worsening. European Jews were attempting to flee Nazi persecution by emigrating to British Mandatory Palestine. In 1938 Niebuhr addressed Hadassah, the women's Zionist organization, supporting a Jewish home in Palestine. Admitting the real difficulty of this occurring on land claimed by Arabs, he first compared it to other situations across the world affected by heavy migration. He assumed the realist perspective that "nothing in the realm of politics can be done without friction." He concluded that "Palestine must not be abandoned," not only due to lack of an alternative location for Zion, but also "because the years of expenditure of energy, life and treasure . . . must not be sacrificed."[17] Addressing the 44th annual convention of the Zionist Organization of America in Cincinnati in September 1941, he said that when all had been said about the problem of relating Diaspora Jews to the Land of Israel, the justice of Zionism enters because "there is no spirit without a body, and there is no body without geography."[18] This is the single most important

16. See Lovin, *Reinhold Niebuhr and Christian Realism*, 10; Rice, "Reinhold Niebuhr and Hans Morgenthau," 255–91.

17. Niebuhr, "My Sense of Shame," 59–60.

18. Niebuhr, September 9, 1941, cited in Brown, *Niebuhr and His Age*, 142.

Zionist statement Niebuhr made, because he connected the Land of Israel with creaturely embodiment and statehood, as they were in the Bible. It also articulates in a nutshell his reconstruction of natural law theory to incorporate freedom, here expressed as "spirit."

Niebuhr's most important publication on Zionism was his 1942 article "Jews after the War." It demonstrates a far-sighted approach unmatched by other Christian ethicists. Reintegrating Jews into Europe would be unrealistic due to prospective post-war impoverishment and endemic anti-Semitism. Assimilation alone would be ethically unacceptable as this would bring about the disappearance of Jews as a nationality. Nationality, not religion, represented that which is unique to Jewish life.[19]

> Jews render no service either to democracy or to their people by seeking to deny this ethnic foundation of their life, or by giving themselves to the illusion that they might dispel all prejudice if only they could prove that they are a purely cultural or religious community.[20]

In this, Niebuhr reflects Louis Brandeis' arguments for Zionism. He astutely observes that poorer Jews had not been able to enjoy the benefits of emancipation and assimilation as richer Jews had, because "majority bigotry" always falls much harder on the poorer members of an ethnic group. Poorer Jews thus had a very strong need to return to the Land of Israel.[21] Zionism was therefore seen as the socialism of poor Jews. Due to Niebuhr's Christian realist critique of Marxism as a myth or religion capable of corrupting politics, he never carried this argument to the logical conclusion expressed in Marxist strands of early Zionism. Those saw emigration to Palestine as necessary for poor Jews to win the class struggle against their more privileged brethren.[22] Christian realism is articulated *in nuce* in his statement that Zionism represents "the wisdom of common experience against the wisdom of the mind, which tends to take premature flights into the absolute or the universal from the tragic conflicts and the stubborn particularities of human history."[23]

19. Niebuhr, "Jews after the War," 134.

20. Ibid., 135.

21. Ibid., 136.

22. On Niebuhr's use and subsequent critique of Marxist ideas, see Gilkey, *On Niebuhr*, 33f. On Jewish Marxist Zionists, see Goldberg, *To The Promised Land*, 113–34.

23. Niebuhr, "Jews after the War," 137.

Niebuhr viewed Israel as an outpost of Western civilization in the Middle East. Indeed, this seems to have become intertwined for him with the idea of a Jewish refuge from persecution as Israel's *raison d'être*. As primary spokesman of the American Christian Palestine Committee, Niebuhr favored free immigration, unlimited settlement by Jews, and the development of a Jewish majority in Palestine empowered to establish a democratic government. He advocated that Palestine should be "set aside for the Jews," and that the Arabs should be "otherwise compensated." It is vital to understand this through the prism of Niebuhr's own German descent, which enabled him to have contact with German Zionists during the Nazi era. This deepens the impact of his painful acknowledgement to American Jews that he was ashamed that "an allegedly Christian civilization" could stoop to the level of systemic anti-Semitism. What surfaces is awareness of the deep cultural link between Western Europe and the United States. Proper appreciation of this very American sentiment is necessary to grasp the importance for Niebuhr of Israel as carrier of Western civilization, specifically one not tainted by the currents that fed Nazi ideology.

In order to defend Christian realism and advance the Zionist cause, he founded the journal *Christianity and Crisis*, soberly telling his American audience that the Nazi regime really intended to annihilate the Jewish people and to destroy Christianity as well. In 1942, forty mainline church leaders and scholars, including Niebuhr, formed the Christian Council for Palestine to support Zionism. On January 10, 1946, Niebuhr appeared before the Joint Anglo-American Committee of Inquiry, formed after the War ended, on behalf of the Christian Council for Palestine, making the following statement: "There is in fact no solution to any political problem. The fact, however, that the Arabs have a vast hinterland in the Middle East, and the fact that the Jews have nowhere to go establishes the relative justice of their claims and of their cause."[24] He supported transfer of Arabs out of Palestine, including Herbert Hoover's idea that they should be resettled in Iraq.[25] Building upon the critical defense of democracy as the only seriously viable form of government that he had developed in his 1944 book *The Children of Light and the Children of Darkness*, Niebuhr then continued:

24. Merkley, *Politics*, 171, citing "Statement to Anglo-American Committee of Inquiry," Reinhold Niebuhr Papers, Library of Congress; also, Central Zionist Archives/box F40/file no. 59; both references in Merkley, *Politics*, 201, fn. 34.

25. Medoff, "Communication: A Further Note on the 'Unconventional Zionism' of Reinhold Niebuhr," 85–88. The British Labour Party also supported transfer.

> Christians are committed to democracy as the only safeguard
> of the sacredness of human personality. . . . The opposition to
> a Jewish Palestine is partly based on the opposition of Arabs to
> democracy, Western culture, education and economic freedom.
> To support Arab opposition is but supporting feudalism and
> Fascism in the world at the expense of democratic rights and
> justice.[26]

While Niebuhr did not explain what he meant by "fascism," the available
historical evidence strongly suggests that he has in mind the active support for Hitler, the *Shoah,* and instigation of Arab attacks on Zionist Jews
in Palestine by Haj Muhammad Hamin al-Husseini, appointed the Grand
Mufti of Jerusalem in 1921 by Sir Herbert Samuels, the British governor.[27]
There are no other serious explanations possible for Niebuhr's use of the
term "fascism" here. The fact that Niebuhr would later complain of the
Eisenhower Administration's combined influence with the USSR in the
United Nations to keep General Nasser in power in Egypt and carry on
with "Nazi measures" (i.e., intention to destroy Israel) corroborates this
judgment.[28]

In 1947 Britain followed Ernest Bevin's advice and referred the
issue of Palestine to the United Nations. In November of that year, the
UN passed a resolution calling for the land to be partitioned into Jewish
and Arab states—the first instance of a "two-state solution." Britain was to
evacuate the land by May 1948. Niebuhr supported this two-state solution
against the idea of a binational state, which was popular with mainline
Protestants as well as Jewish anti-Zionist intellectuals such as Martin Buber and Hannah Arendt.

> The decision of the United Nations Assembly to partition Pal-
> estine and to create a Jewish and an Arab state brings several
> interesting and perplexing chapters of contemporary history
> to a conclusion. On the purely political level it represents the
> first real achievement of the United Nations. . . . The "right"
> of the Jews to Palestine is established partly by the urgency of
> the problem of their collective survival and partly by ancient
> claims and hopes which found their classical expression before

26. Niebuhr, "Statement"; cf. Niebuhr, *The Children of Light and the Children of
Darkness,* 84–104.

27. See Herf, "Convergence: The Classic Case," 63–83.

28. Niebuhr, "Seven Great Errors of US Foreign Policy," 3–5. On Niebuhr and
mainline Protestants in relation to post-war US foreign policy, see Inboden, *Religion
and American Foreign Policy,* 1945–60.

the Jewish dispersion. . . . .The right of the Arabs is quite simply
. . . the right of holding what one has and has had for over a
thousand years.[29]

He went on to say that the Arabs lagged behind the Jews in terms of cultural development, such that "this whole Near Eastern world has fallen from the glory where the same lands, which now maintain only a miserable pastoral economy, supported the great empires in which civilization arose." In response to the argument for a binational state, Niebuhr simply pointed out that the United Nations had already rejected this "primarily because the Arabs were unwilling to grant the Jews any freedom of immigration in such a bi-national state."[30]

Niebuhr defended Israel's wars against its Arab neighbors as defensive wars against intentions to annihilate the Jewish state.[31] Commenting on Israel's victory against the attack of its Arab neighbors upon it as soon as it had declared independence, Niebuhr said:

> It now seems probable that the new state of Israel will be able to establish itself the hard way, by an armed defense of its existence against Arab attacks. . . . The Arabs were, of course, intent upon preventing this new political force from challenging their sovereignty, and also their pastoral-feudal social organization. . . . One cannot speak of this victory as a morally unambiguous one. No political victory can be so described.[32]

He recognized that Christian missionaries to Middle Eastern Arabs had opposed Zionist goals as "unjust invasions of the rights and securities of the Arab world."[33] At the same time, he wanted America to lift its embargo on supplying Zionists with arms, noting that army strategists opposed it for fear of an Arab embargo on oil. Niebuhr seems to have been willing for America to risk losing oil for the sake of arming the Zionists (cryptically saying that lifting the arms embargo would allow Arab self-defense to be organized). He believed such a policy "would have more meaning in preventing a larger war."[34]

29. Niebuhr, "Partition of Palestine," 3–4.

30. Niebuhr, editorial note, *Christianity and Crisis*, 8, 30.

31. For a lucid defense of Israel's wars as necessary to defend the country's very existence, see Lozowicz, *Right to Exist*.

32. Niebuhr, "The Future of Israel," 12.

33. Niebuhr, "Christians and the State of Israel," 3.

34. Niebuhr, "Palestine," 5.

The plight of the Arab refugees who fled or were driven out during 1947–49 concerned Niebuhr, who saw it as a tragic outcome of the foundation of Israel. He was aware of missionary reports of atrocities never reported in American newspapers.[35] In 1951, he endorsed a proposal to resettle these refugees in the surrounding countries, in areas that were controlled by the United Nations. The proposal also included the development of waterways and other material resources in those Arab countries. The funding would have come from Israel and other United Nations member states. The Arab countries refused this offer.[36] Raphael Medoff provides evidence that the prominent American Zionist leader, Rabbi Stephen Wise, privately thanked Niebuhr for publicly supporting the idea of Arab transfer. Jews could not articulate this view publicly for fear of reprisals. Medoff suggests that Niebuhr's support for transfer was part of what Naveh calls his "anti-utopian liberalism," as well as being part of the post-war ethos by which the superpowers effected the transfer of Germans from Eastern European countries for the sake of peace.[37] Critics may argue that Niebuhr's support for the foundation of Israel, even of a two-state solution, constituted a flight into idealism, but it is consistent with his threefold realism. The combination of European anti-Semitic persecution and Arab hostility had pushed Niebuhr to a morally and politically realist support for Zionism alongside liberal Jewish assimilation in the Diaspora.

Responding to the Suez Crisis of the mid-1950's, Niebuhr consolidated his support for Israel's survival as a Jewish-majority state. The central issue was saving Israel from annihilation by its Arab neighbors, especially by Egypt under Nasser. Niebuhr never let go of this central moral goal. He argued that the very existence of Israel was offensive to the Arab world for three reasons. First, Niebuhr argued that "it has claimed by conquest what the Arabs regard as their soil." However, this is simplistic reasoning. The early Zionists legally purchased land from absentee Arab landlords during the time of Turkish and later British rule. Niebuhr may be conflating this with the flight and expulsion of Palestinians in 1947–49.[38] He believed that the second reason Israel's existence was offensive to the Arabs was his own discovery that the Arab states refused to resettle these refugees, and that Israel could not reabsorb them without endangering its security as

35. Niebuhr, "Christians and the State of Israel," 3, 4.

36. Anon., "$800,000,000 Asked for Arab Refugees," *New York Times* (December 19, 1951), 1, 20, cited in Brown, *Niebuhr and His Age*, 142.

37. Medoff, "Communication," 88.

38. See Morris, *The Birth of the Palestinian Refugee Problem*.

the refugees were intrinsically hostile. This problem continues to this day. Niebuhr believed that the third reason for Arab hostility to Israel was the strongest. "The state of Israel is, by its very technical efficiency and democratic justice, a source of danger to the moribund feudal or pastoral economics and monarchical political forms of the Islamic world and a threat to the rich overlords of desperately poor peasants of the Middle East."[39]

He believed the survival of Israel "may require detailed economic strategies for the whole region and policies for the resettlement of Arab refugees." Recommending economic development as a remedy for Arab grievances against Zionism was ironic given that in his visit to the USSR in 1930, Niebuhr had worried that industrial efficiency was elevated above other values.[40] His approach to the Arab question betrays lingering traces of his use of certain Marxist concepts originally used to criticize the Social Gospel movement for its progressivist view of history.[41] Stone gives a thorough analysis of Niebuhr's engagement with Marxism. He argues that "some ideas from his Marxist philosophy remain" in his later writings "but they have found independent justification in his thought."[42] Niebuhr's hope for economic development was also naïve in ignoring the fact that the process of Israel's foundation dealt not only a socio-economic blow to Palestinian Arabs, but constituted Jewish emancipation from centuries of Islamic rule over territory claimed by Islam.[43]

Finally, Niebuhr compared the Six Day War to the combat between David and Goliath. Like many other observers, Niebuhr understood the war as motivated by a serious intention by Israel's neighbors to annihilate it. He bluntly proclaimed that "a nation that knows it is in danger of strangulation will use its fists."[44] At the same time, the survival of Israel was "a strategic anchor for a democratic world" and "an asset to America's national interests in the Middle East." This "special relationship" was to be cloaked in the theologically ambiguous notion of national messianism.

39. Niebuhr, "Our Stake in the State of Israel," 9–12.

40. Stone, *Reinhold Niebuhr*, 61.

41. Ibid., 55.

42. Ibid., 91.

43. Maccoby, *Antisemitism and Modernity*, 150. On Palestinian support for Zionism, see Cohen, *Army of Shadows*.

44. Niebuhr, "David and Goliath," 141.

AMERICA AS A MESSIANIC NATION

Niebuhr drew on the myth, which stretches back to the colonial era of US history, of America's election to forge his notion of America as a messianic nation with a mission. This myth of America as "God's New Israel" has been expressed in two different versions.[45] The first claims God called people out of the old nations to America, which, from the Puritan period onwards, became the "promised land" given to this people and their descendants as a place suitable for the growth of a free society. America was to be "a light unto the nations," an example of a free society for other nations to emulate. Drawing on Puritan roots, this version was important in the American Revolution and lies at the root of isolationist tendencies in American politics. The second version expresses the belief that America is required to spread the fundamental values enshrined in the Bill of Rights and to spread democracy globally. This underlay nineteenth- and twentieth-century American Christian missions and has influenced generations of American foreign policy. Cherry argues that it has "unlovely manifestations" such as imperialism concealing national self-interest and the myth of Anglo-Saxon superiority.[46] Niebuhr's sense of American messianism is a critical reworking of this second version, one that he did not originally espouse. His theology of American messianism was not closely tied to or driven by active interest in American Christian missions abroad.[47]

Early on, Niebuhr had taken a similar view to Berle in viewing the Jews rather than Americans as a messianic people. This was because they embodied for him the values of the Social Gospel movement better than did Protestants. The Social Gospel movement promised redemption within history through moral progress.[48] The reason Niebuhr dropped the link between messianism and Jews was his encounter with Orthodox Jews who regarded literal messianism as blasphemous. This coincided with Niebuhr's disenchantment with the whole idea of the Social Gospel

---

45. Cherry, *God's New Israel*, 19.

46. Ibid., 20.

47. By contrast, many other American mainline Protestants connected foreign missions and foreign policy. See Moorhead, "The American Israel," in Hutchison and Lehmann (eds.), *Many Are Chosen*, 145–66. Niebuhr repudiated Christian mission to Jews in a sermon preached on 10 January 1926. This discovery was made by Dieter Splinter and is recorded in Littell, "Reinhold Niebuhr and the Jewish People," 45–61, citing the Reinhold Niebuhr papers, Library of Congress, Container XIV, 1, Folder 15.

48. Niebuhr, *Leaves from the Notebooks of a Tamed Cynic*, 187–88.

as built on an overly benign understanding of human nature.[49] In *Moral Man and Immoral Society*, Niebuhr denied the kingdom of God would ever be brought to earth.[50] This represented a clear repudiation of the postmillennialism of the Social Gospellers, or the premillennialism of the evangelicals and fundamentalists. Niebuhr never demurred from this conclusion, and this also explains why he remained silent about any possible theological significance to the foundation of Israel in 1948 or its victory in the Six Day War, as these were regarded by premillennialists as the fulfillment of biblical prophecy and as signposts towards the coming millennial kingdom.

The Social Gospel movement held that Israel's end had come in the universalism of the Christian religion, reiterating the traditional Christian understanding of Israel's national supersession.[51] Nevertheless, it was impossible for any subsequent nation to be the exact counterpart to ancient Israel. James H. Moorhead articulates this attempt at balancing notions of Israel's and America's election:

> Individual nations might, by providential circumstances, play a unique role in the advancement of God's purposes, and the Israel of the Old Testament might function as a paradigm for the righteous nation in covenant with God. In this sense, analogies between America and Israel were deemed legitimate and were frequently made; the comparison, however, could never be exact.[52]

What Moorhead does not demonstrate is that the difficulty of making and sustaining the analogy is due to the fact that while Israel's election is a doctrine rooted in traditions of biblical exegesis, notions of America's election obviously cannot be directly based on exegesis, but are built upon speculative providential interpretations of American history. Failure to make this distinction is also a problem in Niebuhr's own writing on the subject. In his 1943 article "Anglo-Saxon Destiny," Niebuhr spoke of America as a nation with a mission to spread democracy and international justice around the globe. This was required by the new Anglo-American alliance, which "must be the cornerstone of any durable world order"; its position was only intelligible for Niebuhr as a manifestation of "destiny."[53] Fleshing out

49. Niebuhr, "The Return of Primitive Religion," 1, 6.

50. Niebuhr, *Moral Man and Immoral Society*, 19–21.

51. Moorhead, "The American Israel," 149.

52. Ibid.

53. In *Christianity and Crisis* 3 (October 4, 1943), reprinted in Cherry, *God's New*

the ethical implications, he compared Amos' view that Israel's destiny as elect gave it a "special peril," not a "special security," to America's supposed destiny as chosen. "God has chosen America in this fateful period of world history. . . . The real fact is that we are placed in a precarious moral and historical position by our special mission."[54] Here Niebuhr's notion of America's being "chosen" by God seems to be a belief in temporary rather than eternal election, as well as based on a political and cultural rationale rather than an inscrutable divine decree. This is evident from the fact that Niebuhr utilized the notions of "chosenness" and "destiny" to account for the fact of Anglo-American global power and influence.

Niebuhr's writings from the post-war period leave the door open for the national supersession of Israel, that is, its replacement by another nation in the providential divine economy. This is closely tied to the afore-mentioned increasing tendency to view America as a chosen nation. In the winter of 1948, Niebuhr questioned whether the Jewish prophets' universal salvific vision betrayed the Jewish claim to the land.[55] However, he did not support this with an exegetical argument that could have opened up ecumenical and interfaith dialogue on the issue.[56] Addressing the First General Assembly of the World Council of Churches, he spoke of the task of Christian mission to entire nations, noting that "Jesus wept over Jerusalem and regretted that it did not know the things that belonged to its peace."[57] This wording echoes the Lucan account of the Lament over Jerusalem.[58] This is an odd choice, given that he included no discussion of parallel Lucan passages readable as references to the sack of Jerusalem, the end of Gentile rule over it and final Jewish acceptance of Jesus. Niebuhr only reiterated traditional Christian teaching that the second Jewish exile was a punishment for rejecting Jesus, without introducing the hope and promise of a second coming. By not grounding his support for Jewish return theologically, he left the door open for covert and overt Christian views that Jewish return was unjustified.

In his 1963 volume *A Nation So Conceived*, Niebuhr unashamedly says that America is a messianic nation.

Israel, 296.

54. Niebuhr, "Anglo-Saxon Destiny," 3.

55. Niebuhr, "The Partition of Palestine," 3.

56. Niebuhr has been criticized for not really engaging in exegetical discussion in his ethics. See Siker, *Scripture and Ethics*.

57. Niebuhr, "The Christian Witness in the Social and National Order," in Niebuhr, *Christian Realism and Political Problems*, 112.

58. Luke 19:41–44.

> Most of the nations, in Western culture at least, have acquired
> a sense of national mission at some time in their history. Our
> nation was born with it. England acquired it after the Revolu-
> tion of 1688 and viewed the Magna Carta retrospectively in the
> light of its newly developed democratic mission. Russian mes-
> sianism was derived from its consciousness of being the "third
> Rome." Like Israel of old, we were a messianic nation from our
> birth. The Declaration of Independence and our Constitution
> defined the mission. We were born to exemplify the virtues of
> democracy and to extend the frontiers of the principles of self-
> government throughout the world.[59]

He does not acknowledge that these older nations' sense of mission
derived from national supersession of ancient Israel. Niebuhr does not
provide an adequate understanding of the convergence and divergence
between older European and American notions of national election to
a mission. His failure to provide theological and exegetical warrant for
American messianism is a problem, because omission of theological and
exegetical sources for his position deprived him of the possibility of connection and debate with other Western Christian and Jewish notions of
messianism. These include various interpretations of the Messiah and/or
Israel as God's suffering servant (based on Isaiah 53), Christian belief that
Jesus is the Messiah anticipated by the Jewish prophets, the succession of
Jewish individuals claiming to be the Messiah through the centuries, political hopes for a Messianic Age, and hopes that a contemporary restored
Israel would be a messianic nation.[60] Given his critique of religion in relation to nationalism, Niebuhr would not have endorsed religious messianic
strands of Zionism.[61]

Niebuhr's view of Israel as an outpost of Western civilization in the
Middle East is linked to its being a democracy, an important element
of his understanding of America. He observed that the "messianic con-
sciousness" of America was "very robust" because of the covenant in the
Constitution, as well as Puritan millenarian and Enlightenment influence.
America would fulfill the Reformation of Christendom. The notion that

---

59. Niebuhr, *A Nation So Conceived*, 123.

60. For a comprehensive survey of Jewish forms of messianism, see Cohn-Sherbok, *The Jewish Messiah*. For studies on biblical material and the early centuries of the
Common Era, see Horbury, *Messianism among Jews and Christians*. On pre-Enlightenment Jewish methods of calculating the coming of the Messiah, see Silver, *A History
of Messianic Speculation in Israel*.

61. Cohn-Sherbok, *The Jewish Messiah*, 153–58.

America's national mission was to safeguard republican democracy became part of the deep fabric of national consciousness, encapsulated by
Woodrow Wilson's view of the First World War as intended "to make the
world safe for Democracy."[62] However, Niebuhr warned that such a missionary and messianic self-belief can be confusing, because nations then
hide from themselves "the will to power" that they posses, behind "the veil
of ideal purposes." The danger is that the nation conceives of its mission
purely in terms of its original content, a comment that reflected his strong
pragmatism. Nevertheless, with a self-confidence that many today would
find difficult, Niebuhr said that "fortunately the substance and content of
our national sense of mission, namely the preservation and extension of
democratic self-government, is more valid than other forms of national
messianism."[63]

Niebuhr was also troubled by Wilson's view of the War because Wilson omitted to give clear notions of how democracy may be universally
valid and neglected to inquire "in what sense it was an achievement of
European culture, requiring political skills and resources which may be
beyond the reach of primitive or traditional cultures."[64] Still relevant is
Niebuhr's question as to whether all countries have "the elementary pre-
conditions of community, the cohesions of a common language and race,"
which helped prepare the way for democracy in Europe. The question
loomed large over whether and to what degree traditional cultures had
acquired the skills to "put political freedom in the service of justice." Finally, Niebuhr was aware that around the world, peoples "desire national
freedom, but have no knowledge of, or desire for, individual freedom except as it has validated itself as a servant of justice and community."[65] With
regard to Palestinian nationalism as well as Israel's other neighbors, this
continues to be a serious theological, ethical, and political question.

Ultimately Niebuhr's cautions about American messianism ring
hollow when applied to Israel because he perpetuated national supersessionism. As long as American mainline Protestant theology ignores the
doctrines of election and providence in relation to Israel, it will also be
incapable of repairing this problem. These factors combined to open the
door to something Niebuhr himself would not have wanted, namely one
of his students suggesting removal of Jews from the Middle East, should

---

62. Niebuhr, *A Nation So Conceived*, 126.

63. Ibid., 127.

64. Ibid., 139ff.

65. Ibid., 150.

support for Israel conflict with American interests.[66] This brings us to inquire into the adequacy of Niebuhr's theology for supporting his ethics.

NATURAL THEOLOGY AS THE BASIS OF NIEBUHR'S ETHICS

Niebuhr's ethics is undergirded by a natural theology,[67] meaning, a realist acceptance of the world external to the psyche that is bound up with a religious acceptance of transcendence, creation, and historical events. In order to understand this, though, we must first understand his theology of revelation. This presumes the classic Christian distinction between natural and dogmatic theology, or in Niebuhr's terms, general and special revelation. General revelation is learned from observation and is constituted by experiences that are inescapable in worldly terms. These experiences lead one to comprehend the presence of a transcendental reality, leading to a sense of moral obligation, a desire to be forgiven and a sense of awe and dependence. Special revelation is required to illumine general revelation. Forms of special revelation correlate with the three elements of general revelation. The sense of moral obligation corresponds to Yhwh's covenantal relation with Israel, and the human desire to be forgiven with the life and death of Jesus Christ. Both "answers" to the human moral sense and desire respectively are historical events in which the eyes of faith perceive divine self-revelation and demonstrate God as Judge and Redeemer. The human sense of awe and dependence grows from perceiving God as the Creator.[68]

Niebuhr also expresses the distinction between general and special revelation (and therefore natural and dogmatic theology) more politically as private versus public revelation. Public revelation is historical and corrects the ambiguities of general or private revelation. However, private revelation came first historically and is bound up with apprehension of external reality. There is a *dialectical* relationship between public and private revelation. This experience is what enables people "to entertain the more precise revelations of the character and purpose of God as they come

---

66. Stone, *Prophetic Realism*, 163–64.

67. This is set out in Niebuhr, *The Nature and Destiny of Man*, i, 141–60.

68. Noting that for Niebuhr these historical events are the key to history's meaning, Robert Song correctly refutes Paul Ramsey's charge that Niebuhr's theology was simply derived from anthropology. Song, *Christianity and Liberal Society*, 54, citing Ramsey, *Speak Up for Just War or Pacifism*, 114.

to them in the most significant experiences of prophetic history."[69] The nature and significance of this political division between the two forms of revelation has not been noted by Niebuhr's critics. It is part of his overall repudiation of mysticism and pietism as anti-political and, as such, irresponsible. Clearly, for him, the history of ancient Israel constituted public or special revelation, yet he does not seem to view the rise of modern Zionism as its continuation.

Two major contemporary Christian readers of Niebuhr, Robert Song and Stanley Hauerwas, have criticized the natural theology that underlies his ethics.[70] Song finds it insufficiently Trinitarian, and therefore inadequate for generating a proper Christian ethic and defending the meaningfulness of history. He thinks Niebuhr declined to use the strongest theological case for this, namely a full account of the incarnation as the divine assumption of human flesh.[71] Turning to Niebuhr's eschatology, Song argues that its structure, coupled with Niebuhr's reluctance to espouse a doctrine of the general resurrection, means his theology "is ultimately focused not on God, but on the project of giving significance to human finitude," and in particular to prompting people to "accept their historical responsibilities gladly."[72] In other words, ethics and politics are driving theology. Song concludes that Niebuhr's God is "more a principle of transcendence than the living God of Abraham, Isaac and Jacob."[73] Song thus unsubtly assumes a theology not fully Trinitarian cannot be a witness to the God of the Old Testament; rather, it is necessarily reduced to being a philosophy.

At the root of Song's criticism is inattention to Niebuhr's Hebraic turn to the Old Testament as source for Christian realist ethics, in contradistinction to what he perceived as the unworldly asceticism of Jesus. Niebuhr taught his students that the Old Testament had given rise to two ethical tendencies: prophetic messianism, fulfilled by Christianity, and legalism, which he believed to have been both resurrected by secular Jewish Zionism as well as fulfilled in the coming of Christ and the eschatological promise of universal peace.[74] Jesus himself was, for Niebuhr, "presented

69. Niebuhr, *The Nature and Destiny of Man*, i, 127, 70.

70. Song, *Christianity and Liberal Society*, 114; Hauerwas, *With the Grain of the Universe*, 115–16, fn. 6.

71. Song, *Christianity and Liberal Society*, 79.

72. Ibid., 82, citing Niebuhr, *The Nature and Destiny of Man*, ii, 332.

73. Song, *Christianity and Liberal Society*, 83.

74. Stone, *Professor Reinhold Niebuhr*, 58ff.

more as a messianic figure rather than as a teacher of ethics."[75] There is a sharp distinction between the perceived legalism and realism of the Old Testament, and the prophetic messianism and unworldly asceticism of Jesus and the New Testament. Essentially, Niebuhr wants to say that legalism was fulfilled both in the coming of Christ and in secular Jewish Zionism. His belief that Jews do not need to become Christians meant that he was unlikely to use the doctrine of the Trinity to undergird his support for Zionism, for example, by arguing its legalism was part of a hidden work of Christ as fulfillment of the Old Testament law. Niebuhr's reluctance to use the doctrine of the Trinity a lot is probably also due to apologetic reserve, deemed necessary when speaking publicly about matters of social justice with non-Christians, including and especially Jews.

In his Gifford Lectures on Niebuhr, Stanley Hauerwas makes the charge that Niebuhr's "god" was merely William James' sense that "there must be more."[76] Hauerwas thinks Niebuhr has not adequately responded to Gustave Weigel. Weigel had criticized Niebuhr for believing in the Trinity "symbolically but not literally," accusing him of believing that the Trinity is little more than an idea attempting to describe our experience of God. Hauerwas expresses surprise that in his pastoral work, Niebuhr did "use trinitarian language without apology."[77] He refuses to take Niebuhr entirely at his word when he wrote that he was incompetent in "nice points of pure theology."[78] The reason is he insists Niebuhr *really* assumes these are "Jamesian over-beliefs that cannot be true or false." This is necessary for Hauerwas' Barthian strategy of rendering Niebuhr a Feuerbachian whose theology is really reducible to anthropology. Hauerwas later makes the revealing admission that Niebuhr's doctrine of creation signifies that "the world in its totality [is] a revelation of His majesty and self-sufficient power."[79]

> Niebuhr observes, and I confess I have never understood what he means, that the biblical doctrine of creation is itself not a doctrine of revelation but the *basis* for the doctrine of revelation. He attempts to explain this claim by observing that the doctrine of creation perfectly expresses the basic biblical idea

---

75. Ibid., 62.

76. Hauerwas, *With the Grain of the Universe*, 122.

77. Ibid., 128, fn. 31, citing Reinhold Niebuhr, "The Hazards and the Difficulties of the Christian Ministry," 129–30.

78. Hauerwas, *With the Grain of the Universe*, 114.

79. Niebuhr, *The Nature and Destiny of Man*, I, 132.

that God is at once transcendent and in an intimate relation to the world. But why do you need the doctrine of creation to express the transcendence and immanence of God? All you need is [William] James's account of the "more."[80]

What Niebuhr most likely means is that the doctrine of creation expresses his notion of general revelation, and that our apprehension of special revelation (what Hauerwas calls, in Barthian fashion, "the doctrine of revelation") depends on our prior acceptance of general revelation in history. Hauerwas is being both mischievous and cynical when he proceeds, despite professing not to understand Niebuhr on this matter, to defend to the hilt his view that Niebuhr is only really a Jamesian. This is his way of discrediting Niebuhr for adhering to a natural theology. It should be obvious that "the Jamesian 'more'" is not enough for Niebuhr, because he does not want to support mystical and pietistic versions of Christianity with their desertion of history and politics. This is why he cites Romans 1:20 to defend his dialectical notion of revelation as both private and public, which Hauerwas himself cites! The relevance of Hauerwas' critique of Niebuhr for Zionism is that Hauerwas wants to set up a parallel with the debate between Karl Barth and Emil Brunner on natural theology in the 1930s.[81] Hauerwas plays the role of Barth with Niebuhr cast as Brunner. This has obvious political resonance, because while Barth feared that Brunner's theology could be used in complicity with the anti-Semitic and anti-Zionist Nazi regime in the 1930s, Hauerwas' tendency is to worry that Niebuhr's natural theology is used to underwrite certain kinds of Christian ethical support for the American state and notions of Western civilization.[82]

Robert Song argues that Niebuhr's theology is dubious because it is serving "the less than ethical requirements of civilization."[83] This requires further elaboration, for the concept of civilization can be linked back to a reading of Genesis as being concerned with the twin rise of agriculture and civilization. In reality, both Genesis and historical research show that agriculture and civilization rose together, and are thus ethically intertwined. Debates over the foundation of contemporary Israel included

80. Hauerwas, *With the Grain of the Universe*, 123, n. 22.

81. Ibid., 115–16, fn. 6; 123, fn. 23.

82. The fact that Niebuhr supported Zionism on the basis of his natural theology, whereas Barth supported Zionism on the basis of a doctrine of election and opposition to the kind of natural theology espoused by Niebuhr, goes unnoticed by Hauerwas. See Barth, *CD* III/3, 211–26.

83. Song, *Christianity and Liberal Society*, 84.

debates about the viability of developing Israeli agriculture. This matters theologically because in speaking of the return of the Jews to the Land, Ezekiel speaks of the Gentiles saying, "This land that was desolate has become like the Garden of Eden; and the waste and desolate and ruined towns are now inhabited and fortified."[84] This is how the Gentile nations will know that the God of Israel is the Lord of all creation. Eden is here a type of the land of Israel. As a garden, it is inextricably linked to the project of civilization. Song's critique misses the real problem, which is lack of serious attention to the very concept of civilization by Christian ethicists. Niebuhr would have been very suspicious of its rejection, given his lifelong view that America is "spiritually a part of Europe," and that the fall of European *civilization* would adversely affect it.[85] Christian ethics would, in his eyes, need to absolve itself of the charge of retreat into the sphere of the church as community of virtue. The Barthian rhetoric of Song's and Hauerwas' criticisms promises more than it actually delivers. Unlike Niebuhr's contemporaries, these critics show little awareness of Niebuhr's Hebraic turn. Also, Song and Hauerwas are respectively British and American ethicists unhappy with any Christian ethic that will support "civilization" and the state. In practice it means that Niebuhr tends to be repudiated on methodological grounds without an adequate appreciation of the link between his method and his substantive commitments.

Niebuhr saw Jewish nationhood as one of the oldest and most legitimate in history, and that it was granted in "a religious covenant experience."[86] This contradicts Eyal Naveh's view that Niebuhr's Zionism was only based on pragmatism.[87] It was based on respect for an ancestral claim, not on dogmatic belief. Niebuhr argued that Christian doctrines were based on biblical myths that had universal significance: creation, fall, redemption, and love. Myth was the dialectical counterpart of logic and rationality, expressed as story, proposition, image, or symbol, grasping "the world as a realm of coherence and meaning without denying the facts of incoherence."[88] The covenant was not one of these myths. Perhaps he believed that its being connected both to the particular history of ancient Israel and to the church threatened to disrupt the universal appeal and

84. Ezek 36: 35.

85. Niebuhr, "America and Europe," 141.

86. Niebuhr, *Discerning the Signs of the Times*, 40, 87; Niebuhr, *The Structure of Nations and Empires*, 161–62.

87. Naveh, "The Hebraic Foundation of Christian Faith according to Reinhold Niebuhr," 42.

88. Naveh, *Reinhold Niebuhr and Non-Utopian Liberalism*, 34.

intent of his apologetic theology. Proof of this is found in his book *Faith and History*, published in 1949, where he compares Abraham, the father of the Jewish nation with whom Yahweh made his covenant, with Abraham Lincoln as the father of America, thus relativizing the uniqueness of the Jewish Abraham and of the covenant made with him. He also criticizes the Jewish prophets for being unswervingly nationalist.[89] This echoes his supersessionist shift from Israel to America as the messianic nation.

THE CRITIQUE OF NATURAL LAW, NATIONALISM, AND RELIGION

Conceiving of Jewishness and Zionism in secular national terms enabled Niebuhr to circumvent debates about the covenant of righteousness that Christians had traditionally used to deny theological validity to Jews returning to the Land before first becoming Christians. Niebuhr managed to connect Zionism to what he perceived as the ethics of the Old Testament, which held nationalism and internationalism in tension. Consequently, the texts themselves require a theological realist reading that does not claim that the entirety of the divine will for Israel's history can be worked out in advance. Basing Zionism on Jewish nationality also enabled Niebuhr to set aside potential Christian theological demands for a coherent system justifying the movement.

Niebuhr begins his essay "Coherence, Incoherence and Christian Faith" by stating the realist claim that "the whole of reality is characterized by a basic coherence. Things and events are in a vast web of relationships and are known through their relations."[90] He argues that coherence must not become the basic test of the truth of an intellectual system for four reasons. First, some things and events are unique, and thus cannot fit into any system. Unique moral situations exist "that don't simply fit into some general rule of natural law." We may understand the founding of Israel as one such situation, given that Niebuhr's theology did not adequately account for the promise of the Land to the Jews and that Niebuhr realized that Zionist and Arab claims to the Land clashed. The second reason that coherence must not be the main criterion of truth is that "realms of coherence and meaning stand in rational contradiction to each other."[91] Here he has in mind theological doctrines such as Trinity and Christology,

89. Niebuhr, *Faith and History*, 23–24, 106.

90. Niebuhr, *Christian Realism*, 165.

91. Ibid., 166.

philosophical attempts to relate being and becoming, essence and existence. This gives away Niebuhr's anti-metaphysical Hebraic tendency and shows why he shied away from developing a fully-fledged systematic theology for his work. Third, some things stand above every system, so man is both in and above nature. Fourth and related, genuine human freedom does not fit into any system. In line with my argument for the first reason given above, a fitting instance of this can be seen in the reality of Jews declaring independence in 1948 and exercising genuine freedom outside the bounds of Christendom.

Niebuhr's suspicion of metaphysics accords with a reluctance to formulate a doctrine of providence, the doctrine Christians often used to deny Jewish aspirations to return to the Land.[92] Providence could easily be joined to natural law thinking to defend the socio-political *status quo* as based on the divine will. John Milbank has criticized Niebuhr for allegedly appropriating Stoicism into his reconstruction of natural law.[93] John Burk astutely refutes Milbank on this, noting that Niebuhr actually wanted to pull Protestant ethics *away from* the excess of Stoicism found in older orthodoxies.[94] This was precisely because he perceived Hellenic thinking as more cosmic and static, less interested in the historical dimensions of human life. For Niebuhr had already written in 1935 that the law of love actually "suggests possibilities which immediately transcend any achievements of justice by which society has integrated its life."[95] Given that at this time Niebuhr was becoming supportive of Zionism, his very support may be viewed as an instance of the "law of love" at work. As Burk explains, Milbank erroneously understands Niebuhr as positing a conflict between the essential (love) and the existential (human life), in a replay of the Stoic conflict between what is ideal and what is real. Actually, what interests Niebuhr are conflicts within the real historical realm of human life. This is precisely why his support for Zionism cannot be dismissed as a flight into idealism based on passionate personal conviction.

---

92. Niebuhr nevertheless insisted on positing providence in order to remind Christians that history is not within our control. However, avoiding a fully-fledged doctrine comports with his theological realist refusal to understand specific events and programs as unfolding a single divine purpose. See his "Providence and Human Decisions," 185–86.

93. Milbank, "The Poverty of Niebuhrianism" in Milbank, *The Word Made Strange*, 233–54.

94. Burk, "Moral Law, Privative Evil and Christian Realism," 221–28.

95. Burke cites Niebuhr, *An Interpretation of Christian Ethics*, 144.

Niebuhr's ethical critique of religion and nationalism aids our understanding of his approach to Zionism. He himself acknowledged Israel's right to choose to be a secular or religious society. He preferred the former because he feared religion's ability, especially when it was espoused as true belief, to identify itself with God's exclusive will on a particular issue.[96] Niebuhr did not give a theological grounding to his ethical criticism of nationalism, because he feared that introducing religion into the conflict would absolutize the issues and render compromise impossible. In other words, it would compromise his threefold realism. He became conscious of this in the 1930s when, as part of his reconstruction of natural law theory, Niebuhr went beyond Marxism in allowing that the interest of the dominant economic classes within nations accentuate conflicts, but are not the only reason for them. Niebuhr saw the conflict between Jews and Arabs in British Mandatory Palestine as an example of such a conflict. There were two key factors: the natural will-to-live of two collective nationalities and religions; and the economic differences between the feudalism of the Arabs and the technical civilization which the Jews were able to introduce into Palestine. "The participants cannot find a common ground of rational morality from which to arbitrate the issues because the moral judgments which each brings to them are formed by the very historical forces which are in conflict. Such conflicts are therefore sub- and supra-moral."[97]

Niebuhr's analysis here is clear-sighted, for he recognizes the mutually exclusive nature of the each party's claim to the land. He also demonstrates how a realist approach would need to be pragmatic, requiring his reconstruction of natural law precisely because the liberal tendency to ground natural law only in reason will not succeed in this conflict. He even prefigures contemporary dimensions of the conflict.

> The effort to bring such a conflict under the dominion of a spiritual unity may be partly successful, but it always produces a tragic by-product of the spiritual accentuation of natural conflict. The introduction of religious motives into these conflicts is usually no more than the final and most demonic pretension. Religion may be regarded as the last and final effort of the human spirit to escape relativity and gain a vantage-point in the eternal. But when this effort is made without a contrite recognition of the finiteness and relativity which characterizes human spirituality, even in its moments of yearning for the transcendent,

96. Niebuhr, *Christian Realism and Political Problems*, 97–98.
97. Niebuhr, *An Interpretation of Christian Ethics*, 126–27.

religious aspiration is transmuted into sinful dishonesty. Historic religions, which crown the structure of historic cultures,
thus become the most brutal weapons in the conflict between
cultures.[98]

Here we arrive at the limits of Niebuhr's legacy for supporting Israel. He
was insufficiently immersed in theology, as opposed to ethics, to be able
to imagine ways in which the different parties could envisage mutual co-
existence by at least partial use of religious discourse. His reconstruction
of natural law privileged individual freedom, yet this is precisely what is
so problematic to Israel's neighbors where Islamic fundamentalism now
thrives.

Niebuhr placed modern Israel and Zionism outside his theology,
because he wanted to communicate with several audiences who did not
share similar theological beliefs. Consequently, the centrality of Zionism to his Christian realism has not been appreciated and his reasoning
for Israel's right to exist as a Jewish state has not been passed on to the
mainline Protestant churches. Instead the idea of the binational state has
reappeared, this time on the grounds of Palestinian Liberation Theology. In addition, Ronald H. Stone, a prominent student of Niebuhr, has
suggested that should the long-envisaged two-state solution not succeed
in abating Islamist terrorism, Jews should be removed from the Middle
East and live in the USA.[99] This contradicts Niebuhr's threefold realism,
which was *moral* and took into account America's relation to Europe as
well as the Middle East. It is incredibly naïve to think that dismantling
the State of Israel would succeed in lessening Islamist terrorism. Terror
would still strike against Western countries, precisely because abandoning
Israel would be perceived as the defeat of the alleged "Zionist-Crusader
conspiracy." America would presumably still need to learn that Niebuhr's
vision of her as messianic was heretical. Christians and others supportive
of Israel's existence living in Middle Eastern countries would face in-
numerable problems. Unfortunately, prominent Niebuhr scholars have
simply ignored his Zionism; so far I have not found rebuttals of Stone's argument in academic literature. Ultimately, Niebuhr lost the opportunity to
articulate a non-supersessionist Christian theology that could undergird
mainline Protestant support for the State of Israel. One result is today's
mainline Protestant ambivalence towards Israel.

98. Ibid., 126–27.
99. Stone, *Prophetic Realism*, 165.

THE PATH FROM REINHOLD NIEBUHR TO POSTLIBERALISM

There is a continuity of approach towards theology and ethics from Reinhold Niebuhr to postliberal theologians and sociologists of religion. This continuity accounts for Mark Jurgensmeyer's sociological approach to apocalyptic violence as a major expression of religious resurgence since the ending of the Cold War.[100] The continuity between Niebuhr, postliberalism and Juergensmeyer comes into sharp focus when we see matters through the handling of Israel. Postliberalism can be conveniently dated from the time of publication of George A. Lindbeck's volume *The Nature of Doctrine* in 1984.[101] Yet in order to understand theologically the path that goes from Niebuhr to postliberalism regarding Israel, we must attend first to a particular variant of liberal theology from the previous two decades, the secular theology of Paul Van Buren.[102] Van Buren was a doctoral student of Karl Barth who departed from Barth's theology of Israel as grounded in the one christological covenant of election, in favor of a type of two-covenant theology.[103] Two-covenant theology is a problem both in systematic theology and in biblical studies (some proponents of the so-called New Perspectives on Paul have adopted it).[104] It is a problem because it has no warrant in the New Testament. It is the belief that God made two covenants, one with the Jews and one with Gentile Christians, for eternity. Gentile Christians are the missionaries to the Gentiles globally, calling them to worship the God of Israel. Jews do not need to believe in Jesus as Messiah. This, of course, flatly contradicts the New Testament, as Jesus and all the apostles who were the first leaders of the early church *were Jewish*. This notion was first suggested by the Jewish philosopher Franz Rosenzweig, and advocated in the USA by Abraham Joshua Heschel.[105] Reinhold Niebuhr took it on, and James Parkes and A. Roy Eckhardt on both sides of the Atlantic sought theological justification for Niebuhr's anti-missionary views, based on the false assumption that Jewish missions had always been "futile."[106] Thus it

100. Juergensmeyer, *The New Cold War?*; Juergensmeyer, *Terror in the Mind of God*.

101. Lindbeck, *The Nature of Doctrine*.

102. Buren, *A Theology of the Jewish-Christian Reality*.

103. Wallis, *Post-Holocaust Christianity*, 2.

104. The first Christian theologian to have espoused a two-covenant theology was the liberal Anglican James Parkes in his *Judaism and Christianity*. On postliberal handling of two covenants and supersessionism, see Harink, *Paul among the Postliberals*.

105. Rosenzweig, *The Star of Redemption*. On Abraham Joshua Heschel's advocacy of a plurality of covenants, see Heschel, "No Religion is an Island," 117–34.

106. Everett, *Christianity Without Anti-Semitism*, 45.

entered the mainstream of American mainline/liberal protestant theology and ethics, riding on the back of a repudiation of Christian mission to the Jewish people, itself based on the false and frankly dishonest assumption that all Christians are Gentile.[107] This stands upon the rejection of *religious* supersessionism of Judaism by Christianity. Typically both liberal and postliberal theologians who espouse two-covenant theology *ignore* the problematic traditional view of the *national* and therefore *political* super-session of Israel by the church. This fact is what permits supersessionist theologians to deny theological and political validity to the modern State of Israel, and what used to permit supersessionist theologians and Christians more widely to deny basic rights to the Jewish people, including and especially the right to exist *if* Romans 9–11 was read in such a way that the Jews' opportunity for conversion to Christ had *already* passed in the first century. In the chapter of "The Star of Redemption" where he pro-pounds the two-covenant theology, Rosenzweig cites Moses Maimonides as a precedent.[108] Maimonides held that Christians worshipped the God of Israel—something that Rosenzweig tells his fellow Jews only a handful of other Jewish theologians had taught. They included Judah Halevi, Mena-hem Hameiri, Jacob Emden, and now himself. Maimonides also believed that Christianity could serve for Gentiles as a preparation for the coming of the Messiah, whom Jews still awaited. He also held that Islam could fulfill the same role.[109] Rosenzweig rejected a missionary and preparatory role for Islam.[110] Heschel, however, seems to follow Maimonides. Postlib-erals have tended to follow this line since the First Palestinian Intifada of 1990, and especially since the Second Intifada of 2000 and 9/11.[111] Thus some theologians have argued that there can be many covenants between the different world religions and God, all under the umbrella of the one

107. James Parkes was particularly vicious, not to say theologically blind, in attack-ing Karl Barth's theology for the Confessing Church as "evil," and in publicly attacking Jacob Jocz, a Jewish convert who was an early adherent of Barth's theology of Israel. See Chertok, *He Also Spoke as a Jew,* 179, 383–84. Parkes like many other liberal Prot-estants never bothered acknowledging Barth's turn to affirm Zionism in 1948.

108. For Franz Rosenzweig on Moses Maimonides, see Rosenzweig, *The Star of Redemption,* passim.

109. Solomon, Harries and Winter (eds.), *Abraham's Children,* 184.

110. Rosenzweig, *The Star of Redemption,* 116–18, 122–24, 164–66, 211–17, 225–27.

111. On Heschel on Islam and Judaism, see Krajewski, "Abraham J. Heschel and the Challenge of Interreligious Dialogue," in Krajewski and Lipszye (eds.), *Abraham Joshua Heschel,* 169–80.

christological covenant.[112] It is evident that such an approach is espoused for the sake of interfaith peacemaking concerning the Israel-Palestine conflict among other things.

In order to understand the line from two-covenant theology to interfaith peacemaking and how it links to the move towards a plurality of covenants, it is necessary to register Van Buren's attempt to forge a secular theology back in the 1960s, when secular theology was a live movement. Van Buren turned away from Barth's method of founding theology on the Word of God. He advanced a version of secular theology in his 1963 publication *The Secular Meaning of the Gospel: Based on an Analysis of Its Language*, aiming to articulate the significance of Christianity for secular men and women.[113] He believed that the idea of a transcendent God was untenable in a scientific age, and expressed agnosticism as to divine existence. By 1980 he was saying that "the language of faith in the Jewish-Christian traditions is expressive of human experience within a particular linguistic community."[114] This illustrates his turn to the later Wittgenstein to conceive of theology as language of interpreting reality, rather than simply referring to reality, thus anticipating the later postliberal turn to Wittgenstein to conceive of theology as grammar.[115] Jews and Christians share a common Way, and their theologians must call us to "our common walk in the Way."[116] By this time, Van Buren believed he was mistaken to have advanced a secular theology, because the Way was "not that of the world," and so couldn't be expressed in worldly language. He termed Israel's story "a narrative metaphysics," as metaphysical language reflected human experience. It is not an accident that his anti-metaphysical turn led

---

112. D'Costa, "One Covenant or Many Covenants?," 441–52.

113. Van Buren, *The Secular Meaning of the Gospel*. His book was subjected to searching philosophical and doctrinal criticism by Eric Mascall, who analyzed it alongside the contemporaneous English expression of a secular theology, Robinson, *Honest to God*. See Mascall, *The Secularisation of Christianity*.

114. Van Buren, *Discerning the Way*, 288.

115. Van Buren's approach is set out in the essays collected in Van Buren, *Theological Explorations*, and Van Buren, *The Edges of Language*. Fergus Kerr's argument that theology can make use of Wittgenstein does not simply focus on language in this way, but studies specific dogmatic topics: anthropology, the immortality of the soul, and the believer's relation to the church and to tradition. Kerr, *Theology after Wittgenstein*. Kerr ends up refuting the common view that Wittgenstein thought of people as "entirely constituted by language," thus pulling the ground from underneath the feet of those who would use his philosophy in the service of a cynical non-realism, as Van Buren was wont to do. Ibid., 209.

116. Van Buren, *Discerning the Way*. 45–67.

him to develop a doctrine of the Trinity within the concept of the Way, pushing him close to a modalist view of the Trinity, claiming that "God is a person." Regarding covenant, Van Buren disliked classic Reformed theologies of covenant, instead opting for the view that covenant was only an Old Testament concept, and designating the New Testament as the "apostolic writings."[117] This seriously undercut both his Christology and his ecclesiology. Israel's existence was defined by God's self-revelation at Sinai. Jesus' attitude towards Gentiles was to call people to "be Jews as he was a Jew, that they be God's Jews."[118] The church's mission to the Jewish people would be to help Israel "be itself" as a nation and carry out its role in God's plan for the redemption of creation.[119] This is because for Van Buren, Israel is still seen in purely secular terms as a nation, not a religion.[120] This is important because interfaith peacemaking is about the nation of Israel and the nation of Palestine. Viewing Israel as a religion has the merit, taken from Barth, of respecting the integrity of the people as a whole rather than privileging religious voices from among them (most Jews, both in Israel and in the Diaspora, are secular). Yet, seeing Israel only as a nation and that only in secular terms involves seeing it purely in empirical terms, reading what is already "visible" to whichever secular worldview is the predominant one in our environment. The idea that Israel is somehow linked to the covenantal purposes of God as part of the providential ordering of the life of nations would not yield such a simple-minded approach, because it would require understanding "Israel" and its purposes as in some sense "hidden with God." Nevertheless, God has spoken to the Jews through the revelatory events of the *Shoah* and the establishment of the state of Israel.[121] Finally, given that Van Buren didn't believe that Jesus or Christians should call Jews to worship Jesus, he believed that the challenge for Christians was how "the God of Abraham, Isaac and Jacob has been and is at work in the People of the Book (Islam), and in the people of many books (Hindus and Buddhists and others)."[122] In summary, we can say that once he turned away from his teacher Barth, Van Buren espoused the two-covenant theology that had been promoted by Reinhold Niebuhr's massive influence over American

117. Van Buren, *A Theology of the Jewish-Christian Reality,* 357–59.

118. Van Buren, *A Christian Theology of the People Israel.* 258.

119. Ibid., 42.

120. Ibid., 31.

121. Van Buren, *Discerning the Way,* 176.

122. Van Buren, *A Christian Theology of the People Israel,* 262–63.

mainline Protestantism, and also turned against any metaphysics to a "narrative theology." He was an experiential-expressivist. He was more radical than Niebuhr in his approach to non-Christian religions. Van Buren has not been alone in this respect. This is closely linked to the fact that like Rosemary Radford Ruether, he reads the resurrection as the disciples' experience of faith born again in them.[123] Bader-Saye charges them with having a doctrine of the Trinity that is Monarchian and a Christology that is "adoptionist at best."[124] What Bader-Saye has not spotted is the fact that this retreat into a subjective, experiential-expressivist understanding of Jesus' resurrection harks back not only to Bultmann, as many will realize, but ultimately to Hegel's Speculative Good Friday as well.[125] Van Buren, like Roy Eckhardt, eventually drifted from orthodox Christian faith, and thus like other secular theologies of the 1960s his method left a void. It didn't take very long for it to be filled by postliberalism. Van Buren had denied the christological covenant regarding salvation, and in doing so had left a vacuum open for a plurality of covenants. Thus with some post-liberals, we have not only two but *many* covenants, thus reproducing and validating the theological pluralism that John Hick sought to ground in theism rather than Christology.[126]

From the above outline it should be clear that Van Buren's turn from orthodoxy was not simply due to his anti-metaphysical turn, but to his theology of covenants. The turn from metaphysics and the problem of a deficient ontology has been at the heart of critiques of postliberalism in recent years.[127] What is missing from such critiques is awareness that post-liberalism from Lindbeck onwards had Israel as a central concern, walking in the legacy of Reinhold Niebuhr and attempting to evade the problems encountered by theologians such as Paul Van Buren. In fact, the post-liberals share a good deal with Van Buren, though their theology of covenants is more christologically rooted.[128] This is partly related to the centrality of christological narrative to their work. The turn to narrative as basic to theology and ethics occurred in the 1970s, as Protestantism got marginalized in Western society. Stanley Hauerwas, whom we encoun-

---

123. Bader-Saye, *Church and Israel after Christendom*, 78.

124. Ibid., 79.

125. Fergusson, *Bultmann*, 112–13.

126. Hick, *God and the Universe of Faiths*.

127. A very incisive such critique is found in Vidu, *Postliberal Theological Method*.

128. See Thiemann, "The Promising God: The Gospel as Narrated Promise," in Hauerwas and Jones (eds.), *Why Narrative?*, 320–47.

tered in section 4, perhaps the chief proponent of narrative theological ethics, was an early student of Niebuhr's work and then rebelled against him. This is important because Niebuhr's approach casts a shadow over Hauerwas, as the latter's Gifford Lectures demonstrate. There is an important continuity between Niebuhr and Hauerwas and Lindbeck, in that Niebuhr speaks of history, whereas Hauerwas and Lindbeck speak of "story." The shift is in the type of narrative. The second way in which Niebuhr casts a shadow over Hauerwas is that Niebuhr himself drew on biblical narrative, or "biblical mythology," in piecemeal fashion to buttress his notion of religion as prophetic but not politically constructive for the state. This has been imbibed by Hauerwas and fits well with his pacifism.[129] Thus narrative theology and ethics for the church has been pursued ironically within Niebuhr's political framework, albeit with much more concentration on ecclesiology than he ever had.[130] The heavy reliance on narrative has prompted an important though contentious critique by the British Roman Catholic theologian Francesca Aran Murphy in her book *God Is Not a Story*.[131] Murphy takes postliberals to task, in a mode that is both satirizing and yet deeply serious, for what she terms "story Barthianism." She rightly argues that this involves the foregrounding of a method, or part of the method of, a favored theologian "rather than the assertions which they make."[132] Narrative theologies "intensify the angular rationalism to which contemporary theology is culturally prone."[133] She astutely notes how Lindbeck called the movement "postliberal" to mimic Barth's supposed "rejection of the efforts of liberal theologians to find common ground with extra-Christian rationality."[134] Murphy argues that this "story Barthianism" is only made possible by the transcendental Thomism that influenced Lindbeck early on.[135] According to her, "an allergy to history is the main legacy of Thomism to narrative theologies," and that in the case of church, Trinity, and eschatology, narrative theology withdraws from

---

129. For Niebuhr on biblical mythology, see Naveh, *Reinhold Niebuhr and Non-Utopian Liberalism*, 187–88.

130. Hauerwas, "The Church's One Foundation is Jesus Christ Her Lord," in Hauerwas, Murphy and Nation (eds.), *Theology without Foundations*, 143–62.

130. Murphy, *God is Not a Story*.

131. Ibid., 5.

132. Ibid., 6.

133. Ibid.

134. Ibid., 15.

135. Ibid.

engaging the temporality of human events.[136] More specifically regarding method, she says that mid-twentieth-century Thomism of the kind that Lindbeck would have learned was "not well-placed to defend the historicity of Scripture," perhaps due to Aristotelian influence. Aristotle preferred tragedy to history.[137] Murphy argues that postliberals accentuate biblical description more than the Word ("more visual than verbal"), thus producing narrative theology that is more like film.[138] She favors contemplation of the Word, having simply accepted the conclusions of historical criticism that the narratives of Genesis to 2 Samuel are not historically reliable.[139] This is rash and unwarranted. The retreat to spirituality is no better than the retreat to story, frustrating Murphy's earlier criticism of the transcendental Thomist allergy against history for corrupting Lindbeck.[140] Lindbeck's notion of religion and theology as languages may be more pragmatist than expressivist, but, as George Hunsinger notes, it still lies within the liberal rejection of propositionalism.[141] It borrows from the later Wittgenstein, thus continuing Van Buren's approach. Lindbeck's stress on our making of the church continues Niebuhr's view that it is we who make history. Importantly, neither Niebuhr nor Lindbeck have strong doctrines of the Trinity and Christology, and this is crucial to their anthropological ecclesiology as well as their shared lack of a doctrine of providence. Last, Lindbeck continues Niebuhr's acceptance of Rosenzweig's two-covenant theology. I shall return in chapter 6 to the problem of postliberal readings of Barth in this respect. What matters here is that all of these themes can be shown to underwrite Mark Juergensmeyer's sociology of violent apocalyptic as one strand of the global resurgence of religion since the end of the Cold War.

APOCALYPTIC VIOLENCE AND THE SCAPEGOATING OF THE SECULAR STATE OF ISRAEL

American sociologist of religion Mark Juergensmeyer has made a landmark study of perpetrators of religious apocalyptic terrorism across

---

136. Ibid., 15.

137. Ibid., 23–26.

138. Ibid., 41–42.

139. Ibid., 293–324.

140. Hunsinger, "Postliberalism" in Vanhoozer (ed.), *The Cambridge Companion to Postmodern Theology*, 42–57.

141

the globe.[142] His work is considered a seminal contribution to the sociological understanding of the violence that has at times accompanied global movements of religious resurgence. His work is of interest both for his analysis of the relationship between secularization and violent apocalyptic forms of eschatology, and for his study of the role of nationalism in religious resurgence since the end of the Cold War. For the purpose of this study, Juergensmeyer is treated as a sociological point of comparison with my reading of Karl Barth in chapter 1, which explored the link between secularization, the loss of eschatology, and the rise of particularly deadly forms of nationalism. The argument is that Juergensmeyer's ethical recommendations for the world religions—to be transformed so as to practice the imaginary cosmic war by nonviolent means—is one paralleled, as far as Christianity is concerned. by Barth in his spiritualization of the doctrine of revolution, and it is a type of attitude widely accepted by Christians and members of many other faiths. Juergensmeyer, however, argues from general principles rather than explicitly theological ones. In this respect, he rightly sees himself as continuing the legacy of Reinhold Niebuhr's thinking. While Barth confines himself to addressing Christians, and does not try to repair the problems of other faiths on the behalf of their members, Juergensmeyer addresses members of all world religions.[143] Mark Juergensmeyer is deeply indebted to Reinhold Niebuhr's approach to religion. What becomes evident upon reading his work is how metaphysical statements are converted into present-day moral requirements. True religion is prophetic and nonviolent; indeed Juergensmeyer appears to imply that it is pacifist.[144] In order for this to be achieved, religions must renarrate their stories of cosmic war.[145] This

142. See fn. 100 above. Juergensmeyer's staff page with complete list of publications can be seen at http://www.juergensmeyer.com. Accessed on 1 November, 2010.

143. The question of whether or to what extent Christian theologians should try to repair the problems of other world religions is important, but neglected in the postliberal literature on interfaith dialogue and Scriptural reasoning. Some questions that ought to be asked in this respect include whether Christian theologians should act as managers for public theological speech. Also, the effect upon different theological debates when this happens needs to be probed.

144. Juergensmeyer, "The Unfinished Task of Reinhold Niebuhr," 884–87. Juergensmeyer authored a volume on appropriating Gandhi for nonviolent conflict resolution early on in his career, Juergensmeyer, *Fighting with Gandhi*; Juergensmeyer, *Gandhi's Way*. This is significant because Reinhold Niebuhr extolled Gandhi in his reflections on Christology.

145. Juergensmeyer, *The New Cold War?*, 153–70; Juergensmeyer, *Terror in the Mind of God*, 148–66.

could in practice mean rejecting propositional views of revelation.[146] We are the makers of history and religion, the performers in the drama of the modern religious sublime.[147] Therefore, we are the ones who have the responsibility of renarrating religion nonviolently, and displaying each other's narratives nonviolently to seek the good of civil society. Underlying these requirements lie an American commitment to natural theology of a particular kind, and natural rights discourse. With Juergensmeyer there is a silence on the theology of covenants, which suggests that his approach is methodologically atheist like that of Peter Berger, allowing either for a minimalist theological reading of his work (there is only one covenant between God and humans), or a maximalist one (there are many covenants). This is typical American pragmatism reinforcing religious pluralism. Looking back to the roots of this sociological thinking, however, it is clear that Juergensmeyer fuses Berger's notion that our action makes the social world and the sacred canopy with Lindbeck's notion that our language makes religious communities and discourses (theology). Ultimately this poietic characterization of both religious discourse and religions, on the one hand, and societies and therefore the life of nations and states, on the other, must be traced back to Hegel and others in the German Enlightenment. These same philosophical theologians presented a flattened theopolitical landscape devoid of the election of Israel or the rise of modern Zionist currents of thought in nineteenth-century Europe.[148] It is therefore no accident that Juergensmeyer, like most sociologists of religion, should present us with a bizarre phenomenology of apocalyptic madness wherein the participants demonize both the state of Israel and the USA for their own problems. Juergensmeyer's first book, *The New Cold War? Religious Nationalism Confronts the Secular State*, tried to look underneath the anti-American rhetoric of resurgent religious nationalism across the world.[149] His other major book, *Terror in the Mind of God*, is extraordinary in that in his overall theorizing based on his case studies, he actually ignores his own evidence showing that nearly all the terrorists he interviewed harbored anti-Semitic and anti-Zionist conspiracy theories. The book was published just after 9/11. Since then, such conspiracy

146. Specifically, this is if particular divine commands in canonical sacred texts have been traditionally understood to permit and enjoin violent treatment of those considered heterodox or non-adherents of the religion in question.

147. On terrorism as dramatization of the sublime, see Eagleton, *Holy Terror*.

148. Tomasoni, *Modernity and the Final Aim of History*.

149. Juergensmeyer, *The New Cold War?*, 22, 56, 73; Juergensmeyer, *Terror in the Mind of God*, 181–85.

theories along with ones about a "New World Order" have mushroomed alarmingly, helped along by the internet. Jurgensmeyer's Niebuhrian method cannot register this problem because it cannot grasp it. It is to the analysis of his findings that we now turn.

The structure of the two parts of *Terror in the Mind of God* reveals the underlying logic of Juergensmeyer's argument. The first part, "Cultures of Violence," presents five case studies of apocalyptic violence from the major world religions. Juergensmeyer tracked down and interviewed the men who had perpetrated these acts. The aim is clear—to attempt to persuade these men to renounce violent attitudes and ways of enacting their religious beliefs. In this respect Juergensmeyer clearly mirrors Western governments' programs of "deradicalization" of Muslim men, attempting to turn them towards identity politics or the politics of recognition instead, as an acceptable way of participating and enacting the dramas of the human condition as viewed through their religious beliefs, in critical participation in Western civil society.[150] Juergensmeyer's book slotted very nicely into the agendas of deradicalization. What is significant, however, is how the first of the "cultures of violence" he studies is the violent fringe of the American Christian anti-abortion movement. Then the sequence goes to religious Zionists opponents of the Middle East peace process, including Yoel Lerner who murdered Yitzhak Rabin, Baruch Goldstein's attack on the Tomb of the Patriarchs in Hebron, and Rabbi Meir Kahane from the Kach Party's arguments justifying violence, as opposition to the creation of a Palestinian government in the West Bank. Third on the list is terrorism by men from an Islamic background, focusing on the 1990 attack on the World Trade Center. Fourth and fifth respectively are Sikh terrorism in the Punjab in 1995, and the Japanese cult Aum Shinirikyo's outlandish attempt to create an Armageddon scenario in a subway in Tokyo in 1995. In the second part of his book, entitled "The Logic of Religious Violence," Juergensmeyer moves from the drama of religious violence enacted in the post-Cold War sublime to an analysis of this as based on an eschatology of cosmic war. He argues that its content involves sacrifice of human victims

---

150. Deradicalization needs to be understood alongside governmental interference in the teaching of Islam in universities. Both initiatives slot perfectly in Western governments' desire to keep orthodox Christians at bay, and to manage and marginalize them insofar as they criticize government programmers that ultimately stem from eugenics population policies, e.g., attempting to redefine marriage, promoting abortion and euthanasia, etc. In this sense, it should be obvious that governments are bound to see Christians and Muslims as equivalent, despite crucial long-standing differences across the board on the ethics of marriage, sexuality, and family life, as well as political theology, which encompasses all of these matters.

and demonization of "others," and that all this emanated from the psyche of marginalized men frustrated in their masculine identities in later modernity. He concludes with a reflection on "the Mind of God." The overall weave of the two sequences should be clear. Apocalyptic violence is happening now because some religious men in all the major world religions feel threatened by the triumph of secularism, whatever that may mean, and resent what they perceive as the unwarranted "softening" of their religions in response to modern ways of thinking and living. Yet the data that Juergensmeyer provides does not simply lead to this conclusion. To stay with him at this point is to focus only on anthropology. With the exception of Sikh-grounded terrorism, all of the case studies have in common a profound resentment and demonization of the State of Israel as both a Jewish and secular state. Israel is the symbol for them of what is wrong with the modern world. My point is that even if the social conditions that made these men unhappy with sexual identity were to be changed in their favor, the demonization and scapegoating of the secular State of Israel might not go away, except perhaps in the case of the religious Jews. It might just find another excuse. Actually, the problem of the Palestinians would remain for them, which complicates the picture further. Reviewing the case studies briefly will demonstrate the problem.

In Juergensmeyer's first case study, we encounter "Christian" neo-Nazi supersessionism in the USA in the form of Christian Identity and Christian Reconstruction movements.[151] These are anti-Semitic American movements that see white Christians as the Aryan race and the replacement of Jews, who are seen as the offspring of Eve and Satan. They are descended from the British Israel movement, which sees Anglo-Saxons as the Ten Lost Tribes of Israel. This is an extreme form of supersessionism. They believe Jesus was an Aryan not a Semite; thus they resurrect the Christology of the German Christians (Nazi collaborators within the mainline Protestant churches). Christian Identity and Christian Reconstruction go against the separation of church and state in the US constitution. They are an extreme wing of the covenantal movement. They espouse conspiracy theories about Jews, Zionists, Freemasons, capitalists, and the US government. They have historically been linked to the Ku Klux Klan. Jews are blamed for liberalism, that is, for frustrating white Christian men's desire to control American society. Logically, they must also resent Jewish emancipation, civil rights, and the establishment of Israel as both a *secular* and *Jewish* state. The second case study is of the Jewish Radical Right

151. Juergensmeyer, *Terror in the Mind of God*, 19–43.

in Israel which is, of course, not at all anti-Semitic.[152] Yet Juergensmeyer misses the significance of their inclusion in his catalogue of apocalyptic violence against the secular state. They agree with Israel being a Jewish state; what they resent is its being a *secular* state. Thus they think that Jews have too little power and sovereignty, and are angry that politicians elected on their behalf are giving it away to Palestinians. They think this goes against the will of God. The third case study is of Islamic-grounded terrorism, which tends to be anti-Zionist.[153] The standard historical actors are involved: Hamas, Fatah, Hizbollah, Islamic Jihad, all of whom either are Palestinian or support the Palestinians. In their eyes, Israel's very existence as both a Jewish and a secular state is an insult, just as it insults Christian Reconstructionists. Islamists are offended because the territorial claims of Islam to Palestine have been broken, thus the power and honor of Allah have been insulted. Muslim men are not in control. The last case study of the Aum Shinrikyo, a Japanese New Religious Movement that propagated prophecies of the coming battle of Armageddon as World War III.[154] Nerve gas attack on Tokyo subway was a sign of Armageddon, that Japan had been captured by the USA and World War III had begun. Juergensmeyer explains that the Second World War was traumatic for Japan given the dropping of the atomic bomb on Hiroshima and Nagasaki. Thus hatred and fear of the USA features in Japanese NRMs' conspiracy theories. Paranoia about Jewish power as Western power is an unsurprising adjunct of such a mentality.

Thus much of the apocalyptic violence at the extreme end of global religious resurgence expresses deep resentment at and scapegoating of secular Jewish emancipation and entry into public life, with all the complexities, political compromises, and pragmatism that life in a secular nation-state involves. The inclusion of the Japanese NRM highlights the utter irrationality of this mentality; there have never been many Jews living in Japan! Juergensmeyer is right in linking the religious scapegoating of his case studies to troubled masculinity.[155] At a theological level we can make sense of this phenomenon. It is founded on the belief that Gentile men, in particular, are only secure in their identity and vocation if they are the sole rulers of national time and space. This is intelligible only if we realize that because of the Bible's historical influence, Israel has been seen

---

152. Ibid., 45–60.

153. Ibid., 61–84.

154. Ibid., 103–18.

155. Ibid., 190–218.

as the archetypal nation. Nations have often modeled themselves on Israel, often seeking to replace her as elected by God.[156] Religious people can fear secular power because it means religious ideologies are not in control of the vision of the good of a nation. Thus a classic reflex of resentment at the loss of religious power and closeness to state power is to turn against the modern State of Israel, because it is secular and an example of mostly secular people doing relatively well in life. This self-righteous religious exclusivism is what lies behind the rising tide of opinion against the very legitimation of the State of Israel among the Western Protestant churches (themselves in decline) since the end of the Cold War and the First Palestinian Intifada.[157] It is pathological in nature. It is not only a generic hatred, as Robert S. Wistrich argued, but also the generic envy and generic paranoia.[158] As such it is also the generic conspiracy theory.[159] All of this fits with arguments Juergensmeyer gives in his book, which is that the visions of cosmic warfare to which the terrorists adhered are in continuity with traditional religious ways of conceiving of warfare, as "presenting an almost cosmological re-enactment of the primacy of order over chaos."[160] It follows, therefore, that attempts to manage religious discourses need to be understood as a form of warfare. Logically this means that both the troubles over masculine identity and the pervasiveness of anti-Semitism and anti-Zionism should therefore be visible in the mainstream of religious resurgence in its various forms. The exclusivist, control-freak nature of anti-Semitism and anti-Zionism explains why men who espouse these generic forms of hatred, envy, and paranoia are also prone to be anti-feminist.[161] Mark Juergensmeyer does argue that religious terrorists are partly motivated by anger and resentment at loss of sexual control. They are especially annoyed by the reality of women being politically emancipated and assuming power in the public arena.[162] (Michael Ignatieff has made this argument regarding the perpetrators of 9/11.[163]) Historically,

156. Smith, *Chosen Peoples.*

157. Anti-Zionism in the Western churches has a long history, briefly recapitulated in Merkley, *Christian Attitudes towards the State of Israel,* 183–94.

158. See Fineberg, Samuels, and Weitzman (eds.), *Antisemitism.*

159. Anti-Semitic and anti-Zionist conspiracy theories have been expressed increasingly openly in the political and cultural mainstream in Europe since 9/11. Ottelenghi, "Making Sense of European Anti-Semitism," 104–26.

160. Juergensmeyer, *Terror in the Mind of God,* 162.

161. I shall explore this problem more deeply in chapter 7.

162. Juergensmeyer, *Terror in the Mind of God,* 202–4.

163. Ignatieff, *The Lesser Evil.*

it is a matter of record that many feminists have been Protestant pro-Zionists. Christabel Pankhurst is a case in point; after suffrage was won, she became a preacher on the evangelical conference circuit, because her own Anglican church denied women ordination at the time, in contrast to the Congregationalist churches, which were the first churches in Britain to ordain women.[164] The newly forming Pentecostals of the day were also more hospitable to women's ministries as well as to Zionism.[165] Pankhurst was a premillennialist and eventually went to live in the United States. Her evangelical theology has been ignored and forgotten by British historians of feminism. The secular nature of the State of Israel has meant that women in Israel have been far more emancipated than in neighboring countries, which have seen Islamic fundamentalist backlash against very moderate feminist gains under Arab nationalism.[166] It is no accident that Israel had the world's first female prime minister—Golda Meir—long before any European country.[167]

Juergensmeyer presents us with a religious and political landscape flattened by inattention to this globalized anti-Semitism and anti-Zionism and the paradoxes and ironies involved—among them the fact that many of the countries in the world that demonize Israel are younger than it, both in terms of cultural memory and of modern statehood. The philosophical consequence of presenting this flattened landscape in which frightening dramas occur and madmen reach for the sublime, is that the implication of Judaism (or Islam for that matter) *in*, not only against, the challenges of modernity are obscured or neglected. The English Jewish philosopher Gillian Rose warned about this throughout her career, in her critique of postmodernist theory's triumph in the academy in the wake of the collapse of Communism and the disgracing of Heidegger for his membership of the Nazi party.[168] Thus she was talking about the precise time when Juergensmeyer was writing. Rose argues that there has been a distinctly modern Western choice by Diaspora Jews to embody Judaism as "politics by other means," that is, a retreat from actual politics to Judaism as ethics (Levinas), Judaism as biblical commentary (Hartmann), and Judaism

164. Christabel Pankhurst's evangelical faith, and specifically her Zionism, have been ignored by English historians of feminism, but recently resurrected by Timothy Larsen of Wheaton College in the USA. See Larsen, *Christabel Pankhurst.*

165. The literature on Pentecostalism and women is vast. On preaching specifically, see Lawless, *Handmaidens of the Lord.*

166. Fuchs, *Israeli Women's Studies*

167. Burkett, *Golda Meir.*

168. Rose, *Mourning Becomes the Law.*

as exilic writing and deconstruction (Derrida).[169] Judaism has been tamed into a religion controlled by the state, as when Napoleon brought a Sanhedrin to France, rather than being a community that shares in the "unequal sharing in the means of violence," which is necessary for maintaining a community.[170] It is clear here that Rose is attacking academic anti-Zionism and the wholescale delegitimization of Israel since 1990, though curiously commentators on her work have missed this. Rose was far from uncritical of Israel, but she situated her critique within an argument that Judaism is properly understood as politics, constituted by successive forms of *Midrash*, and read through her non-esoteric, pragmatist, and aporetic reading of Hegel.[171] This means that she accepts Hegel's speculative union of church and state, perhaps viewing it as succeeding the ancient Israelite union of temple priesthood and kingship.[172] Juergensmeyer would probably rigorously distinguish church and religion construed on a specifically Christian pacifist model, and state as metaphysically distinct, along the American model. This sharp distinction is to be distinguished from the theology of the Church of Scotland, whose establishment is founded in British law, and is closer to Congregationalist and Baptist ecclesiologies, which migrated from Britain to American in the Puritan period. Juergensmeyer appears to conflate pacifism and nonviolence; we can see this from his claim that Christianity before Nicaea was pacifist.[173] Here he is conflating its clear distinction as a spiritual community from the temporal community of the Roman Empire, and of nations in general, with an ethic of absolute nonviolence, which is nowhere categorically enjoined in the New Testament. The necessary clarification is that nonviolence is required of Christians insofar as they comprise the church, but not necessarily of them as individuals participating legitimately in civil society, for example, in the armed forces. Thus what is being asked of the world's religions by Juergensmeyer, and by Western states, is to become like the Protestant free churches—voluntary, noncoercive, and nonviolent in the constitution of their polities. This is the model of "true religion" for him. It is made the ground for asking religious actors to renarrate their sacred histories and visions of cosmic war, in order to construct nonviolent politics that enable them to participate in civil society without behaving violently, and as such

169. Rose, *Judaism and Modernity*. Rose, *Mourning Becomes the Law*, 37–38.

170. Rose, *Mourning Becomes the Law*, 97.

171. Ibid., 75f.

172. Rose, *Hegel contra Sociology*, 51–97.

173. Juergensmeyer, *Terror in the Mind of God*, 25.

against the Western political norm, which is a Protestant nonconformist one in origin, that the state alone should arrogate to itself the legitimate use of force. It is this kind of desire to transform religions by analogy to free church Protestantism that enables postliberal theologians to speak in terms of a plurality of covenants between God and the world's religions. It is not necessary to Juergensmeyer's theory, which is sociological, but the theological space opened up for him by Niebuhr is the same space opened for the postliberal path, as well as for secular and interfaith theologies such as those of Paul Van Buren and John Hick, and Christian interpretations of the work of the Parliament of the World's Religions, for example, Hans Küng. A theological endorsement of a plurality of covenants logically clashes with classic Christian missiology, hence why it has been opposed from various quarters since the 1970s.[174] One who has appeared to be an opponent has been Rowan Williams, Archbishop of Canterbury from 2003 to 2012.[175] A prominent place is given for a critical analysis of his theology in this book. In order to understand his very Anglican postliberal trajectory, we need to turn to his understanding of nationhood and

174. The classic response can be found in D'Costa, Hick, and Knitter (eds.), *Christian Uniqueness Reconsidered*.

175. Williams gives some loose remarks on John Hick's *The Myth of God Incarnate*, published in 1977, in a 2005 interview with Rupert Shortt, saying that "many people felt that this was about as far as a particular kind of rational revisionism could go," and that as a result, some theologians started to turn to Roman Catholic theology as a source, to get out of what he saw as "a certain kind of very insular Protestantism." Williams, "Belief and Theology," in Shortt (ed.), *God's Advocates*, 17. The problem here, however, is that nowhere in his own work does Williams *ever* engage with systematic theology produced by theologians from the free Protestant churches in Britain in the nineteenth and twentieth centuries, despite his own childhood background in Congregationalism and Presbyterianism. Congregationalists, as Alan Sell (himself a major British Congregationalist theologian) has pointed out, comprised the majority of systematic theologians in Britain in the first half of the twentieth century, often involved in setting up new departments of theology in the industrial English cities where many immigrants of all faiths would later come to live. Sell, *Nonconformist Theology in the Twentieth Century*, 11–13, 163. John Hick was a member of the United Reformed Church, formed in 1972 as the ecumenical merger of British Congregationalists and English Presbyterians. He set forth an "Indian laboratory" model of theological pluralism, imported from post-partition India (I am grateful to Kirsteen Kim for pointing this out to me). The URC produced an able and missiologically-experienced critic of Hick in the shape of Lesslie Newbigin. The geographical origin of the debate in Birmingham, England, where both Hick and Newbigin worked, and which contained a sizeable minority of permanent immigrants from the Indian subcontinent, is also very important to note. Hick and Newbigin were debating from experience of encounter with adherents of and converts from the Indian religions. This links nicely with the fact that Indian religions are Mark Juergensmeyer's original area of expertise.

the state of Israel. Williams' understanding of nationhood is discussed in the next chapter. Then in chapters 5 and 6 his approach to Palestine and Israel is analyzed.

3

Wales as a Stateless Nation

Ambivalence Concerning Recognition in Theology and Social Theory

WE NOW GO TO the heart of the issue of nation-state and stateless nation. The case study here is Wales, which forms part of the United Kingdom of Great Britain and Northern Ireland. The question is, whether and to what extent have theologians and social theorists recognized Wales as a stateless nation, specifically as a nation that has lost its own state. A comment is required here explaining why Wales was chosen, and why later in the chapter its treatment is compared to that of Israel. The case of Wales was the one that originally aroused my interest in the question of defining nationhood in the Christian theological tradition. Being Welsh, I have a special concern as a Christian theologian to think through what kinds of commitments and responsibilities are required theologically for recognition of stateless nations. In the framework of the present book, Wales is an ideal case study because it is, strictly speaking, the earliest nation to have come under England's dominion.

As Henry VIII's break with Rome and official sponsoring of the Reformation was connected by himself to absorbing Wales into England, in order to ensure that his Welsh subjects stayed under his own authority and that of the Archbishop of Canterbury, the Church of England was implicated in the loss of recognition, and as high church Anglicanism basically sees itself as the continuation of the pre-Reformation Catholic church in Wales, it is entirely appropriate to look at how Wales' best-known high church Anglican theologian, Rowan Williams, has handled the question.

The examples of his work to be considered are two pieces on Welsh devolution and British identity, one written in 1979 and the other in 2009. I do so in relation to the paper to which Williams responds at the 1979 colloquium on Welsh devolution, by the distinguished Welsh Reformed theologian and historian R. Tudur Jones. While Williams carries over elements of the reception of Hegel by Welsh liberal Congregationalists into liberal Anglo-Catholic theology, Jones works with a larger frame of reference drawn from the biblical and dogmatic work of the Dutch Reformed tradition. I attempt to draw out how aspects of the theology of Herman Bavinck and Abraham Kuyper can supplement Jones' thinking on Welsh nationhood, as well as providing concepts for assessing Williams' approach. At the same time, I open the question of how is it that the two approaches seem consistently to talk past each other, and what further inquiry theology would need to make in order to enable further debate. In the second half of the chapter, our attention is turned to the definition of nationhood in social theory practiced within the interdisciplinary field of nationalism studies. The two main defenders of the concept as pre-modern, Anthony D. Smith and Adrian Hastings, are considered, and I continue the debate they started and left off when Hastings died. The discussion ranges across their analysis of the appropriation of biblical Israel as model of nationhood in European history, the limits to their comparative range, and whether they fail to recognize Wales as a nation due to deficiencies in their concepts or in declining to apply these consistently. In other words, is recognition of stateless nations simply a methodological and hermeneutical problem, or is it a reckoning with a deeper moral challenge.

THE WELSH POLITICAL AND RELIGIOUS SITUATION
BEFORE DEVOLUTION

Before we turn to Jones and Williams, there is a need to sketch the Welsh political and religious situation before the first devolution vote of 1979. In 1997, when devolution was finally won, Wales—unlike Scotland—had no independent institutions that could contain the public memory of independent statehood, lost in 1282 when it was conquered by Edward I and its last king, Llywelyn II, was killed.[1] Only eight years after having conquered Wales, Edward I banished the Jewish population from England

---

1. On the conquest of Wales in 1282, see Williams and Kenyon (eds.), *The Impact of the Edwardian Castles in Wales.*

and Wales.[2] This proved highly symbolic in British history. Back in the eighth century, the Venerable Bede had followed the sixth-century Welsh historian Gildas in casting alternately the Britons and subsequently the Anglo-Saxons as first the Old Israel, subject to divine wrath, and then the New Israel.[3] Alcuin of York emphatically portrayed the Anglo-Saxons as the Israelites driving the Britons out of England/Canaan. Likewise, he portrayed the English monks of Lindisfarne as Israelite in the face of Viking raids in A.D. 793, the latter portrayed as Chaldeans, Babylonians, or Romans.[4] Krishan Kumar points out that England *as* Britain was already a belief among English elites by the tenth century A.D.[5] It was clearly the aim of the Anglo-Saxons from the very beginning to conquer the whole of the British Isles. For Edward as for Bede centuries earlier, England—the Anglo-Saxons now transmuted into Anglo-Normans—was Israel to Wales' Canaan. Thus he had to expel real Jews in order to justify this conquest. The same time period of the late thirteenth century also saw the fall of the Latin Kingdom of Jerusalem, which constituted the Crusader rule over the Holy Land and, under Edward's son Edward II, who succeeded him to the English throne, the dissolution of the chivalric Order of the Knights Templar, which had been formed in 1118 in Jerusalem.[6] Thus while Western nations lost their power over Jews, Muslims, and Christians living in the Holy Land, some turned to persecute Jews and Christian neighbors back home. This wider perspective is central to the thesis of this book. Historically speaking, it can be argued it was the official Reformation as conducted by Henry VIII, and which created the Church of England as a Protestant established church, that led to the loss of recognition of Wales as a stateless nation and entity distinct from England. Wales was legally incorporated into England by the Act of Union of 1536–43. Wales was to remain under the authority of both the king and the Archbishop of Canterbury. Incorporating Wales into England would strengthen this tie, in the face of the fictitious temptation to support Spain should it invade from the south-west of the British Isles.[7] However, when we recall

2. Jews had first come to England and Wales with William the Conqueror in 1066. On their banishment, see Julius, *Trials of the Diaspora*.

3. On Bede's debt to Gildas, see Hanning, *The Vision of History in Early Britain*. On Bede's attitude to the Anglo-Saxons or the English as the new Israel see Ward, *The Venerable Bede*, 114.

4. On Alcuin, see Scheil, *The Footsteps of Israel*, 148.

5. Kumar, *The Making of English National Identity*, 60.

6. On the Latin Kingdom of Jerusalem, see Seward, *The Monks of War*, 23–74.

7. On the Act of Union, see Roberts, "The Union with England and the Identity of

that Wales had been seen as Canaan since before Edward, and Bede had claimed Christianity in Wales to be corrupt and therefore ripe for Roman reforms and re-conversion, the legal denial of recognition to Wales cannot be blamed on an upstart Protestantism contrasted to universalist Catholicism. In practice, the supersession of real Israel, real Jews, by Anglo-Saxon nationalist imperialism was the real problem all along. Faulty, self-serving biblical interpretation was the root problem—as it so often is in the history of European imperialism. Therefore, close attention to biblical interpretation would and will have to be central to any attempts to repair the problem of how Christian theology since Henry VIII recognizes Wales.

The Wales and Berwick Act of 1746 said that "in all cases where the Kingdom of England, or that part of Great Britain called England, hath been or shall be mentioned in any Act of Parliament, the same has been and shall from henceforth be deemed and taken to comprehend and include the Dominion of Wales."[8] This Act of Parliament remained in force until 1967.[9] It was ironic that the Liberal prime minister W. E. Gladstone, popular among Welsh nonconformists, argued that "the distinction between England and Wales . . . is totally unknown to our constitution."[10] In the second half of the nineteenth century, Welsh nationalism was expressed through liberal and radical politics. David Lloyd George, Britain's only Welsh-speaking Prime Minister, also a liberal, described himself as a radical and Welsh Nationalist.[11] The *Cymru Fudd* (Future Wales) movement was founded in 1886, aiming "to secure a national legislature for Wales, dealing exclusively with Welsh affairs, i.e., Home Rule for Wales."[12] "Home Rule" was a divisive issue in Wales, and support for it was weakened by the industrialization of south Wales, because class conflict was found to cut across the liberal-conservative divide, producing fresh support for the new Labour Party. Welsh liberals, who were nationalists, therefore focused their energies on religious and cultural aspirations for the time being. Their two main goals were creating educational institutions, such as the University of Wales, and disestablishing the Church of

---

'Anglican' Wales," 49–70.

8. On the Wales and Berwick Act, see Bogdanor, *Devolution in the United Kingdom*, 144.

9. Ibid., 144.

10. Ibid.

11. Ibid., 146.

12. Williams, *Young Wales Movement*, 3.

England in Wales.[13] As Bogdanor says, the Church was the church of only a minority of Welsh people and Welsh churchgoers, and it had not appointed any Welsh-speaking bishops between 1715 and 1870, despite the fact that most of the population spoke Welsh, and indeed only Welsh, or Welsh far better than English.[14] Disestablishment was achieved in 1914 but was not enacted until 1920. It had been a goal of many nonconformists since the mid-nineteenth century. Free Protestant churches (independent and Baptist) first sprang up in Wales in 1639 in Brecon, and orthodox dissent enjoyed considerable support during the Cromwellian period. They started to proliferate in Wales from the time of the Evangelical revivals of the mid-eighteenth century, and by the mid-nineteenth century, three-quarters of the Welsh population had abandoned the established Church of England in favour of various dissenting denominations.[15] By the early twentieth century, at the eve of the Evangelical Revival of 1904, a quarter of the Welsh population were nonconformist, whereas only 5 percent of the overall population of the UK were. Only 10 percent of the Welsh population adhered to the established Church of England; this means that probably less were weekly churchgoers.[16] Most Welsh people, like most people in the rest of Britain, gained the right to vote after the First World War. Plaid Cymru, the Welsh nationalist political party, was formed soon after in 1925 at Maesgwyn Temperance Hall, Pwllheli. Most early members of Plaid were nonconformists. They had long regarded Wales as a national community. They aspired to fill the vacuum left by the decline of the Liberal Party after the time of Lloyd George. Yet it was the Roman Catholic intellectual Saunders Lewis who was party leader between 1926 and 1939.[17] His personal conviction was that nationalism is a distinct political philosophy, rather than merely being a qualification or degeneration of another ideology. However, Lewis' own approach was to stress the concept of civilization, of Wales as part of European civilization since the medieval period.[18] In 1945, Gwynfor Evans, a Congregationalist, was elected leader. Laura McAllister sees him as "drawing on and adapting many of the principles of nonconformism," saying that this is a reason for "seeing 1945 as

13. On disestablishment, see Morgan, *The Span of the Cross*, 30–37.

14. Bogdanor, *Devolution in the United Kingdom*, 149.

15. Morgan, *The Span of the Cross*, 23–26.

16. McAllister, *Plaid Cymru*, 45.

17. Ibid., 23.

18. Ibid., 53.

the start of the party's modernisation."[19] Evans would become the Party's first Member of Parliament at Westminster in 1966, thereby signaling its growing political leverage.

All of this is needed to put the exchange between R. Tudur Jones and Rowan Williams into perspective. A large part of what accounts for the manner of engagement with the issues in Williams' 1979 essay is his personal trajectory in his youth, moving away from Welsh-medium non-conformity to Anglo-Catholicism. The Williams family had worshipped at Park End Presbyterian Chapel in Cardiff, under the ministry of Geraint Nantlais Williams, until 1961 when they moved back to Swansea. Williams became Anglo-Catholic and persuaded his parents to switch too.[20] Williams differs from Jones in his perspective on devolution also because he stayed in the Oxbridge milieu for longer, and returned to Wales only for a few years.[21] Jones on the other hand had lived in Wales for decades after studying at Cambridge, and knew its central nonconformist theological and political traditions far better.[22] The devolution essay along with an article on Barth were both published in 1979 and were Williams' earliest pieces on political theology. Yet this was not his area of research and teaching. Williams spent the decade leading up to 1979 studying Russian Orthodox theology and the history of Christian spirituality.[23] This proved a convenient way to bolster the Christian socialism he had learned from Welsh nonconformity, so it is interesting that it goes unmentioned in his devolution essay. It is clear from Williams' writings as well that he became part of the movement instigated by Kenneth Leech to develop a left-wing Anglo-Catholicism in response to the "sickly pietism and a right-wing stance in social and political issues" of many Anglo-Catholics.[24] What emerged was the theological manifesto of the Jubilee Group with its foundation in social Trinitarianism.

---

19. Ibid., 45.

20. Shortt, *Rowan's Rule*, 31–32.

21. Williams was Bishop of Monmouth then Archbishop of Wales between 1990 and 2003. Ibid., 185–208.

22. Morgan, in Jones, *Grym y Gair a Fflam y Ffydd*, 6f.

23. Shortt, *Rowan's Rule,* 79–83.

24. Ibid., 83–85.

R. TUDUR JONES AND ROWAN WILLIAMS

Robert Tudur Jones was the most important Reformed theologian and scholar in Wales in the twentieth century. Jones was a Congregationalist minister, lecturer in theology and church history at the theological college of the Union of Welsh Independents at Bala-Bangor Theological Seminary (the seminary of the Union of Welsh Independents in Banor, North Wales), and a founder member of the Evangelical Alliance in Wales, having already been associated with the Evangelical Movement of Wales, a Calvinist non-denominational movement which started in 1948.[25] In his paper of 1979, Jones drew on many modern Protestant theologians to make his case, including Herman Bavinck and Abraham Kuyper, Karl Barth and Gustavo Gutierrez. With Bavinck he taught that humans are naturally religious.

> Just as man is a religious being, so the nation is a religious community, which is to say that it exists to serve God. This is implied in the statement that the nation, like other forms of human community, is rooted in God's covenant with man. To reject the relation between the nation and God's covenant is to assert that it is outside God's dominion and to make an idol of it. . . . In the Christian understanding of society, the service we owe to a nation is discharged within the bonds of God's covenant with man.[26]

On providence, he says:

> Wales shares with other Christian nations the conviction that God has been at work in its history. The conviction goes back to the very dawn of our history when our forefathers began to become conscious of themselves as a specific people as the Roman Empire of the West disintegrated. The conviction can be expressed in many ways. It can be a powerful belief that the nation has enjoyed divine protection during the vicissitudes of its history. It can also be a belief that it is especially favored by God and is an elect nation.[27]

Jones disapproves of this because he thinks it can lead to viewing the nation as one of the ordinances of creation, "a radical form of community created by God." He goes on to say "very closely connected to this conception is

25. Gibbard, *Cofio Hanner Canrif.*

26. Jones, "Christian Nationalism," in Ballard and Jones (eds.), *This Land and This People*, 84.

27. Ibid.

the belief that God in his providence ordains the emergence of nations and their cultural characteristics."[28] He cites the nineteenth-century Christian nationalist Emrys ap Iwan's exegesis of Genesis 1–11 and Acts 17 such that nations are both God's creations and also the products of human activity.

Jones is suspicious of modern state centralization, because it can communicate the atheistic lie that "individual societal structures as bodies [derive] their authority from the state."[29] This was the lie of the Roman Empire. To correct this lie, Jones clarifies his thesis by stating that nation and state are distinct, and that "the nation is a society of societies and the state is one societal structure amongst others in the nation's life." He shrewdly criticizes English Labour and Tory politicians, without naming them as such, for adopting the rhetoric of "nation" to refer to the United Kingdom since the early 1960s, when previous terms from political theory such as "the public" or "the electorate" or "the Kingdom," which spoke in terms of citizens and subjects of state and crown, were used. This was, according to him, a linguistic maneuver to counter the growth of nationalism in Wales and Scotland. Jones detects behind this the assumption long made in England that it is the state that creates the nation, and that this licenses it to suppress other nations it comes to rule.

He draws attention to the interchanging of "nation" and "state" in *Reflections on the Revolution in France*, by the English (Tory and Anglican) philosopher Edmund Burke. Jones ridicules Burke's characterization of the state as "a partnership in all science; a partnership in all art; a partnership in every virtue and in all perfection," pointing out that "the English state (as distinct from the nation) hardly measured up at the end of the eighteenth century to Burke's description." This is important because Burke has long been a favorite philosopher for English conservatives, and indeed conservatives elsewhere, due to his attack on the French Revolution and his defense of social and political traditions. However, Jones did not spare old-fashioned left-wing thought either. He attacked the reality of the scientific state created by modern socialism for having arrogated so many powers—relating to all aspects of life—that stateless minority nations living within it were under threat. He called instead for Welsh people to be given the freedom to direct their own affairs politically, that is, devolved government.

> The central government, almost inevitably, favors the largest partner, its standards, its institutions, its language. It thinks of its

28. Ibid., 85.

29. Jones, "Christian Nationalism," 86–87.

own convenience when dealing with the smaller nations rather than of its duty to enable them to flourish fully as national societies. It creates an internal colonialism in which the undermining of a smaller nation's identity and integrity is interpreted as a civilizing process. And this is precisely what has happened in Britain. It may be argued in a purely academic way that several nations can live amicably under a common government. But the harsh reality as we have experienced it in Wales belies the hope. Government cannot be made the servant of the Welsh identity except by securing for Wales the freedom to construct a political structure that will be subservient to the Welsh people directly. Only then will it be possible to talk realistically of Britain as a partnership of free people in free nations co-operating together in a joint enterprise.[30]

Gwynfor Evans importantly wrote, "Freedom for Wales is the aim of Plaid Cymru. Freedom, not independence. . . . [T]he meaning of freedom in this matter is responsibility. We who are Welsh people claim that we are responsible for the civilization and the ways of social life in our part of Europe."[31] Freedom here means devolution. From our theological standpoint, it is important that Jones draws attention to how successive evangelical revivals have had both a spiritual and a socio-political effect on people's consciousness, "a yearning for greater personal freedom, for the abolition of social privileges, for a more equitable distribution of material wealth, for a wider participation in the process of government and for a more adequate recognition of the maturity of the Welsh nation as a community capable of becoming itself a maker of history."[32] Anticipating both conservative and socialist opposition, he says that "the struggle for liberation has been consistently, and successfully, frustrated by the holders of power either by transposing it into an issue of individual freedom, or into an issue of class privilege."[33] In other words, individuals could succeed and be branded as tokens of liberation, or liberation could be reduced to class matters, and thus lose the cultural dimension and meaning of socio-economic relations. The latter was the pervasive problem among extreme left-wingers and old-fashioned Marxists in the twentieth century. This materialism caught on most in South Wales, where Welsh language and culture had receded thanks to industrialization and British state

30. Ibid., 89.

31. Evans, *Plaid Cymru and Wales*, 43.

32. Jones, "Christian Nationalism," 89.

33. Ibid., 93.

education policies designed to stamp out the language by punishing children for speaking it.[34] It is estimated that in 1801, 90 percent of the Welsh population spoke Welsh. By 1891, the first time a question on the ability to speak the language was asked in the British census, the percentage had dropped to 51 percent. The sharpest drop by decade occurred between 1951 and 1981, the time when Rowan Williams grew up, and the time of the consolidation of a smugly triumphalist postwar British nationalism.[35] It is symbolically noteworthy, in the context of the present book, that this period of the high tide of British and other European imperialistic disfavor to minority languages was also the high tide of European anti-Semitism.

How Rowan Williams responds to this well-rounded argument for devolution is very significant for understanding the roots of his thinking on the political dimensions of theology. Existing commentators on his work have not read this paper, his earliest on political theology, and thus lack a full grasp on his thinking. Williams assumes the notion that the nation is rooted in God's covenant with humans "sails too close to the wind" of the idea of the orders of creation, an idea he thinks cannot be rehabilitated due to the Third Reich.[36] This can't be a serious argument because the Nazi movement sought to corrupt every single Christian doctrine there is; therefore, to take Williams' stance seriously we would have to reject *every* doctrine. To ignore covenant is to ignore its centrality in the Hebrew terminology of the Bible and, ultimately by doing so, to give in to anti-Semitism. What is significant is that Williams never uses the Bible to debate with Jones. Here, it could have been helpful to ask whether by "the universal covenant" Jones meant the Noachide covenant of Genesis 9, carried over to Noah's descendants who were deemed by Jewish and Christian tradition to be the ancestors of the world's nations. We will explore the necessary biblical exegesis below in discussing Herman Bavinck. Williams agrees with Jones that nations are not "orders of creation," but he merely reiterates that "nations are historical constructs," which is a way of saying that they are exclusively made by humans, ignoring their relation to providence—again, a sign of ignoring Genesis 10–11 and its successive reading in Deuteronomy 32 and Acts 17. By the same token there is nothing on the fall of nations as the result of divine judgment to engage Jones' argument that the disappearance of nations is a

---

34. Jones, *Statistical Evidence Relating to the Welsh Language, 1801–1911.*

35. Jenkins and Williams (eds.), *Let's Do Our Best for the Ancient Tongue.*

36. Williams, "Mankind, Nation, State," in Ballard and Jones (eds.), *This Land and This People*, 119.

disaster that must be averted. No comment is made as to whether this attitude ought always to be framed in terms of divine judgment and for-giveness—in practical terms, whether only a Christian revival will bring people back to live a moral life and avert permanent decline in all aspects. Williams wants to cite Aquinas on the state, but this is plainly irrelevant to the reality of Welsh history, where Edward I, self-styled Crusader King, used Catholic doctrine to justify the English conquest of Wales as "Canaan" to England's "Israel." It is more than simply a case of an analogy between Nebuchadnezzar and Zedekiah, on the one hand, and Edward and Llewelyn, on the other, as Williams implies. Aquinas never criticized the Crusades, unlike Joachim of Fiore (whom Williams had in an earlier essay dismissed as a millenarian). Thus the outworking of Crusader ideol-ogy within the British Isles is ignored. As we saw above, even the Papacy supported English conquest of its Celtic neighbors.

Williams is hostile to the idea of national integrity, but does not de-fine what he means by the term. It isn't clear that Wales is a nation for him. He cites the Anglo-Catholic political theorist J. N. Figgis on the state being the "community of communities," which ignores Jones' criticism of the British state as not even coming up to the standard of being a "society of societies."[37] One of the few instances where he connects with Jones is that "liberty and creativity are not properly opposed to tradition."[38] However, which traditions are most appropriate here? The Welsh Protestant tradi-tions that produced the nationalist vision, of a nation participating freely alongside others, are very different from the Catholic ones supported by Williams. They debated biblical exegesis, dogmatics, ethics, and politi-cal theory. Williams rejects the premises of Jones' theological arguments and wants secular, non-theological reason to be used, but using Christian theologians like Dietrich Bonhoeffer and Jacques Maritain. These two were considered to be theologians of secular reason in the postwar period, champions of human rights. Williams' reading of Bonhoeffer in particular is rooted in the British secular theology movement of the 1960s.[39] We shall see in chapter 5 how Williams handles secular thought after 1979, explor-ing in more depth his theological development between then and 2009.

How did Rowan Williams' thinking on Wales developed since 1979? We can see by looking at his essay "This Scepter'd Isle: Culture and Power

37. Ibid., 121–22.
38. Ibid., 122.
39. Ibid., 123–24.

in an Offshore Setting."[40] Matthew D'Ancona, the editor of the volume in which Williams' essay appeared, was the editor of the English conservative political magazine *The Spectator*; as such, it was unsurprising that he would call Britain a nation, in true one-nation Tory fashion. Williams never challenges this designation. In this essay he uses Hegel to show that the Welsh people are the unrecognized "Other" to the English conquests that created the United Kingdom. He starts by saying that "British identity . . . depends first and foremost on history."[41] He gives a sketch of the history of Britain after the Roman Empire, when the Celts regained independence (though he ignores the fact that they had received Christianity from Roman soldiers *before* the Catholic mission sent by Pope Gregory in 597 to convert the Anglo-Saxons). Williams' account of British history almost reads like a parody, because he doesn't use the conventional names for nations and ethnic groups (e.g., he calls the Anglo-Saxons "Germanic tribes," and dubs the Normans "a well-organized military elite from France"[42]). He writes of the conquest of Wales by Edward I thus: "For the next 400 years, during which this elite subdued the Celtic kingdoms of the west (including parts of Ireland) and tried unsuccessfully to do the same in the north, the English state was part of a patchwork of dynastic possession extending over considerable tracts of France."[43] Wales was not a collection of kingdoms, but in fact a unified kingdom—a full nation, a *natio* in medieval Christian political terms. This is *precisely* why it is possible to argue that Wales since then has been a nation that has lost its state—a stateless nation, just like the Jews after the fall of Jerusalem in 587 B.C. and again in A.D. 70; in fact, even more so as they were not dispersed. Williams argues that British history is "characterised by unsuccessful victories."

> "Conquests" occur, but their effect is curiously muted. . . . In an island, there is nowhere else for the defeated to go. Of course defeat leads to exile for some (Scottish and Irish memories will confirm that beyond doubt); but the impression you have from this national story is that the defeated have not been expelled or eliminated and have therefore been around in the memory and awareness of the "conqueror."[44]

40. Ibid.
41. Ibid., 145.
42. Ibid., 146.
43. Ibid., 144.
44. Ibid., 147.

He gives the example of how the legends about an early Celtic defender of Britain—Arthur—became stories about King Arthur as "King of all England" in the high Middle Ages, but omits to say that this was all the responsibility of Edward I.[45] He parallels this with "residual Catholic religion," which returned after the decline of "Bible-based Protestantism," for example, in the outpouring of popular grief at the death of Princess Diana.[46] (This is bizarre—the spirituality that was evident had nothing to do with serious Roman Catholic beliefs. Perhaps Williams means by "residual Catholicism" lighting candles and honoring a deceased mother-figure, vaguely akin to the feast of the Dormition of Mary.) England's unsuccessful victories over Wales and Ireland were deceptive, however. Those who were defeated have not gone away but still live in the same places as before, becoming part of the history of the conquerors.

> What has been for the moment silenced or buried works patiently back to the surface. Hegel wrote of the "cunning of reason," the way in which the overall shape of intelligent human development finds its way infallibly through the chaos of chances of actual history; our island history suggests that there is a "cunning" in defeated cultures, a capacity to infiltrate, inflect and change what thinks of itself as the dominant voice.

There is an unmistakeable echo here of the parable of the Lord and Bondsman from the *Phenomenology of Spirit*.[47] Hegel enables Williams to hint at a notion of providence that he never wants to set out. This is probably because he doesn't want to talk about divine judgment in history via national upheavals.

> The British state maintains, in the face of a lot of rationalising argument, a number of institutions and customs that embody a long past and seem to exist at right angles to anything like a defensible modern polity—the monarchy, the established Church, aspects of legal practice and convention and so on. . . . If we are able to accept without undue anxiety the doubtful "rationality" of some of our institutions as a significant part of our corporate life, we are in effect accepting that there is more at work in that corporate life than our conscious plans and hopes.[48]

---

45. On Arthur, see Biddle with Badham, *King Arthur's Round Table*.

46. On Diana, see Richards, Wilson, and Woodhead (eds.), *Diana*.

47. Hegel, *Hegel's Phenomenology of Spirit*, 111–18.

48. Williams, "This Sceptr'd Isle," 148–49.

In terms of theological method, Williams here has married the liberal Welsh Congregationalist use of Hegel to promote a Christian socialism with his own postliberal reading of Hegel as theologian of recognition and civil society based on "conversation" and "negotiation," drawing on Gillian Rose.[49] Thus we could infer, from comparison with other essays by Williams on Jewish-Christian relations, that Wales is like both Israel and the Canaanites in its place in the history of nations—its people never really went away in the first place.

Rowan Williams' thinking on Wales has changed over thirty years, though it still does not connect with the theological arguments made by R. Tudur Jones. There has to be a way for the two outlooks—liberal Anglicanism and the Reformed tradition—to debate nationhood with each other, rather than continue to talk past each other. I shall focus on two issues relevant to our discussion: imperialism and creation. I shall use Abraham Kuyper and Herman Bavinck to develop a biblically based continuation of the kind of argument Jones was making, which would connect to some themes in Rowan Williams' theology.

ABRAHAM KUYPER AND THE WELSH RECEPTION OF HEGEL

The problem with Rowan Williams is that he is trying to combine a bit of Barth with a bit of Hegel—something Barth himself found tempting but rejected! He is trying to have it both ways—church as gathered community of witness *and* church as civil religion.[50] There is no talk of the foreshadowing in history of the eschatological separation of the righteous and the wicked, or of the overthrow of the kingdom of Antichrist. Abraham Kuyper, by contrast, moves in this direction. In his Stone Lectures at Princeton, delivered in 1898, Kuyper devotes one lecture to "Calvinism and Politics."[51] Kuyper makes a speculative contrast between imperialism and nation-states. First, the reality that the earth is divided into many states does not harmonize with the idea of the human race having been formed from one blood.

---

49. This will be more fully explored in chapter 5 below. For a succinct account by Rose of how Hegelianism can mediate between liberalism and communitarianism, see Rose, *Mourning Becomes the Law.*

50. This was incisively articulated soon after Williams became Archbishop of Canterbury in Hobson, *Against Establishment*, 124–30.

51. Kuyper, "Calvinism and Politics," in Kuyper, *Lectures on Calvinism*, 78–109.

Then only would the organic unity of our race be realized politically, if *one State* could embrace all the world, and if the whole
of humanity were associated in one world empire. Had sin not
intervened, no doubt this would actually have been so. If sin,
as a disintegrating force, had not divided humanity into different sections, nothing would have marred or broken the organic
unity of our race.[52]

Kuyper dismisses "the Alexanders, the Augusti, and the Napoleons,"
international cosmopolitanism as seen in social-democracy, and even an-
archistic political theory, all as "nothing but a looking backward after a lost
paradise."[53] In biblical terms, imperialism is the sin of Babylon, starting at
Babel. It is worth saying here that in seventeenth-century England, many
leading scholars dreamed of recovering the supposedly lost primordial
language of Adam, which was still spoken at Babel. Leading polymaths,
such as John Wilkins, Seth Ward, and George Dalgarno, aspired to invent
a universal language that would reverse the curse of Babel and supersede
the world's many languages.[54] (In the process they contributed to the
mathematization of cryptology, and thus the rising power of the British
imperial project.) This was part of a wider mentality of reading Genesis
alongside the medieval Jewish book of magic *Sepher Raziel* (also known
as the Book of Adam), allegedly given by the angel Raziel to Adam, which
preserved cryptically knowledge of the natural sciences. Francis Bacon
was a key figure in the development of this biblical hermeneutic.[55] Given
all this background, it is therefore possible that Kuyper is here having a
dig at first British and then American imperial aspirations. It is worth
noting that all three movements criticized by Kuyper were anti-nationalist.
International socialism, specifically in its Marxist guise, was nostalgic in
some ways for the medieval era, but in other ways was an eschatological
and even apocalyptic movement. Anarchism seems to have been closer to
a raw form of romanticism about human nature, which may make it more
nostalgic for paradise, and decidedly hostile to the idea of the plurality
of nations. By the time of writing "Common Grace" in 1904, Kuyper had
developed an exegetical approach that conceived of the rise of the global
political empire of the "man of sin" of 2 Thessalonians and Revelation

52. Ibid., 79–80.

53. Ibid., 80.

54. Harrison, *The Bible, Protestantism and the Rise of Natural Science*, 260–61.

55. On Francis Bacon, see ibid., 257–59; on *Sepher Raziel* see Peter Harrison, *The Fall of Man and the Foundations of Science*, 18.

as the full realization of evil enabled ironically by the full realization of common grace. Thus the final empire would be the full realization of the fourth monarchy of Daniel, the empire of Antichrist. Kuyper characterizes this as godless (i.e., secularist), and fears it might appear in the twentieth century. It is thus interesting that John Bolt transforms Kuyper into a public theologian for American globalization![56]

A hundred years before Kuyper, Hegel had argued against looking to prelapsarian society for resolving debates in the Natural Law tradition, arguing that it was outside of our field of vision.[57] He argued against any supposed law of nature at work in the life of nations, arguing instead that the laws found in nations are really formed in response to force, accident, and deliberation, and that these are far more fundamental than any laws of nature deemed universally valid. His work, however, had a somewhat socially conservative cast to it, defending the establishment, as both Bavinck and Kuyper perceived.[58] This is specifically because it was not rooted in biblical debates, and, as such, was well suited to a philosophical defense of older establishment theologies that stemmed from and favored the European established churches. This philosophical defense was negative—it involved repudiating eighteenth-century versions of Natural Law theory both in the empiricism of Hobbes and Hume, and the formalist position of Kant and Fichte. As such, it can be seen as a counterpart to a mystical form of negative or apophatic theology—the style pursued by Rowan Williams. Hegel's position thus appears rather Machiavellian. It is perhaps unsurprising that Williams, with his Welsh nonconformist roots that were familiar with pacifism, might be uncomfortable with this, and as such that his increasing turn to Hegel came about around the same time he started reading René Girard's work on the origins of violence.[59] Girard affords Williams a way of reading the Bible nonviolently, because Girard became a Christian through his own anthropological research on the problem. The problem here, though, is that sin tends to be identified with violence, with the result that large parts of the Bible become alien and unintelligible (on the question of war and permitted killing, for example). Finally, Hegel's approach evaded questions on the origins of society and nations, thus at a stroke repudiat-

56. Bolt, *A Free Church, A Holy Nation*.

57. Hegel, *Natural Law*.

58. Bavinck, "Ethics and Politics," in Bavinck, *Essays on Religion, Science, and Society*, 265.

59. Williams, "Violence, Society and the Sacred."

ing the kind of critique made by Kuyper of political ideologies as nostalgic and primordialist. This left such ideologies intact, free to continue as before.

The question of the origins of nations brings us to the opening chapters of Genesis. Kuyper criticizes modernism and what he sees as the pantheism of Hegel for destroying the doctrinal arguments made possible by Genesis.[60] Modernism tried to mediate between the things that are above and the realism that marks our age. This is surely the microcosm-macrocosm cosmology of the correspondence between the visible world and the invisible world found in all the esoteric traditions. In fact, Kuyper compares it to alchemy and hermeticism. Possibly Kuyper is attacking Hegelianism in the church, as Hegel was known to be interested in these traditions. Kuyper's critique of Hegel as pantheist is set out in "The Blurring of the Boundaries," his speech at the annual transfer of the rectorship of the Free University of Amsterdam in 1892.[61] The metaphysical question to ask here is whether it makes sense to say that Hegel's alleged pantheism prevented theologians from developing a theology of divine government. The answer is that Kuyper appears to link this problem to the exegesis of creation in Genesis. He notes that the Hebrew word *Hammabdil* is used to denote God,

> because He it was who drew lines, first between Himself and the created world, and then throughout the entire domain of the created world. Lines of design, lines of demarcation, lines of distinction, lines of separation, lines of contrast. It is precisely these lines that pantheism attempts to blur. It still knows of distinction but no separation may ever be real. *En kai pan*, one and all, remains the magic phrase.[62]

Indeed, "to the Christian the most essential issues are at stake here." Regarding the exegesis of Genesis 1, he observes that the pantheist does not really believe "in the beginning . . . 'for there was no beginning,' nor does he believe the world to have been created, 'for the world is eternal,' and not 'heaven and earth,' for . . . 'beyond' is an illusion.'"[63]

> In this way, Hegel could pave the way for "something" alongside "nothing," the "here" with the "beyond," the finite with the

60. The main text for Kuyper's critique of modernism in theology is Kuyper, "Modernism," 87–124.

61. Kuyper, "The Blurring of the Boundaries," 363–402.

62. Ibid., 368.

63. Ibid., 374–75.

infinite, the ideal with the real, etc. God is allegedly reduced to a cosmic potency, and thus power is equated with matter, might with right, "accountability" [is dissolved] into a pitiable atavism, private property is equated with theft, and the civil authorities are equated with subjects with both being absorbed into the state. "Communities" replace cities and villages in the political imagination, and "the love of country must dim under the impact of cosmopolitanism. The demarcations of marriage should dissolve into a system of free love. Distinctions of class, lifestyle, or modes of national dress should be no more. Uniformity is the curse our modern life deliberately feeds on." National languages would be abolished and replaced by a kind of Esperanto.[64]

It must be acknowledged frankly that Kuyper's attack on pantheism and Hegelianism, while too extreme, can be applied as a warning to the apophatic use of Hegel to avoid talking about divine providence at work in history.

The reception of Hegel was rather rationalist and optimistic among Welsh liberal Protestants at the turn of the twentieth century.[65] It is precisely their take on Hegel that is the kind of thing that Kuyper and Bavinck criticized as pantheistic and monistic. Kuyper and Bavinck would in fact become key figures for the neo-orthodox wing that responded to liberal Hegelianism, along with the reception of Karl Barth's theology by J. E. Daniel. It was the progressivist and rather triumphalistic Hegelianism of the British Idealists that was imbibed by the liberal nonconformists, including Henry Jones, who lectured in philosophical theology at the School of Divinity at Glasgow.[66] This New Theology shocked many Congregationalists publicly in 1907 when the *Daily Mail* published an article praising it as updating Christian doctrine for the contemporary world in an ethical sense, eschewing traditional Calvinism.[67] The leader of the movement was Rev. R. J. Campbell, minister of the Congregationalist City Temple church in the City of London. City Temple was probably the most famous Congregationalist church in Britain at the time, and was at the center of the activities of the loose social movement known as the Nonconformist Conscience. Campbell had been influenced by Hegelianism, and held a humanistic theology, believing in the divine

---

64. Ibid., 382.

65. Pope, *Seeking God's Kingdom*, 5–8, 16–22.

66. Sell, *Philosophical Idealism and Christian Belief*, 83–93.

67. Pope, *Seeking God's Kingdom*, 11–17.

potential in all people, and linking this to the prospect of socialist renewal. As a monist, he held that the dualism between good and evil and sin and righteousness was not absolute. Evangelical Congregationalists were very displeased with this and accused him of heresy. Campbell was mentored at Oxford by the liberal Anglo-Catholic Charles Gore. Gore managed to turn Campbell slightly towards a more orthodox and metaphysical position by persuading him of the transcendence of God, as well as his immanence. There are anticipations here of the *Honest to God* controversy of the 1960s within Anglicanism, in which Welsh nonconformists would be very interested too. Campbell resigned from City Temple in 1915 and became an Anglican priest. When he died in 1956 he was a minor canon of Chichester Cathedral. The New Theology became very influential in the Welsh Congregationalist churches thanks to ministers such as Thomas Rhondda Williams, David Adams, Ebenezer Griffith-Jones, and John Morgan Jones. The attempt at a Hegelian expression of Christian socialism arose among them as the prestige of the liberal party declined in Britain in the early twentieth century. It was an attempt to grapple with the challenges of industrialization but also with the new questions about social life and progress in the decades after the Welsh Revival of 1904–5, which had appealed to people's need for individual salvation and an experience of the Holy Spirit. Very little academic theological work has been done on this period, which is a pity because the Revival occurred in both Welsh- and English-speaking churches, yet spawned only new English-speaking Pentecostal churches.

Of the liberal theologians, the least theologically coherent was the Congregationalist D. Miall Edwards, who was trained as a philosopher of religion. Edwards supported both nationalism and social reform, and linked the two. He came to believe that Wales should be granted self-determination, because "Welsh civilization could only be reformed by means of the Welsh Nationalist spirit."[68] However, Edwards was never a member of Plaid Cymru. Instead he supported the rather idealistic League of Nations, and hoped rather naïvely for a world state as the logical outcome of the brotherhood of man. Edwards used Hegelianism to argue that Welsh nationalism could contribute to this outcome.[69] Members of the labor movement influenced by a monistic interpretation of Hegel argued that church attendance was unnecessary given the Hegelian teaching that

68. Ibid., 50.
69. Ibid.

God is present everywhere in the world.[70] Robert Pope criticizes the Welsh liberals in that they "viewed the Great War as a historical blip, a minor setback on the path to ultimate perfection."[71] Those who realized that it rendered neo-Hegelianism untenable turned to either Barth or Dutch neo-Calvinism, or a creative combination of both. R. Tudur Jones was a major figure in this trend. As we saw earlier, Jones put together Herman Bavinck's claims that humans are religious animals, and that nations are religious communities insofar as their God-ordained purpose is for their populations to come to worship God. It is not at all clear that Hegel conceived of nations as ordained for this end. The difference between Dutch Calvinists and Hegel in this respect is visible in the doctrines of creation and eschatology. This ultimately stems from the fact that the former use biblical exegesis as a basic source for theology and politics, whereas Hegel does not. In order to get to the bottom of this difference, we need to move beyond Kuyper to Bavinck.

HERMAN BAVINCK AND THE PRIORITIZATION OF THE LITERAL SENSE AS HISTORICAL

Kuyper is infralapsarian in his attitude to the division of the human race into nation-states. He does not see the diversity of nation-states as a positive good, as something that in a sinless world could have come about simply due to the natural limitations of the world. This is why he sees cosmopolitanism and anarchism as nostalgic for paradise. Regarding his view of imperialism as similar, it is possible that he is implying that the sin of Babel is a variant of the sin of Adam and Eve, knowing good and evil on their own terms ("ye shall be like gods"). Ultimately, then, Kuyper would seem to be hinting that he disapproves of all theologies and political theories that are predicated upon an idea of natural, primordial religion as something that needs to be rediscovered through some form of enlightenment. In practice, this would have involved disapproval of esoteric Christian groups that were Deist, Rosicrucian, or Masonic. Kuyper's philosophical and political arguments arise from and point to a biblical hermeneutic that prioritizes the literal sense of biblical narratives concerning nations' place in the divine economy. It is Bavinck who accomplishes this work. He places nations carefully, without overemphasizing their importance, in his

70. Ibid., 62.
71. Ibid., 108.

systematic theology. I am referencing here from "Our Reasonable Faith."[72] The debate on nationhood needs to gather around exegesis of the Bible in this way, otherwise it will have no real theological contours and will merely become philosophy or sociology or religious studies. Hegel can be used for all three of these ends. The framework within which Bavinck works is the distinction between general and special revelation. He references Paul's Areopagus speech in his discussion of General Revelation, saying that "general revelation is directed to mankind in order that they should seek the Lord, if haply the might feel after Him, and find Him (Acts 17: 27)."

> Scripture teaches not only that at the beginning God called the world into being, but also that this world is continuously, from moment to moment, sustained and governed by that same God. He is infinitely exalted above the world not only, but He also dwells in all His creatures in his almighty and omnipresent power. He is not far from every one of us, for in Him we live, and move, and have our being (Acts 17:27–28). The revelation which comes to us from the world, therefore, is not merely a reminder of a work of God which He accomplished long ago: it is a testimony also to what God now, in these our times, wills and does.[73]

The revelation of God is granted to human beings in the reality of their living in nations. Bavinck makes an analogy between God's work in nature and in history.[74]

> He made of one blood all nations of men to dwell on all the face of the earth (Acts 17: 26). He destroys the first human race in the flood, and at the same time preserved it in the family of Noah (Gen. 6:6–9). At the tower of Babel he confuses the language of men and disperses them over the face of the earth (Gen. 11:7–8). And when the Most High divided to the nations their inheritance, and separated the sons of Adam. He determined the times appointed before, and the bounds of their habitation, according to the number of the children of Israel (Deut. 32:8 and Acts 17:26). Although He chose the children of Israel to be the bearers of His special revelation, and permitted the heathen nations to walk in their own ways (Acts 14:16), nevertheless He did not neglect them nor leave them to their own fate. . . . That

72. Bavinck, *Our Reasonable Faith.*
73. Ibid., 39.
74. Ibid., 39f.

which may be known of God became manifest in them, for God showed it to them (Rom. 1:19), in order that they should seek the Lord, if haply they might feel after Him, and find Him (Acts 17:27).

What needs to be said more clearly than Bavinck, with Paul, is that God has appointed the existence of nations for the purpose of human beings seeking God. It seems that living in empires—Babylon being the biblical type of empire—makes seeking God more difficult. This is why the church is drawn from all nations.

> Out of all nations, and kindreds, and peoples, and tongues He gathers His church (Rom. 11:25, Eph. 2:14ff.; and Rev. 7:9), and prepares for that end of the world in which the nations of them that are saved shall walk in the light of the city of God, and all the kings and peoples of the earth shall bring their glory and honor into it (Rev. 21:24–26).

Several questions for debate with the Hegelian perspective arise here. First, there is the modern crisis over the extent of the historicity of biblical narratives. Bavinck, like Kuyper, continued to affirm the historicity of the Genesis narratives regarding nations, even in the wake of the rise of Darwinism. There needs to be careful inquiry into the relationship between this and twentieth-century theological approaches to nationhood (and politics more broadly), because Darwinism triggered the secularization of Social Anthropology, the study of the origins of nations. Twentieth-century theology has shied away from proper debate on the historicity of a prelapsarian state. Bavinck does not pay attention to such problems. What he does do is observe how theologians have tried to arrange these natural and historical witnesses to God into six kinds. For our purposes it is important that he notes the

> remarkable phenomenon that there are no peoples or nations without religion. . . . There are no atheistic tribes or people. This phenomenon is of great importance, for the absolute universality of this religious sense puts us before a choice of one or two positions: either that on this point mankind generally is suffering from a stupid superstition, or else that this knowledge and service of God, which in distorted forms makes its appearance among all peoples, is based on God's existence.[75]

75. Ibid., 41.

He falls back on his doctrine of general revelation, which is close to some early modern notions of natural religion. He believes—against Hegel—that there is a universal moral law, but crucially, he says, agreement on it has been found by the early twentieth century by "the peoples of culture," distinguishing them from "the peoples of nature," who seem to be so-called "primitive" peoples.[76] This nature-culture distinction is from the German Enlightenment, and influenced early social anthropology. It is not a theological distinction and is nowhere to be found in the Bible. It is suspiciously close to John Locke's idea that the American Indians were living in a state of nature, by contrast to the white settlers who lived in political community. Locke made this a warrant for taking their land and possessions.[77] So the Hegelian perspective can actually fulfill a positive role here in interrogating the validity of Bavinck's concepts for defending his biblical exegesis. However, what this requires is moving back to Hegel's metaphysical questions. The second question is that of Babel or Babylon. Here Bavinck is very close to Kuyper, but does more biblical work. Bavinck argues that the confusion of languages at the building of the Tower of Babel "was prepared for already by the break-up into tribes and families of the descendants of the sons of Noah (Genesis 10:1ff.) and by the migration of the descendants of Noah from Armenia to Shinar (Gen. 11:2). The whole idea of a tower of Babel would not have arisen if the threat and fear of dispersion had not already long and seriously presented itself."[78] Thus there is both a positive and a negative aspect to the existence of nations for Bavinck. The fact that he exegetically needs to use the Genesis narratives for this means the problem of historicity is still in view. What this means, plainly, is that if the historicity of these narratives is denied, it is more likely that a historical view of the global empire at the End is denied too. There would need to be a rigorous debate as to whether the Bible necessarily entails a literal political empire when it speaks of the last monarchy, or whether it is speaking in figurative terms about "the kingdom of this world," Augustine's earthly city. There would need to be a debate about the distinction between church and nation, and church and state, in this respect, as well as whether the Bible speaks that in political as well as ecclesiastical terms; historical events foreshadow the final eschatological separation. A Hegelian scheme that pays no attention to the Bible is in trouble here.

76. Ibid., 41.

77. On John Locke, see Ruston, *Human Rights and the Image of God*, 250–66.

78. Bavinck, *Our Reasonable Faith*, 51.

The conclusion that we come to is that Bavinck, via Kuyper's political theological debates, returns the issue of nationhood to biblical exegesis. He does not address all the difficulties involved. Regarding eschatology, Bavinck in particular denied that "all Israel" in Romans 11 refers to all the Jewish nation. He did not believe that Jewish ingathering in the Holy Land constituted a prophetic step towards the Second Coming. This is different from Karl Barth's view, the centrality of the people Israel to the biblical vision of providence. It is also present in Rowan Williams' theology as well. Barth and Williams' approaches to Israel will be the topic of chapter 6. Meanwhile, we need to look at how Israel and Wales have been handled by leading social theorists of nations and nationalism in recent years.

NATION AND *ETHNOS* IN SOCIAL THEORY: THE CASE OF ANTHONY SMITH

Anthony Smith, the foremost contemporary social theorist of nationhood and nationalism, straddles the divide between the perennialist and modernist schools of thought on the origins of nations and nationalism, represented respectively by Edward Shils and Ernest Gellner.[79] For modernists nations as well as nationalism are the product of the forces of modernity. Charles Taylor agrees with Gellner's perspective here.[80] This is ultimately consonant with Hegel's periodization of history, which sees the rise of the (Prussian) nation-sate as an expression of the work of the Spirit breaking loose from the feudal chains of universal Catholic Christendom in the Enlightenment. That Taylor should agree with Gellner is somewhat ironic in view of the recorded fact that Gellner himself harbored an intense dislike for Taylor's espousal of a Hegelian approach to philosophy and the social sciences. Gellner especially disliked both Taylor's reading of Hegel and the politics of recognition as over-complicating public debates, which he thought were better cast in more narrow socio-economic terms, with recognition and identity issues being relegated to the private sphere.[81] Yet Gellner shares the periodization of history that marked off the rise of post-Enlightenment nationalism as the ideology that every nation must have a state in order to flourish. Only Gellner, unlike Taylor, cast this history in socio-economic terms concerning the

79. Shils, "Nation, Nationality, Nationalism and Civil Society," 93–118; Gellner, *Nations and Nationalism*; Gellner, *Nationalism*.

80. Taylor, "Nationalism and Modernity," 81–104.

81. Hall, *Ernest Gellner*, passim.

role of elites in creating nationalism as a means of legitimating industrialization. Clearly this assumes a metaphysically materialist understanding of historical change. Smith by contrast is more nuanced, accepting that nationalism as a specific ideology is modern in dating from the second half of the eighteenth century, though questioning the reduction of nationhood to an instrument of industrialization. Perennialism is an idea that he discerns within the primordialist approach indebted to Shils, but also found in Adrian Hastings' work. We investigate Smith's debate with Hastings in the next section. There is a third school of thought in the social and political theory of nations and nationalism, namely primordialism.[82] Smith attributes its origin to Edward Shils' concept of primordiality, referring to one of a series of human ties, the other being personal, sacred, and civil.[83] The anthropologist Clifford Geertz developed this, including kinship, race, religion, custom, language, and territory within the category of primordial ties, as a means of explaining continued conflict between groups inhabiting the large new post-colonial African and Asian states since the Second World War.[84] Clearly here we are dealing with matters of the collective, deeply symbolic mind of groups. Steve Grosby articulated this in terms of people's belief that certain features of their social existence are life-enhancing, singling out kinship and territory. His focus on the latter in particular, on land as nurturing, is ultimately based on his focus on ancient Israel.[85] The most radical primordialist theorist of nationhood and nationalism is Pierre van der Berghe, who interprets primordialist symbol-theory in sociobiological terms, arguing that ethnicity and nationhood are an extension of kinship ties.[86] Smith claims that primordialism as a school cannot help us with the question of when nations come into being in history, except for Grosby's work arguing that ancient Israel was a nation. Yet it should be obvious that Van der Berghe's argument both goes further back in time than Smith and Grosby as well as challenging their biblical perspective. This is because his sociobiological perspective is essentially, like Gellner's, a materialist and atheist one in making particular features of human materiality as the exclusive cause and motivation of the existence of nations and nationalism. Indeed, once again,

82. Smith, *Nationalism and Modernism*, 145–69; Smith, *The Cultural Foundations of Nations*, 9–10.

83. The foundational essay is Shils, "Primordial, Personal, Sacred and Civil Ties," 13–45.

84. Geertz, "The Integrative Revolution," 255–310.

85. Grosby, *Biblical Ideas of Nationality, Ancient and Modern*.

86. Van der Berghe, *The Ethnic Phenomenon*.

his account is really an account of the origins of nations, given that cause and motive are necessarily things that pertain to accounts of origins. His sociobological perspective, focusing on group dynamics and competition, is not incompatible with Hegel's rejection of natural law theory discussed above. Smith astutely distinguishes between the claim that nations are perennial and that they are natural. He does not believe that the former claim entails the latter. By this he means that nations cannot be considered natural in the same sense as "speech, sex, or geography." Theologically this is an interesting comparison, given that Jewish and Christian tradition have tended to maintain a divine origin for speech and language, a necessary claim for most traditional theories of scriptural inspiration.

As a theologian, it is important to point out that metaphysical clarity is sometimes missing from these discussions. For example, Smith argues against the primordialist claim that nations are natural compared to other allegedly natural features of human activity. This begs the question as to precisely what is meant by "natural." If natural means that something is to be accounted for exclusively through sociobiology or genetics, then it is simply untrue that nations are natural. If nations are natural by comparison to speech, the question is more complex. Clearly the capacity for speech is biologically based, but is it exclusively so? Most of the world's population past and present holds religious beliefs, and at their core lie claims to disembodied speech by divine and spiritual beings. In addition, many cultures, including ancient Israel, have claimed that speech is divinely originating. Thomas Aquinas took up the Aristotelian view that political communities such as nations were natural communities, contrasting this to the church as supernatural spiritual community. The primordialist and perennialist views are, on one reading, secular variants on this view, albeit operating with a transformed understanding of nature. As is well-known, Karl Barth could not accept the view that nations are natural, because in modern Protestantism this had come to mean that they were ordinances of creation, not the outcome of the scattering of peoples at Babel. The perennialist view, especially, can easily fall into the trap of arguing that only those communities that stretch back to antiquity deserve to be called nations, whereas newer ones do not. The problem here is the seeming arbitrariness of assigning a time after which a community that springs up may not be called a nation. At the same time, if the Babel narrative is to be taken primarily in a literal historical sense, it follows that Christian theology cannot go the whole way with primordialism. At the most it can agree to a chastened perennialist perspective where this seems to fit the evidence for particular cases. Primordialism really amounts to a metaphysical claim that Christians must reject for the sake of preserving the moral and hermeneutical integrity of biblical exegesis, theology, and ethics. For if the descent of the Spirit at Pentecost is the spiritual reversal and undoing of Babel, it requires Babel to be an historical event, as Bavinck and Barth, for example, well understood. For primordialism, the shifting division of humanity into nations and languages is the result of immanent human group dynamics. Group survival does not account for linguistic diversity unless group competition is considered basic to their very existence. People competing against each other in war is therefore built into the secular primordialist model on the level of fundamental ontology.

The distinction between nation (understood as nation-state) and *ethnie* is basic to Smith's work. He has developed it in order to explain the resilience of nationalist movements, and their success in motivating populations to support them. *Ethnie* and nations are driven by myth-symbol complexes. He constructs an ideal type of the nation out of the modern nationalist goals of national identity, unity and autonomy. It contains the following elements:

1. The growth of myth and memories of common ancestry and history of the cultural unit of population;

2. The formation of a shared public culture based on an indigenous resource (language, religion, etc.);

3. The delimitation of a compact historic territory, or homeland;

4. The unification of the local economic units into a single socioeconomic unit based on the single culture and homeland;

5. The growth of common codes and institutions of a single legal order, with common rights and duties for all members.[87]

From these elements Smith defines a nation as "a named cultural unit of population with a separate homeland, shared ancestry myths and memories, a public culture, common economy, and common legal rights and duties for all members."[88] He admits that this is a somewhat modernist

87. Smith, *The Ethnic Origins of Nations*, 42; Smith, *Myths and Memories of the Nation*, 104.

88. Smith, *Myths and Memories of the Nation*, 104.

definition but set out to search for parallels for each modernist concept in premodern eras. The fact that he uses ancient Israel and a handful of other entities in antiquity as qualifying examples gives away the fact that he has developed an apologetic for Israel as somehow elected and paradigmatic. Smith defines *ethnies* as "named human populations with shared ancestry myths, historical memories and common cultural traits, associated with a homeland and having a sense of solidarity, at least among the elites."[89] He is of the view that nationhood is closely related to "ethnic phenomena," seeing the former as a sub-category of the latter. Within ethnic phenomena he posits "ethnic communities" as sub-categories of "the global phenomenon of the ethnic category." These are characterized as "cultural units of population with some sense of kinship or ancestry, some common dialects and deities, but too little collective self-awareness, few shared memories, and no common name or territory or solidarity."[90] This definition does not fully make sense. How could any ethnic group be said to exist without a common name, territory, or solidarity? What is required here is specification of the time when a new group is named into being, either by complete outsiders, or by people joining two or more groups together. Smith does not clearly speak of such a specification. It is more plausible to suggest that the lack of coherent historical and mythic memories and of a common name would be due to forgetting these due to the trauma of defeat by an external power, or internal collapse. By the same token, Smith's theory of a general move from weak ethnic categories to strong *ethnics* cannot be corroborated by evidence precisely because the former were far more vulnerable to being defeated by invaders or dissolving due to lack of unity.

Smith sees an *ethnic* as centering around the shared sense of birth and ancestry expressed in the etymology of the classical Greek *ethnos* and the classical Latin *natio*. This sense of shared ancestry may be mainly based on history or myth or both. Does Smith's *ethnie* correspond to the *ethnos*-concept of Greek-speaking antiquity, including the Greek Bible? This is the term translated as "nation" in the generic sense pertaining to the Gentiles. It is itself a translation of the Hebrew term *gôy*. Smith deals with Israel, Greece, and Rome, in relation to the Hebrew, Greek, and Latin terms. In the case of Israel, he acknowledges that a religious culture embracing all its population may have developed slowly, and that "popular participation was much greater in post-Exilic times, especially after the

89. Ibid., 105.
90. Ibid.

Ezraic reforms, and in the area around Jerusalem."[91] Later Judaism of the Mishnaic period was dominated by law, embracing "all Israel." He argued that this saw the dissolution of the distinction between Priests, Levites, and people, replaced by the legal code enjoining rights and duties for every Jewish male.[92] At the same time, Smith recalls that the Mosaic law-code accomplished the latter feat in Israel's early history.[93] Bruce Routledge is critical of Smith's focus on "ethnic cores" as distorting the historical embeddedness of his examples.[94] Routledge distinguishes sharply between an *ethnie*'s shared cultural practice and their objectification as a nation or polity. His example is that the Phoenicians were known in relation to the king of the Sidonians or of Tyre, not in relation to the king of the Phoenicians. Smith elides these distinctions. While acknowledging that the names Canaanite, Phoenician, and Aramaean were used self-referentially as well as by these people's neighbors, that these names formed the basis of political formation cannot be shown. It may be that the distinction between Smith and Routledge turns on the fact that Smith prioritizes the biblical text and other texts over local inscriptions as his main evidence. Ultimately, however, Smith's definition of *ethnie* was deliberately framed to designate a people rather than a form of government. Thus Routledge's criticism is relativized. Regarding ancient Greece, Smith acknowledged the complexity of the overlap between city-states, linguistic subcultures, and the common Hellenic community.[95] Due to its lack of economic and legal unity, ancient Greece is not designated a nation, yet he seems to regard it as an *ethnie*. The question here is, did the Greeks *regard themselves* as an *ethnos*. The classical evidence is that while the *polis* or city-state was the chief form of state from the Archaic period onwards, most of the Greek world was organized into *ethne*.[96] Catherine Morgan's fuller definition of *ethnos* in ancient Greece reveals the complexity and ambiguity of the term.

> [*Ethnos* denoted] a category of state which existed alongside the *polis*, but which is only rarely treated by ancient sources. *Ethne* are diverse, with no single form of constitution. They are

91. Ibid., 107.

92. Ibid., 107–8.

93. Ibid., 119, n. 4.

94. Routledge, "The Antiquity of the Nation?" 213–34.

95. Smith, *Myths and Memories of the Nation,* 109.

96. Raaflaub, "Poets, Lawgivers, and the Beginnings of Political Reflection in Archaic Greece," in Rowe and Schofield (eds.), *The Cambridge History of Greek and Roman Political Thought,* 24.

characterized by the fact that by contrast with *poleis* (which retain total autonomy); individual communities surrendered some political powers (usually control of warfare and foreign relations) to a common assembly. Their inhabitants were thus required to express a range of local and regional loyalties of varying degrees of complexity and strength. By contrast with *poleis*, the role of urban centers in *ethne* varied greatly: settlement structures range from a high degree of urbanization and local autonomy (e.g., Boeotia, which was tantamount to a collection of small *poleis*) to scattered small villages with little urban development (e.g., Aetolia). According to Aristotle (*Politics* 1326b), *ethne* are characterized by their large populations. Although the *ethnos* is sometimes equated with primitive tribalism, social and political developments from the 8th century BC onwards (in religion and colonization for example) often bear comparison with evidence from *poleis,* and the *ethnos* was a varied and long-lived phenomenon. Equally, *ethne* have been seen as the origin or precursors of the federal states created from the 4th century onwards (e.g., the Achaean and Aetolian confederacies). These, however, incorporated many former *poleis*, and relations between citizen groups were thus more formally constituted, often drawing on earlier concepts of *sympoliteia* and *isopoliteia*.[97]

If *ethne* can be said to have existed within the borders of Greece, is it nevertheless possible to speak of Greece being seen by its own population as a meaningful cultural entity to which they felt allegiance? The idea of Greece as a nation in this sense occurs, though solely at critical times such as the Persian War.[98] That the Persian invasion in the fifth century was met by a well-armed, well-organized Greek resistance does suggest that such resistance must have been based on a prior acceptance of common Greek identity transcending city-states and *ethne*. When we turn to the Roman world, matters are different again. Roman citizenship, based on the city-state of Rome, was never transformed into Italian citizenship by the Roman Senate (the name *Italia* designated the Italian peninsula in Roman times). Roman Italy was politically unified by 90 BC.[99] The

97. Morgan, "Ethnicity," in Hornblower and Spawforth (eds.), *The Oxford Classical Dictionary;* Morgan, *Early Greek States beyond the Polis.*

98. Hornblower and Spawforth, "Nationalism," in Hornblower and Spawforth (eds.), *The Oxford Classical Dictionary.*

99. Lomas, "Italy during the Roman Republic, 338–31 BC," in Flower (ed.), *The Cambridge Companion to the Roman Republic,* 199.

Romans saw themselves as a people (*populus*), using this term to stress their sense of superiority over others. At the same time, classical authors such as Cato, Cicero, Sallust, Pliny the Elder, and Tacitus use the term *natio* (from *nascio*, "to be born," hence *natio* means "community of one's birth") for people in the generic sense.[100] The Vulgate Bible translates *ethnos* as *natio*, using *populus* for the Hebrew *ha 'am* (the people), used only for the chosen people of God. This discussion of the Hebrew, Greek, and Latin terms used in antiquity and the Bible show that the distinction between the Bible, on the one hand, and Aristotle and other classical thinkers, on the other, is important. For the latter, *ethnos* is a term somewhat inferior to *polis,* designating that which is not a *polis*. For biblical translators and those using the Bible, *ethnos* can refer to a people whether or not they have their own state or government. It seems that the term *natio* should be allowed equal flexibility, given that it came to be the translation for *ethnos* in the Latin Bible, the most authoritative Latin text of European civilization. Thus the term is primarily cultural even though it is frequently explicitly political. This brings us to the debate between Anthony Smith and Adrian Hastings, as Hastings argued that nationhood is exclusively the product of Christendom.

NATIONHOOD AS PREMODERN: ANTHONY SMITH AND ADRIAN HASTINGS

Adrian Hastings, an English Roman Catholic and one-time historian of Christianity, entered into debate with Anthony Smith concerning the origin of nationhood. He agreed that nationhood was a concept older than the modern period, and dated it to the medieval period.[101] In this respect he argued strongly against the modernist school as represented by the work of Ernest Gellner, Eric Hobsbawm, and Benedict Anderson. Smith for his part debated Hastings' views, but published his criticisms after Hastings' death. There is a discernible move on Smith's part towards convergence with Hastings. In "Nations in History" Smith classified Hastings as a neo-perennialist who defines nation "predominantly in cultural terms, as a 'people,' a community of historical culture linked to a particular ancestral territory or 'homeland.'"[102] He concedes that this definition of

100. *Natio* in Glare (ed.), *The Oxford Latin Dictionary*, 1976–82.

101. Hastings, *The Construction of Nationhood.*

102. Smith, "Nations in History," in Guibernau and Hutchinson (eds.), *Understanding Nationalism*, 14, 19.

nationhood corresponds to his concept of an *ethnie*. Hastings, as Smith notes, was working in the tradition of Johann Gottfried Herder in this respect, making language and literature the chief criteria for nationhood. Where Smith had spoken of both lateral-aristocratic and vertical-demotic *ethnies*, Hastings argued that nations could be either elite or mass groups in terms of real participation.[103] This flexibility is at the heart of the contention over the neo-perennialist definition of nationhood. We met earlier Smith's invocation of the participation of all adult males in ancient Israel in the Second Temple period. Now in debating Hastings he argued that this was analogous to the case of fifth-century B.C. Athens.[104] Such a comparison is reminiscent of Rousseau's fusion of an idealization of the Greek city-states and their cult of male self-sacrifice for the *polis* on the battlefield, with the national exclusivism of Ezra and Nehemiah.[105] Clearly here is one of the many ways in which Smith attempts to demonstrate that Israel is compatible with the modernist family of paradigms, but this time in relation to political and governmental models that were used to promote universal suffrage in the nineteenth century. (The modern Jewish political philosophers who idealized Athens in this manner were Hannah Arendt and Leo Strauss. Gillian Rose provides an attempt to move between Athens and Jerusalem in response to Strauss, in a more Hegelian manner than Smith as we shall see later.) In Rousseau's thinking, idealizing Athens was part and parcel of his civil republicanism with its doctrine of popular sovereignty. This was a different matter than traditional Reformed Calvinist theories of sovereignty, as found in Rousseau's native Geneva. For with Rousseau, God receded to the status of legitimating the social order brought into being by the social contract created by the sovereign people or nation.[106] Smith's assimilation of Israel to Athens does not really stand up historically, not the least because it does not take the complexity of the institution of slavery or the treatment of resident aliens in either polity seriously. It selects one moment in Israel's history, a relatively uncontroversial one that most biblical critics agree happened, namely the building of the nation and at its heart the Second Temple under Ezra and

103. Smith, *The Ethnic Origins of Nations*, 76–89; Hastings, *The Construction of Nationhood*, 26.

104. Smith, "Nations in History," in Guibernau and Hutchinson (eds.), *Understanding Nationalism*, 27.

105. Smith, "Nationalism and Classical Social Theory," 28.

106. This is related to Rousseau's account of the kingdom of God as purely spiritual in an inward sense. He believed that Christian dogmas should play no part in politics. See Rosenblatt, *Rousseau and Geneva*, 173–76, 258–68.

Nehemiah. It proceeds from the perceived end-results of the doctrines underpinning the society rather than their roots. That the norms of manhood were different in Israel than in Athens, even in some ways that they were diametrically opposed to each other, is ignored. Worship was profoundly different in the two states, oriented to profoundly different theological beings and ends. Athens had no sense of exile and return at the core of its history. If Smith is unjustified in assimilating Israel to Athens, then his own question to Hastings as to whether the phenomena in question are sufficiently alike to be covered by the term "nation" can be put to him as well. If Smith's concepts are allowed to cover a range of examples, why not also those developed by Hastings?

In 2003, Smith published a critique of Hastings' theory that nations are the product of European Christendom.[107] Hastings has three core arguments, the first being that many nations, and nationhood as a concept, are premodern. Second, he argues that nations, nationhood, and nationalism were produced by Christianity spreading in Europe, due to the sanctioning of the use of vernacular languages in liturgy and translation of the Bible. Hastings shows how the ecclesiastical hierarchies of several nations weren't interested in biblical translation (e.g., into Irish or Scottish Gaelic).[108] Yet Hastings did also provide the examples of Armenia, the earliest Christian nation, from the third century, where the Bible was translated into Armenian, and Ethiopia, where the Bible was translated into Geʽez.[109] Smith is critical of Hastings ignoring nations outside Christendom, pointing out that literature helped define nations in antiquity as well. Yet Hastings' argument isn't part of a general hermeneutics of the rise of nations, but one of the mimetic appropriation of the Christian Bible. In order to drive the point home, he makes a comparison with Islamic civilization. His claim that medieval Islam was rigid regarding national identity is countered by Smith's argument that early local emirates managed in practice to mobilize ethnic or national identities. The truth of the matter is that the problem with Hastings' overall argument is a subtle one, in that he gives the impression that he is working with the idea of the Bible as literature. This idea derives from Herder, who extolled the Old Testament as Hebrew national folk literature. In this way, the Old Testament could be placed alongside the folk literature of other nations, and read as a model and as an analogue, in the manner of the

107. Smith, "Adrian Hastings on Nations and Nationalism," 25–28.
108. Hastings, *The Construction of Nationhood*, 86.
109. Ibid., 198.

German Orientalism of the day. This hermeneutic subtly eroded respect for the historicity of the narratives, assimilating them to legends and ancient Near Eastern myths. The early medieval Christians who formed the first Christian national kingdoms, by contrast, would have had a much higher level of belief in the historicity of the narratives.[110] Indeed, it is possible to argue that the relative anthropological and social proximity of medieval kingdoms to the world of antiquity rendered the presentism and lack of sense that the past is a foreign country, so typical of medieval writings, plausible and practical.[111] For Hastings, nations are not instances of a kind found universally across history. Really he is arguing that a nation is only a nation if it attempts to model itself on ancient Israel through biblical hermeneutics. Yet this is conflating moral and ontological judgments. The biblical texts do not regard the Gentile nations surrounding ancient Israel in this manner. Hastings may be operating tacitly with the idea that since the coming of Christ, ethnic polities should model themselves on Israel. The end result is logically similar to the modernist problem, which is to argue that a nation is only a nation if it is modeled on the modernist political paradigm of the nation-state. On the underlying logic of Hastings' argument, modern nation-states such as France that have not modeled themselves on ancient Israel are not nations. This is idiotic. There is also a fundamental linguistic problem with Hastings' argument. To suggest that only Christendom contained and produced nations is to rest on the fact that the term "nation" comes from Latin, which was imposed in lieu of European vernacular languages. This contradicts his own argument that nations were built on vernacular languages. Wales forms a crucial test-case for Hastings' arguments here, for the Welsh word for nation, *cenedl*, is not derived from the Latin *natio*, unlike the English word, or terms in the Romance languages. It is significant that Hastings writes that "we are still after more than a thousand years not quite sure where the Welsh stand—an ethnicity within Britain, or even, as at one time seemed the case, within England, a nation within a multi-nation state, even (still to come) a nation-state of their own?"[112] This inappropriate royal "we" was truly bizarre given that Hastings' book was published in 1997, the year Wales was granted a devolved government thanks to popular referendum. In any case, most Welsh people themselves

110. Smalley, *Historians in the Middle Ages*.

111. Hastings seems to realize this in noting that the Old Testament was believed to be historical by scholars until the early nineteenth century. See Hastings, "Holy Lands and Their Political Consequences," 31.

112. Hastings, *The Construction of Nationhood*, 181.

think of Wales as a nation. Why? Because before 1282, Wales was ruled by kings (it was English royalist propaganda that demoted them to the level of "princes") and had its own law-code in the vernacular. Welsh people do not, and never have, thought of themselves as an "ethnic group," a term from 1950s Chicago School sociology only used in Britain for immigrants from the British Empire and the Commonwealth. Hastings does provide medieval evidence to the effect that after their defeat at the hands of Edward I, the Welsh warriors lamented the loss of *nostra nacio* (sic).[113] Ultimately the problem is that Hastings is too close to Smith in having a narrow focus for nation. Smith's insistence, especially earlier in his career, of using the neologism *ethnie*, probably never helped his case against modernism, because nobody apart from him in the academic study of nationalism, and nobody outside the academic world, uses the term. The term "nation," by contrast, is widely used. (It is an occasional gripe among modernist scholars of nationalism that their definition of nationhood has not caught on outside the universities!) If scholars of nationhood, such as Smith and Hastings, truly want to understand what motivates national-ism, they should be more consistent and more respectful of people's own self-designation as nations. This is, of course, at the heart of the politics of recognition. At the heart of the problem with Hastings is that he posits medieval England as "the prototype of the nation and the nation-state in the fullest sense."[114] Here then we have the age-old Israel-England analogy, which goes back to Bede. It is odd that a Christian historian should put forward a second prototype of the nation alongside biblical Israel. Here we are not far from the kind of thinking detected by Karl Barth in his criticism of nationalism as secret unbelief; namely that all unbelief in the modern world is secretly predicated on belief in the ontological primacy of one's own nation, above Israel and the God of Israel.[115]

If the Bible recognizes the reality of nations regardless of whether they have chosen to imitate Israel or not, the problem of how to read the New Testament remains for both Smith and Hastings. Both deny that the New Testament has a political message that could have helped early Christians forge new concepts of nation. They argue that Christians fell back on the Old Testament for lack of New Testament models. This really shows very little understanding of the issues. In practical terms, Christians before the Christianization of the Roman Empire by Constantine were a

113. Ibid., 71–72.
114. Ibid., 4–5, 35–65.
115. Barth, *Church Dogmatics* I/2, 321.

very small population, and channeled their political thinking into the production of apologetic tracts arguing that they could be faithful Christians *and* loyal citizens of the Roman Empire at the same time. Their belief that Jesus is the Lord of history who suffered death on a cross, rather than become a political nationalist zealot for Judea, was key for this purpose. The other important point is that Luke-Acts could be read as implying that God had ordained the existence of the Roman Empire and its rule over the entire known world to facilitate the spread of Christianity. As long as the Empire was not fully Christianized, pre-Constantinian Christians were not needing to come up with their own distinctly Christian political concepts. Not all Christians, however, would have wholeheartedly supported apologetic, as the New Testament authors saw the Roman Empire as at least an instance, if not the instance, of the evil fourth monarchy of the visions of Daniel 7–12. Jesus was considered to have defeated the evil angelic powers ruling over the nations, and as such, all nations were considered to be under his rule, awaiting Christian mission. There was no truly democratic polity in antiquity as there is today, permitting universal suffrage. Government could be monarchical, republican, oligarchic, and so on, but on the whole, it was recognized as resting on the authority of the few over the many. This was true of large-scale priestly religions such as Judaism and Christianity. Early Christians were, in fact, more politically flexible than Smith or Hastings acknowledge. At the right time, they chose to produce apologetics for being Roman citizens. Later, many argued for the Christianization of the Roman Empire, as a reflection of the unity of the world under Christ's rule. Then there were the new Christian kingdoms, invoking not only the Old Testament kingship of David, Solomon, and Josiah, but also the eternal kingship of Christ, king of Israel as well as king of the nations. Early and medieval Christians had a rich christological hermeneutic for reading biblical political concepts as well as interpreting classical and tribal ones. Neither Smith nor Hastings acknowledge this. Perhaps the real problem is that the history of biblical interpretation is not known to most social theorists or historians outside of faculties of theology. The result is a serious distortion of the European and Christian past, and an inability to recognize certain instances of modern nationalism as justifiable in view of the fact that they are motivated by the reality of having been a premodern nation according to the premodern criteria of nationhood. Smith did eventually come to recognize Wales as a nation, but only half-heartedly due to acknowledging the strength of its modern nationalism.[116] He never mentions medieval Welsh kingship and law, the two main criteria for nationhood in medieval Christendom. What this means is that despite having broadened his definition of nationhood to speak of hierarchical, covenantal (more egalitarian), and republican forms of nationhood, he still has not truly grasped the importance of recognizing premodern mechanisms of recognition for the modern politics of recognition.

CONCLUSION

We have seen how reluctant our thinkers are to recognize Wales as a stateless nation. Hastings never recognized it as such. Williams started off with recognition but gave out very mixed signals later. Smith has improved. Ultimately, lack of recognition of Wales as stateless nation is rooted in fear of the intellectual, cultural, social, and political consequences of recognition. If Wales is truly recognized, then the fact that the British Empire was really the *English* empire would come to light in a most uncomfortable fashion. The necessary comparison between the conquest of Wales in 1282 and the subsequent Act of Union, which refused recognition to Wales altogether, and the Act of Union between Scotland and England (sic) voluntarily signed by Scotland in 1707, becomes embarrassingly obvious. Automatically, then, comparisons with Ireland's relationship to England are opened up. Looking further afield, deconstructing the myth of Britain leads to questioning the myth of benign British imperialism around the globe. Logically, this leads to reconsidering the multiple meanings of colonialism, post-colonialism, multiculturalism, and assimilation. We are often rightly reminded, in the face of anti-immigration agitation from far-right voters in England especially, that "Britain is a nation of immigrants." Rightly in the sense that many people who live in Britain are descended from immigrants. Yet the whole point of this chapter has been to show that Britain is a state, but *not a nation*. England, of course, is a nation, yet it is significant that now that Wales and Scotland have attained devolution and thus better recognition, increasing numbers of English people feel left out of the process of recognition. This is nothing less than the direct long-term result of English imperialism starting with Edward I but theologically harking back to Bede. England ironically lost its identity first by styling itself Israel, against real Jews, and second, by styling itself Britain and taking on Welsh, not Anglo-Saxon or Anglo-Norman, political myths,

116. Smith, *The Cultural Foundations of Nations*, 5, 26.

e.g., the return of Arthur, which was used in support of the Tudor dynasty. The term "British Empire" was invented by John Dee, the magus of the Elizabethan court whose parents were Welsh.[117] Dee and others, including Thomas Haklyut, promoted the legend of the discovery of America by the medieval prince Madog, son of Owain Gwynedd, a real king of Wales in the twelfth century.[118] (Owain Gwynedd's descendants include R. Tudur Jones.[119]) The myth of the white Welsh-speaking Indians was but one of the many tales told about the Native Americans in the early modern period, in an attempt to link Native Americans to Welsh ancestry, and to claim America for the British Empire.[120] It was parallel to the idea of the Native Americans being members of the Lost Tribes of Israel. This linguistic claim was investigated by enthusiastic antiquarians, who even claimed to have found a common vocabulary of 500 words between Welsh and one of the Native American languages. The most likely reason for this, however, is that Welsh settlers in the thirteen colonies successfully taught the Native Americans their language as a means of communicating and trading with them. It clearly shows a desire to retain national linguistic distinctiveness in the colonies. With the loss of statehood, religion, language, and culture remained the vehicles of Welsh national consciousness. This is why I think steady Welsh emigration to America from the seventeenth century to the early twentieth century, when universal suffrage for women and working-class men was won in Britain (albeit as a reward for patriotism during the First World War) is so important for understanding Welsh political history. It is not at all surprising that so many of the signatories of the American Declaration of Independence had Welsh, Scottish, and Irish ancestors.[121] There were no less than eighteen signatories who had Welsh ancestors. Many famous American presidents have had Welsh ancestors: John Adams, James Abram Garfield, William Henry Harrison, Thomas Jefferson, Abraham Lincoln, James Monroe, Richard Nixon. Betsy Ross, the legendary maker of the first United States flag, was of Welsh descent too, as was Martha, the wife of George Washington. My own opinion is that emigration to America was the most powerful precursor of Welsh nationalist politics before the twentieth century, as important as support

---

117. On different conceptualizations of the "British Empire," see Armitage, *The Ideological Origins of the British Empire.*

118. Williams, *Madoc.*

119. I am grateful to E. R. Moseley for this information.

120. On the "white Indians," see Senior, *Did Prince Madog Discover America?*

121. For these references, see the relevant entries in Roberts, *150 Welsh Americans.*

for the liberal party, because it was rooted in socio-economic concerns yet seems to have been expressed often in cultural and religious terms. It showed what Welsh men and women could do when they got a real chance. This is why the kind of modernity criticism that many contemporary theologians favor is so questionable, for scratch the surface and we find modernity equals Protestant nonconformity and, bogey of bogeys, the United States of America. It is to this kind of modernity criticism we turn in the next chapter.

4

"Hebrew" Modernity as "Christian Heresy"

John Milbank's Theology and Social Theory *Deciphered*

In the distant medieval past, there was no secular social or political thought. There was peace, love, and understanding—and justice. The entire known world was governed by the Augustinian idea of an "ontology of peace."[1] Yet there were unruly dissenters. Among these was the theologian John Duns Scotus. Scotus' boldness in criticizing Thomas Aquinas' analogical theories of being and language paved the way for the wholescale desecration of theology by social theory in subsequent centuries, going from hardening of Papal authority in the fourteenth century to the rise of a political biblical hermeneutic and ontology of violence with Thomas Hobbes and Baruch Spinoza, and somehow along the way leading to American evangelicals' support for the foundation of Israel in 1948 as the fulfillment of biblical prophecy, ending up with George W. Bush and Tony Blair leading the United States and the United Kingdom into the Second Iraq War in 2003. This, of course, is a very brief summary of the story that the Anglo-Catholic theologian John Milbank tells in his monumental *Theology and Social Theory* and subsequent works of constructive theology. Along the way there are metatheoretical and genealogical critiques of political economy converging on Thomas Malthus and Thomas Chalmers, French sociology from Malebranche to Durkheim, German social theory from Immanuel Kant to Max Weber, and American sociology of religion.[2] Hegel, Marx, Nietzsche, Heidegger, and the French

1. Milbank, *Theology and Social Theory*, 2nd ed., 283–442.
2. Ibid., 51–144.

post-structuralists are treated more favorably as partial allies for the program of an Augustinian sociology.[3] This narrative has been swallowed whole by many Christian theologians in the last two decades. Theology represents an ontology of peace whereas social theory represents an ontology of violence. This has clearly been music to many a theologian's ear, because it repeats the mantra that modernity has been increasingly violent and anti-Christian, culminating in the great evil of modern nationalism. It is worth noting here the criticism that Steven Pinker, an atheist Jew who is a top-flight evolutionary psychologist, levels at this kind of conservative moralizing about history in his massive book *The Better Angels of Our Nature: The Decline of Violence in History and Its Causes,* through showing extensive social scientific evidence to the effect that human societies as collectivities have become less violent in the modern period, thanks to the rise of the modern state. In line with rigorously modern, social-scientific research, Pinker rejects the myth of the noble savage and the peaceful indigenous peoples who used to be popular in sections of philosophy and social anthropology. The modern state has actually led to a *decline* in violence within its boundaries. Of course, it could be argued that Pinker is mistaken to build a progressivist theory of the improvement of human nature on the back of this evidence, and that he too has fallen into the trap of reducing what Christians call sin and evil to violence. Pinker's argument about the positive benefits of the modern state for its own population is also open to serious challenge—the standard one being the Holocaust. Pinker's target is the more socially conservative thinking that insists that violence has been historically on the increase. Naturally, it is possible to take a different perspective and argue simply that Pinker and conservative, pessimistic thinking provide two complementary perspectives on history, given that the number of wars has actually increased through history. What neither Milbank nor Pinker consider is the probability that ideas about peace and war have often *followed* rather than produced advancements in weapons technology as well as surveillance. Milbank in some ways fits the bill for the kind of socially conservative thinker that Pinker targets, only he operates at the level of high theory. Yet at the same time, Milbank does not extol a romantic idea of peaceful primordial peoples surviving today, as numerous anthropologists have done. He does believe in a peaceful human society before the fall, as we shall see. His sense of the entire stream of history is thus declinist. Why then does Milbank look back to the early and high medieval West to situate his

3. Ibid., 147–205, 259–442.

ontology of peace? Is this not an arbitrary and illogical intrusion into the fall from Eden?

"SOCIAL THEORY" AS HERESY: THE COVERT ATTACK ON "JEWISH" MODERNITY

Milbank's book appeared as part of a series of textbooks which actually includes Ingolf Dalferth's *Theology and Philosophy* and Duncan Forrester's *Theology and Politics*. As is evident, Milbank never wrote a textbook. Instead, he wrote a manifesto of "modernity criticism," and sounded the trumpet heralding a series of works of constructive theology. He did claim that his book was an oblique criticism of theologians who use sociology in an ancillary manner to provide description and evaluation for their own work.[4] Given his subsequent attack on Reinhold Niebuhr, which we encountered back in chapter 2, it is possible to imagine that among his targets were Anglican Niebuhrians and Weberians who worked at the interface between theology and sociology in the 1970s and 1980s, such as David Martin and Robin Gill. (Indeed, Milbank never recognizes the work of Martin, Gill, and others which preceded his own.) His manner of argument is heavily based on symbolism plotted in a narrative of the decline of theology and philosophy, which gives it the kind of prophetic aura that is the hallmark of "Christian modernity criticism." At the outset, we must ask what precisely does Milbank mean by "theology"? It is important that he revealed in an interview in 2005 that he had been deeply influenced by his teacher Nicholas Lash at Cambridge, who taught that theology as a discipline has no distinctive object of enquiry.[5] It is thus free to range over a whole range of disciplines. Logically, this must mean that theology does not, and perhaps should not, have God—certainly not the Christian God to which the Bible and the Christian creeds witness—as its primary object of enquiry. Rather, theology is a kind of linguistic discourse that the individual theologian (whatever it means to be a "theologian" in this sense) may freely use to interpret and criticize other disciplines and professions. In the case of Nicholas Lash, this rather unusual idea of what theology is is closely linked to his own preference for negative theology.[6] From the outset, Milbank's actual writings do not give any reliable indication that he has the classical Christian faith in mind

4. Milbank, *Theology and Social Theory*, 1–6.

5. Milbank in Shortt (ed.), *God's Advocates*, 105.

6. Lash, *Believing Three Ways in One God*.

when he speaks of "theology." To be fair, he has made negative comments in passing on "orthodox" kinds of theology enough times by now that readers should have sufficient indicators that this might be a problem. The problem is that many readers have acted as if, or openly assumed, that he is working with creedal orthodoxy in its fullness in mind. We shall return later below to the question of the nature of Milbank's theology. There is also the basic question of what precisely Milbank actually means by "social theory"—and no reviewer of the book has actually posed this question. Most have not spotted the massive problem that Milbank never says what he means by "theology" in the title. What he means by "social theory" is really an amalgam of classical economics or political economy in Britain, classical sociology in France, Germany, and the USA, and classical liberal political theory since Hobbes and Spinoza, as well as liberation theology. Why exactly all this should be classified as "social theory" we aren't told. Milbank's use of the term "heresy" to criticize "social theory" may seem eccentric and over-dramatic, given that normally it refers to ideas that deviate from the central Christian creeds and basic content of the Bible in matters pertaining to salvation, or doctrinal formulations that distort the entire field of doctrine by distorting one or more elements. Once we accept, at least for the sake of argument, that this "heresy" is a "heresy" from an undefined non-creedal "theology," we start to realize that neither term is necessarily meant in a realist sense; rather that they function pragmatically as part of the story of the "fall" of "theology" *and metaphysics and the theory of language* since Duns Scotus.[7] It is important to realize, however, that he devotes two whole chapters to the sociology of religion as a discipline unmasking the primordial truth about religion, and as part of this the intellectual theory of secularization as progressive and irreversible. One of the named targets here is Peter Berger, whom we met in chapter 1, and whom I suggested as a theorist whose work bears resemblance to that of Philip Jenkins. Berger's famous thesis is that to believe in the Christian religion, or any other, today in the modern world is to exercise a "heretical imperative." We are all "heretics" in the literal sense of making choices in order to make symbolic sense of our lives. Indeed, the silent subtext here is that we are all courageous existentialist heroes striking out to conquer the meaninglessness that is the default mood of modernity, especially in its urban settings. Put in sociological terms, this is to say that religious pluralism is the (unhappy) default norm of modern society. As we saw briefly in

---

7. For clarity's sake, I refer here to the first edition of *Theology and Social Theory*, 14, 54, 302–3.

chapter 1, this pluralism was the direct result of legal and social changes pushing religious toleration and various dissenting worldviews, and sociologists of religion and others played an active part in fulfilling their own prophecies encoded in secularization theories and philosophies of history. Milbank's thesis that social theory promoted an "ontology of violence" is stated in highly metaphysical terms, and ranges over problems regarding providence and evil, capitalism and the state. Yet the "violence" that he talks about is not properly defined. In reading *Theology and Social Theory*, it is hard not to get the impression that it is a catch-all term for the social and intellectual conflicts in modernity that happened naturally and inevitably due to demands for religious toleration. His decision to cast social theory as a heresy marks a pragmatist turn towards casting (theological) anthropology in moral terms, judging it by its fruits, which he considers to be "an ontology of violence." It functions not unlike the term "apostasy" in much Protestant discourse, denoting a radical behavioral term against what is deemed the revealed will of God, following its New Testament usage. This is what we might expect given Milbank's aforementioned elision of the distinction between theology and ethics. The term "apostasy" is, of course, stronger than the term "heresy." Generally it is used to suggest that a person or idea has deviated fundamentally from Christianity in a radical way, rather than being the result of an intellectual mistake or moral muddle. Milbank's terms "ontology of peace" and "ontology of violence" suggest precisely this radical turn. The interesting question is, if heresy for Milbank denotes something like apostasy for the New Testament, does he provide adequate means for the conversion of the heretics back to "orthodoxy"? More fundamentally, what exactly is theological "orthodoxy" for Milbank?

Social anthropology gets left out of the critique. This is telling because there is a long tradition of Anglican and Roman Catholic friendliness towards social anthropology due to its link with ethnography (directed at supposedly lesser beings, such as Pentecostals) and ritual studies. At times one suspects that sociology gets put under the intellectual guillotine because it is a discipline that was used against the Catholic and Anglican churches. It is regrettable that Milbank's mostly theological readership have not noticed this. Indeed, Richard Roberts' review back in 1993, one of the earliest, argued forthrightly that the "uncritical adulation" accorded the book by most theologians who read it served merely to underscore "the profound intellectual ghettoization and malaise of much

Christian theology."[8] Roberts even claimed that sociologists were completely unwilling to review the book in their own journals. The obvious inference to be made is that theologians by and large do not read the history of sociology. Equally evident has been the relief that many have felt at the book's appearance, as it has given them permission to stay away from detailed description of social realities altogether.

Ralph Cudworth, the most important theologian among the Cambridge Platonists, is named by Milbank as a forerunner of his thinking.[9] Insofar as both draw up a story of the decline of theology and philosophy based on castigating their targets for not being Christian Neoplatonists, this is an apt comparison. Douglas Hedley has attempted to rescue the Cambridge Platonists from association with Milbank by painting them as pro-natural science, tolerant, and "liberal," even as anti-ritualist.[10] What Hedley ignores is that Cudworth, like Milbank, had a high view of the Hermetic texts, taking them to be a key source in his idea that all religions, at bottom, reflect original monotheism. In this respect, Cudworth differed from Isaac Casaubon, whose text-critical discovery that the Hermetica were forgeries, and not as ancient as previously believed, had damaged their credibility.[11] Hedley ascribes such "Christian Hermetism" and Origenism only to Joseph De Maistre, the eighteenth-century French Catholic Masonic theosophist whom Milbank reads.[12] Hedley's attempt to distance Cudworth from Milbank's appropriation probably evidences liberal Anglican in-fighting. It is also unconvincing as an attempt to paint Cudworth and his ilk as ancestors of modern toleration. As Richard Ashcraft has demonstrated, latitudinarianism did not imply political toleration of Protestant dissenters; it was not "a moderate middle ground between contending extremes" as it portrayed itself, but was "part of the one of the extremes" (Anglicanism).[13] In fact, it was "the acceptable face of the persecution of religious dissent."[14] This was related to the fact

8. Roberts, "Transcendental Sociology?" 527–35.

9. Milbank, *Radical Orthodoxy*, xi.; Milbank, *The Future of Love*, 58.

10. Hedley, "Radical Orthodoxy and Apocalyptic Difference"; Hankey and Hedley (eds.), *Deconstructing Radical Orthodoxy*, 99–116 .

11. On Ralph Cudworth, Isaac Causabon, and the Hermetica, see Assmann, *Moses the Egyptian*.

12. On Joseph De Maistre's influence on French social theory, see Milbank, *Theology and Social Theory*, 1st ed., 54–55, 66–70.

13. Ashcraft, "Latitudinarianism and Toleration," in Kroll, Ashcraft, and Zagorin (eds.), *Philosophy, Science, and Religion in England 1640–1700*, 154–55.

14. Ibid., 155.

that while some Anglicans responded to the crisis of ecclesial authority over worship by arguing that episcopacy is biblically based, mostly "they simply conceded that Anglicanism was a political church, i.e., a religion whose practice depended upon the civil magistrate's authority to enforce compliance with the law."[15] In more modern terms, the Church of England here represents English civil religion, "civilization," and "social cohesion," or, to use the appropriate theological term, "Christendom." The Toleration Act of 1689 had journeyed through Parliament with a Comprehension Bill, designed to bring Calvinist Presbyterians back into the Church of England, the better to isolate Independents, Baptists, Quakers, etc., and facilitate their persecution. Happily, the Comprehension Bill never made it to the legislative stage.[16] The Anglican clergy, most especially the latitudinarians, were myopic in misreading the extent of dissenting opposition to the Comprehension Bill.[17] They were both naive and arrogant in imagining that Presbyterians would side with them, and this did not happen. Such are the delusions of majority power. It is very important that Ashcraft finds the secondary literature on latitudinarianism wanting due to either "seriously underestimating" or ignoring its political commitments, because the very same concealment of political realities is found in Milbank's work.[18] Milbank uses his rather selective reading of Ralph Cudworth to attack his radicalizing reading of Thomas Hobbes, but conceals the fact that Hobbes too was an Anglican—an eccentric type of Calvinist in fact.[19] This is all the more unacceptable in scholarly terms because Milbank uses Hobbes time and time again as a stick with which to beat modern Western social and political theory.[20] Scholarship on Hobbes abounds, because he is such a useful figure for secular political theory and attacks on it. Once his peculiar theology and ecclesiastical provenance are

---

15. Ibid., 153.

16. Bennett, "Conflict in the Church," in Holmes (ed.), *Britain after the Glorious Revolution, 1689–1714*, 161–62. Mensing, Jr., *Toleration and Parliament 1660–1719*, 95.

17. Horowitz, "Protestant Reconciliation in the Exclusion Crisis," 201–17.

18. Ashcraft, "Latitudinarianism and Toleration," 155.

19. Hobbes was a Sabellian. The literature on Hobbes and theology is vast, so it is all the more bizarre that Milbank doesn't reference *any* of it in his work. The most comprehensive discussion of Hobbes as Anglican theologian is in Martinich, *The Two Gods of Leviathan*.

20. See, for example, Milbank, "Sovereignty, Empire, Capital, and Terror," in Milbank, *The Future of Love*, 239.

factored into his thinking, it becomes much more difficult to use him in this way without looking self-serving.

Milbank's attack on Hobbes and Spinoza critically engages a very common path taken in modernity criticism, which is that the Wars of Religion in western Europe, including the English Revolution, provoked a turn to a philosophical approach to politics removed from the matrix of Christian revelation, as a defense against the division of Christendom into independent nation-states, each taking the religion of the head of state. Seventeenth-century political thought, according to this theory, emptied itself of political theology, and thus the secularization of Western thought was born. It is a theory that has been advanced from across the political spectrum of scholars: Leo Strauss, Hans Blumenberg, C. B. Macpherson, Jonathan I. Israel.[21] It has had a knock-on effect on the reading of eighteenth- and nineteenth-century political theorists and philosophers, which ignores their substantive if often heterodox and even esoteric theological commitments. Milbank follows the view that Hobbes and Spinoza and subsequent political theorists are political theologians whose work is based on a new biblical hermeneutic that is distinct from what he calls "Catholic biblical hermeneutics," itself never defined for us. He does not give us close readings of these authors. Eric Nelson's work on the early modern notion of the Hebrew republic gives a more accurate picture of what was involved.[22] Nelson shows that the sixteenth- and seventeenth-century revival of teaching biblical Hebrew in western Europe gave rise to Christian reading of the Bible as the political constitution instituted by God for Israel. Their Jewish teachers passed onto them Rabbinic material that they came to consider as authoritative on these matters. In particular, this perspective challenged the "constitutional pluralism" of medieval Christian political theory, inherited from Aristotle and preserved by Calvin, that there was a range of correct constitutional forms (monarchy, aristocracy, and republic), in contrast with degenerate forms (tyranny, oligarchy, democracy). Mid-seventeenth-century republican theorists began to argue that monarchy as such was an illegitimate constitutional form, and that all constitutional forms that are legitimate are in fact republican. Nelson argues that this was due to Protestant reading of the radical Rabbinic exegesis, which interpreted Israel's demand that Saul become

21. Strauss, *Natural Right and History*; Blumenberg, *The Legitimacy of the Modern Age*; MacPherson, *The Theory of Possessive Individualism*; Israel, *Enlightenment Contested*. I am indebted to Eric Nelson for this insight. See Nelson, *The Hebrew Republic*, 1–22, 141.

22. Nelson, *The Hebrew Republic*.

king as idolatrous. Thus modern schools of political theory are not simply secular in their ethos: they are profoundly *theological*, and very radically biblical, Jewish, and Protestant in the origin and intent. How precisely this illuminates Milbank's political attitudes should be clear: Protestant republican arguments had part of their origins in one strand of Jewish thought. For now, we return to his positioning himself as analogous to Ralph Cudworth.

Milbank's strategy of mounting a critique in advance of sociology via Gillian Rose's reading of Hegel is a dressing up of Cudworth's view that the philosophies of Thomas Hobbes and René Descartes, among others, had already been anticipated as heresies by the church fathers.[23] Common to both Hegel and the church fathers (but not explicit in Gillian Rose's reading of Hegel) is the reality of being steeped in Neoplatonism and Hermeticism.[24] Cudworth believed the materialism, mechanism, and determinism of Hobbes' thought to lead to atheism. Milbank continues this train of thought by applying it to subsequent sociology, arguing essentially that it leads to nihilism, by which he means a counterfeit of *creatio ex nihilo*.[25] In socio-political terms, this seems to be an attack on the belief that humans can recreate society and polity from scratch by means of a naturalist philosophy. The target, predictably for an Anglican theologian, is the French Revolution. Here is where Milbank's conservative Masonic sympathies are important. Many of Milbank's critics fail to understand him adequately because they have not grasped the importance of the esoteric traditions of Hermeticism and "Christian Kabbalah"—mediated via the "Christian Platonism" of the Cambridge Platonists as well as eighteenth-century French Masonic theosophists—to his thinking. The latter had a complex relationship to the French Revolution as well as the Papacy, and some of the contradictions in their thinking come out in Milbank as well. For example, Louis Claude de Saint-Martin, the French popularizer of Jacob Boehme, was not beyond interpreting the *Terreur* of the Revolution as the Word incarnate.[26] Suspiciously, Milbank has nothing to say about this. De Maistre defended papal infallibility, even

---

23. Milbank, *Theology and Social Theory*, 147–76; Rose, *Hegel Contra Sociology*.

24. Sagorin, "Cudworth and Hobbes on Is and Ought," in Kroll, Ashcraft, and Zagorin (eds.), *Philosophy, Science, and Religion in England 1640–1700*, 129; Magee, *Hegel and the Hermetic Tradition*.

25. Milbank, Preface to 2nd ed. of *Theology and Social Theory*, xiv–xv.

26. For a summary of Louis-Claude de Saint-Martin's theosophy, see McCalla, "Louis-Claude de Saint Martin," in Hannegraaff (ed.), *Dictionary of Gnosis and Western Esotericism*, 1024–31.

though Catholics had been officially banned from joining Freemasonry by Pope Clement XII's bull, *In eminenti,* promulgated in 1738.[27] Why precisely the major esoteric traditions should be important for someone repudiating social theory and advocating a Christian sociology is never made fully explicit, yet it is a most important question that no critic has actually posed. Perhaps there are echoes here of the quarrel between the "Ancients and the Moderns" in English Freemasonry in the late eighteenth century.[28] The Ancients wanted to keep Trinitarian symbolism in the rituals, whereas the Modernists were avowed deists, and many suspected this of merely being a cover for atheism and mortalism (denial of the resurrection). The two sides reunited in the formation of the United Grand Lodge of England in 1813. On this account, social theory in Milbank's thought may be a code for the Masonic Moderns. Naturally, not being Trinitarian, deist or modernist Masonic lodges came to welcome Jewish men.[29] It is not insignificant, as numerous critics have observed, that many of Milbank's favorite "counter-Enlightenment" theologians, including Johann Georg Hamann, were either ambivalent to Jewish emancipation or hostile to it.[30] All this was closely related to the Spinozist controversy in the German Enlightenment, which started when the Masonic philosopher Lessing was discovered to be a pantheist like Spinoza.

FROM SPINOZA TO ZIONISM: SCAPEGOATING ISRAEL

Spinoza is considered by Orthodox Jews to be both a heretic, and the first modern Jewish thinker. Milbank, however, includes him in his list of early modern thinkers who are "heretics" against "Catholicism." This is a meta-critical position that hovers above textual exposition and historiography. He assimilates Spinoza to Hobbes, complaining that "political theory achieved a certain highly ambiguous autonomy in regard to theology."[31] The fact that Spinoza is a *Jewish* heretic, and that precisely due to denying the unconditional election of Israel, receives no attention in

27. Clement XII, *In eminenti,* 1738, http://www.papalencyclicals.net/Clem12/c12inemengl.htm; Ridley, *The Freemasons,* 47–58.

28. On the Ancients and the Moderns, see Hamill and Gilbert, *Freemasonry,* 35.

29. On Jews in eighteenth-century Freemasonry, see Katz, *Jews and Freemasons in Europe, 1723–1939.*

30. John G. Betz tries to minimize the problem of Hamann's hostility to Jewish emancipation. See Betz, *After Enlightenment,* 258–90.

31. Milbank, *Theology and Social Theory* (1st ed.), 10.

Milbank's thought. Instead he is painted as someone who attacked "Catholic biblical hermeneutics" via the *Lutheran* principle of interpreting Scripture "only through Scripture" (actually, this comes from the church fathers)![32] It is thus difficult to take seriously Milbank's subsequent complaints about Antiochene tendencies in exegesis, insinuating that they are related to political validation of the biblical text via fulfillment of prophecy.[33] Obviously, he has in mind the millennialist Protestant and Jewish belief that the foundation of the modern State of Israel is a partial fulfillment of prophecy. This is ironic because Spinoza's denial of Israel's election meant that he believed stateless nations, such as the Jews were in his day, would not and should not survive the fatalistic rise and fall of nations in history, but that Jews instead should assimilate into a secularized Christendom.[34] Yet the very notion of the secular is dismissed from the outset by Milbank as having shifted from being a temporal to a spatial notion, thus allowing the secular sphere to be conceived outside of ecclesial time.[35] Unspoken is the annoyance that the Reformation and its consequences saw a challenge to the Roman church's claim to mirror eternity and thus to be a sign of providence. If Protestant and Jewish discourses refused Catholic or Anglican interpretations of providence, their temporal reality had to be accounted for theologically. Logically this means they had to be accounted for as heretics or worse. Thus, the question cannot be avoided, what does "Catholic biblical hermeneutic" mean for Milbank? Repeatedly he argues that medieval theology went wrong in the late thirteenth century, by going the road paved by Duns Scotus regarding the nature of being, which is implicitly linked to a critique of Papal infallibility.[36] Brett Edward Whalen has shown that what counted as such in the high middle ages was the apocalyptic hermeneutic that partly motivated the Crusades, the wars of the Papal armies.[37] This reality is directly relevant to Milbank's attitude to the modern State

---

32. Milbank, *Theology and Social Theory*, 19–20.

33. Ibid., 20.

34. A sharp critique of Milbank's approach to Israel and his uses of Spinoza is made by Scott Bader-Saye in *Church and Israel After Christendom*, 16–21, 154–55.

35. Milbank, *Theology and Social Theory*, 9ff.

36. "Theocratic" construals of Papal authority are deemed to start from the thirteenth century and to be indebted to the rise of voluntarism, in Milbank and Pickstock, *Truth in Aquinas*, 17. Unfortunately, Milbank and Pickstock do not reference the scholarly discussion on this among historians actually reading the relevant primary texts on canon law, e.g., Tierney, *The Origins of Papal Infallibility, 1150–1350*.

37. Whalen, *Dominion of God*.

of Israel in several ways. Milbank constantly claims to espouse an "Augustinian ontology of peace," yet historians have shown how Crusader doctrine was an outgrowth of Augustine's theory that just war could include coercion of heretics, pagans, and Jews, leading to Gregory's notion of missionary war.[38] (Whalen unfortunately ignores the fact that this would be linked to both the Latin West and the Greek East seeing themselves as the millennial kingdom of Christ, the "fifth monarchy" of Daniel. *Amillennial* apocalypticism lent itself directly to medieval Christian imperialisms.)[39] This Augustinian view could justify pacifying non-Catholic Christians, Jews, and Muslims.[40] Such a notion of Christendom, along with Milbank's repudiation of clear thinking on society and the state, and therefore nations, lends itself logically to the repudiation of a two-state solution to the Middle East conflict, and the utopian dream of a "one-state Palestine" (qualifying suitably as "Christendom" due to being anti-nationalist). In medieval terms, this isn't far off the Latin Kingdom of Jerusalem, a very clear instantiation of Latin Christendom in the Holy Land until its demise in 1291, only one year after Edward I had banished the Jewish community from England and Wales.[41] All of this means that Milbank's refusal to make a clear distinction between church and state ought to be revisited. His proximity to the theology of J. G. Hamann to this end, as well as in opposing natural rights, is noteworthy, as the latter opposed Moses Mendelssohn's argument for Jewish emancipation, based on social contract theory.[42] Milbank's conflation of church and state, and church and society, reminiscent of the worst Anglican Erastianism, logically means that he has little positive to say about either modern secular civil society, the modern Western state in general, or the modern Jewish state in particular. As with his "ontology of peace," it therefore has

38. Erdmann, *The Origin of the Idea of Crusade*.

39. Whalen reveals his own bias at the end of his book when he complains that "Christian fundamentalists in the United States support the state of Israel as part of their apocalyptic scenario, still waiting for the 'remnant' of the Jews to enter the Church after the Second Coming of Christ," contrasting this to "the silent majority" who want "universal peace and prosperity . . . with or without the promise of eschatological justice." Whalen, *Dominion of God*, 232. What is required here is closer attention to differences between Protestant and medieval millennialisms, relating to the different church-state and church-society relations envisaged and involved.

40. On Milbank on Augustine and coercion, see Bowlin, "Augustine on Justifying Coercion," 49–70.

41. On the Latin Kingdom, see Seward, *The Monks of War*, 23–77.

42. Milbank, *Theology and Social Theory* (1st ed.), 406–8; Hamann, "Golgotha and Sheblimini!" in Hamann, *Writings on Philosophy and Language*, 164–204.

no contribution to make to modern conflict resolution or transformation. It fits Robin Shepherd's charge that "European hostility towards Israel tends to be more nihilistic [than American types of hostility which proffer a one-state Palestine]—it tends to denigrate and demonize without offering up the pretence of a 'solution.'"[43]

Not only is there little room for Jewish emancipation or a Jewish sovereign state in the logic of Milbank's thinking, but the State of Israel is implied to be at the center of a sinister global conspiracy. The discussion of radical evil in the first chapter of *Being Reconciled* shows that this belief is set within a wider attack on modern theories of evil. Discussing Arendt's theory of "the banality of evil," Milbank notes how she made a link between the debased Kantian view that evil is "a positively willed denial of the good" and the cooperation of a large number of ordinary Germans with the "final solution."[44] As many others have argued, the horror here is that the "final solution" was articulated in rationalist as well as nationalist terms, those of Nazi ideology. It was not articulated in purely nihilistic terms. Milbank focuses on the nationalist element at the expense of its being eugenicist and therefore "positive." Analogously, he defends the Augustinian theory of evil as privative from complicity with modern horrendous evil (genocide), and argues that "the modern, positive [Kantian] theory of evil *is* in a measure responsible for the modern actuality of evil."[45] Such a neat distinction is very difficult to defend with regard to evil, which is so inherently duplicitous and manipulative of human perception. It is also self-serving, as it enables Milbank to draw a moral equivalence between mid-twentieth-century totalitarianism and liberal democracy (which parallels his false equivalence between Islam and Christian theology after Scotus). He goes on to claim that "the presence of genuine socialist ideas allowed the Soviet State later somewhat to reform itself," compared to the faster collapse of Nazi Germany. This is short-sighted. Soviet Communism collapsed within a lifetime; Nazi Germany was defeated by British and American military force and intelligence. Nevertheless, he goes on to make the following claim:

> European and American liberal democracy has also engendered
> a continuous horror almost as grave as the Holocaust, and a
> more troublingly sustainable mode of nihilism; . . . this is the
> sequence of deliberate terror and extermination deployed

43. Shepherd, *A State Beyond the Pale*, 253.

44. Milbank, *Being Reconciled*, 1–3.

45. Ibid., 4.

against civilian populations as primary instruments of war
and neo-colonial power from the Congo and the Philippines
through Hiroshima, Palestine, Kenya, Algeria, and Vietnam to
the Gulf War and Afghanistan.[46]

No argument or evidence is advanced in favor of grouping all of these
conflicts together. No mention is made of widespread support for
terrorism against innocent civilian populations of nation-states in those
countries *from among their own inhabitants,* or to the low level of support
for a two-state solution among Palestinians. At the same time, there is
no acknowledgment in his discussion on the Holocaust that the reason
it is considered unique is ultimately due to the Judeo-Christian doctrine
of the election of the Jews by God.[47] As the Jews are a concrete people
and as such the biblical symbol of all humanity, those for whom Jesus the
Jew first came, the Augustinian understanding that Jesus *is the neighbor*
whom the Good Samaritan serves in his hour of distress, is necessarily
extended to Jews first and thence to all humanity. This exactly mirrors Paul's statement at the start of the epistle to the Romans: "I am not
ashamed of the gospel, because it is the power of God for the salvation of
everyone: both to *Jew first* and to Greek."[48] The history of the Holocaust
requires theological attention by Christians precisely because it is a type of
other genocides. Milbank's insinuation that Israel is continuing the Holocaust because it is a modern state supposedly based on Kantian principles
is strictly nonsense in any case as it was the ideas of Theodor Herzl and
Achad Ha-Am which vied for supremacy among the early Zionists.[49] The
claim is useful for him however because it fits logically with his sugges-
tion that 9/11 could have been a conspiracy masterminded by the Israeli
and US governments.[50] Claiming agnosticism over who perpetrated 9/11
is, of course, necessary for Milbank to exonerate himself of the charge
of upholding a conspiracy theory. Yet it is a denial of the available evidence in favor of the legal verdict already enacted as to the identity of the
perpetrators. It is also, intellectually, related ultimately to a long history

46. Ibid.

47. Ibid.

48. Cranfield, *The International Critical Commentary on the Epistle to the Romans,*
91. Cranfield reads the verse as linked to Romans 11. The *locus classicus* of Augustine's
notion is found in *De Trinitate.* It is repeated in Martin Luther, "The Freedom of a
Christian," and in Bonhoeffer and Barth respectively.

49. Goldberg, *To The Promised Land,* 30–112.

50. Milbank, "Geopolitical Theology: Economy, Religion and Empire after 9/11,"
11.

of conspiracy theories about Jews in general and Zionists in particular harboring malign intentions towards Western society, etc. In such conspiracy theories, the perpetrators (here Jews) are guilty until proven innocent, in contrast to the notion enshrined in British law that those standing trial are deemed innocent until proven guilty. Of course, this harks back to historic Christian anti-Semitism, where Jews were deemed guilty of whatever crime was projected onto them in times of social stress, because by virtue of national descent they were "Christ-killers."[51] A lazy neglect of distinguishing more general theological and social from more specific legal and political categories only lessens intellectual defenses against this kind of thinking. Finally, Milbank has the temerity to caution against "an out of hand dismissal of" the possibility of deliberate conspiracy, because this "would be to imagine that we live in a world in which such an event as the St. Bartholomew's Day Massacre could never really occur."[52] This is hardly an analogy that Milbank can carry off, because the massacre was carried out by a Catholic king against the Huguenots— instigators of Calvinist Reformation that Milbank repudiates in his work. The analogy between the massacre and the paranoid claim that Israel instigated 9/11 is all the more sinister as it insinuates that Israel (and the United States) oppose religious liberty, which is *demonstrably untrue*, especially in the case of the United States. In terms of theological method, the problem is that Milbank is still too wedded to the postliberal fetish for narrative while ignoring close reading of texts and evidence, and the attendant analysis required for making sense of external realities. In truth, it is rooted in his frequent recourse to literary theories that make language constitutive of reality rather than representing it. Such theories may be characterized as de-hebraicized or secularized kabbalah. It is no accident that such a worldview involves a fundamental shift from seeing language stemming from Hebrew as rooted in divine creativity, to seeing language in general (its origins suitably obscured) as rooted in the creativity of the theologian, or guild of theologians. This was the important shift that gradually came about after the Italian Renaissance, and which produced, first, "Christian" Kabbalah, and second, German Romanticism and idealism, then third, French poststructuralism. This genealogy is obscured by Milbank precisely because he seems to think that the post-Hebrew kabbalistic

51. On historic anti-Semitism in England, see Julius, *Trials of the Diaspora*, 105–47.

52. Milbank, "Geopolitical Theology: Economy, Religion and Empire after 9/11," 11.

tradition constitutes true Christianity or "radical orthodoxy." Unfortunately most of his critics have not really spotted this basic problem.

"CHRISTIAN" KABBALAH AND HERMETICISM: AN EGYPTIAN CAPTIVITY IN ENGLAND

Milbank's rewriting of the history of theology as a history of the fall of linguistic theory and metaphysics curiously resembles Gershom Scholem in his understanding of the Kabbalah as counter-history, and a reaction against divine command ethics rooted in Pentateuchal law.[53] While Scholem intended counter-history to be a heuristic device to enable Jewish scholars to research Jewish traditions in a new light, for Milbank, the concept is useful for propping up his narrative of the fall of theology and philosophy, and conspiracy theories about Israel. At the root of such an attitude is a magical view of the power of language to effect human salvation, and to take up the task of co-creation of the world. Milbank's theory of language partakes of the conceptual reduction and simplification of the Kabbalistic legend that God created the world through continuous playful rearrangement of the twenty-two letters of the Hebrew alphabet, which also stood for numbers, to being about language as such.[54] The Jewish legend also ran that God had written the Torah before creation.[55] Furthermore the Torah was believed to have been verbally dictated by God to Moses on Mount Sinai, letter by letter. This belief yielded a hermeneutic of the Hebrew Bible that was at once utterly conservative in its literalism, insisting on keeping all the commandments, as well as capable of accommodating the notion of continuous creation through language as well as numbers, and of human participation in this process. Put simply, the Kabbalistic tradition yields a twofold understanding of language as both descriptive in the ordinary sense and of specifically the Hebrew language as poietic, the language of divine creation. The Christian Kabbalists of the Renaissance were fascinated by the alleged power of Hebrew and sought to appropriate it for apologetic purposes of defending the Trinity, especially to persuade Jews to convert to Christianity.[56] As the Kabbalistic tradition

---

53. Scholem, *Origins of the Kabbalah.*

54. Ginzberg, *The Legends of the Jews. Vol. I.,* 5–8.

55. Schwartz (ed.), *Tree of Souls.*

56. Jews who had converted to Christianity likewise sometimes used this method, especially if this was the catalyst for conversion. For example, Johan Kemper, a Swedish Jew who converted to Lutheranism, believed to have been Emanuel Swedenborg's

contained elements that could be considered to teach "white magic," Kabbalah came to be considered a suitable tool for enhancing the power of theology in a time of crisis. It was also a living exegetical tradition that proved a viable alternative to medieval Catholic scholasticism. The use of Hebrew allegedly guaranteed that the ancient magic of the Hermetic texts that were the other great source of Renaissance Neoplatonism would be free of diabolical influence. The notorious Renaissance occultist Heinrich Cornelius Agrippa saw the name of Jesus as all-powerful, proven by the alphanumeric riddles of the Kabbalah.[57] Like Erasmus in his *Praise of Folly*, Agrippa satirized the vanity of monastic education, in both its scholastic and its occult forms. Like Erasmus too, his insistence on true knowledge as only stemming from the Christian gospel did not lead to the abandonment of monastic learning, nor to occult beliefs and practices. The parallel with John Milbank's thinking is very clear to those who know. There is a chapter entitled "The Name of Jesus" in *The Word Made Strange*, which argues that "Jesus is essentially a linguistic and poetic reality," which surely testifies to a magical, psychic view of language as somehow (re) producing Jesus.[58] (Joan O'Donovan misses this problem because she thinks Milbank is indulging in "Erasmian poetics."[59]) Milbank is closer to Cornelius Agrippa in some significant respects, such as espousing magical thinking. Witness the bizarre fascination with "second sight" in the Scottish Highlands, a sort of traditional clairvoyance which became part of seventeenth-century Masonic lore.[60]

All this is why "the linguistic turn [is] a theological turn."[61] He argues that only since the Renaissance has "the inescapability of culture" been recognized. He tries "after George Berkeley, to elaborate a notion of the real itself as linguistic, and as divine language, and after Robert Lowth and Johann Georg Hamann, to develop a theory of human being as linguistic being which participates in the divine linguistic being."[62] William Warburton is used selectively in order to give an early modern

Hebrew tutor. See Wolfson, "Messianism in the Christian Kabbalah of Johann Kemper," in Goldish and Popkin (eds.), *Millenarianism and Messianism in the Early Modern European Culture*, 139–87.

57. On Heinrich Cornelius Agrippa, see Lehrich, *Heinrich Cornelius Agrippa*.

58. Milbank, *The Word Made Strange*, 3, 145–68.

59. Lockwood O'Donovan, "The Christian Pedagogy and Ethics of Erasmus," in O'Donovan and Lockwood O'Donovan (eds.), *Bonds of Imperfection*, 121–36.

60. Milbank, *The Future of Love*, ix–x.

61. Milbank, *The Word Made Strange*, 84–120.

62. Ibid., 2.

Anglican justification to this linguistic turn.[63] Here again a certain attitude to the biblical Israel surfaces, which is noteworthy. Warburton argued in response to the deists' view that the lack of Old Testament references to immortality undercut the possibility of divine revelation. Milbank rather cryptically reports Warburton's own view as concurring with the deists yet stressing that the lack of resurrection belief indicated the uniqueness of Hebrew religion and politics, as opposed to its identity with the systems of neighboring nations. Milbank goes on to say that "of course there is real historical insight here, but it is ruined by Warburton's crudely positivistic contention that the Hebrew theocracy had its sanctions through a direct providential administration of rewards and punishments in this present life on earth."[64] It is noteworthy that Milbank chooses to criticize Warburton precisely when he gets concerned with earthly rewards and punishments, i.e., the Jewish law. Milbank suddenly introduces the fact that "Warburton concedes the antiquity and independence of Egyptian religion and culture as a prelude to arguing for the independence and integrity of that of the Hebrews."[65] He does not explain why this is important, yet he goes on to emphasize the fact that Warburton "must establish the integral development of the Egyptians and their isolation from 'Mosaic' influence more strongly than his opponents have done," as if somehow it were an established truth that Egyptian and Hebrew religion were really identical. Warburton denies the Hermetic or Kabbalist view of language "that Adam spoke the real divine creative language mystically related to the hidden nature of things."[66] The problem here is that Milbank doesn't discuss the fact that Christian Kabbalists differed from Jewish Kabbalists in not believing that Hebrew was the original language that had this magical mystical property. He wants the esoteric language theory without the reading of Genesis on linguistic origins favored by the Jewish Kabbalists and some Christians. He complains that Warburton holds "a positivistic view of prophecy" and that in so doing he "makes God sound like the most monstrous Egyptian tyrant of all: uttering obscure forecasts in order to keep the Hebrews in further subjugation to his law and to ensure that the Christian revelation be later supported by reliable proofs."[67] The reference to an "Egyptian tyrant" is meant to echo the exodus of

63. Ibid., 55–72.
64. Ibid., 56.
65. Ibid.
66. Ibid., 59.
67. Ibid., 60.

Hebrew slaves from pharaonic Egypt. At the same time, he implies the view that the Jewish kabbalah originated in Egypt, thus assimilating it to the early modern view that the Hermetica preserved ancient Egyptian monotheism as a Gentile precursor of Christian Trinitarianism—the view espoused by Ralph Cudworth. Again we have the problem that Milbank neglects to tell us that he has early modern Anglican precedents for his stance—John Marsham and John Spencer, who gained notoriety for denying the Mosaic authorship of the Pentateuch as they advanced the theory that Israelite religion was Egyptian in origin.[68] Many treatises were written in response by confessionally orthodox theologians, perhaps the most important being the Dutch Reformed theologian Herman Witsius.[69] Naturally, a key problem would have been the elision of the Abrahamic origin of the Israelites for the Egyptophile scholars. Given that Milbank never mentions Abraham in his work, all this leads us to ask whether he thinks the Hebrews were actually from Canaan originally, or whether they were really Egyptians. Analogously, the same problem arises with regard to his view of Jesus. Was he Israelite or was he a Gentile?

Milbank's thinking has an important affinity with Egypt that none of his critics have spotted, an affinity that has clear resonance with his Masonic sympathies. Readers of Milbank's work rarely pay attention to an early piece he wrote with Alison Milbank on their visit to a Coptic Orthodox church with a group from Westcott House. This was published in 1980 in *Sobornost*.[70] It provides a vista into his thinking as it shows a desire to side with the Coptic revival against "encroaching Christendoms." The ingredients of the revival that most impressed the Milbanks are narrative, myth, ritual practices, miracles of a certain kind, and "community": all good postliberal tropes. They side with the Copts in a vision of a counter-Christendom that isn't like any of the others. Presumably these include the Chalcedonian episcopally-governed churches, such as the Church of England and its extension, the global Anglican communion, as well as Presbyterians and evangelicals. The Copts are the true Egyptians in their own eyes. One cannot help but see, in Milbank's later work, an echo of this in his writing on Anglo-Catholicism, England, and Europe: the hint as to who is a true Anglican, a true Englishman, a true European. This quasi-essentialism is essentially nostalgic and fantastical, looking to

68. On John Spencer, see Assmann, *Moses the Egyptian*, 56f.

69. Witsius, *The Question, was Moses the Author of the Pentateuch, Answered in the Affirmative*.

70. Milbank and Milbank, "A Visit to the Coptic Orthodox Church," 57–64.

the past, despite loud protestations in favor of Vico's critique of national mythologies. The reactionary character of the Milbanks' siding with the Copts comes out in the fact that they disdain their myth that Coptic was the original language, but eagerly accept as prophetic truth the story that during the Yom Kippur War of 1973, a Bible was seen floating down the Nile opened at a page saying "Out of Egypt have I called my Son" (Matt 2). If it is not clear whether Milbank thinks the Hebrews were originally from Canaan, typologically we must ask whether he thinks Jesus was from Israel. For he does claim later on that Jesus' birth-place is uncertain, in face of the evangelists' testimony that he was born in Bethlehem, Judea. Egypt symbolizes in positive terms a land of natural wisdom, cosmic learning, and cultural achievement; yet in negative terms it symbolizes a culture of sorcery, magic, and idolatry, which restricts the nation. Concrete Egypt, of course, is a nation that is no more or less equal before God than concrete Israel. The problem with Milbank is that he does not reach these distinctions. He simply plays concrete Egypt off concrete Israel. The real problem with Milbank's entire project is that it is born of reaction against the more Hebraic strand in Christianity, at a socio-political level first and foremost, and dressing this up with theology. Does Milbank think Jesus was born in Egypt? Does his belief that the *Hermetica* were written in the first century A.D. conceal a belief that the Gospel accounts of Jesus were modeled on Hermes Trismegistus, and that Jesus was Egyptian? Actually, Milbank's poetry evidences fascination with a Cornish myth that Jesus came as a child to Cornwall, so to England. Both as a prelude to inquiring further into Milbank's theology and in order to set our understanding of his attitude to social theory on a surer footing, we need to look at how he approaches England and Britain.

Most of Milbank's readers have taken *Theology and Social Theory* to be the key to his work in some sense. In reality, the essays written before that book are the key to understanding him. He has collected many of these in the anthology *The Future of Love: Essays in Political Theology.*[71] Three essays focus on the Christian socialist tradition in Britain, mainly in the Church of England, and two others on Samuel Taylor Coleridge and Matthew Arnold. Milbank's essay on Coleridge is highly illuminating as an interpretation of Coleridge in its own right, but also very helpful for reading his own subsequent work.[72] It finds kinship in Andrew Shanks' idea of a transconfessional priesthood of all intellectuals, also based on

---

71. Milbank, *The Future of Love.*

72. Milbank, "Divine *Logos* and Human Communication," 3–24.

Coleridge, but aimed at the Anglican bishops and the clerics of non-Christian religions who would join a reformed, multi-religious House of Lords in London.[73] I shall return to this affinity in the concluding chapter. Milbank reads in tandem three of Coleridge's prose works, the *Lectures on Revealed Religion, The Friend,* and *Lay Sermons.* The first and earliest of these works will concern me here. Milbank approves of Coleridge's claim that there is a class of inspired people—poets, prophets, philosophers, and legislators—whose roles coincided perfectly only in antiquity, and whose role has been perennially to produce and transmit culture. This inspired class knows the original "real language" of concrete symbols of all humanity, which is derived from nature. The Hebrews (Milbank never calls them Jews or Israelites) also knew this language. God directly granted them their political constitution, according to Coleridge, though Milbank only refers to the Law of Jubilee, the law of tithes, the distribution of land, and the injunction against idols as protecting the people against bloodthirsty gods. He doesn't specify why these are singled out as God-given. What I have shown from Milbank's subsequent work supplies the key to understanding why he singles these out. God, for Milbank, is closely identified with the workings of nature, etc., hence why the original language is the language of nature—an early modern Rosicrucian and "Christian Kabbalist" idea, found in thinkers such as Francis Mercury Van Helmont and Leibniz.[74] What this really means is that the theology of the kabbalah is taken to be the original, primordial, natural religion. Given that God is identified with nature, it should come as no surprise that the Law of Jubilees is singled out from Leviticus, for it follows the "natural" cycle of periods of seven years, a type of the seven days of the week, part of the sequence of months, that is, phases of the moon. The law of tithes is also connected to a naturalist ethic, as is the distribution of land, for private property is seen by Coleridge as original sin. It is important to note that marriage is *not* among the divine institutions. This fits well with the *Poimandres,* the first of the Hermetic texts in Greek, which posits an original androgyne or hermaphrodite, and which implies that the "fall" of humans was constituted by the splitting of the seven hermaphrodite offspring of the original hermaphrodite into males and females.[75] This goes with the view of private property, and therefore inheritance, as original

73. Shanks, *The Other Calling.*

74. Coudert, *The Impact of the Kabbalah in the Seventeenth Century;* Coudert, *Leibniz and the Kabbalah.*

75. For this, see the *Poimandres,* the first of the Hermetic treatises, in Copenhaver, *Hermetica,* 1–7.

sin, which was espoused by Coleridge. The ban on bloodthirsty gods links
back to Milbank's complaint against William Warburton's view of God
as "a bloodthirsty Egyptian tyrant." This really is the imputation that
Jewish monotheism was an invention modeled on Akhenaten's strict
monotheism.[76] Milbank agrees with Coleridge that the prophetic class was
unique in Israel in that they were the initiators, so that there was always a
"culture" in Israel. This is the Renaissance Neoplatonist view that the
initiators of culture are *prisci philosophici*—Shanks' priesthood of all
intellectuals, which he glosses as the order of Melchizedek.[77] Elsewhere,
prophecy was "an achievement of civilization." Prophecy and history
are near-identical for Milbank as for Coleridge, such that the Bible is
considered to be esoteric writing, fictive in the sense of aiming to create
history. Once again, a psychic mind-over-matter view of language is just
beneath the surface. This is fascinating and almost ironic because it echoes
the frequent critique of millenarians as aiming to fulfill prophecy and
"make history" by supporting the creation of modern Israel, "speeding the
Second Coming," etc. Milbank reads belief in Israel in prophecy as part of
a metaphysical trajectory passing from Scotus to Hobbes and so on. This
debate is clearly inconclusive, resting both on entrenched metaphysical
assumptions and a refusal to accept a hierarchy of multiple fulfillments
of prophetic texts, a hermeneutic for which there are ample precedents
in the western Christian tradition. What I want to do here is to push the
discussion forward to show how Milbank's thinking on the Bible, derived
partly from Coleridge, relates to his thinking on England and Britain.

Milbank is very much an English romantic theologian. He has put
his concern for England in a more prominent part of his theology than
Rowan Williams put his concern for Wales in his. He is happy to express
and articulate an identity through allusion, rhetoric, argument, and
poetry. This style is hardly unique, but as he himself notes, it isn't to
everyone's taste. Milbank, like Williams, has also published several
volumes of poetry. These collections shed light on the prose theology,
putting it in more representative and emblematic mode. Milbank's understanding of England, and of Britain as a whole, shines out in *The Legend of
Death: Two Poetic Sequences*, and it is to this, the second of his volumes that
I turn. The first poetic sequence is entitled "On the Diagonal—Metaphysical Landscapes." Milbank lists eight diagonals: culture, the preternatural,
religion, synaesthesia, onomatopoeia, the imagination, spatio-temporal

---

76. Assmann, *Of God and Gods*, 31, 47, 64–68, 81–82, 85–88.
77. Shanks, *The Other Calling*, 1, 3, 14, 20f., 200.

synthesis, and justice.[78] On culture, he says that the surface of the earth is constituted by a "thin crust of organic matter and [a] still thinner crust of the spirit."[79] The "proper work" of human beings is to "perfect nature, to bring it to its aesthetic consummation."[80] This basically characterizes human existence as the Great Work of alchemy.[81] The goal of all religion is a "super-real," "a mattering that is, indeed, also matter."[82] Human beings are to help realize "God," which is also nature. In the poem "Cosmos," Milbank writes of the earth as "our only one and all."[83] This may allude to the Spinozist controversy in the German Enlightenment, where Lessing promoted the slogan *hen kai pan*—one and all.[84] The second poetic sequence, *The Legend of Death*, also furnishes interesting material. Milbank says that "the Christian 'final sacrifice,' which puts an end to sacrifice, is seen as a higher return of a 'saturnian age' of star rather than sun cult, which was a time before the arrival of sacrificial practices in the age of agriculture and the domestication of animal prey."[85] This echoes the classical pagan idea of the Golden Age being the age of Saturn or Chronos.[86] The problem, however, is that this idea of astrology as the original religion is basically antithetical to orthodox Christianity. It is an esoteric or occult idea, and it meshes well with a crypto-polytheism. It is important to realize that historians of astrology tend to show that astrology originated in Babylon, which in the Bible is always the empire opposed to Israel in God's purposes.[87] Indeed, we should recall that astrology and star-worship accompanied the cult of the Golden Calf (Baal or Dionysius), which angered Moses.

The poetic sequence moves geographically from Britanny to Cornwall to other parts of England. The very description Milbank gives of the sequence evidences a complete disregard for Wales. He selects Britanny as the place where (Christian) exiles from "the pagan Saxons" fled, yet claims "many nobles returned" from there to "the old

---

78. Milbank, *The Legend of Death*, 2.

79. Ibid.

80. Ibid.

81. On the history of alchemy, see Maxwell-Stuart, *The Chemical Choir*.

82. Milbank, *The Legend of Death*, 3.

83. Milbank, "Cosmos," in ibid., 82.

84. On Lessing's pantheism, see G. E. Lessing, *Lessing's Theological Writings*, 46–47.

85. Milbank, *The Legend of Death*, 131.

86. See for example Virgil's *Eclogues* and *Georgics*.

87. See Swerdlow (ed.), *Ancient Astronomy and Celestial Divination*.

domain with the Normans," and even that they brought back "much of the corpus of Arthurian myth."[88] The problem with this is that the Arthurian narratives were already preserved in medieval Welsh literature, from an allusion in the seventh-century poem *Y Gododdin* to the ninth-century *Annales Cambriae*, the *Historia Brittonum*, the Black Book of Carmarthen, and "Culhwch ac Olwen" in the *Mabinogion*, only to be later hijacked and manipulated out of recognition by Edward I.[89] Milbank's lack of acknowledgment of this fact militates against his claim to be writing about British origins. He claims the Celts lapsed into paganism when the Angles, Saxons, and Jutes came, but neglects to say this was only true in England, *not in Wales*.[90] He completely ignores the well-attested history of the monks who came from France to Wales, thence to Ireland, Scotland, and finally England, in between the fifth and seventh century.[91] Moving from Land's End north-eastwards, Milbank claimed to invoke "the unique Cornish myth about the journey of the Christ-child to this peninsula."[92] Now this is very telling—because it maps the flight to Egypt onto England, and provides a bridge between Christian Hermeticism and the romantic Masonic view of Celtic religion and Anglo-Saxon "democracy." Milbank acknowledges his poetic interest with Richard Wagner's fascination with the grail cycle and the ring cycle in the medieval Arthurian legends and the Prose Edda.[93] He even suggests that the Germanic high god Woden "may become a kenotic, suffering figure."[94] Again, here is the idea of a Gentile mythical god as prophetic prefiguring of Jesus Christ, an idea derived from the Hermetica, but tacitly rejected by Saint Paul. The Prose Edda, importantly, excludes ancient Israel from its history of the origins of nations.[95] Surely here we have the antique precursor of modern neo-pagan Germanic attempts to get rid of the Old Testament from the biblical canon and the church, and its gradual replacement by Germanic sagas in many

88. Milbank, *The Legend of Death*, 132.

89. On Arthur as historical figure, see Alcock, *Arthur's Britain*. On Arthur in the Welsh literary tradition, see Bromwich, Jarman, and Roberts (eds.), *The Arthur of the Welsh*. On Edward I hijacking the Arthurian stories, see Biddle with Badham, *King Arthur's Round Table*.

90. Milbank, *The Legend of Death*, 132.

91. On this, see Henken, *Traditions of the Welsh Saints*.

92. Milbank, *The Legend of Death*, 132.

93. Ibid., 131–33.

94. Ibid., 133, 172–75.

95. For the genealogy of the Scandinavian peoples, see Snorri Sturluson, *The Prose Edda*, 3–8.

churches in the run-up to the Nazi era.[96] Nobody reading Milbank has any excuse at all to ignore the depth of the problem.

RADICAL ORTHODOXY? TIME FOR DISCERNMENT

Given these misgivings, the time has come to ask, how Christian is Milbank's theology? What led me to ask the question of this section title was simple: does Milbank believe, with the creeds of the Christian churches, that Jesus Christ was raised from the tomb on the third day after his death, his sacrifice once for all on the cross, and in the final resurrection of all people at the second coming of Jesus Christ? When I read through his publications in chronological order once again, I could not find concrete evidence that he does—quite to the contrary, in fact. Most people who have heard of Milbank first did so when *Theology and Social Theory* was published in 1990. Consequently, critical comments on his work tend to start from this book, and to assume without question that the "theology" in the title is that of the Nicene Creed, indeed all the great creeds and confessions shared by all orthodox Christians. While the criticisms of Milbank by philosophers have often been sharper than those produced by theologians, both theologians and philosophers have on the whole neglected the evidence that his early work prior to *Theology and Social Theory* furnishes for understanding his theological thought. Having investigated some of what he has written in relation to culture, we now turn briefly to a chronological overview of his writing on Christian doctrine. The material is remarkably sparse, for in reality, he has concentrated his energies on philosophical and linguistic questions, rather than prioritizing dogmatics.

The earliest article written by Milbank is from 1979, written on Nicholas of Cusa, the fifteenth-century conciliarist theologian.[97] The three main themes are the simplicity of the spirit of the mind-body unity, Jesus' victory at the crucifixion as the culmination of the *via negativa*, revealing the futility of the human search for truth, and the "triumph of the spirit." Here we have not only a suspicious echo of the gnostic idea of the divine spark in each person, via the claim that each person's spirit is simple (contradicting the classical and Thomist idea that only God is simple), but with that a modalist tendency with regard to the Trinity, as

96. Heschel, *The Aryan Jesus,* 44.

97. Milbank, "Man as Creative and Historical Being in the Theology of Nicholas of Cusa," 245–57.

if the Spirit merely followed on from Jesus' expiration at death. Milbank never discusses what Nicholas of Cusa says about Jesus' resurrection. With hindsight, this proves to be important. In the late 1980s, Milbank penned a number of articles focusing on England and Britain, forging a critique of Thatcherism. In "The Body by Love Possessed: Christianity and Late Capitalism in Britain," capitalism is declared to be a Christian heresy, whereas Marxism is the ally of Christian orthodoxy (as defined by Milbank).[98] Here we have a God/Mammon contrast that pervades his entire work, making it appear to be properly biblically rooted. The next year, Milbank published "Divine Logos and Human Communication: A Recuperation of Coleridge," which was discussed above. It is important to realize that what motivated Coleridge to move from unitarianism to Trinitarianism was his search for a critique of liberalism. Hermetism, which was clearly important for him, would be compatible either with unitarianism (or Arianism) and with a subordinationist form of Trinitarianism. Then Milbank published "Religion, Culture, and Anarchy: The Attack on the Arnoldian Vision," exploring with great subtlety the value of Matthew Arnold's work for contemporary social criticism.[99] Then in 1989 came *Theology and Social Theory*. In it, "resurrection" is put in inverted commas, and signifies "the early church's experience of resurrection."[100] This is a realized eschatology in disguise, effectively replacing the requirement of initiation through Pentecost and baptism in the New Testament. In 1991, Milbank published "Postmodern Critical Augustinianism: A Short *Summa* in Forty-Two Responses to Unasked Questions."[101] That Milbank chose to give precisely forty-two "responses to unasked questions" (questions he never indicates in the article) is esoterically symbolic, for forty-two is the number of letters in the secret name of God according to kabbalistic tradition.[102] (What it signifies cryptically is that Milbank's theology is pantheist.) It is also one of the symbolic numbers of the Beast in the book of Revelation. Point 26 runs as follows:

98. Milbank, "The Body By Love Possessed," 75–112.

99. Milbank, "Religion, Culture and Anarchy," 25–35.

100. Milbank, *Theology and Social Theory*, 132, 162.

101. Milbank, "Postmodern Critical Augustinianism," 337–51.

102. The great medieval kabbalist Abraham Abulafia considered that the forty-two-lettered divine name supposed to be concealed within the first forty-two Hebrew letters of Genesis 1, mentioned as lost by Nachmanides, to have been recovered. See Idel, *Kabbalah in Italy, 1280–1510*, 65.

Resurrection is no proof of divinity, nor a kind of vindication of Jesus' mission. And no very good "evidence" survives, only the record of some strongly insisted-upon personal testimonies. What we have is the memory of communion, of "ordinary" conversation, of eating and drinking, continuing beyond death. Without this element, there could not really be a memory of a moment of "perfect" community, for this is normally inhibited by the forces of nature as we know them, and by death especially.[103]

The last supper involved only men. The women were the first to see Jesus once he was raised from the dead. Privileging the memory of the male disciples over the "strongly insisted-upon personal testimonies" is deliberately selective and arguably misogynistic. It insinuates that the women's testimonies are fantasies, produced by wilfulness—or perhaps "voluntarism"—the loaded term used by male modernity critics such as Milbank to attack lay and nonconformist movements, which often allowed women to minister! It inverts exactly the implication of the Gospels, which is that the male disciples stubbornly refused to accept by faith the testimonies of the women to having seen the risen Jesus bodily. Their scorn for evangelical Pietism clearly derived in no small part from resentment of the place women had in the movement, not to mention the suppressed envy that intellectuals can have towards those who have a simple and direct faith.

Milbank's language on resurrection in relation to death is slippery. For example, in his response to Helmut Peukert, he says that "resurrection, as its intimate link with the eucharist shows, is *not* the return of a 'present' subject to whom justice can again, or after all be done, but rather the manifestation of remembered and narrated life, of life 'shed' in time as self-giving to the other, as after all 'real' life beyond the possibility of death."[104] Here life, not blood, is shed for us. This switch is crucial, because if it is Jesus' life not his blood that is the main subject of the verb "shed," then the wounds on Jesus' resurrection body are unimportant. It is *not* clear whether Milbank is using "life" as a synonym for "blood" or not. On page 139 Milbank does say that "the resurrection of Christ, still bearing the marks of his death, exposes this death as in reality the completeness of the divine-human person." What exactly does Milbank think the marks of Christ's death are? More importantly, what exactly does he mean by "the

103. Milbank, "Postmodern Critical Augustinianism," 346.
104. Milbank, "A Critique of the Theology of Right," 18.

resurrection of Christ"? It turns out that the answer to these questions is anything but straightforward. In "The Name of Jesus," Milbank argues that Luke's passion narrative requires Jesus to be a resister to Roman rule, that is, a revolutionary.[105] The idea of Jesus as revolutionary originated with the German deist Hermann Samuel Reimarus, whose *Ramen der Geschichte Jesu* were published posthumously by Lessing, a well-known Masonic philosopher and playwright.[106] It is important here that theologians who characterize Jesus as a revolutionary leader almost never cast him as a zealot (i.e., a Jewish nationalist), but as the instigator of some sort of wider revolutionary. Of course, in the hands of Lessing and others, Jesus could be cast as a role-model for Masonic social and spiritual revolutionaries. More recently, it is not hard to see kinship with ideas of Jesus as a proto-communist revolutionary, which would definitely make him anti-nationalist. As Reimarus was also the originator of the "Quest for the Historical Jesus," it is important that Milbank assumes two "stories of Jesus" in the canonical Gospels, the first the "apparently 'historical' tale" of the life of Jesus, the second a commentary or "metanarrative" on this story.[107] His understanding of Luke's writing is that he wanted to avoid portraying Jesus as "suicidally courting death at the hands of his enemies." In narrative terms, it is a major clue that Milbank doesn't believe Jesus was raised from the dead. Indeed, he characterizes the Gospel accounts as "drastic textual alchemy," reinterpreting Jesus' death as a sign of "life and victory," and at the same time that "Christianity itself is this recoding."[108] Jesus himself is merely designated as the founder, not the ruler of the new city, the new Israel that is the church. Apparently, we are empowered by Jesus to "continue atonement" through linguistic and ritual practices. In an inversion of language, traditional objective theories of atonement and sacrifice are dismissed as "esoteric," examples of "doctrinal propositionalism."[109] We should note here the deliberate use of the term "esoteric" against orthodox Christian doctrine, signaling thereby an attack upon the tradition of orthodox Christian criticisms of esoteric types of biblical hermeneutics and theology. What this amounts to is a bizarrely entirely visible ecclesiology, which of course suits Anglicanism perfectly. Yet Jesus is said to "arrive simultaneously with the Church,"

---

105. Milbank, "The Name of Jesus," 139.

106. Lessing, *Lessing's Theological Writings*, 9–29.

107. Milbank, "The Name of Jesus," 146.

108. Ibid.

109. Ibid., 148.

and concomitantly, "the resurrection" will not be until "the eschaton." Jesus' body will only be united with other bodies "with the cancellation of physical death," yet at the same time, "united bodies are the resurrection," "the making of words effective and life-giving."[110] This sounds as if the existing empirical church *is* "the resurrection body of Jesus" for Milbank. Analogously, he reinterprets the symbol of Chalcedon as follows. Jesus' "physical individuality, consciousness, will, etc., were fully and purely human." The "divine personhood" only functions as a "propositional belief" *if* it is also understood as "a pragmatic instruction to go on re-narrating and re-realizing 'Christ.'"[111] Christian worshippers bestow upon God, upon Jesus Christ, his divinity. There is no temporal distinction between Jesus' first coming and his return. Jesus Christ has arrived "only in terms of his final, eschatological arrival which is yet to come."[112] Frederick Christian Bauerschmidt has overlooked these massive problems of Milbank's Christology in his review of *The Word Made Strange*.[113] He thinks Milbank veers towards docetism and even monophysitism in his critical response to Hans Frei's Christology. Although he notes the priority of the ecclesial body to Jesus' "natural" body for Milbank, he misses the processual understanding of Christ's divinity as the backdrop to this, and the ultimately Hermetic origin to it. Given that "the resurrection of Jesus" for Milbank does not mean what it means on a plain reading of the New Testament, but that it refers only figuratively to the growth and extension of the church through history, it is reasonable to ask what he means when he says in the foregoing chapter that "the resurrection of Christ, still bearing the marks of his death, exposes the death as in reality the completeness of the divine-human person."[114] Meister Eckhardt made out the suffering of Christians to be "divine," a mark of living "in Christ."[115] It isn't impossible that for Milbank, "the marks of Christ's death" born by "the resurrection of Christ" really only refers to the "suffering" of Christians. Bauerschmidt notes the rather startling claim that Christ "opens himself out to re-crucifixion" in his "historical, Eucharistic giving," accusing Milbank of conflating two modes of Christ's real presence

110. Ibid., 152.

111. Ibid., 157.

112. Ibid., 159.

113. Frederick Christian Bauerschmidt, "The Word Made Speculative?" 417–32.

114. Milbank, "A Christological Poetics," 139.

115. Milbank evidences fondness for Eckhardt in the Preface to the second edition of *Theology and Social Theory*, xxvi–xxx.

in Catholic theology.[116] Nevertheless, he misses the deeper problem here, which is that Milbank believes that Christ's sacrifice is repeated at each eucharist. This means Christ is *re-crucified* at each eucharist, and must mean Christ is reincarnated also. We need to ask whether beneath this perpetuation of Christ's sacrifice there is logical opening to holding Jesus to be a reincarnated person, because in some esoteric traditions, Jesus is at times considered a reincarnation of Hermes Trismegistus, also considered to be Enoch, and ultimately, of Adam.[117] Such a view typically goes hand in hand with a belief in the transmigration of souls—the "revolution of souls" believed by the Cambridge Platonist Henry More.[118] The question is, are there traces of this in Milbank's work?

In "Can Morality Be Christian?" (1995), Milbank contrasts "five marks of morality" (reaction, sacrifice, complicity with death, scarcity, and generality) with "five notes of Christianity" (gift, end of sacrifice, resurrection, plenitude, and confidence).[119] Again, his treatment of resurrection is entirely subjective. Murder is wrong for Christians because "it repeats the Satanic founding act of instituting death, or the very possibility of irreplaceability, and absolute loss."[120] Murder is "not wrong because it removes something irreplaceable," that is, a unique human life. The origin of death is the origin of the fact of an individual life being ir-replaceable. Of course, it makes no sense to suppose that an individual life is truly replaceable, for the intrinsic meaning of an individual is that it is unique and irreplaceable. What this really means is that Milbank believes that the reality or idea that each person's life is unique and ir-replaceable was originated by *Satan*, not God; that it came in at a cer-tain point at or after the fall. Before then, human lives were presumably not only immortal but replaceable. Why? Because Milbank believes in a Neoplatonist cosmology of correspondences, where everything is replace-able with everything else. The transmigration of souls was a Neoplatonist belief. One body is replaceable, from a soul's point of view, by another, in a series. Behind this lies the kabbalistic idea of *Adam Kadmon*, the "plas-tic" hermaphrodite mythical ancestor. For Milbank "resurrection cancels death . . . and ruins any possibility of a moral order" that presupposes the

116. Bauerschmidt, "The Word Made Speculative."

117. On Jesus as a reincarnated being in Sethian Gnosticism, see Stroumsa, *Another Seed*, 96.

118. Almond, *Heaven and Hell in Seventeenth-Century England*.

119. Milbank, "Can Morality Be Christian?" 219.

120. Ibid., 229.

absoluteness of death.[121] Many readers will have assumed by this, Milbank only argues that resurrection means Christians must not kill and must not adhere to any sort of Just War Theory. In reality, there is an esoteric meaning to Milbank's words here. First, if the absoluteness of death is on the same par as the idea of individual uniqueness and irreplaceability, resurrection—which, remember, for Milbank, is the "experience of Christ in our lives"—is noetic, involving our acceptance that through language and ritual the divine spark in each of us, the conscience, is being reintegrated into the unfolding process of the cosmic Christ, the second Adam Kadmon. Second, this ruins any possibility of thinking in terms of death as our final enemy. Death is not necessarily one's gateway to hell, and the real reason is a secret adherence to reincarnation. When Milbank says in the resurrection there is only "natural law," life, the meaning is cryptic. For Milbank, humans were originally immortal, but their bodies became mortal due to the fall, or, in accordance with Hermetic lore, they acquired (sexed) bodies at the fall. The problem here is that we are not told how many souls there originally were at creation. What was the fall exactly for Milbank? Was it a fall on earth, or a fall *to* earth from heaven, as the Cappadocians and Origen believed? The latter idea is also found in the Hermetic corpus. The latter set of ideas makes it possible to believe that the fall involved physical death, for the reason that souls became united with animal bodies at a particular point in evolution.

We turn finally to Milbank's attitude to Christ's sacrifice on the cross. He asserts that "in dying, as God, [Christ] already receives back from us, through the Holy Spirit which elevates us into the life of the Trinity, our counter-gift of recognition."[122] Milbank denies that we should read Hebrews on Jesus Christ having made a one, all-sufficient sacrifice plainly; he says this is to read it "over-literally and naively."[123] For Milbank, Christ passes into "the heavenly sanctuary as both priest and victim." His earthly self-giving death is

> but a shadow of the true eternal peaceful process in the heavenly tabernacle, and redemption consists in Christ's transition from shadow to reality—which is also, mysteriously, his "return" to cosmic omnipresence and irradiating of the shadows (Hebrews 9: the middle Platonic element here is essential). . . . [T]he

---

121. Ibid. 229.

122. Milbank, *Being Reconciled*, 100.

123. Ibid.

> heavenly altar that is purified is, for the author of the *Epistle to the Hebrews*, the psychic realm: "your conscience."[124]

This is microcosm-macrocosm cosmology. The individual subtly replaces Christ and/or is identical with him ontologically. Christ enters into the heavenly sanctuary, the heavenly tabernacle, at his death, according to Milbank. As this is really a metaphor for the conscience of individuals, this really means that Christ is broken and diffused into the lives of all people—a sort of Gnostic divine spark. In a nod to those who would connect theology to ethics, he argues that to be ethical is to believe in the resurrection, and somehow to participate in it. Indeed, "outside this belief and participation there is, quite simply, no 'ethical' whatsoever."[125]

What does the letter to the Hebrews in its entirety teach about Jesus Christ's sacrifice? Hebrews 9:11 says that "through the greater and more perfect tabernacle (not made with hands, that is, not of this creation) he entered once for all into the Holy Place." The heavenly tabernacle is what is being referred to. It is "not of this creation," not made with human hands. He took "his own blood" into "the Holy Place." Milbank does not account for this. He ignores the shedding of Christ's blood. Does Milbank believe that Jesus' blood was actually shed on the cross or not? Does he actually believe that the Roman soldiers wounded Jesus? Does he actually believe that Jesus was crowned with a crown of thorns? If the sacrifice of Jesus Christ in the heavenly tabernacle is not once for all, how can it be a new covenant? If the heavenly sanctuary simply is the individual conscience and not the eternal realm, then Milbank's theology is pantheist. It means that the phrase that Christ entered "into heaven itself, now to appear in the presence of God on our behalf" is meaningless, for "God" is only considered to live already within the individual. Hebrews then goes on explicitly to say:

> Nor was it to offer himself repeatedly, as the high priest enters the Holy Place yearly with blood not his own; for then he would have had to suffer repeatedly since the foundation of the world. But as it is, he has appeared once for all at the end of the age to put away sin by the sacrifice of himself. And just as it is appointed for men to die once, and after that comes judgment, so Christ, having been offered once to bear the sins of many, will appear a second time, not to deal with sin but to save those who are eagerly waiting for him. (Heb 9: 25–28)

124. Ibid.
125. Ibid., 148.

This is crucial because it actually rules out the very kind of Christology espoused by Louis Claude de Saint-Martin, one of Milbank's conservative Masonic role-models. In reality, Saint-Martin's Christology is the closest analogue to Milbank's, yet so far, critics have not realized this. For Saint-Martin, the sacrifice of Christ fulfills the history of blood sacrifice of "reparators" of the fallen human condition in the pagan religions since the dawn of history. Only transformed humanity as a whole can and will complete Christ's work of reintegrating all beings. Indeed, by imitating him, "men of desire" can by the "gift of the Spirit" go beyond Christ in sanctifying the cosmos through their suffering.

Precisely what the implications are for those readers of Milbank who have assumed his "theology" to be Christian are as follows. Can their co-option of his social ideas, his genealogy of "social theory," and his own constructive work continue to be used even though its avowedly esoteric and counterfeit nature has been shown? There have been a number of criticisms of his genealogy of "violence," but none have suggested that it may conceal a nostalgia for the rule of the Latin Kingdom of Jerusalem by the Knights Templar. Perhaps people might feel silly writing about this, perhaps afraid of being stigmatized as "conspiracy theorists." Yet we are not talking here about whether or not there are still "Knights Templar" around today, secretly pulling the strings of history. We are not concerned with such occult "alternative history." We are simply concerned with one person's ideas about the medieval past. If anybody has spotted the suppressed nostalgia, one suspects that this perception may have been quietly shelved, in no small part due to the recent campaign to demonstrate that the actual medieval Knights Templar were not apostates from Christian orthodoxy. This campaign gained publicity and sought to argue that despite having confessed heterodox beliefs and repugnant practices, those Templars who did so in the early fourteenth century did so under torture and therefore were not to be believed. An alternative apology has been that these confessions were truthful, but that the verbal apostasy and repugnant practices were insincere, and were in fact inculcated in the Templar initiation rites as means of concealing their Christian orthodoxy from prospective Islamic captors.[126] Personally, I find the latter explanation disingenuous, clearly protesting too much. It is fascinating here that Milbank's own attitudes concur much more with the kind that the Templars confessed under torture than with the Christian orthodoxy that was that of the medieval Latin church. This may help us understand

126. Frale, "The Chinon Chart," 109–34.

one of his more bizarre arguments, made in *Being Reconciled*, namely that "watching violence" is "more violent" than actually committing it.[127] This argument is made explicitly in reference to our attitude to previous generations' actions. The Templarist nostalgia may be the real reason why Milbank favors eighteenth-century French (and Scottish) Masonic counter-revolutionary theosophists. For it is they, in particular Andrew Michael Ramsay (David Hume's patron, no less), who invented the idea that the Knights Templar were forerunners of the Freemasons.[128] This ran parallel to the idea that the Essenes were earlier forerunners of the Freemasons, and that Jesus was initiated into their sect, invented by the eighteenth-century German Freemason, Johann Georg Wachter, but having precedents among the Counter-Reformation Carmelites.[129] When Milbank talks about the need to think of the continuation of the incarnation, and the collective but never individual "Resurrection Body of Christ," we need to ask whether he is possibly lamenting the interruption of Templar beliefs by the fall of the Latin Kingdom of Jerusalem, in a similar manner to lamenting the withdrawal of Britain from the Palestinian Mandate in 1947. In an article in the Australian media in 2010, he asserted that Islam had taken a "dangerous" non-mystical and political turn in the wake of the "premature collapse of the western colonial empires."[130] The entire logic of his thinking, however, suggests that a similar attitude towards Jews and Judaism would fit with this statement, for Milbank clearly privileges the kabbalistic tradition within Judaism as more authentic. Thus, British imperial rule over the Holy Land is implied to have been necessary to reform Islam, and perhaps also Judaism, and to keep them "mystical." (It is perhaps not an accident that Freemasonry, which has freely borrowed and reinterpreted choice ideas and practices from both Sufism and Kabbalism, has a long history within the British armed forces and elites.) Do the events of 1947–48 represent the incursion of the "ontology of violence" in the history of the Holy Land and the world for him? Ultimately, this whole preoccupation with "an ontology of violence" is highly questionable. It has the capacity to become an idol, to become more important than truthfulness. It is a target for resentment, regret, nostalgia, and scapegoating. The problem with it, as with the populist campaign to exonerate the Knights

127. Milbank, *Being Reconciled*, 28, 37–43.

128. On Andrew Michael Ramsay, see Milbank, "Hume versus Kant: Faith, Reason and Feeling," 276–97.

129. Wachter, *De primordiis Christianae religionis*.

130. Milbank, "Christianity, The Enlightenment and Islam."

Templar of apostasy, is that it puts nonviolence above every other value, above all truthfulness and the public character of knowledge, a value stressed by all great theologians in the actual Augustinian tradition, and by non-esoteric philosophers from Thomas Reid to Jürgen Habermas.

CONCLUSION: IN PRAISE OF SCOTTISH DUNCES

If Milbank's negative approach to "social theory" is linked to a resentful attitude to orthodox Christian theology and to the state as it has developed since the middle ages, the negative approach to political forms of Jewish thought and Israel needs to be understood logically as part of this. In this respect, it is especially important to recall the observation made by Alain Touraine, that "sociology in France has been almost completely Jewish—and in the United States too."[131] At first glance, Milbank's rejection of Peter Berger's sociology of religion, and his call for a renewed Trinitarian doctrine of participation, together with his argument that "only theology overcomes metaphysics," might lead us to assume that he doesn't think Christianity (as he sees it) can be made "plausible" by any external means. Yet now that we have deciphered the story that is the backbone of *Theology and Social Theory*, and of his entire theology, we see it is the story of the decline of a "Christendom" in the Holy Land since the fall of the Latin Kingdom of Jerusalem and the disbanding of the Knights Templar. If this is what made Milbank's version of Christian theology and Christendom increasingly invisible and thus implausible, it follows that reinstating it somehow would make it visible and plausible again. The question is, what or who is the obstacle to this happening? The answer is not hard to find: the State of Israel and the Palestinian Authority— Jewish and Arab national independence from European Christendom, be it Byzantine, Catholic, or British imperial rule. Israel, for Milbank, is the latest instantiation of "the ontology of violence," which "rebelled" against "Catholic Christendom," and nearer to our time, the British Empire's Mandate over Palestine (1917–48). Thus the plot of Milbank's project can be interpreted somewhat parodically as follows.

Once, there was no nationalism. There was peace, love, and understanding—and justice. The entire known world was under the sway of the Pope and the Holy Roman Emperor, and the Holy Land was governed by the Latin kingdom of Jerusalem, courtesy of the kings of France and the Knights Templar. Theologically, this was the world of Thomas Aquinas and Meister Eckhart. It was also the world of the Crusader kings and their castles, not the

131. Touraine, *Un désir d'histoire*, 76.

least of whom was Edward I of England. As such, it was the world in which the United Kingdom was gradually formed. Yet there was resistance to this great and noble idea of participation. First the Welsh, then the Irish, then the Scots, fiercely resisted, and under the leadership of their kings, defended their national independence, only to be defeated or to give in. Among the resisters in Scotland was none other than John Duns Scotus, whose theology and philosophy is believed to have lent itself to the wording of the Declaration of Arbroath supporting Scottish independence and a contractual theory of kingship.[132] Scotus' boldness in criticizing Thomas Aquinas' analogical theories of being and language paved the way for the wholesale desecration of theology by "social theory" in subsequent centuries, in partnership with the contractual theory of government (kingship being contractual in much of the Celtic tradition), passing through Thomas Hobbes and somehow along the way leading to American evangelicals' support for the foundation of Israel in 1948 as the fulfillment of biblical prophecy, and George W. Bush and Tony Blair leading the United States and the United Kingdom into the Second Iraq War in 2003.

Presumably, Scotus—the theological classroom dunce—is now to be blamed for Alex Salmond campaigning for greater independence for Scotland within the European Union, not forgetting to blame him for Thomas Reid's influence upon the American Declaration of Independence ("We hold these truths to be self-evident"). Naturally as the United States has always supported the project of the European Union, Duns Scotus must be considered an extremely powerful hypostasis behind world history, almost as powerful as Walter Scott was sycophantic regarding the Crown Jewels. One gets the feeling from some of Milbank's recent writing that what Israel/Palestine *really* needs is to be governed by British imperialists again. The sons of Japheth must "dwell in the tents of Shem" once more. Curiously, however, the Anglican theologian who has intruded the most with a proposal for Israel/Palestine has not been English, but Welsh: Rowan Williams. Tending the interfaith flock makes sense for one who has lauded the Cistercians in his story of Christian spirituality, for they were the parent order of the Knights Templar, as well as responsible for introducing sheep-farming to Wales.[133] Without further ado, we must pick up our reading of Williams where we left it, in Wales, and move from there to the Holy Land.

132. Broadie, "John Duns Scotus and the Idea of Independence," in Cowan (ed.), *The Wallace Book*, 77–85; Cowan, *"For Freedom Alone."*

133. Williams, *The Wound of Knowledge.*

5

Rowan Williams as Hegelian Political Theologian

Resacralizing Secular Politics

ROWAN WILLIAMS' ATTEMPT TO speak for the common good and rein in the extremes of liberal individualism is at the core of his Hegelian co-ordination of ecclesiology and political theology. His is a managerial approach, which co-ordinates his Anglican ecclesiology with a Hegelian political theology. Behind the approach of Rowan Williams lies a common liberal Anglican tradition of absorbing large tracts of Hegel's work to forge a political theology that is wedded to a liberal establishment ideology of managing not only the established Church of England and the global Anglican provinces, but also alternately co-opting and marginalizing other more orthodox Christian theologies and churches.

In this first part of a two-part essay, I shall show how Williams' political thinking was secular from his first publication on politics, a paper on Welsh devolution based on an address given in 1979. This secular approach is rooted in a theological approach that advocates divine retreat from the world. I then critically analyze Williams' reading of Hegel in the three papers he wrote in the 1990s as he climbed the Anglican episcopal ladder. Reading Hegel enables Williams to theologize his secular post-Kantian political theory. I argue that Williams strives to read Hegel in a non-esoteric style, evading the hints towards Hegel's esoteric and pagan roots found in Gillian Rose and Andrew Shanks, to whom he is indebted for his reading of Hegel. I conclude with three judgments on Williams' project by Theo Hobson, which forms the bridge to the second part of the essay.

MARGINALIZING PUBLIC SPEECH ABOUT GOD

Rowan Williams' political theology has received far less critical analysis than his ecclesiology, for understandable reasons. Nevertheless, as his political theology underwrites so much of his public discourse it is imperative that we develop a deeper understanding of its root commitments and trajectory. With the exception of comment on his 2008 lecture on Islamic law in England, hardly any of the existing secondary literature on Williams deals with his political theology.[1] An understanding of the theological ferment that produced the arguments in the 2008 lecture requires retracing our steps all the way back to Williams' first public address on a political topic, namely the first vote on devolution in his native Wales in 1979.[2] Williams commends the Anglo-Catholic political theorist J. N. Figgis' construal of the state as "community of communities" as a way of understanding Wales as a nation, in the sense of its being a stateless nation, having lost its state due to being conquered by King Edward I in 1282.[3] Thus he both echoes and rejects Jones' idea that the nation is a people and thus a "society of societies," with "the state as one societal structure among others in a nation's life," an idea that enables Jones to argue for Wales as a distinct nation that should be granted political and legal expression.[4] Williams slips from describing the state as "community of communities" to saying that it is "like other societies" that associate in a legal federation. Consequently, "the freedom of national communities is a matter comparable to the freedom of a church, a union or a charitable trust."[5] This simply makes no sense at all of the very old Welsh sense of nationhood, or the very old Scottish, English, or Irish sense of nationhood, for that matter. It also avoids the implication of a theological defense of popular sovereignty from the Protestant (or the Catholic) side; an idea that would open up debates about the relationship of Anglican establishment to models of sovereignty. Equally troubling, especially from a theological standpoint, is the purely empirical and visible

---

1. Higton provides a descriptive introduction in Higton, *Difficult Gospel,* 112–34. The only other piece on political theology that could relate to concerns about civil society is Russell, "Dispossession and Negotiation," 85–114.

2. Williams, "Mankind, Nation, State" in Ballard and Jones (eds.), *This Land and This People,* 119–25.

3. Ibid., 121–22, citing Figgis, *Churches in the Modern State,* 54–93.

4. Jones, "Christian Nationalism," in Ballard and Jones (eds.), *This Land and This People,* 87.

5. Ibid.

definition of church invoked. There is a deep irony here, in that Williams was baptized a Congregationalist but converted to Anglo-Catholicism as a teenager, and is debating with Jones who was Wales' most eminent Reformed theologian, also a minister in the Union of Welsh Independents, the Welsh-speaking Congregationalist denomination. The Congregationalist ecclesiology of the gathered church is frequently alluded to in cryptic terms in Anglican polemic as "voluntarist," even though it is profoundly Puritan and has a strong notion of the invisibility of the true church as the creature of the Trinity. Williams' purely visible notion of church cannot help but be voluntarist insofar as it is compared to a charitable trust or other secular communities. The total lack of Trinitarian mooring for the church here means that baptism as the sign of inclusion is ignored. The fact that Williams slides between stateless nation as society and stateless nation as community is one thing, but the completely non-theological foundation of the concept of community (which in any case originated in classical sociology, and thus was bound to be purely empirical), would prove troublesome in his 2008 lecture on Islamic law in England as well. In subsequent work, the ambiguity over community is revealed to be also an ambiguity over baptism, as evidenced from his 1986 essay "Trinity and Revelation," in which he argues that the confession of the lordship of Christ "generates a communal life increasingly distinct from other contemporary options," which assumes that Christian commitment starts off as somehow simply being "a community" in general.[6] Pastoral controversies over issues such as "baptismal policy in secularised areas . . . are essential stages in the 'hermeneutical spiral' whereby the significance of Jesus, the *divinity* (the decisive generative quality) of Jesus, is recovered." What is significant about the questions Williams asks of the two types of baptismal policy is that he frames them in wholly secular terms about belonging in or exclusion from "community."[7] By 1990 it is difficult to see why he thinks baptism matters, as he advocates Raimundo Pannikar's Trinitarian theology of religious pluralism, assuming in the process that the object of interfaith dialogue is "the discovery of how the Christian can intelligibly and constructively unite with the Buddhist or Muslim in the construction of the community of God's children."[8] Traditional theological reasoning—that only Christians who are baptized, whether as

6. Williams, "Trinity and Revelation," reprinted in Williams, *On Christian Theology*, 144.

7. Ibid., 143–44.

8. Williams, "Trinity and Puralism," reprinted in Williams, *On Christian Theology*, 178.

infants or as confessors, are "children of God"—is replaced here by the implication that members of all religions (but not all people regardless of religion) are children of God.

Returning to the 1979 lecture, Williams argues that God has created the world as "an integral network of agencies (at the personal and sub-personal level) with its own 'good,' its own principle of welfare or survival."[9] This means that "the life of 'grace' is . . . the dimension in which the whole world and the whole of history is differently apprehended, newly structured by the imagination of faith, by Bonhoeffer's *disciplina arcana*."[10] He approvingly cites Simone Weil's dictum that "God has abandoned it." This divinely-given freedom for the world "to be the world," much celebrated in the secular theology of the 1960s, means that "the explicit referral of political, aesthetic or economic questions to the express will of God rests upon a misunderstanding."[11] Williams would subtly modify his denial of public speech about God in his 1989 essay "Postmodern Theology and the Judgment of the World," where he writes:

> There may be a "naked public square," but, before the churches rush into it, they have to ask whether the space opened up is genuinely a *public* one, or is simply the void defined by a system that can carry on perfectly well in the short term with this nakedness.[12]

This is an important about-turn, because in 1979 Williams took the view that politics can manage perfectly well on secular presuppositions. What really happened in the intervening decade is that Williams selected only internationalist topics (apartheid and nuclear weapons) for Christian engagement and critique. Wales specifically, and Britain more broadly, received little comment apart from a piece on Scotland written for the newly opened "Centre for Theology and Public Issues" at Edinburgh University.[13] The final problem with the 1979 essay is that Williams makes

9. Williams, "Mankind, Nation, State," in Ballard and Jones (eds.), *This Land and This People*, 123.

10. Ibid.

11. Ibid.

12. Williams, "Postmodern Theology and the Judgment of the World," reprinted as "The Judgment of the World" in Williams, *On Christian Theology*, 35.

13. See Williams, "Violence and the Gospel in South Africa," 503–13; Williams with Collier, *Peacemaking Theology*; Williams, *Star Wars: Safeguard or Threat?*; Williams, "Nobody Knows Who I Am till the Judgment Morning," in Honore (ed.), *Trevor Huddleston*, 135–51; Williams, "The Ethics of SDI," in Bauckham and Elford (eds.), *Nuclear Weapons Debate*, 162–74; Williams, "Christian Resources for the

the arbitrary claim that the question "why liberty and equality should be seen as social goods" is metaphysical, whereas the question of how they are to be achieved and whether society is preventing this, is not.[14] This not only undercuts the possibilities of Christian political engagement, but also undercuts the possibilities of Christian critique of politics from other theologians. How Williams would permit himself—but not others—to overcome this chasm, was through forging an apophatic Hegelian political theology.

THE NON-ESOTERIC READING OF HEGEL

There are three major essays in which Williams handles and appropriates themes in Hegel's philosophical theology. They are "Between Politics and Metaphysics: Reflections in the Wake of Gillian Rose" (1991), "Hegel and the Gods of Postmodernity" (1992), and "Logic and Spirit in Hegel" (1998).[15] These span his time as Anglican Bishop of Monmouth (he was elected to the see in 1991 and consecrated in 1992, and appointed Archbishop of Canterbury in 2002). In an interview with his biographer Rupert Shortt, Williams acknowledged his indebtedness to both the late Gillian Rose, secular Jewish philosopher who was baptized into the Church of England on her deathbed, and his friend Andrew Shanks, Canon Theologian of Manchester Cathedral, in returning to read Hegel as a political theologian, having been put off by Russian Orthodox readings of him.[16] His complaint was that these tended to assume that people could say whatever they wanted using Hegel. In his 1991 essay on Gillian Rose, taking up her reading of Hegel, Williams wants to retrieve metaphysics in a way that "doesn't immediately descend into the quagmires of fantasy," but, unfortunately, doesn't explain what constitutes fantasy metaphysics.[17] His foil however is postmodernist "post-realism," by which general metaphysical inquiry has been marginalized, in which is advocated a merely negative theology of "absences, blanks and pauses in the exchange, unthematisable

---

Renewal of Vision," in Elliott and Swanson (eds.), *Renewal of Social Vision*, 2–7. Note the deployment of the managerial language of "resources," by which Williams now permits himself to use choice concepts from beneath the surface of the tradition of Christian political theology to manage public engagement.

14. Williams, "Mankind, Nation, State," 124.

15. I use the versions reprinted in Higton (ed.), *Wrestling with Angels*.

16. Shortt, *God's Advocates*, 16–17.

17. Williams, "Between Politics and Metaphysics," 53f.

and alien to will and reflection." The twofold ethical upshot of this state of affairs is that, first, humanity is believed to be purely "constructed and enacted in speech"—speech that is "without privilege, in the sense that it is not amenable to closure or stasis." No discourse holds an objective authority, it is implied, so no perspective exists that enables controlling linguistic "exchange." The result is akin to the confusion of languages after Babel.[18] The second problem is that people aspire to "a non-historical freedom" (i.e., absolute individualism) and cease to ask questions about the power imbalances involved in argument. Thus social reality is envisaged not as "negotiation" (what Williams hopes for) but "coexistence of projects" (live and let live, without close and continuous dialogue and mutual confrontation).

We can recognize this state of affairs as the picture given by conservative and radical Marxist critics of the liberal human rights paradigm. Williams formulates a response to this static situation, based on construing human sociality as fundamentally dynamic insofar as individuals are brought out of their social solipsism into negotiation for the common good. In conversational terms, "my desire and project redefines or rethinks itself in symbiosis with others." Therefore, argues Williams, "a practice in which the presence of scarcity ceases to be simply an occasion of 'war' is avoided." The (social) environment comes to be perceptible as "one of potential abundance."

It is striking how reminiscent this picture is to eighteenth-century Social Contract theories, in assuming as a baseline humans as individuals who opt into civil society. It is likely it also draws on the pluralist political theory of J. N. Figgis. It is already slipping into the metaphysical fantasy and evasion of investigating power imbalances in the social fabric, which Williams decried earlier. Possibly aware of this problem, he asks "is this, then, simply a plea for philosophy to produce a transcendental ground for political options already determined?" He proffers the view that "classical metaphysics arises from the impulse to look for a ground in the discussion of justice and injustice in political affairs."[19] What he has in mind is Plato's *Republic*, the construction of "a city in speech," which has "mathematical, moral and aesthetic conditions of judgment" (the true, the good, and the beautiful). He doesn't want us to worry about the metaphysical status of "the structures Plato believes he has uncovered" (i.e. the forms).

18. Ibid. 55. "After Babel" is my gloss on Williams, echoing Jeffrey Stout's study, *Ethics After Babel*. This makes sense of Williams' espousal of the postliberal reading of the later Wittgenstein's argument that religions are like languages.

19. Williams, "Between Politics and Metaphysics," 56.

Apparently, it doesn't matter that "a parallel world of occult objects exercising an eccentric variation of ordinary worldly causality" has been found. Rather, a discourse has been articulated "that is confidently about something other than casual states of affairs."[20] This is an incredibly brazen way of thinking—any old metaphysics will do, just so long as we are confident about it!

Much scholarship through history has been devoted to arguing that Plato's philosophy had an esoteric side too. This is evident from Plato's astrological beliefs, displayed in *Timaeus* 41 D-E, where the number of stars is correlated by the demiurge to the number of souls. Before birth, each soul chose a life, and this choice was validated by the Fates.[21] Each soul then went to sleep and fell down Creation through the planetary spheres to be born in a body. This kind of belief was common in pagan antiquity and made its way into Gnostic currents that shadowed early Christianity. In addition, Plato set store by the astronomical-astrological concept of the Great Year in his thinking on providence, a concept that returned to Western culture at the Renaissance, and more recently with the New Age movement. There is now plenty of scholarship on the history of astrology that shows it persisted and was championed by many Christian clergy through history, with only the Puritans, evangelicals, and Jesuits opposing it in early modern Britain, while the high Anglicans, to whom Williams looks back, were deeply involved in astrology.[22] What was at stake included rival theologies of providence and politics. The Puritans looked to the final salvation of the Jews, and to the return of the Jews to Israel, as well as increasingly to religious toleration. The Laudian Anglicans and their Calvinist counterparts on the other hand, clung to establishment and religious repression. It is worth pointing out here that early on in his career, Rowan Williams published two sets of poems along with friends as part of a group called Gemini Poets, so-called because all were born under the astrological sign of Gemini.[23] The money was donated to the Christian Movement for Peace. Did this constitute a realist belief in astrology of some kind, or was it the kind of poetic and psychological flirtation indulged in by C. S. Lewis in writing the Narnia Chronicles?[24] We might never know, but Williams' cavalier "don't bother

---

20. Ibid.

21. Maxwell-Stuart, *Astrology*, 24–25.

22. Thomas, *Religion and the Decline of Magic.*

23. Williams (ed.), *The Gemini Poets.*

24. Lewis was deeply nostalgic for the cosmology of correspondences between the

with inquiring into Plato's metaphysics" looks rather suspicious in light of his poetry. When we correlate this to his non-esoteric reading of Hegel, we may infer that flirting with astrology did involve pulling back from serious metaphysical questions about providence and divine judgment over nations. This somewhat corrects the view of Vincent Lloyd that Williams focuses his theological recovery of Rose on metaphysics not ethics.[25] Williams in reality uses the *idea* of metaphysics to talk about a spiritual and political dispossession as the root of ethics.

Having dismissed potentially troublesome questions about Platonic metaphysics, Williams's states his central thesis, which is that human existence is characterized as work or production.[26] (Apart from the oddity of coming from an apophatic theologian and thus sidelining contemplation, this claim isn't developed out of biblical exegesis, e.g., the *problem* of work in being enveloped under a curse, in Genesis.) This involves production of something that is either needed or receivable for someone else. He thinks this applies to "the entire range of communicative activity from cookery to philosophy to mysticism."[27] This categorization of activities that tend to be conducted by individuals is significant, because by the end of the essay, it appears that what preoccupies Williams, and why he reads Hegel through Gillian Rose, is the production of some sort of political ideas and entities, possibly institutions of various kinds—definitely not things that are produced by individuals. Here we must realize that the metaphor of production employed for politics is intelligible as a substitute for the older notion of craft (as in "statecraft"). Richard Sennett's elegant exploration of the centrality of craftsmanship to life conveys some of what Williams wants to convey, but with greater perspicuity, for Sennett admits that the metaphor is used to claim that we make ourselves.[28] It is at this point that Williams introduces the idea that production, specifically when it "issues in the changing of the environment, material or conceptual or imaginative," involves accepting conventions "outside the power of the producing agent."[29] This sounds

stars and planets and human personalities, which had been swept aside by the Calvinist Reformation. Ward, *Planet Narnia*.

25. Lloyd, "The Secular Faith of Rose," 705. Lloyd himself reads Rose as developing a kind of virtue ethics, but doesn't want to read her work as an apologetic "in advance" for a christological reading of "the Broken Middle."

26. Williams, "Between Politics and Metaphysics," 57–58.

27. Ibid., 58.

28. Sennett, *The Craftsman*.

29. Williams, "Between Politics and Metaphysics," 58.

rather too obvious to need to be said, but might need to be said given that he appears to have started off from civil society being a collection of individuals and their "projects." The likely reason for introducing conventions is he wants to condition the reader to be willing to accept the concept of theological tradition standing behind modern political theories. Keeping in mind that he hasn't specified what kind of product is imagined, he worries that the product may be thought of as "intelligible in entire abstraction from the condition of its production (including the motivation of the producer). The problem with this is "it ceases to be either risky for the producer or difficult for the interpreter."[30] The "otherness" of the work therefore hovers uneasily between "the ineffability of the (quasi-) sacred" and "the reflexivity of something that can be conscripted in to the projects of the interpreter." He takes up Gillian Rose's Hegelian critique of modern social theories because she plunges into the heart of this problem.

If we conceive of nations as works or products in the sense that Williams describes, we can perceive the theological limits of his approach. Some nations, usually strong ones that have imperial pasts, tend to conceive of themselves as almost eternal, simply "being." England is one of the best examples in the world of this self-presentation, and its national religion, liberal Anglicanism, likewise. The temptation of idolizing "the ineffability of the quasi-sacred" is an apt description here, long predating postmodern negative theology, reposing instead in the subdued but confident mood of the English "stiff upper lip" and its connotations of cultural and class hierarchy.[31] Again, as Hegel sought to create a metaphysics for Germany (which wasn't yet a nation-state in his day), Williams appropriates Hegel in an essay in 2009 to imply a rather uneasy metaphysical assumption of the United Kingdom centered on England.[32] It does mean that Matheson Russell's concurrence with Williams that he is more "internationalist" than Hegel himself needs qualification.[33] Russell admits that this stems from Williams' use of Hegel's kenoticism for ecclesiology

---

30. Ibid., 59.

31. It is significant that the popular song "There'll Always Be an England" was written and published by Ross Parker in the summer of 1939, at the eve of the Second World War. Such claims to the eternity of a nation tend to be made when it feels itself threatened. A defence of the stiff upper lip style of Englishness (as if it constituted the essence of English culture) is found in Scruton, *England: An Elegy.*

32. Williams, "This Scepter'd Isle: Culture and Power in an Offshore Setting," 145–53.

33. Russell, "Dispossession and Negotiation," 104–5.

rather than politics. Of course, the fuzzy boundary between church and civil society, and church and state, originates partly from Hegel's deliberate "speculative" conjoining of church and state, suits the quite peculiar political and legal foundation for the establishment of Church of England with the English monarch as its "supreme governor," and is perpetrated by both Williams and Russell ignoring Hegel's denial of Jesus' resurrection, ascension, and return. Instead church and state are held together as a necessary tension that is required, so to speak, to expose "illusions of peace," which Russell glosses as "the illusion that peace is found in disengagement and passivity."[34] Noting that for Williams this tension is the condition for the possibility of "movement," which is "life," and by a leap of faith, "kenotic movement is divine life," Russell complains that eschatological hope and rest become unintelligible as a result. His complaint is too anthropocentric as it centers upon a need for an end to tension, and his citation of Revelation without prior attention to biblical narrative comes too late to rescue him from that possibility. Attending further to eschatology here would be to run ahead of the argument, so for now, let us stay with the use of Gillian Rose.

Rose argues that we learn about each other through recognizing that we falsely perceive each other, and that learning involves reimagining and reconceiving the self.[35] This constitutes encountering "the violence" that is alleged to be inevitably involved in our relation both towards others and towards ourselves.'[36] Paraphrasing Rose, Williams makes the following claim:

> In reality, love is always found to be involved in violence, and the attempted reversions to a beginning or an end free from violence found in writers like Thomas Mann or René Girard in fact condemn the human agent to the alternatives of an *agape* beyond structures and negotiations or a conflict without

34. Ibid., 106.

35. The best introductions to Rose's work are the interview conducted with her by Vincent Lloyd, 201–18, and her autobiographical volume *Love's Work*; Caygill (ed.), "The Final Notebooks of Rose," 6–18; and Rose, *Paradiso*. These display her work without too much theological commentary, whereas Shanks and Giles Fraser give a theological interpretation of her, which was only possible after her death, immediately preceded by baptism into the Church of England. There is, therefore, the danger of reading her as if her theologization by such figures as Shanks, Williams, and John Milbank, were both a foregone conclusion and theologically warranted. See Shanks, *Against Innocence*.

36. Williams, "Between Politics and Metaphysics," 60.

containment. Love and violence are both involved in law—that is to say, in strategy and social form."[37]

This claim shows traces of the absorption of Darwinism by liberal Anglicans around the same time as they absorbed Hegel. Thus it illuminates Williams' silence on work as a problem in the Genesis narratives. In addition, the definition of law as "strategy and social form" is very Hegelian and reminiscent of Hegel's attack on natural law theory in the non-Trinitarian versions of Kant and Fichte.[38] Williams approvingly cites Rose's reading of Kierkegaard's "suspension of the ethical" as a "protest against 'the essentialising of violence.'"[39] Instead, "violence is only to be thought of as the risk entailed in power." The phrase "the essentialising of violence" suggests that violence has become an essence in the metaphysical sense, almost primordial. Alternatively it may denote the elevation of violence to a necessity and its placing at the apex of a hierarchy of values.

To understand the interconnection with Hegel, we need to return with Williams to the coming together of individual makers learning to work according to existing customs and, by implication, traditions. For Williams, "thinking is ineluctably a pattern of self-displacement."[40] Thus he asks Hegel's question, "how, historically, we come to think of thinking in the framework of disposession," answering that "this requires a history that can be told as the narrative of the absolute's self-loss and self-recovery," which Hegel reads as the Judeo-Christian narrative. What makes this possible is the historical covenant of God with the Jewish people and with humanity in Jesus Christ. Disposession is instanced when "Israel's identity becomes bound up with exile, Jesus' identity with the cross, and the Church (in some of its more primitive self-reflection) with the imagery of the 'resident alien.'"[41] Williams says no more doctrinally than this. This is highly significant because Hegel favored Jewish assimilation into German society, rather than Zionism, and disbelieved in Jesus' resurrection, ascension, and second coming.[42] He substituted a Boehmean pansophic apocalyptic for the elements of Joachim of Fiore's apocalyptic, which involved the final conversion of the Jews and their return to Israel. Hegel's repudiation of Zionism matters for the rest of this chapter, be-

37. Ibid., 61–62.

38. Hegel, *Natural Law*.

39. Williams, "Between Politics and Metaphysics," 64.

40. Ibid., 71.

41. Ibid., 72.

42. Tomasoni, *Modernity and the Final Aim of History*, 107–58.

cause Gillian Rose ends up parting from him in this respect. For now, it is important that Williams concludes that Hegel's reading does not assume that Christian doctrine specifies a particular metaphysical structure. This is untenable as a reading of Hegel, who reinterpreted the Christian story to fit his esoteric metaphysics and theology. It is to this problem we now turn.

HEGEL'S ESOTERIC ONTOTHEOLOGY

Hegel's philosophical theology is both Hermetic and Rosicrucian at heart, according to recent scholarship published by Glenn Alexander Magee.[43] Rowan Williams ignores the extensive and profound rootedness of the theology that underwrites Hegel's program in the esoteric traditions of Hermeticism, magic, alchemy, and Kabbalah. This is also a serious failing of Matheson Russell's critique of Williams (written long after Magee's book was published), who claims that "Williams' insistence on giving full weight to the theology underlying Hegel's philosophical system mirrors a general trend in recent Hegel scholarship," which follows the work of Peter C. Hodgson, Robert M. Wallace, and Andrew Shanks.[44] Neither Williams nor Russell mention the work of scholars who have read Hegel as an ontotheologian and contributed towards uncovering these roots, such as Eric Voegelin, Claude Bruaire, Albert Chapelle, Walter Jaeschke, Emil Fackenheim, Glenn Alexander Magee, and Cyril O'Regan.[45] To be sure, Williams does not read Hegel in a non-metaphysical way, as Klaus Hartmann and others have done.[46] Rather, Hegel's theology is appropriated in a disenchanted de-esotericized form. This is highly convenient for established Anglicanism because it mediates between Williams' own attempt to assimilate Hegel to more orthodox forms of theology, or slightly more "enchanted" versions of Anglo-Catholic theology such as that of John Milbank, and "secular" non-metaphysical or anti-ontotheological readings that still persist outside the church. My concern here is not to pursue a blanket anti-esoteric agenda, but to draw attention to the fact that Hegel's profound indebtedness to important strands of these traditions

43. Magee, *Hegel and the Hermetic Tradition*.

44. Russell, "Dispossession and Negotiation," 91, n. 20.

45. Voegelin, "On Hegel," in Voegelin, *Published Essays 1966–1985*; Bruaire, *Logique et religion chrétienne dans la philosophie de Hegel*; Chapelle, *Hegel et la religion*; Jaeschke, "Speculative and Anthropological Criticism of Religion," 345–64; Fackenheim, *The Religious Dimension of Hegel's Thought*; Magee, *Hegel and the Hermetic Tradition*; O'Regan, *The Heterodox Hegel*.

46. Hartmann, "Hegel: A Non-Metaphysical View," in MacIntyre (ed.), *Hegel*.

raises some serious questions as to the appropriateness of his work for a Christian ethic and political theology such as developed by Williams.[47] Methodologically this is because Christian ethics and political theology are by nature non-esoteric in the sense of being in principle public and open about its sources and methods. Substantively, it is because Hermeticism is founded on a fictitious account of Hermes Trismegistus being a Gentile prophetic type of Jesus Christ and supposedly teaching the Trinity better than the Bible.[48] This is called into question by Paul's warning to the Ephesian church that the gospel of the incarnation was never previously communicated to Gentile nations.[49] Finally, Hermeticism was also important in underwriting both Islamic and Arian esotericism and alchemy in premodernity.[50] Renarrating Christianity through utilizing them as Hegel does could well lead to acceptance of varieties of unitarianism, and exclusion of Trinitarian theologies, which do not incorporate these esoteric traditions.

There is a twofold problem with Hegel: first, his denial of the classical view of creation as good, of the fall, Jesus' resurrection, ascension, and second coming, and his concomitant denial of immortality, the general resurrection, and last judgment.[51] Second, Magee characterizes his entire system as a Hermetic initiation and progression, starting with the *Phenomenology of Spirit*.[52] This constitutes an initiation rite in which the mind is raised above the sensory and mundane to prepare it to receive wisdom. Second, the *Encyclopaedia of the Philosophical Sciences* corresponds to the Hermetic ascent to the Absolute. Third, the *Science of Logic* constitutes

47. The Western esoteric traditions have been explored by the theologically-minded at various times as a means of aiding cosmology, not the least because of their fittingness with Neoplatonism. Frequently, the type of political theory allied to a Neoplatonist cosmology is the hierarchical one involving the idea of a "great chain of being." Lovejoy, *The Great Chain of Being*.

48. Fowden, *The Egyptian Hermes*.

49. Eph 3:1–6.

50. On the migration of Hermeticism from Graeco-Roman Egypt to Persian culture and then Arabic learning, see Van Bladel, *The Arabic Hermes*. The most famous espousal of Arianism in relation to a particular reading of Hermeticism, specifically the Emerald Table, is Sir Isaac Newton. See Dobbs, *The Janus Face of Genius*.

51. O'Regan's work analyses each moment of Hegel's "swerves," as he puts it, from Christian orthodoxy, with unsurpassed depth and breadth. He diagnoses Hegel's heterodoxy as indebted not only to an imaginative renarration using select reading of sources such as Eckhardt and Joachim of Fiore, but also to the profound influence of Jacob Boehme's theosophy on Swabian Pietism, and detects important affinities therein with Valentinian Gnosticism.

52. Magee, *Hegel and the Hermetic Tradition*, 257.

Hegel's ontotheology, encompassing the Kabbalah of Isaac Luria (Magee does not say that it has been removed from its mooring in biblical Hebrew), and influences from Jacob Boehme and Raymond Lull. The *Logic* is important for the doctrine of creation, because it uncovers the divine mind before creation. God—for Hegel, as for Hermeticism—is incomplete, and he must know himself in order to complete himself. This entails seeing himself reflected in an Other. Hence a speculative doctrine of the Trinity can be constructed. Fourth, the *Philosophy of Nature* envisages the world as mirroring God, and the world is full of "intelligible anticipations of Spirit." The writings for the fifth stage are the *Philosophy of Spirit*, the *Philosophy of Right*, the *Philosophy of World History* and the lectures on "the three moments of Absolute Spirit," which are art, religion, and philosophy. These set forth the "return" of creation to God through humanity. (This is why defenders of Hegel can say against postmodernists that there is no "return to the same" in his program. Theologically, this somewhat misses the point, given the heretical doctrine of God that is assumed.) It is humans who bring about the actualization of God through what Magee terms "progressively more adequate embodiments": first, in institutions and practices of all kinds (which correspond to Williams' productions of human labor); second, in culture, that is to say art and religion (which also correspond to Williams' human productions); and third, in Hegel's own system of speculative philosophy, which he says *is* "the Word made flesh." (Would Williams be comfortable with admitting such a poietic role to theology?) Magee observes that Hermes Trismegistus appeared in early German Freemasonic rituals that would have been familiar to Hegel, as he was very sympathetic to Freemasonry in his youth, though there is no surviving evidence that he was initiated into a lodge.[53] This may be because he found Freemasonry to be politically too liberal. This would fit with his later sympathy for Rosicrucianism and its defense of church establishment.[54] As Magee argues, in Frances Yates' terms, Hegel *was* a "Rosicrucian."[55] How would this relate to Hegel's heretical approach to the biblical narrative witnessing to Jesus Christ? Cyril O'Regan has produced the deepest and broadest analysis of Hegel's theology and its mystical esoteric roots to date. While not quite agreeing with Hans Küng, Eberhard Jüngel, James Yerkes, and Emilio Brito's judgment, that Hegel's Christology is the key to his ontotheological enterprise, he follows them in

53. Ibid., 53.
54. Ibid., 248–57.
55. Ibid., 254.

bringing it back from the margins to the structural core of Hegel's theology, noting that it constitutes one of its earliest components.[56] Hegel is apparently "impatient with the Chalcedonian definition" (though O'Regan misleadingly dubs him a "monophysite" thus eccentrically assimilating him to Coptic theology!), and proclaims that the "Christ of faith" must surpass "the historical Jesus."[57] If we return this to the *Phenomenology of Spirit*, dubbed an initiation rite by Magee, we discover that Christianity is the *culmination* of natural religion, and Hegel has the ancient Greek cult of Dionysius in mind as its anticipation—very similar to the idea of Hermes Trismegistus as a Gentile type of Christ.[58] It is important then that by the time he delivered the third portion of the *Lectures on the Philosophy of Religion*, Hegel focuses on Jesus' teaching as "a defining feature of his unique individuality," characterizing it as a polemic "subverting the established ethical order" and heralding the kingdom of God.[59] Crucially, it is this world only that is the horizon of Jesus' teaching. It is logical therefore that Hegel rejects both Jesus' resurrection and by implication the general resurrection. O'Regan is too generous to Hegel in arguing his motive for this was "dissatisfaction with the empirical-rationalist advocacy of the resurrection appearances and the phenomenon of the empty tomb."[60] Philosophically this links to the fact that Hegel only values "the truths of reason," following Lessing.[61] A more likely motive for Hegel's denial of the resurrection and its sequelae would be his Rosicrucian affinities. In the late eighteenth century, Freemasonry had incorporated elements of Rosicrucianism by creating the 18th Degree of the Rose Croix. Its initiation ritual commemorates the death of Jesus on the cross as a Masonic "brother," but is silent on his resurrection, ascension, and return.[62] This ritual of course is open only to men who have already been initiated into the lower pagan degrees (Rose Croix is deemed a "Christian" degree open only to men who profess faith in the Trinity). This makes sense of Hegel's ecclesiology, or his notion of the spiritual community. He denies both the satisfaction and sacrificial theories of atonement.[63] The

---

56. O'Regan, *The Heterodox Hegel*, 189–234.

57. Ibid., 191.

58. Ibid., 193.

59. Ibid., 204.

60. Ibid., 213.

61. Lessing, *Lessing's Theological Writings*.

62. Jackson, *Rose Croix*.

63. O'Regan, *The Heterodox Hegel*, 207–8.

spiritual life therefore is constituted by mystical union with the Absolute, the acceptance of one's sonship vis-à-vis God, and the transformation of the profane by the sacred. Hegel believes Lutheranism succeeds and Catholicism fails here. (It is not irrelevant that the Papacy had banned Catholics from belonging to Masonic lodges back in 1738.) While Hegel wants to say that the mystical body is "a democracy of spirit," this is not a "free church ecclesiology" in the sense of the Puritan or Pietist divines.[64] This is because he also recommends an exoteric public religious hierarchy, with sacraments and an "ethical form of life," and an esoteric core in which philosophers are an isolated caste of priests.[65] There is a special regard for mystics who have ascended from the realm of representation to that of pure thought. What this really means is that Hegel allows for and even encourages a heretical Rosicrucian, quasi-Arian core of priests and theologians to the established churches, who manage and control the orthodox Trinitarian lower clergy and laity.

LIBERAL ANGLICAN HEGELIANISM: BETWEEN DIONYSIAN RELIGION AND NEGATIVE THEOLOGY

All of this presents major problems for Williams' continued absorption of Hegel, problems that, as we are seeing, he prefers to ignore. This is at the peril of the integrity of his political theology as properly Christian. To understand the depth of this problem, we turn to Andrew Shanks' reading of Hegel, which has influenced Williams deeply. Shanks wants to keep Karl Barth's Trinitarian radical critique of natural theology, due to its being validated as critique of Nazi ideology, but he also wants to use Hegel to defend Anglicanism as civil religion, against Barth's repudiation of such a thing.[66]

Shanks reads Hegel through Gillian Rose.[67] He approves of how Rose "systematically identifies the highest wisdom with the virtues of the good, mediating peace negotiator," hence the title of her book *The Broken Middle*.[68] His biblical warrant for this is Paul's claim that he has

---

64. Ibid., 248.

65. Ibid.

66. Shanks, *Civil Society, Civil Religion*, 69.

67. Two clear overviews of Rose's work by philosophers who haven't Christianized her prematurely are Caygill, "The Broken Hegel," 19–27, and the touching obituary by Wolf, "The Tragedy of Rose," 481–88.

68. Shanks, *Against Innocence*, 32; Rose, *The Broken Middle*.

become "all things to all people" (1 Cor 9:22). Yet Paul was speaking missiologically here, about making the gospel intelligible, not about reconciling opposing ethical or religious standpoints. According to Shanks, Rose wants her ideal negotiator to be all things "quite literally 'to all people,' all those whom one ever encounters."[69] This literal-mindedness is frankly neurotic and if applied either to Christology or to Christian individuals, destroys any understanding of their nature. Importantly, Shanks describes this as joining Hegel's "bacchanalian revel of Spirit," which he elsewhere identifies as the Speculative Good Friday.[70] This appeals to Shanks because "Hegel's metaphor is meant to conjure up the sheer impossibility of ever genuinely fixing spiritual truth into any sober, settled form of correctness," as if this were Paul's primary concern (or Jesus', for that matter). He claims that Pontius Pilate's crime against Jesus, authorizing his murder, is "the denial of the broken middle." This is difficult to substantiate because as a rationalization of the crucifixion, it raises a number of questions. First, can a mythological figure such as Dionysius (or Hermes Trismegistus for that matter) legitimately be read as a Gentile prophetic type of Jesus Christ similar to how the historical figures of the Old Testament have been read in Christian exegesis?[71] Second, if the answer is "yes," does this not mean that the death of *any* man (or woman) can equally well function as representing "the broken middle" in and for a particular society? And if so, does this not go some way to explaining not only the logic of scapegoating but also the logic of human sacrifice in so many pagan religions? In relation to ancient Israel, why did *Jesus* have to die if he was a type of Dionysius? Jesus was a type of the sacrificial lamb of the Day of Atonement, and of Isaac, whom Abraham prepared to be a passive victim but who was never slain and was never an active negotiating figure. Was Dionysius himself a "peace negotiator" in mythology? It is possible here to imagine a critique which says that not seeing Jesus in these Dionysian terms as "the good, mediating peace negotiator" amounts to an "exclusive Christology" which Shanks elsewhere deplores as "kitsch."[72]

Dionysius is necessary for Shanks' Hegelian "inclusive Christology," and his defense of established liberal Anglicanism as supposedly speaking of and for "true Christianity." It is necessary for his stigmatization of other Christologies as "exclusive" in the sense of emphasizing Jesus' particularity

---

69. Shanks, *Against Innocence*, 35.

70. Ibid., citing Hegel, *Phenomenology of Spirit*, 27.

71. On Dionysius in ancient Greek culture, see Kerényi, *Dionysos*.

72. Shanks, *Hegel's Political Theology*, 1–4.

and distinction from the rest of humanity, along with theories of penal substitutionary atonement and sacrifice.[73]

Of course, the larger question looming behind this is the evidence that the cult of Dionysius and its parallels was implicitly forbidden to ancient Israel. This would explain the paraphrasing of Euripides' *Bacchae* in the third conversion narrative of Paul in Acts.[74] Luke is implying that Dionysius is the counterfeit of Jesus Christ, a view that the church fathers would take up.[75] Those who would read this passage otherwise, as affirming Dionysius as a legitimate type of Christ, would need to explain again why Paul denies in Ephesians that the gospel had already been communicated to the Gentiles before the incarnation, as well as tackle the theological and ethical questions raised above. Thus Hegel's move from the historical Jesus to the Christ of faith becomes *necessary*, and the Athenian *polis* supersedes Israel. This accords with ignoring Paul's warning to the Ephesian church, which expressly repudiates assimilation of the Christian gospel to pagan mystery religion by saying,

> In former generations this mystery was not made known to humankind, as it has now been revealed to his holy apostles and prophets by the Spirit: that is, the Gentiles have become fellow heirs, members of the same body, and sharers in the promise in Christ Jesus through the gospel.[76]

Shanks' reading of Hegel goes deep into Hegel's pagan sources, but prefers to ignore his Rosicrucian-inspired denial of the resurrection and the consequently clear, Spirit-induced distinction between church and society, state and nations. It is clear that Shanks and Rose follow Hegel's preference for an idealized Athenian political religion glossed as a "Greek" political theology where Dionysius is a prophetic type of Christ, in opposition to the twin alternatives of Roman state religion and the religion of the beautiful soul. These are clearly stereotypes invented by Hegel to discredit Roman Catholicism and free church Protestantism respectively.[77]

---

73. Ibid., 4–15.

74. Acts 9:4, see the parallel suggested with Euripides, *Bacchae* where Bacchus/Dionysius confronts Pentheus from heaven (vv. 784–95), in Barrett, *A Critical and Exegetical Commentary on the Acts of the Apostles*, 449–50.

75. On the problem of the Alexandrian tradition relating Dionysius to Christology, see Jourdan, "Dionysos dans le Protréptique de Clément d'Alexandrie," 265–82.

76. Eph 3:5–6, NRSV.

77. Rose, *Hegel contra Sociology*, 119–28.

In "Hegel and the Gods of Postmodernity," Williams expresses a desire to construct a Hegelian type of negative theology, which would be "a moral and spiritual dispossession and recreation, inseparable from the process of a corporate making of sense."[78] He warns against "the risk of a negative theology in abstraction," saying that this gives a purchase to "a depoliticised or even anti-political aesthetic." This is important because another comment made in the 1979 lecture on Wales was that politics is like art in being an activity governed by immanent principles, and thus as we saw, "the Christian is not entitled to introduce 'God' or 'the will of God' as part of the furniture of the argument."[79] Significantly Williams has never taken up Welsh Congregationalist theologians' Hegelianism, which had been forged expressly to advance Christian socialism.[80] Two decades after this episode, Williams turned to Russian Orthodoxy to articulate what the Welsh Hegelians had attempted, an eccentric move given that Orthodoxy has never been a form of Christianity incarnated in Britain, and that its twentieth-century battles were with Communist socialism's hostility towards it![81] Thus Williams moved from sacralizing the secular to re-enchanting it, by moving towards a "Greek" political theology. Back in 1979 also, Williams delivered his Westcott House lectures on the history of Christian spirituality published as *The Wound of Knowledge*, and also published a major article on Vladimir Lossky's style of negative theology.[82] He recalls this obliquely in the 1992 Hegel article by naming Lossky as a type of Hegelian negative theology that he wishes to develop.[83] (This is ironic because he later claimed to dislike Russian Orthodox readings of Hegel.)[84] He defends his turn to Hegel as one that does not "endorse the Hegelian system in all its ambition and complexity," rather to use some themes to "undermine a sacralizing of absence and inception at the expense of the work of social meaning."[85] Apophasis was always central

78. Williams, "Hegel and the gods of Postmodernity," 30–31.

79. Williams, "Mankind, Nation, State," in Ballard and Jones (eds.), *This Land and This People*, 123.

80. On Welsh nonconformist Hegelians, see the excellently fair and perceptive diagnosis by Pope, *Seeking God's Kingdom*, passim.

81. Williams, *Sergei Bulgakov*.

82. Williams, "Lossky, the *Via Negativa* and the Foundations of Theology," 1–24.

83. Williams, "Hegel and the Gods of Postmodernity," 30–31.

84. See footnote 3. Williams says he "got very impatient with what seemed a vast edifice of speculative metaphysics, where really you could say pretty much anything you liked." This is deeply ironic.

85. Williams, "Hegel and the Gods of Postmodernity," 31.

to Williams' approach, and what we saw in the 1979 essay was a refusal to think of nationhood in relation to divine presence, absence, action, and judgment. Effectively he sacralizes the repudiation of God-talk from public Christian engagement via an apophatic approach to spirituality developed in parallel to his "post-Bonhoeffer" secular politics. Just over a decade later, Williams started to resacralize his own politics by means of Hegel, but could only do so by ignoring the huge problems with the roots of Hegelian metaphysics and stick to his narrative (a typical post-liberal move), which Williams insists, against the most accurate readings, is Christian. We are told that "Hegel's structuring narrative is, of course, that of incarnation."[86] He even goes as far as claiming that Hegel's cross is "the historical cross," in which "the negative" is understood "speculatively" as "the denial of human spirituality in oppression, suffering and death." (This already collapses the subjective appropriation of "taking up one's cross" into the historical event at Golgotha.) Beyond the cross lies the need for new conditions for thought "in which the concrete denial of spirit is overcome." This is held to be the condition for any further talk of identity. According to Williams, this is why Hegel links the cross with "the spiritual community." In "Logic and Spirit in Hegel" (1998), Williams takes up this point by citing Hegel's claim that "the reversal of consciousness beings at Calvary," made in the 1831 Lectures on the Philosophy of Religion.[87] Here is where the categories of making and violence, which he has learned from Gillian Rose, come into play again.

> The absolute difference between Spirit's reality and what is humanly constructed must be shown not only in the retreat of Spirit into the inner life (as in the preaching of Jesus) but also in the violent repudiation of this interiority by positive, *de facto* authority.[88]

This is very odd, as the Spirit cannot be said to retreat only into the inner life in the Gospel texts. Certainly Jesus breathes the Spirit onto the disciples after his resurrection, though this finds no mention in Hegel because he tacitly denied the resurrection. Yet Williams claims that for Hegel, the doctrine of the Trinity is only conceivable in terms of incarnation, crucifixion, resurrection, and Pentecost.[89] This entails understanding "what it is to think history at all," which is "the dispossession and recovery

---

86. Ibid., 32.
87. Williams, "Logic and Spirit in Hegel," 44f.
88. Williams, "Hegel and the Gods of Postmodernity," 46.
89. Ibid.

that is mental life." This sundering of the mental life from bodily life is disturbing and unwarranted from the New Testament. Williams suggests a theology of mental relating as a vestige of the immanent Trinity—the kind of analogy of being of which Barth would have been suspicious. "Our history has already told us all this, though in ways that have yet to reach full self-consciousness."[90] Psychologically, this is a curiously Jungian reading of history, leaping over the metaphysical chasm left by Freud, though fitting as Jung used similar esoteric sources to Hegel. This kind of move is specifically repudiated by Gillian Rose as offering "an alternative mysticism."[91] For Williams, nevertheless, God is "the guarantor of the thinkable and reconcilable nature of our world." The result is that "if a universally shareable, self-cognisant freedom is not possible, we had better abandon all pretence to be thinking subjects or political subjects."[92] The problem with this is that Williams has co-opted Hegel's redemption narrative, thus collapsing the distinction between church and society, or church and nation, or church and international community, and getting rid of the second coming as the symbol of Christian hope. Thus his warning that we should abandon our "pretence" if we cannot think of "a universally shareable, self-cognisant freedom," really turns out to mean that we should abandon it if we can't accept his reading of Hegel.

Williams admits in his 2001 essay "Beyond Liberalism" that he needs Hegel for his project. "Hegel understood that without a 'myth' of spirit or self-reflexivity as fundamentally a self-staking and a self-risking, politics could not happen; we should remain at the level of oppositional goods, deprived of a full account of the good that is irreducibly social and humanly universal."[93] This seems rather desperate and suggests a long-term over-reliance on Hegel at the expense of a variety of possible other sources. Basically this leaves critics of Williams with very little intellectual or political honor or dignity ascribed to them (his royal "we" notwithstanding), an unpleasant situation that evidences a dark side to his thinking. This is the managerialist subtext of Rowan Williams' theology. It is very important within our discussion of secular political theory trumping Christian political theologies and ethics, because it is precisely this kind of intolerance yoked to baptizing Hegel that is at the core of the constant stream of high-minded rhetoric about allegedly "extremist" or

90. Ibid., 47.
91. Rose, Interview with Lloyd, 217.
92. Williams, "Hegel and the Gods of Postmodernity," 50.
93. Williams, "Beyond Liberalism," 71.

"fundamentalist" religion by both scholars and clerics. This is the logic of Andrew Shanks' commendation of Hegel's "inclusive Christology" wedded in Dionysian religion, opposed to more orthodox "exclusive Christologies."

The predominantly "liberal catholic" reading of Hegel is undoubtedly at the root of this focus on philosophical theology at the expense of relating to broader currents in dogmatics, ethics, and biblical exegesis. Theo Hobson argues succinctly, and persuasively, how Williams' underlying approach to Anglican theology evidences a tacit belief in the superiority of Anglicanism over both Catholic and Protestant forms of theology on church and society.[94] He links the liberal Anglican penchant for Hegel to this, and to the project of co-ordination the church, and to England the beginning of the church as a body distinct from Papal authority. He goes on to claim that "Williams' theological project may be seen as the attempt to Christianize Hegel, or to exorcise his liberalism, and introduce an eschatological horizon." The social import of this is his belief expressed in "Logic and Spirit in Hegel" that "the ideal human society 'is adumbrated but not realized by the Church.'"[95] The first judgment is the closest to the truth, in that it understands Williams annexes features of Hegel's approach that enable theological validation of his political vision. The second needs revision, for Williams like Hegel really incorporates liberal individualism. The third judgment is more complex and Hobson doesn't follow it through. The question is, to what extent does Williams underwrite his Hegelian vision with a Christian eschatology, to make good for Hegel's eschatological deficit, and to what extent has his eschatological outlook been influenced by his annexation of Hegelian thinking. This shall be the concern of the rest of this chapter, leading into an explication of how it transforms Williams' secularized political theology set out back in 1979 into the sacralization of religious and political pluralism via Hegel. The tensions within this program will be shown to account for the arguments made in the 2008 lecture on Islamic law in England.

In his assessment of Williams as an Anglican Hegelian, Theo Hobson suggests that Williams is attempting to introduce an eschatological horizon to his Hegelian political theology.[96] Correct as this judgment is, it needs to be seen as paradoxical, for Williams' approach to eschatology is apophatic, as is his approach to creation "out of nothing." The specter of Hegel looms large over the shape and content of Williams'

---

94. Hobson, "Williams as Anglican Hegelian," 290–97.

95. Ibid., 296.

96. Ibid., 296.

thinking on these twin dogmatic poles and upon the enclosed political theology. One concrete example of Williams' program is the use of his Hegelian apophasis to manage Islamic theological-legal discourse, as evidenced in his lecture "Civil and Religious Law in England," on the subject of the recognition of Islamic law in English law, delivered at the Royal Courts of Justice in London in 2008. Williams' lecture is underpinned not only by J. N. Figgis' idea of community, but also by his Hegelian political theology learned from Gillian Rose. This brings into sharp focus the central public concern about the possibility of force being used by Shariah courts in Britain. The problem underlying Williams' work is that Figgis' notion of community is nonviolent, whereas Rose sees Judaism as a midrashic political community—one permitted to participate in the use of force. Conceiving of the Islamic community (or the Diaspora Jewish community) in Britain in this way would be unacceptable to most people. Thus I am critical of those commentators who have defended Williams as proposing a "politics of the middle" that safeguards the secular realm. Understanding the political theology that underwrites "Civil and Religious Law in England" requires understanding that its seeds were sown back in 1979, when Williams rejected traditional Reformed options in ethics and political theology, and implicitly parallel Catholic options, opting to affirm a post-Bonhoefferian notion of the secular "world come of age," as far as domestic politics was concerned. He did so using Figgis' pluralism, then co-opting this into his non-esoteric reading of Hegel through Rose and Shanks. This is intertwined with an apophatic approach to biblical exegesis. It appears that Williams is gesturing hopefully towards a similar move from Islamic scholars. To understand the theological import of this, we need to turn to his thinking on eschatology and creation.

"WORLD WITHOUT END, AMEN"

In order to dig deeper into the theological framing given for Williams' managerial approach, I turn to a theologian who is very affirmative of Williams. Mike Higton simply sets out the kernel of Williams' political thinking as being that politics is "a process of bringing all of our limited perspectives, all of our partial understandings, together in order to seek the common good that might emerge from their interaction."[97] This suggests a poietic understanding of the common good, implying that we make the political future. Higton states

97. Higton, *Difficult Gospel*, 125.

that Williams' vision of politics is a vision of future peace, contrasting this with the possessive individualism of liberal political theory and rights theory.[98] The problem with this politics-as-future-peace notion is that it ignores the picture painted by Jesus himself of the time of the church and the nations until his return. The history of nations and states is not tending towards politics as peace in any lasting, christologically based sense.

Rowan Williams' apophatic approach to eschatology, politics, and peace lend credence to the suspicion that he does not believe in the *parousia*, and therefore is not a punctiliar end to history enacted by God. This first surfaces in a 1974 essay on pneumatology.[99] Williams attempts in this early paper to develop a theology of the Holy Spirit using insights from Russian Orthodox theologians, such as Florensky, Bulgakov, Lossky, and Evdokimov. He starts with Paul's statement that God "has given us the pledge of the Spirit" (2 Cor 5:5).

> The new life which the Christian believer enjoys is nothing other than the life of the Kingdom of Heaven, the beginning of that participation in the divine nature which the 2nd Epistle of Peter describes as our final destiny. . . . If, then, we are to see the Holy Spirit is that mode of the divine presence and activity which is associated with the coming Kingdom, we may see also that He is primarily to be apprehended and experienced in the dimension of *hope*, the sense of a promise of the future which is in no sense conditioned or determined by the limits of the present and the past. Throughout the Old Testament, the theme of the "newness" of God's action is very much to the fore: the Exodus is a *new* act, it may be spoken of (as it is in the Psalms) in mythological terms of the formation of being out of chaos and conflict; again, the return from Babylon, as described in Second Isaiah, is a "*new* thing," "hidden and unknown to you, created just now, this very moment" (Is. 48: 5); and so forth. . . . History goes on, but a fresh level of God's activity has been manifested in it, and thus new levels of *human* activity have been made possible.[100]

There are hints here of the amillennial reading of 2 Peter 3:1–13, and of the founding of an account of Israel on the exodus story rather than on Abrahamic election, typical of both Liberation theology and the Hermetic tradition, which saw Moses as equivalent to Hermes

98. Ibid., 114, citing Williams and Collier, *Peacemaking Theology*, 13–24.

99. Williams, "The Spirit of the Age to Come," 613–26.

100. Ibid., 614.

Trismegistus.[101] Williams follows the eastern Orthodox theologians in opposing premillennialism.

> History goes on, and therefore we must beware of simply saying that there is some identifiable point in time at which the "present age" is supplanted by the "age to come," for this is in fact to deny the absolute newness and distinctiveness of the age to come by reducing it to one more period in a succession of periods. Paradoxically, if we say that the present age, the present world-order is to be swept away totally by the inbreaking of the new age, we are in danger of undervaluing not only the present age, but the future one too. It is too radical in that it denies any real positive value in the present except insofar as it is something which can be set over against a totally positive future; it presumes, in fact, a gulf between nature and grace which is in sharp opposition to any genuinely Christian doctrine of creation; it makes hope a thing so totally divorced from present reality, from experience and reason alike that it ceases to be a genuinely and credibly *human* phenomenon.[102]

His critique is a fairly stereotypical "Alexandrian" one, accusing premillennialism of an overly carnal eschatology. At no point are any premillennialist theologians (e.g., the majority of the ante-Nicene fathers, some early modern Anglicans) engaged in exegetical and dogmatic debate.

> And this scheme is not radical enough, because the new age which it sees coming in is essentially something on exactly the same level as what has gone before, another member of an historical *series*; grace is swallowed up in nature, hope is reduced to the mere expectation of another tomorrow, in which only the scenery and dialogue are new: the stage is the same. Such a concept of the coming age has little to do with the Christian hope, the eschatological hope: it represents a confusion of the eschatological with what Bulgakov has called the "chiliastic" plane, that set of ideas—so often disastrous in history—of "the thousand years of the reign of the saints upon the earth," an essentially finite historical utopia.[103]

What is important here is the lack of attention to the christological contents of the Christian hope—the hope of Christ's return has dropped below the horizon, almost eclipsed by a focus on human social

---

101. On Moses and Hermeticism, see Assmann, *Moses the Egyptian*, 18ff.

102. Ibid.

103. Ibid.

transformation by the Spirit. There follows a rather breathless dismissal of Montanism, Joachim of Fiore, and the ecstatic among the Spiritual Franciscans, for their division of history into the successive ages of Father, Son, and Holy Spirit. Notwithstanding the fact that the scholarly retrieval of Joachim was underway at this time, Williams goes on to claim that the "Third Age" is a feature of "the extremist groups at the time of the Reformation, in the Wars of Religion in the 17th century, among the Russian radicals of the 19th century and, of course, up to our own day in the less sophisticated varieties of Marxism, and perhaps, in some statements of the 'Death of God' theology."[104] It must be said frankly, however, that Williams is closer to the errors ascribed to these when he speaks above of the Spirit as a "mode of the divine presence"! Williams' criticism that the idea of the "new age" breaking in is "too radical" because it devalues the human and the present creation is a very poor criticism, as belief in a radical new age breaking into creation only makes sense on the assumption of divine initiative. There should be no problem theologically with divine initiative into history and creation. We must realize that Williams radically and eccentrically denies that there is to be a point in time when the "new age" begins, and that by this he seems to be denying not only the millennium (over which there has never been agreement) but the New Heavens and the New Earth. It must also be said that he doesn't concede that premillennialists also believe that after the millennium, God will usher in the New Heavens and the New Earth.

Is Williams' eschatological silence apophatic or is it tacit denial of the *parousia*? We cannot tell without knowing his mind on the general resurrection. What we can discern, though, is that his apophasis has ideological and political motivation behind it.[105] One clue to this is his attitude towards the resolution of moral debates. He does not think that contemporary Western Christian debates on homosexuality, capitalism, or nuclear deterrence will be settled by appeal to "the literal sense of Scripture."[106] Ethical divisions aren't taken to reflect the problem of disobedience to God. While it is true that he is trying to say that exegesis alone won't solve them, grouping debates over homosexuality (which seems to be referred to, at least in terms of certain actions, in the Bible) with capital-

---

104. Ibid.

105. Greg Clarke wishes Williams to speak of eschatological sabbatical rest to Muslims in his public engagement. The problem is that this isn't a serious possibility given the level of Williams' reticence about eschatology. See Clarke, "The Beauty of God in Cairo and Islamabad," 202f.

106. Williams, "The Discipline of Scripture," 57.

ism or nuclear deterrence (which are not) is not the most helpful way of clarifying the problem of scriptural sources for ethics.

What Williams does say about the future of the church and ethics is that the covenant community's history produces Christ and that this is expressed by the Chalcedonian symbol. Even if the covenant community here is Israel, the idea that it "produces Christ" is a problem given that he mentions neither the Father nor the Spirit as the sources of the Son. He concludes by stating that "we are not promised . . . a final theological resolution," which is rather consonant with the lack of acceptance of Christ's judgment upon us in his theology. Yet he famously asks that the literal sense of Scripture be reconceived as eschatological.[107] This seems to mean that acceptance of the literal sense should be deferred until the *eschaton*—but the problem here is that there is no evidence that Williams believes in the *parousia*. It is so obvious that appeal to the literal sense cannot neatly resolve Christian debate on nuclear deterrence for reasons that have little to do with exegesis, and that is because Christian debate on nuclear deterrence is unlikely to affect the relevant decision-making, partly because it has to remain secret and away from influences outside secret spheres of state. The real value of Christian debate on nuclear deterrence is in enabling Christians to organize themselves vis-a-vis the state.

The upshot of Williams' approach to ethics as well as politics and peace, is that he tends towards a monistic and uniform view of the future. There is no foreshadowing of the final eschatological judgment of Jesus at his return, and no warning of repeated apostasy, deceitful teaching, and betrayal of the faithful by wolves in sheep's clothing. Rhys Bezzant rightly argues that Williams privileges the *vision* of God over the *reign* of God, and *union* with Christ over *justification* by Christ because he opts for mystical theologies.[108] He notes that Williams lacks an understanding of "our sinful and cursed union with Adam," which corresponds to the lack of understanding of work, including theological work, as laboring under Adam's curse.[109] There is nothing either of the revelation of God's wrath and righteousness in history as a somber foretaste of the Day of the Lord.[110] What needs saying here is that all of these problems are inherent in Hegel's theology too. Indeed, another commentator in the same critical volume astutely notes how Williams tends to "Hegelianize" his favorite

107. Ibid., 58.

108. Bezzant, "The Ecclesiology of Williams," 16.

109. Ibid. 18.

110. Ibid.

theologians.[111] Greg Clarke observes that Williams opts for the beatific vision as "the least problematic expression of the Christian understanding of the future" in his 2005 address at the Islamic University in Islamabad.[112] What this means is that Williams avoids the question of the world's future ending and enables the hearer to conceive of the vision of God as attainable immediately upon death.

CREATION "OUT OF NOTHING"

So much for the End of Days, but what about their beginning? Does the doctrinal candle get burned at both ends? Clarke astutely notes that Williams is sympathetic to Rosemary Radford Ruether's criticism of the traditional Christian linear understanding of eschatology (though he would have been more accurate in pinpointing this as a view of history as a whole).[113] He expressed this concern in the fourth Eric Symes Abbott Memorial Lecture in 1989, reprinted as "On Being Creatures." It is important to note Williams in this text is attending to the doctrine of creation "out of nothing" as it has been articulated in the Latin West. He sympathizes with the view that it is to be criticized for being analogous to "historical action as heroic rupture, breaking away from the natural and timeless, a kind of imitation of the primordial rupture between nothing and something which is the authoritative word of creation."[114] Ruether's concern is a feminist one that seeks to deny that human history involved human liberation from nature. She is critical of the Hebrew understanding of creation as an understanding produced by a supposed male consciousness, contrasting this with the Babylonian and Canaanite versions ("creation is a movement of self-regulation within a single continuum, 'the matrix of chaos-cosmos'").[115] Williams sympathizes with her claim that "the Hebrew version paves the way for the more drastic hierarchicalism and alienation of the Greek model of the world's making, where human consciousness (implicitly male) is recognized as akin to the primary agency of God as mind, and foreign to the realm of matter."[116] It isn't clear from this article how far Williams is willing to

111. Moody, "The Hidden Center," 35 fn. 56.
112. Clarke, "The Beauty of God in Cairo and Islamabad," 202.
113. Williams, "On Being Creatures," 64–78.
114. Ibid., 64.
115. Ibid., 77.
116. Ibid.

go with the doctrine of creation. Clarke wants Williams to extend his eschatological reflections to include the concept of rest. The problem is that Clarke appears to operate with a premillennialist theology of hope for Christ's return, inaugurating a future millennial kingdom of peace, but omits framing the discussion as such. Israel plays a central role in such an eschatology, though there are amillennial eschatologies where Israel has a place too. Israel's survival, according to this eschatology, is derived from the providential activity of the triune God, and those who oppose Israel's very existence are considered to do so because ultimately they oppose Christ's role as Messiah and only Son of God. There is no eschatological Sabbath rest for them without repentance.

In his 2001 article "Beyond Liberalism," Williams claims that "the Christian narrative affirms that the self-emptying or 'decentering' of spirit is first the rationale of creation and then the content of the story of Jesus and the call of the believing assembly."[117] Here we have Hegel's "kenotic" understanding of creation, which is a *creatio ex Deo* model (of what kind is a question of some dispute).[118] Thus we need to ask what Williams makes of creation "out of nothing." To do so we need to return to his 1989 lecture. Here he draws on Aquinas' treatment in a way that raises suspicions first found in his earlier discussion of Ruether. According to Aquinas, "'Creation' simply because it points us to the existing reality in relation to a creator."[119] Apparently "it does not explain some enormous event which would explain everything that came later; as Aquinas realized, the doctrine is equally compatible with thinking the universe had an identifiable beginning and thinking it existed eternally."[120] Williams distances himself from viewing creation as God's monarchy and government, because "if God creates freely, God does not need the power of a sovereign; what is, is from God. God's sovereign purpose is what the world is becoming."[121] This basically constitutes emanationism and panentheism. The rest of the essay is spent discussing how this limited understanding of God as creator implies a contemplative understanding of personhood and action. He throws in his objection to nuclear weapons as supposedly based upon this.[122]

---

117. Williams, "Beyond Liberalism," 71.

118. O'Regan, *The Heterodox Hegel*, 144–51.

119. Williams, "On Being Creatures."

120. Ibid., 68.

121. Ibid., 69.

122. Ibid., 77.

Williams' silence on his own opinion on the eternity or otherwise of the world (meaning the universe, not simply the earth) is a serious problem. Not distinguishing between the universe and the earth is a problem if he wants to talk about nuclear weapons, which threaten the earth specifically. He probably had in mind a critique of Ronald Reagan's support for deterrence along with his fear of a nuclear Armageddon in line with his interpretation of biblical prophecies concerning Israel and the nations in the latter days. This silence may be an example of Williams' attempt to take an apophatic approach to doctrine in order to invite people to question their own doctrinal and exegetical certainties as God-given. While eschatology as a field of doctrinal articulation lends itself particularly well to apophasis, given its very nature as peering into "the last things" and the "End of Days," however understood, the juxtaposition of an unfinished discussion on the eternity of the world alongside a hasty denunciation of nuclear weapons capable of bringing human history to an end offers small hope of thinking things through properly. Put bluntly, if Williams does believe in the eternity of the world, it is small comfort for a humanity threatened by the possibility of nuclear warfare. Affirming, or hinting at belief in the eternity of the world is not going to encourage people to give up nuclear deterrence or beliefs in Armageddon, because the theatre of such concerns is human history and not that of the universe in general.

It is difficult to take seriously Williams' criticism of the panentheism seemingly enjoined by Ruether along with Mathew Fox, as his own thinking appears to affirm it, in that he views history—the future, peace —as something that *we* create. On one hand, what needs to be clarified here is the distinction between the contingency of the universe, the finitude of the earth, and the finitude of the present age of history (the time of the church and the time of nations). The last two suppositions follow on from the first one. On the other hand, a distinction is required between the idea of the limitless duration of the earth seen from our historical vantage point, and the ending of the present age at the second coming followed by the recreation of heaven and earth. In conclusion, it appears that an apophatic approach has been deployed rather clumsily to ward off awkward questions on the doctrine of creation as well.

This twin apophatic approach to eschatology and creation "out of nothing" allows Williams to do two things. First, it allows him to avoid entering into debates about the place of politics in relation to different Christian eschatologies. Second, it conceals the possibility of reading

Genesis 1–3 as Hegel read it, in opposition to Martin Luther's sequential reading of the narrative, along with rejecting Luther's commitment to a punctiliar moment of creation *ex nihilo*. Where Williams would take leave of Hegel is in understanding the creation in general and humans in particular as good, rather than intrinsically evil, despite the reality of original sin. The first moment allows him to avoid clashing directly with Christian theological warrants for Zionism, be they premillennialist or amillennialist, which have (often wrongly) been charged with deriving their support primarily from eschatology. The second moment has proven influential in the liberal Anglican reception of Darwin and modern cosmology. Both these moments together parallel premodern and early modern recourse to Neoplatonist metaphysics by Christian theologians. As such, they parallel premodern Islamic recourse to Neoplatonist metaphysics in the exegesis of the Qu'ran and its narratives of the creation of man and woman, which closely resemble the biblical narratives. What this entails is that Williams' apophatic Hegelianism, a sort of modernized apophatic Neoplatonism, enables the management not only of Christian scriptural exegesis but also of Islamic scriptural exegesis, insofar as he is called upon to be a pre-eminent religious leader who represents religious communities in public debate. The apophatic approach to eschatology appears to give his political and legal vision an eschatological horizon, thus keeping at bay Islamic apocalyptic beliefs, which have tended to be more homogeneous than Christian apocalyptic beliefs. According to David Cook, an academic expert on Islamic apocalyptic, Muslim apocalyptic writing was dominated by the 'ulama (conservative religious leadership) until the mid-twentieth century; that is, until the foundation of Israel.[123] The defeat of the Arabs by Israel in the Six Day War proved a crisis in that it defeated the modernist secular vision of Islam and the Arab world, especially strong in Egypt under Nasser. The Islamic response was the rise of radical or political Islam, and the rise of Muslim apocalyptic. Conservative writers tend to oppose popular apocalyptic and try instead to downplay the expectations of the faithful. This does not mean that they do not believe the basic thrust of Islamic eschatology, but that they are wary of attempts to date the hour (the final judgment and the end of the world), or to specify components of the narrative. These conservative writers also tend to be the academics who are more interested in metaphysics. Thus Williams' apophatic metaphysical approach signals a

123. Cook, *Contemporary Muslim Apocalyptic Literature*, 15f.

window to engagement with them as "official" representatives of Islamic communities.

APOPHATIC THEOLOGY MANAGES ISLAMIC LEGAL THEORY

The apophatic tradition has tended to focus more on the individual spiritual journey than on political ethics. Just as it would be impossible to have an esoteric Christian ethics, so too it would be extremely difficult to have a thorough-going, apophatically-derived Christian ethics. This may explain why many critics find Williams' approach to ethics and politics so lacking. Its high valuation of the (monastic) individual parallels the rise of a secular individualism in deistic forms of the Enlightenment (Kant). The absorption and transformation of this high spiritual valuation of the individual in a mystical direction by Hegel is continued by Rowan Williams.[124] As such, it is also important in what I call "the liberal catholic" form of "religious resurgence," the "action and contemplation" style of spirituality and "social activism" of Thomas Merton, which deeply influenced Williams as a student.[125] This mystical approach reverses the empiricist argument that scientific reasoning surpasses religion in its rationality. In this account, it is the kataphatic and exoteric religion of most Christians that is prone to empiricism, and that needs to be either managed or marginalized in public discourse.

Williams' studiously apophatic approach to eschatology and the doctrine of creation as the poles between which his annexation of Hegel moves provides a suitable window into his approach to Islam. This emerges with clarity in the interview with Rupert Shortt in 2005. Williams says two basic things in response to the question of whether Christians and Muslims believe in the same God. First, we share "the pre-history, as you might say, of Christianity and Islam—the history of the Jewish narrative, the Abrahamic narrative."[126] Second, we share "the later history, the medieval history of intellectual exchange and the painful definitions of common ground and the marking out of boundaries in that context, which comes in the exchanges of the great medievals: St Thomas, Ibn Sena, Maimonides."[127] First of all, this is all rather extraordinary coming

124. Williams, *The Wound of Knowledge*, 132–39.
125. Shortt, *Rowan's Rule*, 157–58.
126. Shortt, *God's Advocates*, 20.
127. Ibid.

from someone who has consistently maintained that Israel was formed out of the exodus event, rather than by the election of Abraham. As a matter of fact, the concept of election and the evocation of Abraham only enter Williams' theology when he wants to talk of Anglican interfaith dialogue. One wonders what he actually believes himself. Here already his perspective has been profoundly colored by an approach that is distant from the Bible. The "Abrahamic narrative," and many other narratives, are considerably revised in the Qu'ran, serving different ends, partly because Qur'anic Christology is an anthropological one, aimed explicitly *against* the Trinitarian Christianity of the Middle East of the seventh century.[128] Yes, Islam is "Abrahamic" in claiming the Ishmaelite line, but this is insufficient ground for putting it simply alongside Christianity (whether of a supersessionist or non-supersessionist type) without further comment. What Williams really wants to concentrate upon is his second, apophatic response.

> Jews, Muslims and Christians can agree about a very great deal concerning the definition of what it's like to be God. God is not an item in the world. God is not confined by the agency of others. God's will and God's being coincide. God is wholly free to express what God is without interruption, without frustration.[129]

ISLAM AS COMMUNITY: BETWEEN J. N. FIGGIS AND GILLIAN ROSE

A crucial question is what does Williams mean by characterizing Islam, especially in Britain (or in the West generally), as "a community." This question needs to be pursued by reading Williams' commendation of J. N. Figgis' notion of the state as a community of communities along-side Gillian Rose's later work on Judaism as a community constituted by midrashic politics.[130] In his lecture, Williams speaks numerous times of Islam as "community": (religious) community as generic type, and the notion of "community cohesion" are mentioned in the abstract and

---

128. On Qu'ranic narratives in relation to the Bible, see Reeves (ed.), *Bible and Qur'ān*. On Qu'ranic Christology and its theological limits, see Parrinder, *Jesus in the Quran*.

129. Shortt, *God's Advocates*, 20.

130. Figgis, *Churches in the Modern State*; Rose, *Mourning Becomes the Law*.

throughout the lecture.[131] The Islamic community in general is termed correctly the *ummah* in the body of the lecture.[132] Finally he refers to "the majority community" within the state and its likely disapproval of some Shariah provisions which were rooted in the Qu'ran.[133] Rose promotes the idea that Judaism is midrashic politics, not a "religion" in the enlightened sense of the term.[134] The purpose of this is to forge a critical engagement with the modern State of Israel. For Rose, a community is one that is allowed to participate in "the unequal sharing of the means of violence," whereas a religion in the post-Enlightenment usage is not, because it is modeled on the Christian church.[135] By "Judaism" she means the people "Israel" as political community, both in the sense of the state, and of Diaspora communities. So she seems to be allowing for Diaspora communities to participate in the arrogation of force normally relegated to the state in modern times. No Jewish community in any country outside Israel is allowed this *qua* Jewish community. Rose's recommendation is too ambiguous to be safely and responsibly appropriated. She does not say whether she has in mind that Diaspora Jewish communities are to be allowed to participate in the arrogation of the use of force by having military chaplains, for example, which might symbolically validate Jewish participation in a Gentile state's armed forces as Jewish. The community right to use force in distinction from the state's use of force is what modern political theory denies to religious communities. *If* Rose in her latest phase is the voice that underlies Williams' argument in his lecture on Islamic law, this is a big problem, for a major problem with Islamic law in Britain and the West is the requirement to give up the right to use force. Unlike Israel, Islam has no one historical event such as the Bar Kochba Revolt that forced it to reckon with wholesale defeat and loss of polity, and thus loss of the capability and assumed right to use force. It did not and does not possess a canonical narrative of exodus like Israel does. What is actually being asked of Islam today by the West is to cease to be a "politics" in Rose's sense of participating in the means of violence, and to become what others would call a "politics of recognition." Back in 2003 in his

---

131. Williams, "Civil and Religious Law in England," 262.

132. Ibid., 265.

133. Ibid. 268.

134. Rose, *Mourning Becomes the Law*, ch. 4.

135. Ibid., 94, 97.

book *Lost Icons,* Williams' "more-than-liberal politics" was still politics of recognition, based on Gillian Rose and Charles Taylor's reading of Hegel.[136]

It is possible that Williams' comparison of Islamic law and legal theory to Orthodox Jewish law as practiced in England draws on Gillian Rose's thinking about Judaism as political and not only ethical, and as deeply implicated in the problems of modernity just like non-Jewish philosophies, but he may be mixing up Rose's meaning of community with Figgis' meaning.[137] Rose criticized the reduction of Judaism to ethics (Levinas), writing (Derrida), and criticism (Adorno), dubbing them the reduction of Judaism to pursuing politics by other means, paraphrasing Von Clausewitz on war.[138] Rose opposed the tendency for modern thinkers to opt either for "Jerusalem" or "Athens." She cites Levinas as one who opted for "Buddhist Judaism," "the sublime other of modernity," the New Jerusalem, as this detracts from the basic features of Judaism.[139] She also criticizes those who opt for Athens instead.[140] Against Levinas she advocates Rabbinic Judaism's practice of *midrash.*[141] It is evident that she thinks her characterization of it is congruent with her reading of Hegel.[142] Rose argues that "to oppose new ethics to the old city, Jerusalem to Athens, is to succumb to loss, to refuse to mourn, to cover persisting anxiety with the violence of a New Jerusalem masquerading as love."[143] Here the slippery meaning of "violence" for Rose, and Williams' reading of her, must be understood, especially as it is unclear whether it underlies Williams' recommendation for two-way dialogue between Shariah and secular legal thinking and practice. "New Jerusalem" here is any sort of "Christendom" model, such as historically supported by the different Anglican parties, though she specifically has John Milbank's work in

---

136. Williams, *Lost Icons,* 91–105.

137. Rose, *Judaism and Modernity.*

138. Rose, *Mourning Becomes the Law,* 37–38.

139. Ibid.

140. Rose, *Judaism and Modernity,* passim.

141. Rose, *Mourning Becomes the Law,* passim.

142. This is profoundly important for understanding the theological use of Rose by Williams. Hegel's esoteric roots included the Kabbalah of Isaac Luria detached from its roots in biblical Hebrew in the manner of the Christian Kabbalists. Leading modern scholars of the Kabbalah have argued that traces of this de-hebraicized Kabbalah can be found in the nihilistic postmodern theory of Jacques Derrida. Rose wants to return Jewish and secular political thought from the nihilism of Derrida to the constructive project of Hegel, which allows for a more poietic approach to law and texts, thanks to his notion of spirit. See Rose, *Dialectic of Nihilism.*

143. Rose, *Mourning Becomes the Law,* 36.

Theology and Social Theory in mind.[144] So, the secular legal sphere isn't simply the "Hebrew republic" of the early modern period, nor is it simply an idealized secular "Athens." Yet her notion of the "broken middle" as the "true politics" that lies between "Athens" and "Jerusalem" is more "Dionysian," like Andrew Shanks and Giles Fraser's understanding of the Church of England and the Anglican Communion.[145] As the Dionysian mystery religion was the religion that was considered to bind Athens together, her model is ultimately closer to "Athens," but in a less ethically idealized form than in some thinkers.

Accordingly, Rose extols Hegel's notion of Greek "ethical life" (*Sittlichkeit*) against the modern notion of legal status with its privileging of individual subjective rights, whose real interest is apparently "without substance."[146] Rose's characterization of law as "the falling towards or away from mutual recognition, the triune relationship, the middle, formed or deformed by reciprocal self-relation," is fanciful.[147] She says that her characterization of law as "triune relationship" is "the meaning of spirit in Hegel." This evokes the "social trinity" idea that was popular with Williams' erstwhile colleague David Nicholls as a way of supposedly countering the "violence" of a covertly Arian monotheism that ruled the Christianized Roman Empire after Constantine.[148] What is missing here is a robust discussion of the christological grounding for the theology of law. This is precisely where a comparison between Christian and Islamic approaches would encounter serious and probably irreconcilable difficulties. Law, for Rose, appears to have a teleological but not really a deontological character, simply because she speaks of it as part of an immanent search for a theory that mediates between recognition of individuals and recognition of the common good or "right" of the political community by focusing on how they are forever intertwined in mutual misrecognition.

It is possible that beneath the surface of Williams' lecture lies a hope for Islamic legal thinking to move from the deontological to the teleological pole, much as Williams' own sexual ethics has done. The problem

144. See Rose, *The Broken Middle*, 277–96. On the legal foundation of the Church of England, see Lockwood O'Donovan, *Theology of Law and Authority in the English Reformation*.

145. Rose discusses the figures of Dionysius and Orpheus in chs. 5 and 6 of *Mourning Becomes the Law*.

146. Rose, *Hegel contra Sociology*, 36–77.

147. Rose, *Mourning Becomes the Law*, 75.

148. Nicholls, *God and Government in an "Age of Reason"*; Nicholls, *Deity and Domination*.

then would be, as with Williams' own liberal Anglican sexual ethics, a tendency towards historicism.[149] Williams' notion of "human dignity as such" is not directly indebted to Rose, but his argument that it involves having a voice in the shaping of a common project harks back to his reading of Rose in 1991, where he uses her to take up the enlightened notion of social contract. It is possible that the latter move was intended also to incorporate the ideas of J. N. Figgis in a Hegelian framework. The problem is that such a theory perpetuates dangerous illusions about social situatedness, power, and oppression. At the theoretical level it does not help that Rose was never very sympathetic to feminism, and that Williams has little interest in secular feminism.[150]

The question of whether Williams means "community" in Figgis' nonviolent sense or in Rose's sense of participating in the arrogation of force is not answerable from Williams' lecture alone, but from studying his response to a question afterwards.

> Regarding Williams' claim that "the Abrahamic faiths" are needed to defend "human dignity as such," commentators have largely ignored Williams' response to a question afterwards, recorded in the printed version of the lecture, as to whether Islamic law could play a role in finding a solution to the Israel-Palestine conflict.[151] Williams' answer is entirely consonant with his reading of Hegel through Gillian Rose: "The principles of Islamic law, as outlined by the Muslim jurists I have read, are principles that lay heavy stress on dignity and respect; which, even though they are crafted in the context of a good deal of fierce conflict, nonetheless retain a sense that the "otherness" of the Other's identity is not something that can be extinguished by force. Now that is an ethical principle that Islam holds entirely in common with Judaism and Christianity: the other-ness of the Other cannot be ironed out by force. I think that, in that sense, there is a real convergence, which ought to help us to look at this, and other situations, in depth.[152]

This is an extraordinary answer because it evokes a generic, non-christological construal of "the other," which is a term used by modern

---

149. See for example Williams' remarks in "Incarnation and the Renewal of Community," reprinted in Williams, *On Christian Theology*, 225–38.

150. Rose, *Love's Work*, passim.

151. The argument that justice is constituted by inherent human rights, and that such a theory requires a theistic foundation, is made in Wolterstorff, *Justice*.

152. Williams, "Civil and Religious Law in England," 277.

theologians reading continental philosophy to denote the biblical concept of *the neighbor*. For Martin Luther, following Augustine, from whose biblically rooted metanarrative Hegel "swerved," *Jesus Christ* is the neighbor and we can only know who our neighbor is through first learning the Christian gospel.[153] (This theme is developed by Karl Barth in the 1930s against the counterfeit gospel of National Socialism).[154] Williams, on the other hand, is trying to talk about the potential of Islamic law to safeguard the recognition of "the Other," which shifts the ground for recognition away from a Trinitarian understanding of God to a shared theism.

It is very important that Williams' discussion of the shared theism of Christianity and Islam is set out in apophatic, not kataphatic terms, and that this corresponds profoundly to his apophatic approach to the Bible. In 1979, the same year as his address on Welsh nationalism, Williams published an essay on the Russian Orthodox theologian Vladimir Lossky, drawn from his PhD thesis. Near the beginning he writes, "we do not encounter God primarily through language or through the contemplation of words allegedly referred to him."[155] We need to understand this as a repudiation of all doctrines of Scripture that presuppose verbal inspiration of the text. Williams' studiously apophatic approach to the doctrine of creation catches up with him here, and is revealed as the deep counterpart of an apophatic rejection of a high doctrine of Scripture. All of this matters with regard to Islam because the logical development of his theology over nearly forty years strongly suggests he is optimistically gesturing towards an apophatic theology and exegesis of the Qur'an among Islamic scholars, similar to his own, which would somehow affect or converge upon would-be Islamic reformers of Islamic jurisprudence and legal praxis. As with the implausibility of esoteric Christian ethics, so with an apophatic approach to divinely rooted law; the question is whether the idea is coherent and therefore possible. In his own Christian theology, Williams skirts shy of notions of authority, yet these must be confronted when discussing law theologically. This matters fundamentally because it is very telling that in his lecture, he does not talk of mutual recognition between "Others," only recognition of "the Other" by a type of divine law. This keeps his discourse at a paternalistic level, yet

153. Luther, "The Freedom of a Christian," in Lull (ed.), *Martin Luther's Basic Theological Writings*, 585–629.

154. Barth, *CD* I/2, 401–54.

155. Williams, "Lossky, the *Via Negativa* and the Foundations of Theology," 2.

this is undercut by the speculative foundations undergirding his argument and the apophatic underpinning of his theology in general.

Existing scholarly analyses of Williams' speech have not probed this thoroughly into the theological hinterland which enabled him to make the extraordinary arguments he makes. For example, fellow Anglican Mark Chapman merely reproduces approvingly the secular or immanent elements of Williams' thinking without probing the roots found in Williams' idiosyncratic theology. Chapman argues that in his lecture, Williams relies on J. N. Figgis' political theory as advocating "interactive pluralism" as the right approach to the Church of England's relation to the state, in the wake of the breakdown of "the religiously monolithic state since the Enlightenment."[156] This is an extraordinary distortion of history. In reality, the challenge to Anglican absolutism and hegemony came with the Puritans—supported by roughly half of England and Wales' combined populations.[157] At the same time, it is impossible to ignore historic Roman Catholic opposition to Anglican absolutism. Anglicans really are not at liberty to ignore these facts. Indeed, Chapman even says it is this "breakdown" since the Enlightenment that means "in the modern world churches . . . have become voluntary organizations to which nobody can be compelled to belong." Again, this is totally untrue. Without resurrecting the charge of theological voluntarism, the idea nobody can be compelled to belong to a church was born among the Puritans—specifically the Independent or Congregationalist martyrs John Penry (a Welsh man) and Henry Barrow—in the time of Elizabeth I.[158] Their theological stance moved between infant baptism for believers' children and confessional baptism, and thus tacitly to a clear distinction between the nation as community of first birth, and the church (however conceived) as community of spiritual birth. (Again, Roman Catholics at this time would have seen themselves as a persecuted church outside the Anglican system of baptizing every infant in the Anglican parish.) This distinction between nation and church clearly militates against the absorption of Hegel into Christian theology. This highlights a curious anomaly in Chapman's account, which claims Williams probably "long ago faced up to the reality that Christianity was a minority religion."[159] In reality Williams appears torn here; he wants to continue using Hegel

---

156. Chapman, *Doing God,* 88.

157. Coffey, *Persecution and Tolerance in Protestant England,* 1558–1689.

158. Morgan, *Wales and the Word,* 91–92, 109.

159. Chapman, *Doing God,* 100–101.

to advance Christian-derived arguments for managing public discourse, which is simultaneously both multi-religious and secular. Thus he behaves *as if* Anglicanism isn't a minority religion, but a majority one that continues to have the right and the responsibility to manage other Christians and other religions. The clear metaphysical distinction between church and state, and church and society, in most Protestant theologies (including that of the established Church of Scotland), as well as in modern Roman Catholic theology, has probably contributed partly to the speedier demise of Hegelianism in the relevant churches.[160]

What is important, and has gone unnoticed by prior commentators, is the extent to which Williams' approach to religious pluralism, framed by his particular style of apophasis, has ultimately derived from his rejection, back in 1979, of the biblical narrative concerning the life of nations and states under God. Williams' 2008 speech thus sent out signals to those who represent the "religious resurgence" of Islam since the late 1960s, when Shariah Law was re-introduced in some Islamic countries, and when some modern radical movements sprang up in other countries.[161] In interfaith dialogue, he has pulled back from the temptation to co-opt Islamic theological motifs into an "interfaith public theology," and also from optimism concerning reform of basic Islamic theological beliefs (e.g., supersession of Judaism and the Jewish nation).[162] This statement was made in 2005 in the third "Building Bridges Seminar" on "Prophecy in Biblical and Quranic Perspectives," held at Georgetown University in Washington, DC. In other words, Williams was more realistic then in his acknowledgment of the Islamic belief that the modern State of Israel should be superseded by one binational Palestinian state ruled by Islamic law. Yet, he doesn't spell all this out in such explicit terms in 2005. His caution back then is undercut by his optimism in 2008 about Islamic law being an asset in the Israel-Palestine conflict. What Williams does not discuss is the problem that Islamic law as it stands, not in the idealized reformed version he envisages along with reformers, is very repressive in the Palestinian areas, and is wedded to an Islamic ideology of hope for Islamic government of the entire Holy Land as the land of Allah. Williams is not at liberty to ignore the *theological* root of this problem. He can only continue to maintain his "managerial" approach to Islamic theology

160. On Hegelianism in the Church of Scotland, see Fergusson, *Scottish Philosophical Theology,* 135–60; Sell, *Defending and Declaring the Faith,* 64–88.

161. On Shariah law being reinstated in some states since the early 1970s, see Peters, *Crime and Punishment in Islamic Law.*

162. Williams, "Analysing Atheism." Ipgrave (ed.), *Bearing the Word,* 1–10.

and law precisely because his apophaticism allows him to maintain the creedal formulations of the Trinity while distancing himself from biblical exegesis as the root of political theology and ethics. In this respect, he reproduces the antinomy found in liberal Anglican theology since *Essays and Reviews* was published in 1860, and later in Charles Gore's essay in *Lux Mundi*, published in 1889.[163] These essays date from the ascendancy of Hegelianism among liberal Anglicans, and from the spread of Anglicanism worldwide riding on the back of the British (English) Empire. For the last thirty-one years of its existence, Britain ruled the Holy Land, and concluded by designing the two-state solution in 1947 and presenting it to the United Nations. It was rejected by the Arab Muslim side and accepted by the Jewish Zionist side (which was mostly secular in its outlook). It was rejected by the Islamic leaders of the Palestinian Arabs not because there was unanimous objection to a pragmatic compromise among Palestinians, but because the leaders adhered naturally to the view that the entire Holy Land is the land of Allah, and as such must ideally only be governed by Muslims.[164] This is no more friendly to the pragmatist compromises required in politics than is the medieval idea that the Holy Land must only be governed by Christians.

Immediately, of course, such a view evokes historical debates about the Crusades. The question then is, were those who represented them Christians? I do not mean this question in the pacifist sense that questions whether soldiers can ever be Christians, nor in the sense of whether the Crusades could be justified, for they were wars to recover land that was legally Christian, with majority Christian populations, though invaded and conquered by Muslims. I am asking the question of who is taken to represent the Crusaders from among the Crusaders as Christian soldiers. Probing into this matter a little will show why this question matters for a longer view of Williams' attempt to manage both Christian and Islamic theological discourse, and of his overall theological approach to nations.

FROM THE TEMPLARS TO HEGEL AND BACK

None of the commentators have probed into the significance of the institutional matrix of Williams' lecture. His lecture was delivered at

163. On this problem, see Seitz, "Scripture Becomes Religion(s)," Bartholomew, Greene, and Möller (eds.), *Renewing Biblical Interpretation*, 40–65.

164. Hillel Cohen provides evidence from as far back as 1881, when the Jewish Zionists first settled in the Holy Land, for this mentality. Cohen, *Army of Shadows*.

the Royal Courts of Justice as part of the Temple Festival 2008, run by Temple Church in London, commemorating the 400th anniversary of the granting of a Royal Charter in 1608 by King James I to the Inns of Court to use Temple Church in perpetuity.[165] The Master of the Temple, the priest of the church at the time, was the Anglican theologian Richard Hooker. Williams and many other liberal Anglicans look to Hooker for the model of what Anglicanism stands for, rather than looking to the legal foundations in the Henrician and Elizabethan period.[166] At the same time, given the strong criticisms from international politicians and journalists of Williams' rather optimistic statements about Islamic law being reformed, he is very fortunate indeed that he was not asked to deliver the lecture at Temple Church, unlike subsequent lecturers in the series. This is because Temple Church is the oldest church of the Knights Templar in Britain, and this has a symbolic bearing upon our earlier discussion of his evasion of the esoteric roots of Hegel's theology. (It is also the case that Temple Church actually appears in the *Da Vinci Code*—a fact that would have further undermined Williams' credibility.) Temple Church was the chapel of the headquarters of the Knights Templar in the Temple area of London. The church is modeled on the Church of the Holy Sepulchre in Jerusalem, and was consecrated in 1185 by Heraclius, Patriarch of Jerusalem. This was the time of Richard the Lionheart's participation in the Third Crusade against Saladin. The website of the Temple Church comments on effigies of the Knights therein, and states unambiguously the premillennialist doctrine that the millennial reign of Christ will be ended by the final battle in Jerusalem of the saints who came alive to reign with Christ at the first resurrection, including the Knights Templar themselves.

> By 1145 the Templars themselves wore white robes with red crosses. White was linked with more than purity. In the Book of Revelation the martyrs of Christ, clad in white robes washed in the blood of the Lamb (Rev 7.14), are those who will be called to life at the "first resurrection." For a millennium they will reign with Christ; at its end Satan will lead all the nations of the earth against "the beloved city" (Rev 20.9). The final battle will be in Jerusalem. Our knights have good reason to draw their swords. For buried in "Jerusalem," in Jerusalem they shall rise to join the Templars in the martyrs' white and red. Here in the Temple, in our replica of the Sepulchre itself, the knights are waiting for

165. The historical information on Temple Church is taken from its website. http://www.templechurch.com

166. Williams, "Richard Hooker (1554–1600)," 24–39.

their call to life, to arms and to the last, climactic defense of their most sacred place on earth.[167]

King Edward I took over the Temple in 1307 after the Order of the Templars was abolished by Pope Clement V due to a charge of heresy. Edward gave it to the Knights Hospitaller, who let it out to the lawyers of the Inner and Middle Temples, and they also used the church. At the Reformation Henry VIII abolished the Knights Hospitaller and resumed control of the church, appointing a priest called the Master of the Temple. To this day, the Master is under the jurisdiction of the crown, not of the Anglican Bishop of London. The Temple became the scene of a battle between the Calvinist and liberal Anglicans of the time of Elizabeth I. Walter Travers, who along with Thomas Cartwright was the leading figure of English Calvinism, was appointed Reader of the Temple in 1581. Richard Hooker was appointed Master in 1585. They differed considerably on soteriology and ecclesiology. Travers wished England (and therefore Wales) to become a "godly commonwealth" like Calvin's Geneva. Hooker argued that Roman Catholics could be saved. Both men were moved to other churches by the Archbishop of Canterbury, John Whitgift. Hooker thereupon wrote his *Laws of Ecclesiastical Polity*, extolling natural law as the universal expression of divine law.[168] Finally, in 1608 James I granted a Royal Charter to the Inns of Court, allowing them to use the Temple in perpetuity. The Royal Courts of Justice, where Williams delivered his lecture, are enclosed by the Inns of Court.

Had the lecture been delivered at Temple Church, international media attention would undoubtedly have focused on what I have just discussed: the Templar connection, with the history of the Crusades against Islam (which also resulted in massacre of Jews and eastern Christians), the accusation of heresy leveled against the Templars, related concerns about the Freemasons as they have an eccentric idea of the Temple of Solomon at the heart of their rituals, concerns about how many members of the Bar are Freemasons, conspiracy theories believed by many Muslims in the Middle East about "Zionists and Freemasons" controlling world events, premillennialist beliefs (which Williams himself admits he doesn't understand but nevertheless has frequently stigmatized), and the *Da Vinci Code* connection. None of this would have been good publicity for either the British legal profession, the Church of England, or Rowan Williams. The fact that the authorities of Temple Church were responsible

---

167. http://www.templechurch.com/TC_History/timeline2.html

168. Faulkner, *Richard Hooker and the Politics of a Christian England.*

for Williams giving the lecture is symbolically significant, though in relation to Hegel, for as we have seen, Hegel was very friendly to esoteric traditions, and a Rosicrucian Christology stands at the heart of his mature theology. Moreover, the "foaming chalice" of the Holy Grail, about which legends abounded in the high medieval period, was believed by many to have been owned by the Knights Templar, and is placed in the Rosicrucian Christology of Hegel's Speculative Good Friday. I have argued above that this also serves as Hegel's vindication of the 18th Degree of the Rose Croix of the Ancient and Accepted Scottish Rite of Freemasonry. Many Anglican clergy joined Freemasonry in the late nineteenth century, the time as we have seen when they turned to Hegel and when Anglicanism spread across the British Empire.[169]

Last, but not least, the allegation of idolatry and apostasy and various vices made against the Templars in 1307 have exercised enduring fascination throughout the centuries. In 2003 Vatican historian Barbara Frale discovered the Chinon Parchment in the Vatican Secret Archives, which shows that Clement V had absolved the Templars of heresy in 1308 before disbanding them in 1312.[170] Frale was able to establish some of the secret initiation rites of the Templars, most importantly being asked to denounce the cross and spit on the crucifix.[171] This was justified as "practice" in case they were captured by Muslim soldiers. The Vatican evidence shows the Templars were guilty of the abusive behavior of which they were accused, but the only reason they were deemed not guilty of heresy was the excuse given that they still maintained inward secret fidelity to the cross. This is frankly a specious argument. The New Testament teaching is clear that Christians are not free to deny Christ with their lips in such a way.[172] Ergo, anyone who does so *is* an apostate. In any case, had their ritual been orthodox, it would not have needed to be secret. It is clear that christological heresy was really a problem among the Templars. It is, therefore,

169. In response to private correspondence leaked to the London newspapers, "Dr Williams' spokesman said: From the end of the 19th century a lot of Anglican clergy got involved in Freemasonry. In the 20th century a number of very senior clergymen were Masons. In the 1960s people started turning against the idea of secret societies and a number of Anglican ministers saw it as possibly Satanically inspired." Bennetto, "The 'Satanic' Brotherhood with Clergymen in Its Ranks."

170. Frale, "The Chinon Chart," 109–34.

171. Ibid., 126–27.

172. See the saying cited by Paul, "if we deny him, he will also deny us" (2 Tim 2:12). The passage in which this is written is prefaced by the injunction to "Remember Jesus Christ, raised from the dead, a descendant of David—that is my gospel" (2 Tim 2:8). This is the gospel Hegel denies.

important that the members who survived torture by the Inquisition were absorbed into other religious orders, and treated more leniently in England than elsewhere. Given what we know of the rituals of the Templars, and their hypocritical distinction between their heretical content and their own alleged inward orthodoxy, the comparison with Hegel— outward, exoteric Trinitarianism but esoteric denial of the full history of Jesus Christ that provides the *telos* of the crucifixion, is irresistible. Thus the fact that Rowan Williams, who denies that there is a serious problem with his own continued used of Hegel to bolster his political theology, accepted to give a lecture in a series organized by Temple Church, which maintains the Templars were orthodox and that they will participate in the first resurrection of the saints, is seriously significant. The fact that the historical "myths" about the Templars have become so deeply woven into popular culture has contributed to a culture where discussion of them is relegated to the merely comical and the ridiculous. Yet their affinity with Hegel only serves to show the comical dimensions of Williams' stubborn insistence on using Hegel to bolster his political theology, culminating in a completely speculative approach to the problem of reforming Islamic law in Britain and Western countries, not to say speculating that it can help Palestinian civil society when he had previously admitted that Islam was not going to give up on its supersessionism vis-à-vis the people Israel. This is all done as if it were the job of a Christian clergyman and theologian to help another religion that still aids and abets the persecution of Christians to "be itself" even more truly! What this constitutes is a continuation of liberal Anglican and English imperialism by a managerial discourse using Hegel, long after the demise of the Empire, in the midst of the global fracturing of Anglicanism, and in the wake of repeatedly published evidence demonstrating Hegel's completely heretical leanings. Perhaps the most important thing that we learn from this long excursus on "the art of apophatic management" is that Williams has been apophatically managing the problems with Hegel so that they don't come to light!

Williams designed an apophatic approach to political theology because he was already fusing Hegelian opinions with genuinely apophatic theology, such as that of Vladimir Lossky and Saint John of the Cross, back in the 1970s. Yet, of course, apophasis *cannot* found ethical and legal discourse and never has done. Apophasis in Williams' hands is not only used to manage and marginalize other theologies, by its very nature it undercuts the possibility of public theological ethical debate. Williams is not really silencing himself when he is writing apophatically: he is marginalizing other Christians (the kataphatic majority) who have never trodden the path he trod from 1979 onwards. At the same time, this is how he can seem to engage in interfaith dialogue with Muslims: theologically, he only really engages those Muslims who use the apophatic tradition within Islam. Williams' Anglican supporters have claimed that he defends "the secular" and the rights of religious people.[173] What my argument over this entire chapter has shown is that he has not really done this over the long term. There is a remarkable lack of critical analysis of Williams' political theology from within Britain, with what little that has been done coming from outside Britain.[174] Given what has been demonstrated in this essay, this means that there is a deficit in the debate and dissent needed for theological speech as well as secular reason to flourish.

173. See Higton, "Williams and Shariah."
174. See the collection edited by Matheson Russell, *On Williams.*

6

Israel and Jesus

Recognition, Election, and Redemption

NOW THAT WE HAVE caught a glimpse into how Williams handles recognition of Palestine, obliquely in relation to his use of apophatic theology to manage Christian and Islamic theological reasoning, we turn to look at how he handles the recognition of Israel. We do so in comparison with how Karl Barth handled the same issue. The way in which interfaith dialogue is made to circle around Jesus is how Williams has chosen to drawn near to the mystery of Israel. Then we pursue the way in which Williams' theology touches the apophatic void and sidesteps the Old Testament prophetic injunctions to silence, and how this relates to the recognition of Israel. The eschatological horizon unfolding before this vision provides the occasion for turning to consider Karl Barth's theological account of Israel since 1945, and to connect this back to features of his eschatology that were outlined in the first chapter. This brings us ultimately to the need for a theological theory of recognition of nations that stems from reading Israel's history as one of election through Abraham.

JESUS, ISRAEL, AND INTERFAITH DIALOGUE

Williams approaches the topic of Israel from a variety of standpoints. First, there is the recognition of the enormous vulnerability and fallibility of theological language, especially in light of the long history of Christian anti-Semitism and anti-Zionism. He strives to take seriously the insights of liberation theology that political domination and oppression can and do seriously distort theological thinking and therefore Christian ethics and practices. His work is also informed by the realization that debates on salvation are often stuck at an objectivizing level, paying scant attention to the reception of models of salvation in people's lives. Important for Williams is the discovery that attending to the concreteness of Israel can be a means of responding practically to the challenge of interfaith relations more constructively than John Hick. Finally, we will examine his role as Archbishop of Canterbury in representing the Church of England and the Anglican Communion in interfaith dialogue. Most of these standpoints concern theological method rather than doctrinal and exegetical substance. Nevertheless, there are substantive theological writings to which we must turn.

The key text for grasping Williams' approach to Jesus, Israel, and interfaith dialogue is "The Finality of Christ."[1] Political intrigue rather than collective sin is blamed for the crucifixion. This is surely linked to the lack of a theology of atonement in Williams' writing. Certainly the latter problem is closely paralleled in Hegel's theology, which eschews both the sacrificial and satisfaction models of atonement. It is also important not to miss the Hegelian overtones of blaming the Romans for the crucifixion, for Rome stood for Roman Catholicism among the German esotericists and romantics, at least as far back as Hermann Samuel Reimarus' portrayal of Jesus as a revolutionary (perhaps a Spartacus figure). Williams argues that Christianity is "the first self-contained 'religion' in history."[2] What needs saying here, what he does not argue, is that this is due to the metaphysical distinction between church and nation in the New Testament, with the nation as the community of first birth and the church as the community of second birth. (This brings into focus the root meaning of *natio* encountered in chapter 3.) This has an interesting parallel with Jesus' words to Nicodemus: "If I have told you earthly things and you do not believe, how can you believe if I tell you heavenly things?" (John 3:12). Nicodemus was "a teacher of Israel." He didn't cease to be an Israelite in the national sense when he confessed his faith in Jesus. By defining Christianity as a "self-contained religion," Williams tacitly repudiates supersessionism, that is, denies the teaching that the church as the Christian religious body was destined to replace the nation of Israel wholly in its mission. However, having disposed of one theological problem, he introduces another, namely a processual understanding of the relationship of

1. Williams, "The Finality of Christ," 93–106.
2. Ibid., 96.

Israel to Jesus and therefore the church. He says that there is "a more intense unity or consistency" in Israel culminating in Jesus.[3] He argues that
the movement of Israel's hope and history converged on the figure of Jesus
to such an extent that to decide for his "claim" on Israel's identity was to
decide for the "true" Israel first summoned into being by God in exodus
and covenant. This is a judgment clearly indebted to modern historical-
critical elision of the historicity of the patriarchal narratives. It evokes the
idea of pre-exilic "Yahwism" as supposedly superior to post-exilic Second
Temple Judaism. Abraham as the ancestor of the Jews is nowhere to be
found in Williams' theology. As we saw in the previous chapter, the focus
on the exodus is, of course, part of the stock-in-trade of liberation theologians, but also of an earlier and much more cunning style of evading
the patriarchal narratives and the election of Israel—Hermeticism. Thus
Williams believes that the Israelites came into being at the exodus, which
suggests he believes they were really Egyptians. The divine *fiat*, which
appears odd here given his typical hostility to what he regards as
arbitrary divine power, is responsible for this (on what grounds could this
be just unless the patriarchal narratives are taken as historical accounts of
leaving Canaan?). Gradually, "God's free utterance alone" comes to be
seen as what is behind creation and Israel. This is where Williams cites
Aquinas on what creation means.[4] He also states his belief that the gift
of the Law "is anchored in the great festivals where Israel returns to the
formative events of Exodus and desert wandering, to *become again* the
people whom God chooses; festivals whose origins were probably agrar-
ian are transformed into historical recollections so as to serve the distinctive vocation of Israel."[5] He approves of this as "a very pervasive and
organized 'sacramentality'; a sign-making consciously extended to an
enormous range of activities."[6] The belief that the Canaanite festivals were
transformed into memories of Israel's history since the exodus is unsub-
stantiated by any references. It evidences a typically Anglo-Catholic typology of "Christ transforming culture," which is ultimately rooted in a
Dionysian Christology, and which echoes the Coleridgean approach we
encountered in Milbank's work. Certainly in the previous chapter we
saw how Williams' work is heavily indebted to Gillian Rose's advocacy of
the Dionysian Christology of the "broken middle," and the question was

3. Ibid.

4. Williams, "On Being Creatures," 68.

5. Williams, "The Nature of a Sacrament," 202.

6. Ibid.

raised as to whether Williams' reading of Rose did not lie silently beneath his approach to Islam and Palestine. The question now is whether it has not also been made to underwrite Williams' theological handling of the State of Israel. Williams criticizes the supersessionist theology advanced by Timothy Radcliffe, which asserts that Israel's calling was to "become truly the people of God in ceasing to be a people at all."[7] Against this, Williams attacks the long Christian tradition of the "counter-claim" of being a chosen or "peculiar" people, the "new Israel." The route that he takes to criticize this replacement of Israel by the Christian church is not one providing a more careful definition of nation as opposed to church. Rather, he stays with the term "people," and says that "insofar as the Church has not ceased to be a people, with the institutional and political defenses appropriate to a people, it has no right to question Israel's continuing existence as a people, as 'Judaism.'"[8] The problem here is that there simply *isn't* one, institutional church. It may be that Williams is taking the romantic Anglo-Catholic view here that the Anglican church is but a branch of the Catholic church. This is the only way to make sense of the implied sense that the church now has "institutional and political defences." The fact that he then goes on to claim, "the vocation of the Jewish people remains," a life shaped under God, still does not say anything about the state. What he does say is that the modern State of Israel is guilty of "ersatz messianism," without citing any references or naming any political thinkers, and without having given a positive theological account of the State of Israel.[9]

More dangerous forms of abstraction and spiritualization are found when he says that "the church runs a greater risk than Israel, in that its institutional life is committed to the preservation, by word and sacrament, of its own questionability . . . because of this, it is not free to claim finality for itself."[10] If we render this thought truly concrete by reading "Israel" as "the State of Israel" for the sake of argument, we find that this statement simply does not make sense. Any state—and especially Israel—is not free to "risk" preserving "its own questionability" because its very job as a state is to preserve its population from external and internal threats to their very existence. The nature of the risks it faces are different than the ones the church in general faces. This is because, metaphysically, church and

7. Williams, "The Finality of Christ," 99, citing Radcliffe, "The Old Testament as Word of God," 266–75.

8. Williams, "The Finality of Christ," 99.

9. Ibid., 102.

10. Ibid., 100.

nation are distinct. Comparing the two as if the one had a "greater risk" than the other is probably the result of having subsumed church and nation under the generic category of "community" back in 1979, when Williams tried to shoehorn the recognition of Wales as a stateless nation into the pluralist theory of J. N. Figgis. It didn't work then, and it won't work with Israel as nation-state.

His approach gets played out in a rather troubling argument suggesting an idea of who is a "true Jew." Williams implies that he thinks Jesus enables Jews to become Jews, but declines to pursue this line of argument.[11] Instead he wants to develop Jesus' role in enabling Jews to become Jews (or perhaps more Jewish in a specific way) to "the specific politicization of Jewishness at specific moments of history," rather than in relation to "an essence of messianic Jewishness." What he has in mind first is that "the crucified Jesus puts God's question to the various styles of political defence of Jewishness in the first century of the Christian era" (i.e., zealotry mainly among the Essenes).[12] This is where the argument surfaces that Jesus' "anti-messianism" can be part of critique of the "ersatz messianism of the modern state of Israel," following Rosemary Radford Ruether. The problem here is that Williams had never made a theological case for the State of Israel before choosing to criticize it. In addition, the equivalence of first-century zealotry with a certain type of modern Zionism is interesting. Zealotry was a liberationist movement for independence from Roman rule. Zionism before 1948 *may* have had some analogies with zealotry (undoubtedly modern Zionists thought so, given their prizing of Masada as a national icon, with IDF soldiers being sworn in there). However, zealotry lost its battle against Rome, whereas Zionism *won* its battle against the British Empire (and Roman Catholic anti-Zionism).

Again the parallel with his thinking on Wales needs to be drawn out. Williams seems to harbor a remarkably submissive attitude to the imperializing state. Regarding Wales in 1282, we recall that he compared it to Israel being attacked by Babylon. This suggests it "deserved" to be conquered and imperialized. At the same time, it makes England, or the Anglo-Norman monarchs, out to be "Babylon" or "Rome." At this point we must recall Williams' strong Hegelian affinities, for Hegel preferred Greece over Rome as symbolizing freedom among other things. In these terms, 1948 saw Israel throwing off the shackles of "Rome." The subtext is that the challenge for Israel is to live according to the values of the "broken

11. Ibid., 101.
12. Ibid.

middle." The problem is that this involves a rather compromised Christology. Williams tries to say that the Christology he is offering is one that eschews the temptation for Christians to control religious meaning, but the unacknowledged Dionysian affinities of the "broken middle" concept with which he works open up uncomfortable questions that he avoids. For example, if Hegel, for Williams, is the only real resource for political discourse in our time, a sentiment encountered in the previous chapter's discussion, this must mean that this Christology is deemed the only one acceptable for a theology that is to be politically aware. Far from eschewing control, what this actually does is to fix Christology in the affirmation of a prior pagan culture and its gods—and when we recall that Dionysius was equivalent to Baal, the idol for whom the Golden Calf was built (the calf or bull being Dionysius' astrological symbol), we see here what Milbank means by the coming of Christ (in esoteric tradition) involving the return of the ancient "Saturnian" astral religion. This is the very idolatry that Israel of old was constantly being asked by God, through Moses and the prophets, to *give up!* It can be understood as yet another variant on pantheism, where God and Nature are secretly identified, and star-worship funds a "Christian polytheism" that becomes a tritheistic model of the Trinity based on the Egyptian triads (Osiris-Isis-Horus). The question now is, how does Williams conceive of the alternatives to his approach.

In the same breath as criticizing "the ersatz messianism of the state of Israel," Williams turns to the Third Reich as acting out "chiliastic fantasies."[13] The problem with this move is twofold. First, the term "chiliastic" is typically a derogatory academic term for premillennialism—by far the predominant form of eschatology among Jewish believers in Jesus, both today and historically. It is also not uncommon among religious Jews. Second, as a result, throwing out the concept of "chiliastic fantasies" stigmatizes premillennialism as inherently fantastical (as if other forms of eschatology harbor no fantastical elements!), and subtly draws close to the Israel equates to Nazi analogy, which has become so regrettably common in some circles, and which originated with Soviet propaganda influences on the German Democratic Republic during the Cold War.[14] The third problem is that Williams' comparison is bolstered by the claim that the Nazi state was "a parodic Church, a purified community of the last days."[15]

13. Williams, "The Finality of Christ," 102.

14. On the use of the Israel-Nazi analogy in contemporary left-wing European intellectual circles as a badge of European identity, see Markovits, *Uncouth Nation*, 150–200.

15. Williams, "The Finality of Christ," 102.

Now purely in relation to the Nazi state, this is a common theological account, though it has to be said there are parallels to be made between the pro-Nazi approach to Christianity and the one we saw advanced by Milbank, which is basically Germanic and neo-pagan, and as such, stands in far too close proximity to Williams to be passed over in silence. For Milbank's fondness for the Scandinavian Eddas and the Germanic sagas as Gentile precursors of Christianity was, as we saw, *exactly* the attitude of those German Christians from the nineteenth century onwards who replaced Israel with Germany. The real problem is replacing Israel's tradition with that of another country. It doesn't really matter, theologically, whether this be Germany, ancient Greece, England, Wales, ancient Egypt, or Canaan. It all amounts to the same thing—replacement theology and supersessionism. In other words, it amounts to non-recognition of Israel's "right" to be a nation (which it needs if it is to be a "people" in the biblical sense, fulfilling its vocation). On what grounds, precisely, can Williams criticize Israel for being "chiliastic" and really like Nazi Germany, when his own theological account of Israel is secretly implicated in the same neo-pagan sources as Milbank and the Western esoteric tradition within the churches?

The next question to ask now is why was Williams interested in talking about Jewish-Christian tensions in this article written in 1990? The answer is that the First Palestinian Intifada had happened by then, and he was becoming interested in interfaith dialogue with Muslims as well as Jews. How he conceived of Jesus continues to be important in reading this essay. "To be a Christian is to claim that the Jewish story with its interruption and repristination in Jesus is the most comprehensive working-out of this moment of dispossession," that is, the loss of the God who is defined as belonging to us and our interests.[16] He means, of course, the loss of an image of God as exclusively belonging to one group of people and interested only in their welfare. The problem here is that to see Jesus as "the most comprehensive working-out" of anything is to fall into the trap of equating other human beings with Jesus in spiritual potential, which again suggests a semi-Arian cast of mind. This is unsurprising given Williams' Hegel-like preference for mystical theologians when dealing with the Christian life at the expense of "objective" accounts of the work of Christ.

Williams takes an anthropocentric view of Israel's rejection of Jesus as the Messiah, writing that Israel's history is

> about a community . . . unable to make a decisive act of faithful-
> ness to its own original nature and calling because its history

16. Ibid., 104.

has not only preserved but also obscured that distinctive sense
of identity and mission. Its hopes and desires have become
sufficiently unclear for there to be no means of recognizing what
it would be for them to be fulfilled. In the language of Amos, the
desired Day of the Lord has come and is darkness not light.[17]

This passage is fraught with problems. As we have already seen, he wants
to blame Second Temple Jewish traditions for the fact that Israel as a
nation rejected Jesus. The problem here is a combination of resorting to epistemic reasons and neglecting the clear witness of the New
Testament texts. The New Testament texts engage in a constant dialectical pattern between individuals and the nations to which they
belong, much like the Jewish prophets when they speak of Israel and
the Gentile nations. The very term *ethne*, translated in English as
"Gentiles," clearly stands for both individuals who are Gentiles and
not subject to the strictures of the Torah, and the nations as whole
entities. As regards acceptance or rejection of Jesus, it is clear from the
New Testament that national Israel is divided between those individuals
who accept him and those who reject him. The book of Acts ends with this
distinction as a cliffhanger, with Paul telling the reader that he does
not hold Israel in judgment. In the service of interfaith dialogue, then,
Williams effectively repeats the old-fashioned generalization that "the
Jews rejected Jesus," but putting this down to the decline of religious
traditions (from which period, he doesn't say). In the New Testament,
however, it is not the history of Israel that has created an epistemic
confusion for ordinary Jews, but certain ways of interpreting the Law.
Some have argued that one reason that many Jews did come to believe
in Jesus, especially in the Galilee, was that they were expecting the Messiah to come early in the fifth millennium.[18] The idea that the Day of
the Lord had come "but was darkness" can only be read as a Christian
interpretation of Jewish rejection of Jesus. Of course those who didn't
recognize him as the Messiah would not have believed the Day of the Lord

---

17. Ibid., 97.

18 Silver, *A History of Messianic Speculation in Israel*, 6f. "When Jesus came into
Galilee, 'spreading the gospel of the Kingdom of God and saying the time is fulfilled
and the kingdom of God is at hand,' he was voicing the opinion universally held that
the year 5000 in the Creation calendar, which is to usher in the sixth millennium—the
age of the Kingdom of God—was at hand." Citing Mark 1:14–15; see also Mark 9:1;
13:30; Matt 10:3. Silver's cites 4 Ezra 14:48, "'And I did so in the seventh year of the
sixth week of 5,000 years of the creation, and three months and twelves days" (ibid.,
16).

had come at all, so it is an odd thing to say in the context of trying to find a way of accounting for rejection of Jesus in interfaith terms. It is more important, however, as a hint of how Williams thinks about eschatology. Nowhere in his work does he acknowledge a future Day of the Lord or the possibility of double temporal fulfillment of Old Testament prophecies about the Messiah upon which the notion of the second coming is built. This would explain Matheson Russell's suspicion that Williams historicizes eschatology. It also recalls the discussion in the first chapter of the present book as to the nature and motivation of attacks on premillennialisms.

More laudably, Williams does not want to "devise hasty Christian theologies of (definitions of?) the Jewish experience in this century."[19] However, he is perhaps in danger of doing just that when speaking of Jesus' sinlessness. He cites Donald MacKinnon's notion of "historically achieved innocence" when speaking of judgment passed on "the entirety of a life in which the inevitable damage done by human beings to each other has not sealed up the possibility of compassionate and creative relationship."[20] Williams thinks modern Jewish writers' relating Jesus to post-Holocaust Judaism hints at what sinlessness might mean, but doesn't cite any Jewish writers to back this up. The problem here is the semi-Arian notion of achieved sinlessness as far as Jesus is concerned. Jesus was not a man who inevitably damaged others insofar as he was a man, unless he was sinless only by virtue of the work of the Spirit, not his own divine-human makeup as the New Adam. The link made between Jesus the Holocaust is misplaced, as it attempts to equate victimhood as such with absolute sinlessness—perhaps the long shadow of victim theories of atonement in Latin Christianity is felt here too. Alternately, it is possible that here we have some sort of inclusive Christology, whereby all people including Jews are deemed already included in Christ, but may "fall" if they turn to violence. This would fit with the tendency for Williams to reduce sin to violence in a Girardian fashion. The Pelagian and Kantian overtones of such thinking ought not to be ignored. In the terms of the politics of recognition, there is something badly wrong with the preference of many theologians to speak of the Jewish people in terms of the Holocaust rather than speaking of the modern Israeli state. It clearly reflects a stark preference for seeing Jews as victims to be pitied, yet never quite respecting the human need for state protection—odd for theologians who were mostly born after the Second World War, so were never responsible for the

19. Williams, "Nobody Knows Who I Am 'Till Judgment Morning," 287.
20. Williams, "Trinity and Ontology," 157.

Holocaust. In an address to the Building Bridges interfaith dialogue seminar in 2005, Williams at least attempts to balance the two factors in his thinking about Jews as a nation.

> Can Christianity and Islam sustain themselves against the accusation of promoting a theological imperialism which has, from a Jewish point of view, nakedly and often murderously political implications? And once again, there are answers that may emerge. Christians (Christians other than the extreme dispensationalist Christian Zionist anyway) will often find difficulty in offering a theologically positive valuation of the continuing identity of the Jewish people, but may still believe that it is necessary to work at this, if only in terms of the people of Israel as the radical sign of the Church's incompleteness and the priority of the covenant people into whom non-Jews are now believed to be incorporated.[21]

Here we have a leveling of Christianity and Islam "from a Jewish point of view," yet it looks as if the underlying point is really from an *Israeli* Jewish point of view. In other words, Israel's problem is that there are Christian and Islamic worldviews that would deny that Israeli Jews have the right to be recognized as a distinct nation-state under God, alongside other nation-states. According to these worldviews or theologies, the Middle East conflict should really be resolved by a reversion to either a Christian or an Islamic state for all the Holy Land. This is Christian and Islamic anti-Zionism and anti-nationalism. Indeed, it is not too much to argue that Christian and Islamic anti-nationalism today *is* Christian and Islamic anti-Zionism. Anti-nationalism is intrinsically anti-Zionist. It is unfortunate that Williams doesn't explain precisely what he means by "extreme dispensationalist Christian Zionism." Is there a dispensationalism that is not "extreme," or is it inherently "extreme" in relation to some other type of eschatology? As we saw with John Milbank, it is perfectly possible for a Christian theologian to be anti-Zionist and prefer the dream of a Christian one-state solution harking back to the Latin Kingdom of Jerusalem and British Mandate Palestine. If this is amillennialism, it *is* extreme in its anti-Zionism and its "nakedly political implications." When we turn to the term "Christian Zionist" used by Williams, it is important to note that this term is typically used in a negative sense by academics in state-funded universities. It is almost never simply a description of someone's position. This is confusing, because the term tends to be used

21. Williams, "Analysing Atheism."

of dispensationalists who believe all the Holy Land should be ruled only by Israel, and perhaps only inhabited by Israeli Jews too (the two are not the same, and not everybody makes the former belief a basis for the latter). It is doubly confusing because Zionism is a form of nationalism first and foremost, and as a lot of Israeli writing shows, is not necessarily incompatible with willingness to recognize the right of Palestinians to national sovereignty within their own areas within the Holy Land. Stephen Spector has provided useful corrective information about American dispensationalists in this respect, showing how pragmatist some are prepared to be in moving to recognize Palestinians as a nation within the Land as well.[22] It remains to be seen whether Spector's work will have a genuine impact on critics of dispensationalism and so-called "Christian Zionism." Finally, the multiple possible meanings concealed under the term "Christian Zionism" makes the term deeply misleading as the tendency for many to conflate it lazily with dispensationalism (and to assume that dispensationalism and premillennialism are identical, or that either of those exhausts the range of Christian beliefs about prophecy and providence) leaves no room for recognition of Christian thinkers who recognize and accept Zionism in a modest form.[23] A lot of this is down to the self-righteous unwillingness of many contemporary scholars to distinguish between nationalism and imperialism. Failing to observe these fine distinctions is not good news. It has the adverse effect of galvanizing those people who believe Palestinians should not be allowed even to live within the Holy Land into a defensive action, portraying themselves as the only true supporters of Zionism (defined in a very particular way).

The reality is the position that Israel's future is guaranteed providentially has always existed within the church, and has never been the sole preserve of dispensationalists. With regard to modern dispensationalism, its founder, John Nelson Derby, was an Irish Anglican clergyman.[24] One wishes that, as with Milbank reading Hobbes, Williams had acknowledged that his debate with dispensationalism was very much an *Anglican in-house* debate. Dispensationalism was never a majority position among

22. Spector, *Evangelicals and Israel*.

23. A theologian who attempts to account for and recognize these shades of difference among Christians is Walter Riggans, in his book *Israel and Zionism*. It is worth pointing out that Riggans was a minister in the Church of Scotland, a denomination which has always had a balanced *amillennial* theology of Israel. The truth is that *most* modern academic critics of Christian Zionism—who conflate it with dispensationalism—seem ignorant of this.

24. Spector, *Evangelicals and Israel*, 13–15.

Anglicans, but historic premillennialism was common among them in the past, and also had a doctrine of Israel, though not one that posited two distinct covenants for Israel and the church. In Britain, the best modern exponents of a theological account of Israel have been Scottish theologians working within the long Scottish reformed (and amillennial) tradition, pre-eminently T. F. Torrance and David W. Torrance.[25] To dismiss these as marginal extremists would really take some nerve. Both have interestingly acknowledged and drawn from the theological account of Israel given by Karl Barth, who—as was argued in chapter 1—can be said to have attempted to correct aspects of dispensationalism in developing his doctrine of providence, and what we have of his mature eschatology.

THE STATE OF ISRAEL AND THE PALESTINIANS UNDER GOD

In terms of method, Williams' theology is in many ways the opposite of that of the Reformed theologians mentioned, as it is heavily indebted to an apophatic retreat from certain kinds of overly transparent liberal theologies of recognition found in the interfaith movement.[26] In terms of method, this represents a continuation of his concern for Christology being safeguarded in the face of John Hick's theology of religions. What Williams is doing is preserving the liberal approach to Israel, which tends to be rationalist and tends to iron out paradox, irony, and mystery from the understanding of providence, under an apophatic cloud. Finally, the failure to reckon with stateless nationhood properly means he never gets round to addressing issues regarding the Palestinians. Ironically, we see this in his much-discussed address, delivered in absence, to the Sabeel Ecumenical Centre in 2004.[27] Israel means two things for Williams: "Israel under God" (i.e., the Jewish people as "bearers of covenant and witnesses to God's revealed justice") and the State of Israel ("a contemporary and secular political reality, which is also seen as the homeland for 'Israel under God'"). He cites Paul to the effect that God's promise does not fail (Rom 9:6), and then asks what the covenant is for. It is for Israel

25. Torrance and Taylor, *Israel God's Servant*.

26. See, for example, Markham, "Theological Problems and Israel," in Fry (ed.), *Christian-Jewish Dialogue*, 123–26.

27. Williams, "Holy Land, Holy People," 14 April 2004, http://www.archbishop-ofcanterbury.org/articles.php/1840/lecture-to-the-5th-international-sabeel-conference-holy-land-and-holy-people-jerusalem.

to be a paradigm nation. Williams draws on Gary Burge's arguments in discussing the theological significance of the land of Israel. He turns to Leviticus 25, neglecting Yhwh's promise of the land to Abraham in the book of Genesis. Israel has a mission, not to "manifest God's supreme and arbitrary power in choosing and shaping a nation, but God's wisdom and justice as the pattern for human society."

> In Deuteronomic terms, God chooses a small and oppressed people to demonstrate this, lest his justice be confused with a powerful and successful nation. Take away this vocation and the history makes no sense. A "chosen people" that has become not only powerful but oppressive in its practice has made nonsense of God's calling to them.

This is a statement that should occasion profound suspicion as it reveals a deep-seated unease with "Jewish power," which, of course, is *essential* to political sovereignty. Power, as Stephen Sykes has argued, has been poorly theorized in Christian theology historically.[28] There is a terribly dangerous bias towards powerlessness in certain styles of Western Christian theology that can reinforce a tendency to pacifism, which in practice means no nation has a right to defend itself against imperialists, and a mindless paternalism towards minorities, keeping them in a subordinate "place," doomed to play a pseudo-Christian role as reminders to the powerful of the "need" for weakness. To be powerless and a victim is good. (This is echoed in Williams' commendation of MacKinnon's incoherent idea of Jesus' "achieved sinlessness.") Aside from this, there is a need to distinguish between power and authority in the case of Israel. Does Israel's mission include witnessing to divine authority?

Williams' publicly stated desire to forge a liberation theology for the Holy Land is beset with problems. First, it is clearly attempting to answer both to the Palestinian Liberation Theology of Sabeel and to dispensationalism. Second, liberation theology typically draws heavily on Marxist categories to read the Bible and formulate doctrine and ethics. The problem with this is Marxism is inherently supersessionist and anti-Zionist at its roots. Anybody who seriously wants to forge a liberation theology for Israel and the Palestinian territories would need to study very deeply those Jewish Zionist movements that were strongly indebted to Marxism, and also the history of the Arab reception of Marxism, before being able to think empathically and responsibly about how a Christian liberation theology for Jewish and Gentile believers in the Land could be viable, as it would be inevitably perceived

28. On this, see Sykes, *Power and Christian Theology.*

through the respective Jewish and Arab experiences of absorption. The Jewish Zionist reception of Marxism and socialism produced the Labor Zionism that was in power for the first few decades of Israel's history up to the election victory of Menachem Begin. The Arab reception of Marxism, on the other hand, came via modernizing trends in Islam, and the fact that much of this occurred within the USSR while the Soviets attempted to systematically wipe out Christianity and Judaism is something no serious thinker on the subject could ignore, as it fits with the supersessionist mindset of both Marxism and Islam towards Jewish sovereignty within the Holy Land. The question of whether Marxist economic and cultural categories can truly be divorced from supersessionism is therefore of paramount importance, and whether alternative categories can be found that do the critical job at least as thoroughly.

A more explicit problem is Williams' claim that "the problem increasingly lies less with aggressive neighbours than with failure [on the part of the State of Israel] to tackle the underlying issues about regional stability."[29] This is a key statement in the speech, especially in the wake of the Second Intifada, the rejection of the two-state solution by Yasser Arafat, and the very serious threat posed by Iran to Israel, not least through its funding of Palestinian and Lebanese militia. He then returns to say that this is why the land increasingly "becomes a prison, not a gift," citing unnamed Israeli commentators who say that "the spiral of overwhelming violent reaction to the indiscriminate violence of suicide bombings and the consequent desperate anxiety over security creates more and more barriers and walls." Finally, Williams makes the strangely flat claim that "fear and instability erode law," claiming that these are the root of violence. It could just as well be said that fear demands law-making, and that instability requires it. He alleges that this fear pushes Israel towards defensiveness that "sits lightly on national and international law and inexorably undermines wisdom in its policy and polity." He asks Israelis and Palestinians to encourage lawfulness in each other, saying it is Israel's gift under God to the nations. Nations who are aware of this are required to reflect this back to Israel "to hold Israel accountable to itself and its God." This is a very strange thing for a Christian to say, as the God of Israel *is also* the God of the nations. There can be no question of demanding Israel be held accountable to God without the surrounding nations and the international community being held accountable before God for their treatment of Israel, not to mention their total lack of genuine effort to repatriate

---

29. Williams, "Holy Land, Holy People."

generations of Palestinian refugees. Neither Egypt nor Jordan showed any desire to create a Palestinian state in Gaza and the West Bank between 1948 and 1967; this is why the modern West Bank is called the *West Bank*—of the river Jordan. Why should we imagine that they will now? Israel's Islamic neighbors are, of course, very well aware of the giving of the Torah to Israel—it is treated at length in the Qur'an. They refuse to recognize Israel as a state in legal terms because to do so would require observing international laws of war and thus acknowledging them as a higher authority in practice than Islamic codes of war; alternatively, it would be a question of adjusting Islamic approaches to war. Moreover, Israel's neighbors never lose an opportunity in the meantime to talk of how it should observe human rights laws which they themselves regularly flout in domestic terms. Thus Williams' claim that back in 2004 Israel was the main problem ignores the fundamental problem, which is not lack of awareness by Gentile nations but a defiant refusal to acknowledge that Israel's God is also their God—the kind of thing for which the Israelite prophets repeatedly warned judgment would come upon the Gentile neighbors of Israel. This judgment is continued throughout the eschatology of the Old Testament prophets, which is the basis of the eschatology of the New Testament authors. On the matter of judgment, however, Williams tends to fall silent.

TOUCHING THE APOPHATIC VOID

As an apophatic theologian, Williams is appealing to many who wish theology to be seen as concerned with the sheer mystery and transcendence of God. However, there is in reality a serious disjunction between the generally mystifying language that he employs, which frequently serves as a strategy for evading historical reading of the Bible, and the New Testament texts that speak of mystery exclusively with regard to the mystery of Christ made known in the End of Days. The Greek term *to musterion* is employed by Paul and John in the Jewish sense of being a heavenly reality formerly kept secret and disclosed in the End of Days as necessary for salvation. This is a more recent scholarly discovery thanks to the long study of Qumran texts. Before 1947—before the establishment of Israel—the term "mystery" was believed by many scholars to indicate that Paul especially was using the terminology of the Greek Dionysian mystery religions to speak of Christ, and moreover as such transforming the mysteries christologically. This way of thinking found its way into the church as far back as the Alexandrian fathers and especially among the Greek fathers in the aftermath of Nicaea. The New Testament authors designate as mysteries the salvation of "all Israel" (Rom 11:25b), the resurrection of the righteous at the last trumpet (1 Cor 15:51–58; Rev 10:1–7, 11:15–19), and the revelation of Jesus Christ (Col 1:15–20). Mystery is clearly eschatological in a temporal as well as an ontological sense in the New Testament, as Paul's comments in Ephesians demonstrate about "the fullness of time" (Eph 1:9–10, cf. 3:4, 6:19). The triple mystery in the New Testament does not call so much for endless apophasis as assent and indwelling as well as repentance. By its very eschatological nature it calls into question the monistic Hegelian poietic peacefulness envisaged by Williams as a self-soothing fiction. At the same time, it demands engagement with the whole complex of divine providence. To what extent he intends to do this can be seen in his reading of the Jewish philosopher Simone Weil, who converted to Catholicism without being baptized.

Williams' writing on Weil shows that he is prepared to use her extreme apophaticism against biblical witness to God.

> To imagine God is, Weil implies, to conceive a state of affairs, a determination of circumstances, which will inevitably be conditioned by my needs, and will be a falsehood. Even if I imagine *as an object in my mental world* the God who is characterised by the selfless abandonment, the creative letting-go of reality which is, for Weil, the crucial element in truthful speech about God, I am thereby kept away from the God who can be truly talked about precisely because God has been brought into my mental world, in which all objects are—so to speak—tainted by the particularised wants of the unredeemed subject. So to "believe" in God, if it is not to be the manufacture of a "false concordant composition," becomes an intensely paradoxical affair: if God is in our minds, God must be "imagined" as not existing, not involved in any real or imaginary circumstances.[30]

Williams draws from this premise the conclusion that

> the *grammar* of our talk of God can appropriately be refined, so that we know what we are talking about—that is to say, there is a proper place for objecting, "You can't say *that* about God," when faced with models of a vindictive or arbitrary divine power

---

30. Williams, "The Necessary Non-Existence of God," 54.

(such as Simone Weil identified in the Jewish Scriptures and in much of the rhetoric of the Catholic Church).[31]

The problem with this argument is the assumption that the entry of the concept of God into one's mental world is necessarily an *idolatrous* reduction of God to being One who merely exists to fulfill one's vengeful desires, as opposed to being an entirely necessary accommodation to human finitude. It is very telling Williams follows Weil in rejecting biblical depictions of divine vengeance and power, dismissing them as "arbitrary." There are shades of the animus against "voluntarism" in Duns Scotus and William of Ockham recycled by Milbank and others in what amounts to an anti-Reformed stance—anti-Reformed because it's cynical about ideas of divine sovereignty, freedom, and election. The more appropriate theological term would have been to denote the less pleasant depictions of divine action and speech as inscrutable, as this would have allowed more for the sense that the reader or hearer always has plenty more to understand of God. As things stand, this is yet another instance of Williams abusing his much-vaunted apophatic method to police biblical exegesis.

Typically, Williams moves from discussing the existence and non-existence of God in Weil's philosophy to the question of the holiness of the believer's life. The problem is that this is done by bypassing the role of biblical reading in the formation of the believer. I do not think that the remedy to the defects here is simply to counsel "believing the Bible" to be historical, although it is part of the issue. Mike Higton's favorable judgment is that Williams is most at home with historical reality:

> To some extent, Williams is academically most at home not with the big statements of philosophy, but with the painstaking attention to detail of history: working with extraordinary care through, say, the masses of unruly evidence that remain to us from fourth-century theological debates, trying to undermine any all-too-easy telling of the story. This, too, is no accident: it is deeply connected to Williams' theology of the Incarnation, and to his recommendation of contemplation (of paying attention to what we do not control).[32]

On the contrary, he really is very *evasive* of the historical reality to which the Old Testament especially witnesses. John Webster has criticized Williams for his thin view of the Bible, and suggested that seeing the Bible

31. Ibid., 54.
32. Higton, *Difficult Gospel*, 9.

as a gift from God under which we must live is the way forward.[33] While in the absolute sense this is right, it probably isn't really an approach that will work in the short term. It is reminiscent of the attitude of too many conservative Reformed theologians, which is to spend a lot of time establishing a doctrine of scriptural inspiration, inerrancy, and infallibility, as a basis for establishing the authority of biblical texts. This is a modern attitude that has done little or nothing in practice to enable recovering the sense of the Bible as authoritative in the sense of being realistic. Partly this is because it is an approach that does not and cannot deal very subtly with how different literary genres in the Bible are authoritative. In reality, it has operated in a negative sense as a means of setting a boundary for what may not be countenanced morally by successive generations of Christians. Given Williams' concern with human experience, I propose adopting a self-conscious stance of reading the history of Israel alongside the history and culture of one's own nation. This should, ideally, evoke not only a necessary empathy but also a critical distance vis-à-vis one's own national perspective. Such a distance is rendered near-impossible by associating too closely with theologies of replacement.

George Steiner describes the Hebrew Bible as the textual homeland of the Jewish nation. Unending commentary on the Bible is elemental in Judaism.[34] The text of the Torah, the biblical canon, and the concentric spheres of texts about these texts, replace the destroyed Temple. Modifying these arguments, we could say that as Christian theology has become exiled from its Jewish roots, it has become exiled from the biblical text.

Williams has published some poetry in English, and some translations into English of Welsh poetry.[35] He has also published some writing on Christian poetry. Williams' own poetic style is free—not at all using the choices of strict metrical styles available in the Welsh tradition. Thus he lies, like his favorite R. S. Thomas, outside the mainstream Welsh poetic tradition, which has always been the pre-eminent national artform, just as preaching has always been the pre-eminent Welsh form of theology. Both Williams and Thomas are high Anglicans with an extremely apophatic approach to theology. Their apophasis meshes well with their choice not to adhere to Welsh metrical traditions. (And perhaps

33. Webster, "Williams on Scripture," in Bockmuehl and Torrance (eds.), *Scripture's Doctrine and Theology's Bible*, 105–24.

34. Steiner, *Real Presences*, 40.

35. Williams, *After Silent Centuries*; Williams, *Remembering Jerusalem*; Williams, *Headwaters*.

with the fact that Williams has never published either poetry or theology in Welsh. His extremely loose style of writing wouldn't be suited to Welsh, which like most languages has tighter grammatical rules and a smaller vocabulary than English.) There is a deep analogy here between Williams' attitude to Welsh poetry and his attitude to the biblical text. In his lecture "Christian Imagination in Poetry and Polity: Some Anglican Voices from Temple to Herbert," Williams displays a very typical Anglo-Catholic discomfort with the Puritan Commonwealth "when the Episcopal Church of England was proscribed and persecuted; and when those who had perhaps too readily lived in a 'William Temple' style of world suddenly found that they were no longer at the centre of things, they were no longer deciding the fate of the country."[36] He connects theologically the poetry of George Herbert with the theology of Richard Hooker, and with the poetry of Henry Vaughan, a Welsh Anglican. From there he concludes via T. S. Eliot and R. S. Thomas. In reality most Welsh poetry historically has been both metrical and wedded to a more kataphatic style of theology. At the same time, Welsh literature possesses very early prose epics, the *Mabinogion*, which shaped prose writing in the medieval period. This combination of both secular (demythologized) prose and poetry so early in Welsh literary history mirrored the Bible in a way that was not the case in early German and Scandinavian literature, which had preserved the euhemerist folk memory of the "gods" in a pagan polytheistic form.

Petra Heldt, a Lutheran patristic scholar working in ecumenical circles in Israel, draws a link between eschatology, nationhood, and biblical hermeneutics. Criticizing Rosemary Radford Ruether's anti-Zionist theology, she says that "when supersessionism is abandoned and Christians acknowledge the right of Jews to be in their biblical homeland, room is created for Christians to consider how the Land is theologically important for them too."[37] Astutely, she notes that modern supersessionism in the mainline churches is partly rooted in historical-critical readings of the Bible (the documentary hypothesis is singled out), which destroyed the potential for reading biblical narratives as realistically historical. She proposes that this realism can be recovered in modern Israel because it has been kept alive "in spite of analysing the text critically since the time of the Second Temple."[38] She suggests that

36. Williams, *Christian Imagination in Poetry and Polity*, 33.

37. Heldt, "For Brothers to Dwell Together," in The Council of Christians and Jews (ed.), *The Mountain of the Lord*, 60.

38. Ibid., 62.

this realism is "still accepted as life-shaping" because of "the synchronism of the language" and "the synchronism of the landscape," that is, Israelis know the landscape of the Bible intimately, and archaeology has enabled rediscovery of places named in the Bible, authenticating the biblical narratives as historical.[39] It is worth saying here that as Protestants have lacked a tradition of pilgrimage to the Holy Land, it should be unsurprising that they have embraced historical-critical skepticism the most. The fact that Protestantism spread in modern industrializing societies distanced Protestants further from the type of society that could render the biblical world "plausible," and thus it is not accidental that those Protestants who have continued to read the Bible historically have been very supportive of biblical archaeology. She suggests that Christians need "a Halakah of Aliyah," focusing on Isaiah 2:3, Jeremiah 8:23, and Romans 15:9. She points out that "the Book of Zechariah also closes with the vision that those who once persecuted Jews will instead go up to Jerusalem to worship with them the Lord of Hosts."[40] This is startling because she is drawing our attention to Zechariah's eschatological vision as one of reconciliation between enemies after the final battle of this age. The unnerving question here, naturally, is how a christological, and as such figurative, reading of this passage might unfold; would it be militarist or eschew militarism? I shall suggest a way forward below with Barth.

Having proposed immersion in the twin synchronicity of Hebrew and the Land, I also propose that the concept of mystery as it appears in the New Testament become the focus of contemplation and *lectio divina* along with a refocusing of *apophasis* on prophetic injunctions to silence before the mystery of the Day of the Lord.

> "But the Lord is in his holy temple;
> Let all the earth keep silence before him." Hab 2:20

> "Be silent before the Lord God. For the Day of the Lord is at hand." Zeph 1:7

> "Sing and rejoice, O daughter of Zion; for lo, I come and I will dwell in the midst of you, says the Lord. And the Lord will inherit Judah as his portion in the holy land, and will again choose Jerusalem. . . . Be silent, all flesh, before the Lord; for he has roused himself from his holy dwelling." Zech 2:10, 12–13

39. Ibid., 42–43.
40. Ibid., 37.

The Minor Prophets call upon the people of Israel to be silent before Yhwh on the day of his coming. The call and command to silence in the Old Testament is always linked to the day of God's judgment. It is never an idea or a technique initiated by human beings to sharpen their cognitive faculties, such as is much apophatic theology. Habbakuk commands silence as a means of evading the idolatry of the Chaldeans (Babylonians), who are the first of the four empires of Daniel's prophecies. Zephaniah commands silence because the Israelites have spoken and acted against the will of God and offended against his holiness, and even pretended that he will not exercise just judgment on sin. Zechariah, by contrast, enjoins all human beings to be silent because God will come down to bless Jerusalem and the people dwelling in the land of Israel. This is the vision fulfilled at both the first and second coming of Jesus Christ (Gospels; Revelation 1 and 19). While all of this merits a lengthy article or more, the point is clear enough—there is a serious contrast between the reason for the prophets' call to silence before God, and the kind of apophasis that Williams tends to advocate. The one is born of an utterly realistic belief that God acts in history and judges nations. The other shies away from this and even goes as far as questioning and subtly denying that this really has been and will be the case. The kind of silence that would come over the hearer of Habakkuk, Zephaniah, and Zechariah is a profound experience of being struck dumb by the majesty, righteousness, and reality of God. It is the kind of sense of awe that for many people has been their response to the establishment of the state of Israel in the twentieth century. It is certainly what seems to have struck Karl Barth. I am not saying that this event was "the Day of the Lord," but it seems clear to me, as to millions of other Christians around the world, that it is a sign that there *will be* a future Day of the Lord. Hegel did not see this event in his lifetime. Those who follow in his footsteps today have seen it and do not understand it in the light of the Day of the Lord, probably because they don't really believe in this end to history.

The very establishment of modern Israel has had an important effect on Christian theological speech. In the words of T. F. Torrance, it has provoked an epistemological crisis that has threatened to rupture the coherence of theology. Responses have varied. Many have simply ignored the challenge and thus, wittingly or not perpetuated, a supersessionist approach to the nation of Israel. Others have labored hard to overcome centuries of anti-Semitic prejudice, and these scholars tend to fall into different groups. Many have sought to acknowledge Judaism as a religion with continued theological validity. Others have focused on Jewish culture and nationality, and yet others on the Jewish roots of Christianity. Finally, there are a number who have turned against the State of Israel and against the Jewish roots of Christianity. In most cases, Christians have written a huge amount about Jews, Judaism, and Israel. Those who have written more concisely about Israel—Karl Barth, T. F. Torrance, David Torrance—have understood the mystery, and the compact style of writing suggests a prior experience of awe at the foreshadowing of the Day of the Lord. Their response has not been a continuous advocacy of an evasive apophasis, but a continued reading of the biblical texts as witnessing to the history of the covenant. Some recent Messianic Jewish theologians have also advocated a more reserved approach to eschatology than dominant premillennialism, though they still hold that Israel has a providential role as a nation preserved by God and journeying towards christological fulfillment.[41] Karl Barth's theology is cited as a major source for this approach. It is fitting then that we now turn to his work on Israel.

THE ELECTION OF ISRAEL AS SEEN WITHIN THE DOCTRINES OF CREATION AND PROVIDENCE

Karl Barth developed his doctrinal account of Israel over a long period of time, beginning in the doctrine of election in the second half-volume of the *Church Dogmatics*, written during the Second World War. He then continued to develop it in his doctrine of creation, his theological anthropology and his doctrine of reconciliation and eschatology. Thus Israel spans the major dogmatic loci in Barth's *Church Dogmatics*. For Barth, all humanity is elect in Jesus Christ. The election of the community of the people of God—Israel and church—is enclosed within this. Membership of the Israelite nation and people was as logically indispensable to the incarnation as was his incarnation as a man. As the election of the Jewish people is enclosed within the election of all people, they are neither superior nor inferior to their fellow human beings. The survival of the Jews as a nation is hinted at as a parable or fulfillment of Ezekiel's vision of the valley of the dry bones in Barth's doctrine of creation, published in 1945.[42] Herein, the covenant is the internal basis of creation. According to Genesis 2:7, man was created from the dust. Barth links this to God's calling of Abraham and his formation of Israel. As man is formed "from a

41. Harvey, *Mapping Messianic Jewish Theology*, 223–61.
42. Barth, *Church Dogmatics* III/1, 248.

handful of dust taken from the rest," so God elects Abraham and his seed "from a multitude of nations, thus causing the body of Israel to come into being and fashioning it as a distinct and peculiar people, but one whose nature is like that of all peoples . . ."[43]

God ratifies his choice of Abraham by making a covenant with Israel, and giving it "a prophetic Spirit," by which the people will receive a soul and will become "in contrast to all other nations, a living people." This is the *ethnos/laos* (nation/people) distinction made in the biblical Greek, translating the Hebrew *gôy* and *'am*.[44] The events of the Red Sea, Sinai, and Jerusalem confirm God's promises to Abraham. Man's inevitable return to dust at death is analogous to Israel as a nation (*ethnos*), doomed to sink and perish in the mass of the nations. This actual disappearance proves that Israel's only hope is in God, and that indeed God is the only hope of man and of the whole world. Barth goes on to say that Ezekiel 37 (the narrative of the dry bones) is "the most powerful commentary on Gen. 2:7." In this passage "it has reached the climax of its history, and this climax is the end which always threatened and has now come." The prophetic Spirit was not killed when Israel became a valley of dry bones. Barth's christological reading of this is important.

> If he really spoke of the fulfilment of its history as this took place in Jesus Christ on the far side of Israel's destruction, he did not prophesy in vain but in the name of God. For what took place in Jesus Christ is precisely the resurrection of Israel from the dead by the power of the prophetic breath of life which for the sake of the nations had created it as a nation, and which was not killed and did not die with Israel.[45]

The analogy between Israel and human beings arises from the representative role of the typology of Adam and Jesus Christ, as representatives of the creation. In this respect, it is very important to observe what previous commentators on Barth have not, which is that the fact that he connected creation and covenant was not merely a dogmatic move on Barth's part, but an exegetical and hermeneutical one as well. Breaking with the Documentary Hypothesis, Barth argues that "the *toledoth* [generations] of the heavens and the earth" in Genesis 2:4a, rather than being a late editorial imposition, could be the original title of

43. Ibid., 247.

44. See *ethnos* and *laos* in Kittel and Friedrich (eds.), *Theological Dictionary of the New Testament*, 201–2, 499–505.

45. Barth, *CD* III/1, 248, 33.

the section that source critics claim runs up to Genesis 3:24. Most source critics, proponents of the Documentary Hypothesis, argue that the P source is the origin of the text enclosed within Genesis 1:1 and Genesis 2:4a. Confessional readers, especially in the Reformed tradition, have long argued in response to criticism that the repetition of the Hebrew sentence "these are the generations of X" throughout Genesis indicates the textual division intended for the whole book. As a result, they argue that the section starting at Genesis 1:1 actually finishes at Genesis 2:3. Since the seventeenth century, Reformed orthodox theologians and Orthodox Jewish exegetes have argued the latter case, and their approach has been closely linked to the defense of the Mosaic authorship of Genesis and the entire Pentateuch. Following this hermeneutical path allows Barth to show that creation ("heaven and earth") and history (starting with the genealogies of Adam, Noah, etc.) belong together, constituting the "pre-history and history of Israel." Furthermore this fits nicely with Barth's supralapsarian doctrine of election, arguing that God created creation in order to graciously elect man. Given that Jesus Christ *is* the true and elect man for Barth, this means this is his way of articulating the doctrine of "incarnation anyway," found as far back as Maximus the Confessor and Duns Scotus, and more recently popularized by Schleiermacher and Isaac Dorner.[46]

The traditional doctrine of Israel's survival and rebirth as a nation is that the prophets and Jesus prophesied the scattering of the nation across the world as a punishment for rejection the Messiah, yet at some unspecified time before the return of Christ to return to the promised land for good. Barth transposed this doctrine into the sphere of the doctrine of election, thus making it something that God foreknew all along. Any claim that Israel's existence as a nation is a fulfillment of Old or New Testament prophecy is now to be tested against the christologically grounded doctrine of election, which links closely to the form of Barth's doctrine of creation and covenant, and of providence. Barth wrote of the creation of the State of Israel within his doctrine of creation and his doctrine of providence. Providence for Barth must be understood christologically, not in a deist or correlationist manner. This is especially because Hitler was fond of the term "providence."[47] It should be noted here that Barth did regard Hitler as a type of the antichrist.

46. On supralapsarian Christology, see the excellent study by Van Driel, which includes two whole chapters on Barth, *Incarnation Anyway*.

47. Barth, *Church Dogmatics* III/3

Israel's creaturely existence is only secured by God's fidelity to his covenant.[48] Barth tells us that "the divine ruling" is decisive for his doctrine of providence. It is the ruling of God the Father. God the Father is the King of Israel, in the New Testament as well as the Old. He is "the same Lord of the same covenant."[49] Barth has three principles on the divine ruling. First, God rules alone. Therefore he is the goal to which his rule directs humanity and indeed all of creation.[50] This means God is not constrained by natural processes.[51] Second, God rules by establishing order.[52] Third, the people of the King of Israel includes non-Jews, and still includes Jews as Jews.[53] In this way, Barth argues that they are a light to the nations. His identity as the King of all nations is not fully revealed in the Old Testament, but is in the New. The divine ruling is not revealed through the movement of history, but only by its biblical form. From this we learn "world-occurrence generally stand under the same lordship and has the same relationship, because the King of Israel is its King too."[54]

Barth believes there are "signs and witnesses" within world-occurrence that have a special relation to the history of the covenant and salvation, and therefore to "that one revelation of the divine world-governance."[55] There are four witnesses: the history of Scripture, the history of the church, the history of the Jewish people, and the limitation of human life. They are "a permanent riddle" in relation to the rest of history, only explicable from the perspective of the God who rules history. Only those with the eyes and ears to see and hear them will. For Barth the history of the Jews begins in A.D. 70. He thinks they are now fulfilling their Isaianic mission to be a light to the Gentiles. God's love is what has sustained the Jewish people as a people.[56] Barth would situate Israel even more clearly within the history of redemption in the fourth volume of the *Dogmatics*, which involved reworking his theology completely.

48. Ibid., 84.
49. Ibid., 176, 179.
50. Ibid., 158–59.
51. Ibid., 160–61.
52. Ibid., 164–67.
53. Ibid., 181.
54. Ibid., 196–97.
55. Ibid., 199.
56. Ibid., 218–19.

THE HISTORY OF ISRAEL PREFIGURES THE HISTORY OF THE MESSIAH

In his doctrine of the Little Lights, within his doctrine of reconciliation, Barth characterizes Jesus Christ as the true witness to God. He contrasts the prophets, who are only witnesses to the covenant and not by way of their lives true types or adequate prefigurations of Jesus. Rather, Jesus can be compared with "the glory of the history of Israel . . . in its character both as a divine act and as the experience and action of the men of Israel, and in its character as an unbroken sequence of new events of divine faithfulness . . . as contrasted with the great unfaithfulness of man."[57] The prophets' witness and activity does not "bring to expression the history of Israel," but only serves to "confirm and record that this is what happens." This is because the history of Israel is grounded in the Word of God as speech and declaration, and as Word in the flesh. Prophecy occurs with the history. Barth then goes on to argue that this is why "the Old Testament is every-where, and not merely in explicit narration, a book of history."[58] Thus he undercuts any possibility of his own work, or the Bible, being read accord-ing to a "narrative theology" or "narrative ethics." Narrative as a category represents a truncation of the notion of history from being referential to merely formal, reproducing the problems with postliberal theology we saw in chapter 2. In order to drive this point home, Barth refers to the later prophetic writings and the Psalms as being supremely concerned with the history of the covenant past, present, and future. The very fact that the Psalms are connected to King David is a sign that they are bound up with promise and fulfillment in David, and at the same time David himself as the promise of a future fulfillment of royal hopes for Israel. Wisdom literature also ultimately has to do with the history of the covenant.[59] The history of Israel, like that of Jesus, is "the city on the hill which cannot be hid."[60] It is "the light of the world lighting every man."[61] This is very important. The history of the modern State of Israel today is one of the little lights in creation that witnesses to the light of the world who is Jesus Christ himself.

57. Ibid., IV/3, 1, 53.
58. Ibid., 54.
59. Ibid., 55.
60. Ibid., 56.
61. Ibid., 65.

Old Testament prophecy as a whole is universal, even though individual prophets are not universal in the scope of their addresses. Barth then cites a string of Old Testament passages that have historically been used by the Protestant philosemitic tradition to speak of the second and final return of the Jews to Israel, and the growth of the church in relation to this process.

> It is obvious that this whole witness to the universal significance, scope and meaning of the history of Israel has an eschatological character. It was its future or final course which was presented to the Old Testament witnesses in this universal prophetic character. But we should not lose sight of the fact that it was still the familiar past and present history which was presented to them in this final course and therefore in this character.[62]

In other words, the prophets themselves were not given photographic representations of the twentieth century and beyond. The prophecies were not couched as straightforward predictions in the scientific sense. They were given as events in antiquity functioning as figures or types for subsequent listeners and readers to use as criteria for discerning the signs of the times. Nevertheless, Barth addresses Pietist concerns that these writings are speaking of events since 1948. He notes that this history "even now hurries relentlessly to this future."[63] In other words, it was *not* fulfilled with the founding of the church in the first century. Barth is able to read these passages in this way because of his notion of the threefold *parousia*, with eschatology being rooted in Christology. Jesus' first coming is the incarnation, the second *parousia* being Pentecost, and the third being eschatological. Thus it is plausible to read these passages as prefiguring both the growth of the church after Pentecost and the growth of the church after the return of the Jews to Israel in the twentieth century, but as part of one overall moment. This is also why Barth's postwar Old Testament exegesis is so historical—he sees Old Testament so-called "eschatological" passages as a window into contemporary history, reading the Bible in one hand and the newspaper in the other. (Typically, Barth scholars miss this and only link his comment about Bible and newspaper to his Christian socialism. Yet both socialism and Israel were secular parables of the kingdom for Barth, thus he must have had both in mind.) This history he narrates up to the "catastrophe of Samaria and Jerusalem" and "the new exile and return." He is reluctant to dismiss what are considered

62. Ibid., 59.
63. Ibid.

nationalistic overtones in the prophets, and equally reluctant to read these passages only in an eschatological sense, given that they clearly also have a historical sense. He even goes as far as arguing that in terms of the ends of history, the later prophets agree with the apostles and the New Testament.[64] What is meant is that the universal international vision of Old Testament prophets is balanced by the universalism of Romans 9–11, which is in fact concerned with the moment of inclusion of Jews into the community worshipping Jesus as the Messiah. The universalism of the prophecy of Jesus was evident to the New Testament church from other writings of Paul, John, and Luke.

ELECTION AND REPROBATION IN THE HISTORIES OF JESUS AND ISRAEL

Central to Barth's doctrine of reconciliation is the contention that the Word became *Jewish* flesh.[65] This illustrates what Bruce McCormack has correctly understood as Barth's turn from Platonic metaphysics to forge a new metaphysics of actualistic divine ontology: God's being is in his acts.[66] Though McCormack does not say it, a large part of Barth's reason for his turn from classical metaphysics is precisely his doctrine of the election of Israel as well as Jesus. Barth's talk of Jesus' suffering the suffering of Israel refers both to the cross and to him suffering with Jews in the *Shoah*. This is because the histories of both Israel and Jesus are histories of humiliation and suffering. The Son of God exists in solidarity with Israel. Like Job, he is silent. Barth even argues that "we can and must think of the history of the Jews right up to our own day."[67] While this is deeply offensive to many ears, it is logically linked to Barth's view that the foundation of the State of Israel is a symbol of the resurrection of the people in Ezekiel. Thus we can make the following argument. Israel's history is a type of the history of Jesus. The history of Jesus is the history of the election and rejection of human beings in the one, elect Son of God. It is therefore also the history of the election and rejection of Israel in the elect son of God. Thus, we can improve on Barth's theology and say the history of Israel before the incarnation prefigures Jesus' history, and the history of Israel after the exile

64. Ibid., 60.

65. Barth, *Church Dogmatics* IV/1, 167.

66. McCormack, "Grace and Being," in McCormack, *Orthodox and Modern*, 183–200.

67. Barth, *CD* IV/1, 175.

of A.D. 70 is also a type of Jesus' history, of "the Way of the Son into the Far Country." These two phases of Israel's history are not simply dichotomized as the church already existing in the Old Testament and the "blind synagogue" of medieval anti-Judaism. This is because both promise and fulfillment, and judgment and grace, are to be found in both Testaments. Rather, the two phases together represent both the election and reprobation of Israel insofar as they are understood as linked to the one covenant wrought in Jesus Christ.

What is vital to realize is that, for Barth, *Israel is God's servant nation.* It history is an "exact prefiguration" of the Messianic prophecy of Jesus Christ.

> In all its autonomy and singularity, and therefore in all its distinction, it is a true type and an adequate pattern. To use a much abused but in its true sense valuable expression, it is Messianic prophecy, and indeed complete Messianic prophecy. And when we say this, we mean that as a declaration of the divine wisdom controlling it, it is fore-telling.[68]

Clearly addressing dispensationalist, broader premillennialist, and prophetic concerns, Barth argues that Israel's history and its prophecy are fulfilled in Jesus and therefore cannot run further. The history of Jesus is true history for Barth, because Jesus is the true witness. Thus the history of Israel is true history insofar as it is bound up with the history of Jesus Christ. This sounds as if he is dismissing the history of Israel after Christ's first coming completely. In reality, we already know that for Barth, Israel survived because of Christ's providential grace and election. Therefore, what he is emphasizing is that people learn to read the meaning of Israel's history in the light of Christ's coming.

> What might seem to be [fulfillment of prophecy in the present day] are only recollections of their former occurrence which is now broken off and concluded. As such they may be very impressive. They may even be a kind of proof of God, as the history of what is called Judaism has been called. . . . As abstract recollections they have always a notably unsubstantial and unprofitable character, with no true or genuine prophecy, because even at best their prophecy is only the old without the new, without the fulfilment at which it always aimed even as the old, and which it has long since found in the new.[69]

68. Ibid., 65.
69. Ibid., 69–70.

To be precise, what Barth wants to avoid is the kind of reading of biblical prophecy and contemporary events that views them as *only* having to do with the history of Israel and not with the election of Jesus Christ. It has to be said, however, that his idea of history constituting "recollections" is odd. It seems to gesture towards the idea that God arranged the post-biblical history of Israel such that it would imitate its prior history figuratively, perhaps as a negative witness. Immediately after this caution, Barth goes on to insist that the history of Israel is not "outmoded, replaced or dissolved," because the one covenant between God and man in the election of Jesus "was its basis, content and goal." Thus he rules out all theological justifications for replacement of Israel by other nations, or denial of the validity of Israel's existence as a nation. Finally, there is only one Prophet, Jesus, to which both Testaments witness, as the New Testament is latent in the Old, and the Old is patent in the New. The one covenant of this one Prophet has a twofold form, "first concealed" in the history of Israel, then revealed in the history of Jesus Christ. This implies that Barth can make sense of the covenant with Abraham concerning his physical descendants inhabiting the Land (Gen 15) *within* the election of Jesus Christ.

ISRAEL'S HOSTILE NEIGHBORS AND THE TURN TO WORSHIP GOD

Barth spoke of Israel in his final articulation of the doctrine of providence in *CD* IV/3.2, published in 1959. Therein Barth says that his doctrine of providence published in *CD* III/3 back in 1948,

> has nothing whatever to do with an optimistic evaluation of the world. In the sense indicated it follows very soberly from the necessity of understanding the first article of the creed in the light of the second, which refers in closing to the *sessio Filii ad dextram Patris omnipotentis.*[70]

The example that Barth gives of the providence of God ruling world history is the Old Testament depiction of the Gentile nations living alongside Israel as the one people of God. Israel's history is the inner circle and the history of its neighbors is the outer circle. Election therefore is not imagined in an exclusive manner. Thus Barth starts with the narratives of creation in Genesis, "which are unmistakeably understood and fashioned in retrospect of the guidance and experience of Israel and therefore in the

70. Ibid., IV/3, 2, 688.

light of the inner circle."[71] This, of course, is close to Niebuhr's historical-critical evaluation of Israel's covenant and biblical writings as based on her covenant experience; though, as we have seen, Barth goes deeper into hermeneutics and its relation to dogmatics and ethics. He stresses that through Abram "shall all the families of the earth be blessed" (Gen 12:3), and that even Ishmael, ancestor of the Arabs, also being the son, was to be circumcised and protected by God. He stresses that the peoples of Moab and Ammon are relatives of Abraham, and that Jacob and Esau's dispute ends in reconciliation, such that "the race of Edom, later to be another unpleasant neighbour of Israel, is given a place in the account of the patriarchs."[72] Moving on through the history of hostility of the native Canaanites, Midianites, and Philistines down to the war with Rome in A.D. 70, Barth comments on the mysterious fact that

> no nation in world history, when it has come to the end of its independent existence, has been so little assimilated, or has been able so mysteriously and yet so genuinely and distinctly and continuously to maintain its identity in the sea of surrounding, overflowing and absorbing alien peoples, of *goyim* old and new with their own histories and languages and cultures, as has the people of Abraham, Isaac and Jacob.[73]

The Jews are *not* disinherited from the promises of nationhood for Barth. He goes on to say that perhaps the Jews will survive "the modern powers" just as they survived those of classical antiquity, with or without the help of the State of Israel. Indeed, he observes how they outlasted Hitler's "thousand-year Reich." This comment on the Nazi regime being set up in opposition to the existence of Jews is important, as it is meant in a generic sense to argue that *any* national regime set up in deliberate opposition to the existence of Israel as a nation will not fare very well in the long run. Barth was writing in 1959, a year after Yasser Arafat had founded Fatah. Barth would live to see the founding of the Palestinian Liberation Organization in 1964. Thus, while Barth does not comment on the right of Palestinians as Gentiles to inhabit the promised land alongside Israel, he does tacitly condemn any overt or especially covert intention by Palestinian organizations to dismantle Israel as a Jewish nation-state, as being an instance of the denial by their members of their own election in and through Jesus, the Jewish Messiah. Once again,

71. Ibid.
72. Ibid., 689.
73. Ibid., 690.

Barth scholars have ignored this. They are not really entitled to do so, for Barth's train of reasoning here matches exactly the criticism he made in the aftermath of *Kristallnacht*, of European nations who intended to destroy the Jewish nation. In 1967, he criticized severely European Christians who came out against the Six Day War.[74] On 3 July, the Working Committee of the Prague Christian Peace Conference had "pronounced against Israel's fight for existence." In August 1967, Barth was invited to write an essay for a collection entitled "Jewish-Christian Solidarity in the Third Reich." He could not meet this invitation, but sent a note saying that there was a contemporary need to resurrect the Jewish-Christian solidarity that arose during the Nazi period. Unless this happened, in the face of Israel having to fight for its very existence, the solidarity of the Nazi era would be rendered meaningless. This was to be a covenant-based solidarity. We can also say that this was to be covenant-based recognition of Israel as nation-state. It is from this rootedness in election, moving in between the election of Israel in Abraham—himself from the line of Noah and thus linked to the division of the human race into nations by language and location (but not on any ontological grounds)—and all of this is part of the eternal election of the Son, that a theological form of recognition of every nation, be it a nation-state or a stateless nation, can be given. It must be given as part of missiology.

Commenting on the surrounding nations, Barth lists individual figures from among them who worshipped the God of Israel and who supported Israel's cause and existence. He also instances the repentance and conversion of the entirety of Nineveh in the book of Jonah. Thus he can say that "it is only in co-existence with the people of God, and not as the subject of independent or neutral interest, that the nations appear on the canvas of the Old Testament."[75] It is God who rules over their history with Israel. It is God, not Israel, who is truly magnified in its history with its neighbors—yet the Gentile nations, too, only exist because God allows them to. Barth then cites a string of citations from the Psalms concerning the praise of the nations to the God of Israel, the eschatological deliverer of Jerusalem.

In a passage that at first sight seems to contradict his lifelong opposition to the idea of nations as orders of creation, Barth says: "God has created the nations (Ps. 86:9). In fact He is already their King (Ps. 47:8). Hence their raging against His people is already futile (Ps. 2:1). This is the

74. Lindsay, *Barth, Israel and Jesus*, 84.
75. Barth, *CD* IV/3: 2, 691.

decisive thing which the Old Testament sees and says concerning them in the light of its own theme and centre."[76] Is Barth here overturning his lifelong view about the orders of creation? Not necessarily. The term "nations" refers both to all Gentile people and to individual nations across time and space. What we see here is the coordination of both senses, in line with the enclosure of the doctrine of providence within a christologically grounded doctrine of creation. To say God "created the nations" here is not to claim that they were present at the moment of *creation ex nihilo*, for Barth has said nothing to undo his commitment to the genealogies of Genesis 1–11. It is a statement about how the very existence of Gentile nations is bound up with the existence of Israel, all are spheres governed by God, and their cultural and political continuity is under divine judgment and grace. This is precisely the implication of the entire metanarrative of the Old and New Testaments. (It must be said at this point the guild of Barth scholars has tended to ignore passages of this kind, preferring the attack on the orders of creation, largely because the reading of Barth has been divided according to confessional battles over ethics, especially sexual ethics, in the Protestant churches).

What this means is that for Barth, the rage of *modern* Israel's neighbors, which are in fact descendants of its ancient neighbors (Egypt, Lebanon, Syria still exist; some of the Palestinians see themselves as Philistines or Canaanites), is ultimately futile. Nevertheless, it is vitally important to realize that the surrounding nations are *not annihilated* in Barth's reading of the prophets' eschatology. Their struggle against Israel's existence is futile, irrational; indeed they can be understood as a striving against their own election, because sin for Barth is the absurd striving to live an autonomous life against election. There *is* hope for them and their inhabitants in turning to worship the God of Israel who has revealed himself through Jesus Christ. Therefore we do not see in Barth any of the populist scenarios about nuclear warfare in the Middle East, or war destroying the surrounding nations completely, nor do we see a rapture of the saints to escape the coming Armageddon. We do not even see the church in triumph over the nations—hardly surprising given Barth's seriously reserved ecclesiology in the wake of the Nazification of the mainline Protestant churches after 1933 and the failures of the confessing church. *Jesus alone* is the victor over evil and the true witness to the Father on earth.

76. Ibid., 692–93.

CONCLUSION: KARL BARTH AS HEIR OF PIETISM—THE CHALLENGE TO THE "MAINLINE" CHURCHES

The greatest weakness in the scholarship on Barth's politics and eschatology by those who have concentrated most on these, is they completely ignore the evidence for Barth working within the Pietist or evangelical prophetic tradition concerning Jews and Israel. From knowing the world of Barth scholarship inside, it is not hard to see why. With a few exceptions, Barth scholars are PhD students disgruntled with evangelical churches. They fall easily into the trap set by the younger Barth himself of differentiating sharply between himself and the Pietists, or himself and the seventeenth-century Reformed orthodox. Barth's massive ego speaks to their own quest for identity as theologians. In the United States in particular, because dispensationalist formulations of Zionism are a staple of evangelicalism, persons disgruntled with the latter are apt to run a mile from theological accounts of Israel. Of course, there are other reasons why scholars of Barth's work may choose to ignore or minimize the importance of his work on Israel. They range from disinterest in the Old Testament as Scripture to the doctrinaire anti-nationalism criticized at the outset of this book.

Happily, there are now newer works on Barth that are more guided by intellectual curiosity than by reaction. The writing of Christian T. Collins Winn on Barth's debt to the Blumhardts proves particularly helpful regarding Israel.[77] Barth's theological approach to Israel is not fully intelligible until we acknowledge his profound debt to the German Pietist preacher Johann Christoph Blumhardt, and his son Christoph Friedrich Blumhardt. Christian T. Collins Winn has demonstrated from a mass of documentary and comparative evidence that Blumhardtian understanding of themes such as the kingdom of God in relation to Christian socialism and eschatology deeply influenced Barth from his break with liberalism onwards. Along with Eberhard Busch, he uncovers Barth's self-serving tendency to call his favorite German Pietists "non-Pietistic," propping up his youthful caricature of them as religious individualists and subjectivists. J. C. Blumhardt (1805–80) was born into a strongly Pietistic family in Stuttgart. The family believed in the millenarian eschatology of Johann Albrecht Bengel, a major biblical exegete of the movement who had predicted that the millennium would

---

77. Winn, *"Jesus is Victor!"*

begin in 1836.[78] They seriously expected final tribulations of the faithful and the coming of the Antichrist, which they seem to have interpreted as the Napoleonic wars of the time. Both Blumhardt theologians rejected this apocalyptic eschatology, but carried on its tendency to read the "signs of the times" in God's kingdom.[79] J. C. Blumhardt studied theology at Tübingen and became a pastor in Basel, serving in the Basel Mission house (1830–37) teaching Hebrew, physics, chemistry, and mathematics. The interest in Hebrew was no accident as Blumhardt was passionate about missions to the Jews. Winn says this was grounded in a dual stress on Christ's humanity and an apocalyptic eschatology.[80] The incarnation was the ground for Christian solidarity with Jews. Conversion of the Jews as a sign of the coming kingdom of God was an old Pietist belief, not only espoused by Bengel and Karl Kollner, as Winn says, but going right back to Philip Jakob Spener, the founder of German Pietism in the seventeenth century. The belief that there would be mass Jewish conversion to Christ is found throughout Blumhardt's written works, linked to his idea of the "time of grace," when the whole earth would be renewed by God to prepare for the *parousia*.[81] This is a conviction that goes right back to the dawn of Protestantism, sixteenth-century Christian Hebraists among both the Reformers and the Humanists. In fact, it goes much further back than this to sections of the early church.

Blumhardt's eschatology was formed by a christocentric reading of the Hebrew prophets, which is unsurprising given that his job was to teach Hebrew. He preferred them to the book of Revelation. Winn backs up this point by citing Blumhardt's view that the prophets gave descriptions of the *eschaton* that were "more straightforward, concrete and filled with hope," unlike Revelation, which is vastly more difficult to understand.[82] The younger Blumhardt had abandoned his father's concerns for Jewish mission and healing mission in favor of social activism, "the healing of the body politic."[83] *Barth refused to dichotomize his interests in this way.* Nevertheless, Barth did not repudiate what he had learned from the younger Blumhardt, namely that he had discarded his father's "loosely periodized theology of history," a kind of dispensationalism. Instead, Barth allows,

78. Ibid., 79.

79. Ibid., 77.

80. Ibid., 79.

81. Ibid., 79–90, fn. 45.

82. Ibid., 80, fn. 48.

83. Ibid., 110–54.

without describing historically, the ongoing erruption of the kingdom of God in Jesus detectable in parables of the kingdom. Barth follows J. C. Blumhardt in being reticent about the millennial kingdom of Christ and in rejecting the notion of a second or final tribulation and other aspects distinct to dispensationalism. Blumhardt believed the delay of the time of grace was due to the church's failure; that is, God was waiting for the church to be faithful. He did not believe that the time of grace needed to be preceded by a final tribulation and destruction. Instead he taught that there would be a final and sudden outpouring of the Spirit before the final judgment, through which "many who are far off might be brought back."[84]

Blumhardt nevertheless did not do what amillennialists in the tradition have done, which is to date the millennial kingdom of Revelation 20 from Pentecost due to Peter's citation of Joel 3:1f. The reason is that the millennium in Revelation comes to an end with conflict and judgment. Instead, Blumhardt taught that the time of the Spirit since Pentecost was a time of grace during which God's kingdom would progress in history. The transition from history to eternity would be more a day of forgiveness. This can be characterized as postmillennialism. We see this belief carried over into Barth's (unfinished) eschatology, his notion of the threefold *parousia*—Pentecost, the return of Christ, and between the two the global outpouring of the Holy Spirit. It should be clear that this is Barth's way of talking of a kind of "revival" or mass conversion, the "final battle" of Jesus against evil *in lieu of the militarist Christology of some forms of dispensationalism*. This is surely *extremely* important because it constitutes a constructive *alternative*—something not provided by scholarly critics of dispensationalism as we have seen.

Among these scholarly critics is Williams. How does the foregoing account of Barth's theological approach to Israel challenge Williams' approach? Barth and Williams stand in many ways diametrically opposed to each other. This is important to realize, particularly because Williams likes citing Barth as if Barth is a figure who can be assimilated into his own outlook. In reality, Barth represents a major challenge to it. Although Williams is very affirmative of the view that God created humans out of love in order to delight in them, it is not clear that this leads to a supralapsarian doctrine of election. We see that Williams' Christology harbors adoptionist overtones, suggesting an infralapsarian view of the incarnation as a response to the fall. Whereas for Barth, Abraham is a historical figure, the father of Israel, it is not clear whether Williams really believes

---

84. Ibid., 105.

he was historical. Israel started at the exodus for Williams, suggesting that he clings to a Hermetic view of Israel, and that he has no theory of the origin of nations following Genesis. God is definitely not a process for Barth, which means that providence does not involve our cooperation in completing creation, let alone ushering in global peace and justice by our own efforts or programs. Barth's view that the history of Israel is a figure of the history of Jesus, both as election and reprobation, is also a type of the history of all nations. Hermeneutically, Barth derives this from reading Isaiah as the Fifth Gospel.[85] Williams, by contrast, does not make much use of the Old Testament for eschatology and ethics conjoined. As we have seen, his attitude seems to be we produce "peace." It is significant here that there is no mention of the second coming of Jesus Christ in any of Williams' theology. Jesus is not represented as coming to judge the nations in his work. By contrast, Barth's unfinished eschatology, so rooted in his Christology, strongly suggests the idea of a nonviolent *parousia* where Jesus' judgment is really the final, gracious outpouring of the Holy Spirit upon all nations—a final revival, so to speak. Meanwhile, of course, Christian mission must continue, as it is rooted in the Great Commission.

This brings us back to the challenge of the recognition of nations for theology. Mission involves not only preaching but also hearing and listening, and acceptance or rejection of the message. It should go without saying that addressing people in mission requires addressing them in the fullness of their reality. Part of that reality is that God has placed people to live in nations. If this dimension of their lives is ignored, or goes unrecognized, either by tacit omission, or by pretending that the nation to which certain people belong is of little worth, or isn't really a nation because to be a nation means to have one's own state, then those people are far less likely to listen to the message. Ignoring the secular, or slighting it as something that shouldn't exist, involves in practice slighting or misrecognizing national identity. The entire critique of Williams and Milbank in this book has amounted to this, that *they have not given nationhood its due regard as a topic in theology*, and that this shows up in their handling of both Wales and Israel. As heirs of a colonialist, imperialist tradition, they are really stuck here. Of course, their denomination in practice does recognize different kinds of nation, but the theologians seem to have serious trouble finding the right intellectual tools for doing so. If my analysis is correct, there is an eerie parallelism between the difficulties they have recognizing Israel, and the reluctance, for so many reasons, to recognize Wales as a

85. Gignillat, *Barth and the Fifth Gospel*.

nation. If this is the case, and I believe I have shown it is, then no wonder our theologians have so much trouble even beginning to see the sense in the idea that Palestinians constitute a stateless nation in yet another sense, a nation that has never had its own state. When we compare these with Karl Barth, it is evident that there are two traditions of the recognition of nations here, one based on the state as having the ultimate power to recognize what or who is a nation, and one based on the biblical view that it is language, culture, and location—the ties that bind a people—that are the criteria. These two traditions clash. Their attitude to the origin of Israel, and their attitude to the Old Testament as inspired Scripture, is at the root of this clash.

7

Conclusion

How ARE OUR THREE themes interrelated? We have seen how ambivalent attitudes to nationhood yield an unreliable commitment to respecting the State of Israel's "right to exist." It is *not* the case Rowan Williams has a clear, stable, reliable, theological notion of this. John Milbank operates within a profoundly esoteric approach to nations specifically, and to theology generally. Reinhold Niebuhr's conception of Israel is stable and unwavering, but non-theological. Effectively, he puts the United States at the center of world history through its commitment to Israel. The problem with Niebuhr is that however reasonable and careful, his approach could not carry through to subsequent generations of Protestants because it was insufficiently theologically rooted. There was consequently a heightened danger that Israel would become America writ large, thus almost inevitably inviting the post-1967 and especially post-1990 backlash in some quarters. Only Karl Barth has a commitment that is both stable and theologically rooted. Of these four theologians, Barth is the only one who speaks plainly about Gentile nations existing only at the mercy of God. Barth also scores above Niebuhr, Milbank, and Williams in actually engaging in a constructive manner, albeit nevertheless with insufficient detail of reference, with the Pietist and millenarian traditions. His basic attitude was that even where these committed what he saw as theological errors, they were at times errors in the right direction. This should cut through the dramas of secularization, desecularization, and religious resurgence, which we dissected in the first chapter.

Many will not like what I have shown of Barth's actual thinking in this book, because he will strike them as too close to the millenarian traditions. The question that must be asked here is what precisely is the problem. The animus against beliefs about Israel in relation to prophecy is often, underneath, really the expression of annoyance at any notion that divine providence might be concerned with events outside the history of the churches. It punctures the bubble of those who consider the church more important than worldly bodies. As Barth himself well understood, such annoyance is also, secretly, annoyance at the implication that because elect Israel is still with us, we are being reminded that all nations, every nation that has ever existed and every nation that has ever perished or will yet come into existence, survives ultimately at the mercy of God. Every nation is under judgment. I am deeply suspicious of the narrow church-centeredness of theologies that deny a place for Israel. They seem to be motivated for the purity of the church and Christian doctrine at the expense of being interested in making Christian sense of *history*. It is to Barth's credit that he moved beyond the disastrous churchly exclusivism of the confessing church to support early Zionism, and on the grounds that what was needed was Christian support for the human rights of Jews. Unfortunately, this maturing in Barth's perspective has been lost on many of his readers, and I happen to know that there are some very influential scholars of Barth's work who react with annoyance when I've told them precisely how Barth came to think about Israel. Unfortunately for them, this is an unacceptable form of censorship, and if this book will have contributed to the small but necessary pool of scholarship that corrects readings of Barth that choose to ignore Israel, that will be a good thing.

Two basic challenges present themselves: the biblical witness, as suggested above, and also the fact that there is an undeniable link between eschatology and one's understanding of providence. Barth's theology cleverly confronts this evasiveness in advance, by positioning Israel within a Trinitarian understanding of providence and election and the inter-twining of creation and covenant, rather than inserting it straightaway within eschatology and/or prophecy. These large dogmatic themes could well provide a robust framework within which to develop an understanding of the ongoing existence of Israel as somehow related to the vision of the prophets, above all of Christ's prophetic office. At the same time, I hope to have shown in this book how Barth's dogmatic method, based on his christological reading of election, effectively meant that while he didn't pay close enough attention to them, Gentiles living within the Holy Land can be recognized as equal in their right to live there alongside Jews. Straightaway this goes against some contemporary formulations of dispensational eschatology, which deny the Palestinians have an equal right to live in the land, or which make it conditional upon various moral considerations while making Jews' rights unconditional.

At the same time, however, it is true that Barth shares with premillennialists the belief that there will be some sort of final battle or confrontation. The question is, what might this actually mean according to his theological formulation? Barth refrained from developing any sort of detailed apocalyptic narrative, though what he does cite regarding the growth of the church uses the same sources as dispensationalists and historicists, as well as amillennialists who believe Israel's existence to be a sign of prophecy. This focus on the church is very important. Barth's belief is spelled out explicitly in the *Church Dogmatics*. He believed that ultimately, if the surrounding nations were to try to defeat Israel and get rid of it, they would lose, but not be annihilated (unlike many dispensationalist scenarios). He held out hope, based on a figurative reading of the story of Jacob and Esau, of reconciliation between all the nations involved. The source of the possibility of reconciliation would not simply be the church, however, but the final outpouring of the Holy Spirit, which seems to accompany the second coming in his eschatology. As Barth never lived to finish his eschatology, it is impossible to work out whether this really means that he had some sort of "timeline" in mind. What we do know, however, is that he did not believe that when Jesus returns, he will fight a physical war against the leaders of the nations, a belief prominent dispensationalists hold. The final battle was, for Barth, a figure for the war of the Lamb, the sword coming out of Jesus' mouth being the sword of the last judgment, the sword of the Spirit, and as such the outpouring of the Spirit upon all flesh. Thus, we could fill in the gaps left in Barth's eschatology as follows. The reading of Revelation is of the kings of the nations assembling together against Jerusalem, not only figuratively in the sense of being against Christ and the church, but also literally. The peoples living in the Holy Land would want to defend it against neighboring nations. Yet because of the primacy of figural reading for Barth, as for the theological mainstream historically, there would be no literal final battle fought by Christ. Instead, the battle would be the war of the Spirit against all flesh in the form of some sort of Pentecostal conversion or revival. Here it is clear that Barth is an heir of sorts to the evangelical wing of German-speaking Pietism.

Barth's eschatology is arguably the best we have in Western Protestant terms of handling Israel. It is significant, however, that it shies away from the question of dividing the land. What do we know about Barth's theological approach to the land of Israel? We do know that in accordance with much Jewish exegesis, he saw it as the Garden of Eden, where Adam and Eve dwelled. Barth argued in his commentary on Genesis that the survival of the people Israel and the foundation of the state constituted an analogy or parable of creation, and of the resurrection of the dry bones in Ezekiel. This is a common Jewish view.

Barth's notion of secular parables of the kingdom was applied by himself to the State of Israel, as he had done to socialism earlier in his career. It meant he could speak theologically of modern Israel as enclosed within the accompaniment of Israel and of world history by Jesus Christ, without resorting to predictive prophecy, and thus without being open to accusations of harboring a two-covenant theology or dispensationalism. The implication is that Christ is the true inheritor of the land, because he alone is righteous. In the Sermon on the Mount, Jesus says "the meek shall inherit the earth." As this is an allusion to Psalm 37:11, originally written in Hebrew, there is the possibility this is a play on the words *ha aretz*, meaning *both* the earth *and* the land of Israel. Yet who is meek, righteous, and a peacemaker except Jesus Christ? And if Christ's words were a historical prophecy on only one level about human beings inheriting the land, why have generations of non-Christian Gentiles and Jews been allowed to live in the land since the ascension? Theologically, we must reckon with a providential reason here. A clue is found in Barth's doctrine of election. First, grace is unconditional for Barth. Second, Jesus is Jewish because he was born of a human mother, and human because he was born of a Jewish mother. He is the new Adam. Adam is the father of all humans, Jews and Gentiles, for whom Jesus died. Given these two truths, we can construct a theological framework for understanding the issue. Christ was crucified and rejected by both Jews and Gentiles. The Jewish nation was dispersed from the land, and reunited on it in 1948. There they encountered Gentiles again, who refused to leave. Some were Christians, most were Muslims. Given that the land is really Eden, that Jesus is the inheritor of the land, that his grace is unconditional, it must follow according to Barth's theology that Gentiles have just as much a right to live on the land as Jews. Thus Barth's theology has to be opposed to any plans to remove Palestinians from the land. Such plans constitute a counsel of despair. They also involve a misunderstanding of the contours of the biblical witness on the gift of the land.

Now we can move to what Barth says about nations. Barth recognized that there was such a thing as stateless nations as well as nation-states. Does this mean we can employ Barth's theology to argue that within the Holy Land, there is the nation-state of Israel, and the Palestinians, who are a nation but without a proper state? I have deliberately not tackled the question of Palestinians in this book, as this would have been to go beyond the remit. To be precise, Palestine, considered a stateless nation, cannot be considered a stateless nation in the same way as Wales (or Scotland), because unlike them, it has not lost a state in the past. Many hope that it will gain a state in the future. It would take a whole book to handle the question of Palestine as nation properly. Let me say here that there are certain themes and approaches that might prove promising: reviewing what Western and Eastern theologians have written about Palestinians since 1948, looking at the history of Christian Arabs and historic Christian Arabic theology produced by people living in the Palestinian areas, looking at documents of Western missionaries to the Arabs in the modern period, looking at the treatment of Palestine and Palestinians in the discipline of nationalism studies, in Islamic studies, etc. Readers can readily appreciate the magnitude of such a task. Yet the approach I have taken here has drawn back from such a task, and I chose to look first at whether Western theologians can even handle a less difficult, less complex form of recognition.

Important Western theologians are ambivalent about proper recognition, either of Israel, or of a nation that has lost its state, such as Wales. This is not very surprising, when we consider the annoyance at ideas of the continued election of Israel discussed above. There is also the complexity of recognition as a discourse and attitude. Recognizing Wales as a stateless nation is a different matter than recognizing Scotland, because of the manner in which each came to be governed from London. Recognizing Catalans and Basques would be different. Recognizing Native American peoples as stateless nations would entail specific challenges well outside the scope of this book. In reality, this might be a test-case for the social theory of nationalism. The pre-eminent scholars in the field have not really looked at so-called indigenous peoples, who tend to be the province of social anthropology, not sociology. John Milbank might have gotten away with penning a highly metaphysical polemic against modern sociology in the eyes of Western theologians, but a similar polemic against social anthropology would have been shot down in flames in many quarters, given the much higher degree of disciplinary self-awareness and reflexivity in social anthropology, and the even greater hostility to Christianity among anthropologists than sociologists, in large measure because of the atrocities committed against small nations by the imperial "Christian" powers. Not only that, but anthropology, once a colonial discipline, has come home to roost, and some anthropologists, like some scholars in religious studies, produce ethnographies of academia. Writing a manifesto of the style of *Theology and Social Theory* about anthropology might have attracted an ethnographic study of theology in Britain, and that could prove rather interesting . . .

Recognition involves paying close attention to how people designate themselves culturally, linguistically, and politically. It involves accepting that they have both the right and the responsibility to do so. The naming and defining of a nation is never only the work of its enemies. Naming in the Bible has profound significance. In Genesis, the concern about the builders of the Tower of Babel is they have desired to make a *name* for themselves against God. They are not interested in receiving the name God might have for them. The scattering of human beings into nations is a paradox, in that it prevents the possibility of a unified universal polity "making a name for itself," instead ordering the world into nations that must now all learn each others' names and remember that they all have a common ancestor. In other words, they are all faced with the challenge of recognition. Recognition is a challenge because Babel is reversed at Pentecost. The coming of the Spirit does not bring a new human language to replace national languages. Receiving the Spirit does require people to recognize Israel. Paul is very clear in Romans 11 that Gentile cruelty towards Israel is an occasion for God to forfeit Gentile salvation. Hereby, Paul continues the promise of God to Abraham, "I will bless those who bless you, I will curse those who curse you," applied to Abraham's descendants. Often, this promise gets read as referring exclusively to Jews. Others read it in the exact opposite way, as referring only to the church. In the literal-historical sense, it clearly refers to *Israel as nation*. However, given that Abraham is deemed the father of the faithful in the New Testament, it must *also* be read in ecclesial terms. Barth clearly read this promise in its dual sense. The problem with this is that it can be deemed terribly exclusive, as if Christians ought to favor Jews and Israel while being given *carte blanche* to treat other nations in a less respectful manner. Indeed it is important to admit that such tendencies are not exactly absent from contemporary Christianity. How might a theological approach that wants to go with Barth on this avoid falling into this temptation? When Paul asks

Gentiles not to "boast over the branches" or be arrogant towards Jews, he focuses on Jewish election by God. This was effected through Abraham. Recognition of election as the means of our salvation should eventually drive us to look at how Abraham was related to other nations—for example, Ishmael, the son of Abraham, is considered the father of the Arabs. Barth preferred to speak of them through the figure of Jacob and Esau. Perhaps Barth's preference for figural reading was wise here, in that it can open the theological imagination rather than fixing it, for Jacob and Esau are a type of recurring quarrels over election in Barth's theology. Ultimately, his clear teaching is that *all* have been chosen in Jesus Christ, but all must still hear the message, turn, and accept their election as part of conversion.

As for the third theme of the book, how selected social theorists have compared to theologians, I looked not only at nations but also at discourses on secularization and religious resurgence. It became evident that recognition is an important practice in this line of work too, though recognition of the world's religions clearly takes precedence over recognition of nations. This is important because there is no serious discussion among the social theorists handled in this book about concepts of nation in non-Christian religions. Thus, insofar as social theorists fail to investigate this, they probably collude with the statist view of nations, and as such, fail to represent the complexities of history. Such simplification and reductionism of nation to state, even if a nation had a state in the past, and indeed the refusal to countenance seriously the distinction between nation and state, is often a hallmark of secularist thinking. Certainly it flies in the face of the priorities implied in Genesis and Acts. Nevertheless, I have not made this a reason to attack the whole discipline of social theory, for it is a historically situated discipline, and as we saw, the possibility of recognition within it is not entirely absent.

Ultimately, as this book has tried to show, social theorists when taken singlely tend to correspond to specific modes of theology. There is no point in simply advising theologians to beware "social theory" on the grounds that it is secular. The very dichotomy between "theology" and "social theory" has now been exposed as predicated upon an unorthodox, esoteric approach to the former, and to a narrative of decline from the Latin Kingdom of Jerusalem. While there are many esoteric traditions, like there are many confessional Christian traditions, and several Christian traditions that attempt to co-opt esoteric discourses, this book has also shown the affinities between Hegel as a major representative of the Western esoteric traditions within theology, and Rowan Williams. If Gillian Rose is right that sociological discourses, social theory, all ultimately makes sense when traced back to Hegel, perhaps the problem is Hegel's attitude to nations, and to the Bible.

We are now inbetween Karl Barth and the Dutch Reformed theologian, where we were in chapter 3 in the discussion on Wales. As hinted in the last chapter, the real problem is that we have basically before us two opposing traditions of recognition of (and therefore definitions of) nations, which are related to two very different traditions of theology. A choice must be made between them in Christian missiology. What I hope to have shown in this book is that how theologians approach the State of Israel reveals a lot about how they approach their own countries, whether the latter are subtly made more important than Israel, and therefore whether those theologians' attitude to providence, eschatology, and missiology, can be trusted.

Bibliography

Alcock, Leslie. *Arthur's Britain: History and Archaeology, 367–634.* 2nd ed. London: Penguin, 2001.

Almond, Philip. *Heaven and Hell in Seventeenth-Century England.* Cambridge: Cambridge University Press, 2004.

Armitage, David. *The Ideological Origins of the British Empire.* Cambridge: Cambridge University Press, 2000.

Ashcraft, Richard. "Latitudinarianism and Toleration: Historical Myth Versus Political History." In *Philosophy, Science, and Religion in England 1640–1700,* edited by Richard Kroll et al., 151–77. Cambridge: Cambridge University Press, 1992.

Assmann, Jan. *Moses the Egyptian.* Cambridge: Harvard University Press, 1997.

———. *Of God and Gods: Egypt, Israel, and the Rise of Monotheism.* Madison, WI: University of Wisconsin Press, 2008.

Bader-Saye, Scott. *Church and Israel After Christendom: The Politics of Election.* Eugene, OR: Wipf and Stock, 2009.

Barnard, F. M. *Herder's Social and Political Thought.* Oxford: Clarendon, 1965.

Barrett, C. K. *A Critical and Exegetical Commentary on the Acts of the Apostles.* Vol. 1. chs. I–XIV. Edinburgh: T. & T. Clark, 1994.

Barth, Karl. *Church Dogmatics* III/1. Translated by J. W. Edwards, O Bussey, and R. Knight. 1958. Reprint. London: T. & T. Clark, 2004.

———. *Church Dogmatics* IV/1. Translated by G. W. Bromiley. 1956. Reprint. London: T. & T. Clark, 2004.

———. *Church Dogmatics* IV/3: 1. Translated by G. W. Bromiley. 1961. Reprint. London: T. & T. Clark, 2004.

———. *Church Dogmatics* IV/3: 2. Translated by G. W. Bromiley. 1961. London: T. & T. Clark, 2004.

Bauerschmidt, Frederick Christian. "The Word Made Speculative? John Milbank's Christological Poetics." *Modern Theology* 15 (1999) 417–32.

Bavinck, Herman. "Ethics and Politics." In *Essays on Religion, Science, and Society,* 261–78. Grand Rapids: Baker Academic, 2008.

———. *Our Reasonable Faith.* Grand Rapids: Eerdmans, 1956.

Beckford, James A. *Social Theory and Religion.* Cambridge: Cambridge University Press, 2003.

Bennett, G. V. "Conflict in the Church." In *Britain after the Glorious Revolution, 1689–1714,* edited by Geoffrey Holmes, 155–75. New York: Saint Martin's, 1969.

Bennetto, Jason. "The 'Satanic' Brotherhood with Clergymen in its Ranks." *The Independent,* 15 November 2002.

Benson, Bruce Ellis, and Peter Goodwin Hetzel, editors. *Evangelicals and Empire: Christian Alternatives to the Political Status Quo.* Grand Rapids: Brazos, 2008.

Berger, Peter L. *The Precarious Vision: A Sociologist Looks at Social Fictions and Christian Faith.* New York: Doubleday, 1961.

———. *Questions of Faith: A Skeptical Affirmation of Christianity.* Malden, MA: Wiley & Sons, 2003.

———. *Redeeming Laughter: The Comic Dimension of Human Experience.* New York: de Gruyter, 1997.

———. "Reflections of an Ecclesiastical Expatriate." *Christian Century,* 24 October 1990, 964–69. Online http://www.religion-online.org/showarticle.asp?title=232.

———. *The Sacred Canopy: Elements of a Sociological Theory of Religion.* New York: Doubleday, 1967.

Berle, Adolf A. Sr. *The World Significance of a Jewish State.* New York: Kennerly, 1918.

Bertram, G., and K. L. Schmidt. "*Ethnos*" In *Theological Dictionary of the New Testament,* edited by Gerhard Kittel and Gerhard Friedrich, 201–2. Grand Rapids: Eerdmans, 1985.

Betz, John G. *After Enlightenment: The Post-Secular Vision of J. G. Hamann.* Oxford: Blackwell, 2012.

Bezzant, Rhys. "The Ecclesiology of Rowan Williams." In *On Rowan Williams,* edited by Matheson Russell, 1–24. Eugene, OR: Cascade, 2009.

Biddle, Martin, with Sally Badham. *King Arthur's Round Table: An Archaeological Investigation.* Woodbridge, England: Boydell, 2000.

Black, Anthony. *The History of Islamic Political Thought: From the Prophet to the Present.* Edinburgh: Edinburgh University Press, 2001.

Blumenberg, Hans. *The Legitimacy of the Modern Age.* Cambridge: MIT, 1986.

Bogdan, Henrik. *Western Esotericism and Rituals of Initiation.* Albany, NY: SUNY, 2007.

Bogdanor, Vernon. *Devolution in the United Kingdom.* Oxford: Oxford University Press, 2001.

Bolt, John. *A Free Church, A Holy Nation: Abraham Kuyper's American Public Theology.* Grand Rapids: Eerdmans, 2001.

Bowlin, John R. "Augustine on Justifying Coercion." *Annual of the Society for Christian Ethics* 17 (1997) 49–70.

Bretherton, Luke. "A New Establishment? Theological Politics and the Emerging Shape of Church-State Relations." *Political Theology* 7 (2006) 371–92.

Broadie, Alexander. "John Duns Scotus and the Idea of Independence." In *The Wallace Book,* edited by Edward J. Cowan, 77–85. Edinburgh: Donald, 2007.

Bromwich, Rachel et al., editors. *The Arthur of the Welsh: The Arthurian Legend in Medieval Welsh Literature.* Cardiff: University of Wales Press, 1991.

Brown, Charles C. *Niebuhr and His Age: Reinhold Niebuhr's Prophetic Role and Legacy.* Philadelphia: Trinity Press International, 1992.

Bruaire, Claude. *Logique et religion chrétienne dans la philosophie de Hegel.* Paris: Éditions du Seuil, 1964.

Bruce, Steve. *Secularization: In Defense of an Unfashionable Theory.* Oxford: Oxford University Press, 2011.

Buber, Martin. *A Land of Two Peoples: Martin Buber on Jews and Arabs.* Edited by Paul R. Mendes-Flohr. Chicago: University of Chicago Press, 2005.

Burk, John. "Moral Law, Privative Evil and Christian Realism: Reconsidering Milbank's 'The Poverty of Niebuhrianism.'" *Studies in Christian Ethics* 22 (2009) 221–28.

Burke, Kathleen. *Old World, New World: The Story of Britain and America*. London: Abacus, 2007.

Burkett, Elinor. *Golda Meir*. London: Gibson Square, 2009.

Campbell, Colin. *Towards a Sociology of Irreligion*. London: Macmillan, 1971.

Casanova, José. *Public Religion in the Modern World*. Chicago: Chicago University Press, 1994.

Caygill, Howard, editor. "The Final NoteBooks of Gillian Rose." *Women: A Cultural Review* 9 (1998) 6–18.

Chapelle, Albert. *Hegel et la religion*. 3 vols. Paris: Éditions Universitaires, 1964–1971.

Chapman, Mark D. *Doing God: Religion and Public Policy in Brown's Britain*. London: Darton, Longman and Todd, 2008.

Cherry, Conrad. *God's New Israel: Religious Interpretations of American Destiny*. Chapel Hill, NC: University of North Carolina Press, 1998.

Chertok, Haim. *He Also Spoke as a Jew: The Life of the Reverend James Parkes*. Portland, OR: Mitchell, 2006.

Choueiri, Youssef M. *Islamic Fundamentalism: The Story of Islamist Movements*. 3rd ed. New York: Continuum, 2011.

Churton, Tobias. *Aleister Crowley: The Biography*. London: Watkins, 2011.

Clark, Victoria. *Allies for Armageddon: The Rise of Christian Zionism*. New Haven: Yale University Press, 2007.

Clarke, Greg. "The Beauty of God in Cairo and Islamabad." In *On Rowan Williams: Critical Essays*, edited by Matheson Russell, 186–204. Eugene, OR: Cascade, 2009.

Coffey, John. *Persecution and Tolerance in Protestant England, 1558–1689*. Harlow, England: Longman, 2000.

Cohen, Hillel. *Army of Shadows: Palestinian Collaboration with Zionism, 1917–1948*. Berkeley, CA: University of California Press, 2008.

Cohn-Sherbok, Dan. *The Jewish Messiah*. Edinburgh: T. & T. Clark, 1997.

Cook, David. *Contemporary Muslim Apocalyptic Literature*. Syracuse, NY: Syracuse University Press, 2005.

Coudert, Alison. *The Impact of the Kabbalah in the Seventeenth Century: The Life and Thought of Francis Mercury Van Helmont (1614–1698)*. Leiden: Brill, 1999.

———. *Leibniz and the Kabbalah*. Dordrecht: Kluwer Academic, 1995.

Cowan, Edward J. *"For Freedom Alone": The Declaration of Arbroath, 1320*. Edinburgh: Birlinn, 2008.

Cranfield, C. E. B. *The International Critical Commentary on the Epistle to the Romans*. Edinburgh: T. & T. Clark, 1975.

D'Costa, Gavin. "One Covenant or Many Covenants? Toward a Theology of Christian-Jewish Relations." *Journal of Ecumenical Studies* 27 (1990) 441–52.

D'Costa, Gavin, John Hick, and Paul F. Knitter, editors. *Christian Uniqueness Reconsidered: The Myth of a Pluralistic Theology of Religions*. Maryknoll, NY: Orbis, 1990.

Dalferth, Ingolf. *Theology and Philosophy*. Oxford: Blackwell, 1989.

Davis, Moshe. *America and the Holy Land*. Westport, CT: Praeger, 1995.

Dittmer, Jason, and Tristam Sturm, editors. *Mapping the End Times: American Evangelical Geopolitics and Apocalyptic Visions*. Farnham, England: Ashgate, 2010.

Dobbs, Betty Jo. *The Janus Face of Genius: The Role of Alchemy in Newton's Thought*. Cambridge: Cambridge University Press, 2002.

Eagleton, Terry. *Holy Terror*. Oxford: Oxford University Press, 2005.

"$800, 000, 000 Asked for Arab Refugees." *New York Times*, 19 December 1951, 1, 20.

Enayat, Hamid. *Modern Islamic Political Thought*. London: Macmillan, 1982.

Erdmann, Carl. *The Origin of the Idea of Crusade*. Princeton, NJ: Princeton University Press, 1977.

Evans, Gwynfor. *Plaid Cymru and Wales*. Llandybie, Wales: Llyfrau'r Dryw, 1950.

Everett, Robert. *Christianity Without Anti-Semitism: James Parkes and the Jewish-Christian Encounter*. Oxford: Pergamon, 1993.

Fackenheim, Emil. *The Religious Dimension of Hegel's Thought*. Bloomington, IN: Indiana University Press, 1967.

Faulkner, R. K. *Richard Hooker and the Politics of a Christian England*. Berkley, CA: University of California Press, 1981.

Fergusson, David. *Bultmann*. London: Chapman, 1992.

———. *Scottish Philosophical Theology, 1700–2000*. Exeter, England: Academic, 2007.

Figgis, J. N. *Churches in the Modern State*. Longmans: London, 1913.

Fineberg, Michael et al., editors. *Antisemitism: The Generic Hatred. Essays in Memory of Simon Wiesenthal*. Edgware, England: Mitchell, 2007.

Ford, David. *Christian Wisdom: Desiring God and Learning to Love*. Cambridge: Cambridge University Press, 2007.

———. *The Future of Christian Theology*. Oxford: Wiley-Blackwell, 2011.

Forrester, Duncan B. *Apocalypse Now? Reflections on Faith in a Time of Terror*. Aldershot, England: Ashgate, 2005.

———. *Theology and Politics*. Oxford: Blackwell, 1992.

Fowden, Garth. *The Egyptian Hermes: A Historical Approach to the Late Pagan Mind*. Princeton, NJ: Princeton University Press, 1986.

Frale, Barbara. "The Chinon Chart Papal Absolution to the Last Templar, Master Jacques de Molay." *Journal of Medieval History* 30 (2004) 109–34.

Frykhom, Amy Johnson. *Rapture Culture: Left Behind in Evangelical America*. New York: Oxford University Press, 2007.

Fuchs, Esther. *Israeli Women's Studies: A Reader*. New Brunswick, NJ: Rutgers University Press, 2005.

Geertz, Clifford. "The Integrative Revolution: Primordial Sentiments and Civil Politics in the New States." In *The Interpretation of Cultures*, edited by Clifford Geertz, 255–310. New York: Fontana, 1973.

Gellner, Ernest. *Nationalism*. London: Weidenfeld and Nicolson, 1997.

———. *Nations and Nationalism*. Oxford: Blackwell, 1983.

Gerber, Haim. "The Limits of Constructedness: Memory and Nationalism in the Arab Middle East." *Nations and Nationalism* 10 (July 2004) 251–68.

Gibbard, Noel. *Cofio Hanner Canrif: Hanes Mudiad Efengylaidd Cymru 1948–98*. Bryntirion, Wales: Gwasg Bryntirion, 2000.

Gignillat, Mark S. *Karl Barth and the Fifth Gospel: Barth's Theological Exegesis of Isaiah*. Aldershot, England: Ashgate, 2009.

Gilbert, Martin. *Israel: A History*. London: Black Swan, 2008.

Gilkey, Langdon. *On Niebuhr: A Theological Study*. Chicago: University of Chicago Press, 2000.

Ginzberg, Louis. *The Legends of the Jews. Vol. I. Bible Times and Characters from the Creation to Jacob*. Philadelphia: The Jewish Publication Society of America, 1909.

Goldberg, David J. *To The Promised Land: A History of Zionist Thought*. London: Penguin, 1996.

Goodricke-Clark, Nicholas. *The Occult Roots of Nazism: Secret Aryan Cults and Their Influence of Nazi Ideology*. London: I. B. Tauris, 2004.

Greenberg, Gershom. *The Holy Land in American Religious Thought, 1620–1948: The Symbiosis of American Religious Approaches to Scripture's Sacred Territory*. Lanham, MD: University Press of America, 1994.

Grosby, Steve. *Biblical Ideas of Nationality, Ancient and Modern*. Winona Lake, IN: Eisenbrauns, 2002.

Hall, John. *Ernest Gellner: An Intellectual Biography*. London: Verso, 2010.

Hamann, J. G. "Golgotha and Sheblimini!" In *Writings on Philosophy and Language*, 164–204. Cambridge: Cambridge University Press, 2007.

Hamill, John, and R. A. Gilbert. *Freemasonry: A Celebration of the Craft*. London: Greenwich Editions, 1992.

Handy, Robert T. *A Christian America: Protestant Hopes and Historical Realities*. New York: Oxford University Press, 1971.

Hannegraaff, Wouter J. *New Age Religion and Western Culture: Esotericism in the Mirror of Secular Thought*. Leiden: Brill, 1996.

———. *Swedenborg. Oetinger. Kant: Three Perspectives on the Secret of Heaven*. West Chester, PA: The Swedenborg Foundation, 2007.

Hanning, Robert W. *The Vision of History in Early Britain: From Gildas to Geoffrey of Monmouth*. New York: Columbia University Press, 1966.

Harink, Douglas. *Paul among the Postliberals*. Grand Rapids: Brazos, 2003.

Harrison, Peter. *The Bible, Protestantism and the Rise of Natural Science*. Cambridge: Cambridge University Press, 1998.

———. *The Fall of Man and the Foundations of Science*. Cambridge: Cambridge University Press, 2007.

Hartmann, Klaus. "Hegel: A Non-Metaphysical View." In *Hegel: A Collection of Critical Essays*, edited by Alasdair MacIntyre, 101–24. Notre Dame, IN: University of Notre Dame Press, 1972.

Harvey, Richard. *Mapping Messianic Jewish Theology: A Constructive Approach*. Milton Keynes, England: Paternoster, 2009.

Hastings, Adrian. *The Construction of Nationhood: Ethnicity, Religion and Nationalism*. Cambridge: Cambridge University Press, 1997.

———. "Holy Lands and Their Political Consequences." *Nations and Nationalism* 9 (2003) 29–54.

Hauerwas, Stanley. "The Church's One Foundation is Jesus Christ Her Lord: Or, In a World Without Foundations, All We Have is the Church." In *Theology Without Foundations: Religious Practice and the Future of Theological Truth*, edited by Stanley Hauerwas, Nancey Murphy, and Mark Nation, 143–62. Nashville: Abingdon, 1994.

———. *With the Grain of the Universe: The Church's Witness and Natural Theology*. Grand Rapids: Brazos, 2001.

Hayes, J. H., and F. C. Preussner. *Old Testament Theology: Its History and Development*. London: SCM, 1985.

Hazony, Yoram. *The Jewish State: The Struggle for Israel's Soul*. New York: Basic, 2001.

Heddendorf, Russell. *From Faith to Fun: The Secularisation of Humour*. Cambridge: Lutterworth, 2009.

Hedley, Douglas. "Radical Orthodoxy and Apocalyptic Difference: Cambridge Platonism and Milbank's Romantic Christian Cabbala." In *Deconstructing Radical*

Orthodoxy: Postmodern Theology, Rhetoric and Truth, edited by William J. Hankey and Douglas Hedley, 99–116. Aldershot, England: Ashgate, 2005.

Hegel, G. W. F. *Hegel's Phenomenology of Spirit*. Translated by A. V. Miller. Oxford: Oxford University Press, 1977.

———. *Natural Law*. Philadelphia: University of Pennsylvania Press, 1975.

Heldt, Petra. "For Brothers to Dwell Together: Re-Thinking Christianity in Israel." In *The Mountain of the Lord: Israel and the Churches*, edited by the Council of Christians and Jews, 30–48. London: Council of Christians and Jews, 1996.

Henken, E. R. *Traditions of the Welsh Saints*. Cambridge: Brewer, 1987.

Herf, Jeffrey. "Convergence: The Classic Case. Nazi Germany, Anti-Semitism and Anti-Zionism during World War II." *Journal of Israeli History* 25 (2006) 63–83.

Hermann, Tamar. "The Bi-National Idea in Israel/Palestine: Past and Present." *Nations and Nationalism* 11 (2005) 381–401.

Heschel, Abraham Joshua. "No Religion Is an Island." *Union Seminary Quarterly* 21.2 pt.1 (1966) 117–34.

Heschel, Susannah. *The Aryan Jesus: Christian Theologians and the Bible in Nazi Germany*. Princeton, NJ: Princeton University Press, 2008.

Hick, John. *God and the Universe of Faiths*. London: Collins, 1977.

Higton, Mike. *Difficult Gospel: The Theology of Rowan Williams*. London: SCM, 2004.

Hobson, Theo. *Against Establishment: An Anglican Polemic*. London: Darton, Longman and Todd, 2003.

———. "Rowan Williams as Anglican Hegelian." *Reviews in Religion and Theology* 12 (2005) 290–97.

Hodgson, Peter C. *Hegel and Christian Theology: A Reading of the Lectures on the Philosophy of Religion*. Oxford: Oxford University Press, 2005.

Hoezl, Michael, and Graham Ward, editors. *The New Visibility of Religion: Studies in Religion and Cultural Hermeneutics*. London: Continuum, 2008.

Horbury, William. *Messianism among Jews and Christians: Twelve Biblical and Historical Studies*. London: T. & T. Clark, 2003.

Hornblower, Simon, and Anthony Spawforth. "Nationalism." In *The Oxford Classical Dictionary*, 3rd ed., edited by Simon Hornblower and Antony Spawforth, 1027–28. Oxford: Oxford University Press, 2003.

Horowitz, Henry. "Protestant Reconciliation in the Exclusion Crisis." *Journal of Ecclesiastical History* 15 (1964) 201–17.

Hume, David. *Dialogues concerning Natural Religion*. London: Penguin, 1990.

Hunsinger, George. "Postliberalism." In *The Cambridge Companion to Postmodern Theology*, edited by Kevin Vanhoozer, 42–57. Cambridge: Cambridge University Press, 2006.

Idel, Moshe. *Kabbalah in Italy, 1280–1510: A Survey*. New Haven: Yale University Press, 2011.

Ignatieff, Michael. *The Lesser Evil: Political Ethics in an Age of Terror*. Edinburgh: Edinburgh University Press, 2004.

Inboden, William. *Religion and American Foreign Policy, 1945–1960: The Soul of Containment*. Cambridge: Cambridge University Press, 2008.

Israel, Jonathan I. *Enlightenment Contested: Philosophy, Modernity, and the Emancipation of Man, 1670–1752*. Oxford: Oxford University Press, 2006.

Jackson, A. C. F. *Rose Croix: The History of the Ancient and Accepted Rite for England and Wales*. London: Lewis Masonic, 1980.

Jaeschke, Walter. "Speculative and Anthropological Criticism of Religion: A Theological Orientation to Hegel and Feuerbach." *Journal of the American Academy of Religion* 48 (1980) 345–64.

Jenkins, Geraint H., and Mari A. Williams, editors. *"Let's Do Our Best for the Ancient Tongue": The Welsh Language in the Twentieth Century.* Cardiff: University of Wales Press, 2000.

Jenkins, Philip. *God's Continent: Christianity, Islam, and Europe's Religious Crisis.* New York: Oxford University Press, 2007.

———. *The Jesus Wars: How Four Patriarchs, Three Queens and Two Emperors Decided What Christians Would Believe for the Next 1,500 years.* London: Harper Collins, 2011.

———. *The Lost History of Christianity: The Thousand-Year Golden Age of the Church in the Middle East, Africa and Asia, and How it Died.* Oxford: Lion, 2007.

———. *The New Faces of Christianity: Believing the Bible in the Global South.* New York: Oxford University Press, 2006.

———. *The Next Christendom: The Coming of Global Christianity.* 3rd ed. New York: Oxford University Press, 2011.

Jones, Dot. *Statistical Evidence Relating to the Welsh Language, 1801–1911=Tystiolaeth Ystadegol yn ymwneud â'r Iaith Gymraeg.* Cardiff: University of Wales Press, 1998.

Jones, R. Tudur. "Christian Nationalism." In *This Land and This People,* edited by Paul Ballard and Huw Jones, 74–97. Cardiff: Collegiate Centre of Theology, University College, 1979.

———. *Grym y Gair a Fflam y Ffydd: Ysgrifau ar Hanes Crefydd yng Nhgymru.* Swansea, Wales: Gwasg John Penry, 1998.

Jourdan, Fabienne. "Dionysos dans le Protréptique de Clément d'Alexandrie: initiations dionysiaques et mystères chrétiennes." *Revue d'Histoire des Religions* 223 (2006) 265–82.

Juergensmeyer, Mark. *Fighting with Gandhi.* Revised edition. San Francisco: Harper Row, 1984.

———. *Gandhi's Way: A Handbook of Conflict Resolution.* Berkeley: University of California Press, 2005.

———. *The New Cold War? Religious Nationalism Confronts the Secular State.* Berkeley: University of California Press, 1993.

———. *Terror in the Mind of God: The Global Rise of Religious Violence.* 3rd ed. Berkeley: University of California Press, 2003.

———. "The Unfinished Task of Reinhold Niebuhr." *Christian Century,* 12 September 1973, 884–87.

Julius, Anthony. *Trials of the Diaspora: A History of Anti-Semitism in England.* Oxford: Oxford University Press, 2010.

Kant, Immanuel. "The Contest of Faculties." In *Kant: Political Writings,* edited by H. S. Reiss, 176–90. Cambridge: Cambridge University Press, 2003.

Karsh, Efraim. *Palestine Betrayed.* New Haven: Yale University Press, 2010.

Katz, Jacob. *Jews and Freemasons in Europe, 1723–1939.* Cambridge: Harvard University Press, 1970.

Kerényi, Carl. *Dionysos: Archetypal Image of Indestructible Life.* Princeton, NJ: Princeton University Press, 1976.

Kerr, Fergus. *Theology After Wittgenstein.* London: SPCK, 1997.

Kidd, Colin. *British Identities Before Nationalism: Ethnicity and Nationhood in the Atlantic World, 1600–1800*. Cambridge: Cambridge University Press, 1999.

———. *The Forging of Races: Race and Scripture in the Protestant Atlantic World, 1600–2000*. Cambridge: Cambridge University Press, 2006.

Krajewski, Stanislaw. "Abraham J. Heschel and the Challenge of Interreligious Dialogue." In *Abraham Joshua Heschel: Philosophy, Theology and Interreligious Dialogue*, edited by Stanislaw Krajewski and Adam Lipszye, 169–80. Wiesbaden, Germany: Harrassowitz, 2009.

Kumar, Krishan. *The Making of English National Identity*. Cambridge: Cambridge University Press, 2003.

Kuyper, Abraham. "The Blurring of the Boundaries." In *Abraham Kuyper: A Centennial Reader*, edited by James D. Bratt, 363–402. Grand Rapids: Eerdmans, 1998.

———. "Calvinism and Politics." In *Lectures on Calvinism*, 78–109. 1898. Reprint. Grand Rapids: Eerdmans, 1931.

———. "Modernism: A Fata Morgana in the Christian Domain." In *Abraham Kuyper: A Centennial Reader*, edited by James D. Bratt, 87–124. Grand Rapids: Eerdmans, 1998.

Larsen, Timothy. *Christabel Pankhurst: Fundamentalism and Feminism in Coalition*. Rochester, NY: Boydell, 2002.

Lash, Nicholas. *Believing Three Ways in One God*. London: SCM, 1992.

Lawless, Elaine J. *Handmaidens of the Lord: Pentecostal Women Preachers and Traditional Religion*. Philadelphia: University of Pennsylvania Press, 1988.

Lehrich, Christopher I. *Heinrich Cornelius Agrippa: The Language of Demons and Angels*. Leiden: Brill, 2003.

Lessing, G. E. *Lessing's Theological Writings*. Edited and translated by Henry Chadwick. Stanford, CA: Stanford University Press, 1957.

Lindbeck, George A. *The Nature of Doctrine: Religion and Theology in a Postliberal Age*. London: SPCK, 1984.

Lindsay, Mark. *Barth, Israel and Jesus: Karl Barth's Theology of Israel*. Aldershot, England: Ashgate, 2007.

Littell, Franklin H. "Reinhold Niebuhr and the Jewish People." *Holocaust and Genocide Studies* 6 (1991) 45–61, citing the Reinhold Niebuhr papers, Library of Congress, Container XIV, 1, Folder 15.

Lloyd, Vincent. "The Secular Faith of Gillian Rose." *Journal of Religious Ethics* 36.4 (2008) 683–705.

Lockwood O'Donovan, Joan. "The Christian Pedagogy and Ethics of Erasmus." In *Bonds of Imperfection: Christian Politics, Past and Present*, edited by Oliver O'Donovan and Joan Lockwood O'Donovan, 121–36. Grand Rapids: Eerdmans, 2004.

———. *Theology of Law and Authority in the English Reformation*. Atlanta: Scholars, 2000.

Lomas, Kathryn. "Italy during the Roman Republic, 338–31 BC." In *The Cambridge Companion to the Roman Republic*, edited by Harriet I. Flower, 199–224. Cambridge: Cambridge University Press, 2004.

Lovejoy, Arthur O. *The Great Chain of Being: A Study of the History of an Idea*. New York: Harper and Row, 1960.

Lovin, Robin W. *Reinhold Niebuhr and Christian Realism*. Cambridge: Cambridge University Press, 1995.

Lozowicz, Yaacov. *Right to Exist: A Moral Defense of Israel's Wars*. New York: Anchor, 2003.

Luhmann, Niklas. *Religious Dogmatics and the Evolution of Societies*. Translated by Peter Beyer. New York: Mellen, 1984.

Luther, Martin. "The Freedom of a Christian." In *Martin Luther's Basic Theological Writings*, edited by Timothy F. Lull, 585–629. Minneapolis: Fortress, 1989.

Maccoby, Hyam. *Antisemitism and Modernity: Innovation and Continuity*. New York: Routledge, 2006.

MacPherson, C. B. *The Theory of Possessive Individualism: Hobbes to Locke*. Oxford: Clarendon, 1962.

Magee, Glen Alexander. *Hegel and the Hermetic Tradition*. Ithaca, NY: Cornell University Press, 2008.

Markham, Ian. "Theological Problems and Israel." In *Christian-Jewish Dialogue: A Reader*, edited by Helen P. Fry, 123–26. Exeter, England: Exeter University Press, 1996.

Markovitz, Andrei S. *Uncouth Nation: Why Europe Dislikes America*. Princeton, NJ: Princeton University Press, 2007.

Martin, David. *On Secularization: Towards a Revised General Theory*. Aldershot, England: Ashgate, 2005.

———. *Pentecostalism—The World Their Parish*. Oxford: Blackwell, 2002.

Martinich, Aloysius. *The Two Gods of Leviathan: Thomas Hobbes on Religion and Politics*. Cambridge: Cambridge University Press, 2002.

Marty, Martin E., and R. Scott Appleby, editors. *The Fundamentalism Project*. 4 vols. Chicago: Chicago University Press, 1993–95.

Mascall, E. L. *The Secularisation of Christianity: An Analysis and Critique*. London: Darton, Longman and Todd, 1965.

Maxwell-Stuart, P. G. *Astrology: From Ancient Babylon to the Present Day*. Stroud: Amberley, 2010.

———. *The Chemical Choir: A History of Alchemy*. London: Continuum, 2008.

McAllister, Laura. *Plaid Cymru: The Emergence of a Political Party*. Bridgend, Wales: Seren, 2001.

McCalla, Arthur. "Louis-Claude de Saint Martin." In *Dictionary of Gnosis and Western Esotericism*, edited by Wouter J. Hannegraaff, 1024–31. Leiden: Brill, 2006.

McCormack, Bruce L. "Grace and Being: The Role of God's Gracious Election in Karl Barth's Theological Ontology." In *Orthodox and Modern: Studies in the Theology of Karl Barth*, 183–200. Grand Rapids: Baker Academic, 2008.

Medoff, Raphael. "Communication: A Further Note on the 'Unconventional Zionism' of Reinhold Niebuhr." *Studies in Zionism* 12 (1991) 85–88.

Mensing, Raymond C. Jr. *Toleration and Parliament 1660-1719*. Washington, DC: University Press of America, 1979.

Merkley, Paul Charles. *The Politics of Christian Zionism, 1891-1948*. London: Cass, 1998.

Milbank, John. *Being Reconciled: Ontology and Pardon*. London: Routledge, 2003.

———. "The Body By Love Possessed: Christianity and Late Capitalism in Britain." In *The Future of Love: Essays in Political Theology*, 75–112. Eugene, OR: Cascade, 2009.

————. "Christianity, The Enlightenment and Islam." ABC Religion and Ethics, 24 August 2010, http://www.abc.net.au/religion/articles/2010/08/24/2991778. htm?topic1=home&topic2.

————. "Divine *Logos* and Human Communication: A Recuperation of Coleridge." In *The Future of Love: Essays in Political Theology,* 3–24. Eugene, OR: Cascade, 2009.

————. *The Future of Love: Essays in Political Theology.* Eugene, OR: Cascade, 2009.

————. "Geopolitical Theology: Economy, Religion and Empire after 9/11." Posted online 16 May 2006. No Pages. Online http://theologyphilosophycentre.co.uk/ papers/Milbank_GeopoliticalTheology.pdf. Reprinted in *The Impact of 9/11 on Religion and Theology,* edited by Matthew J. Morgan, 85–112. New York: Palgrave Macmillan, 2009.

————. "Hume versus Kant: Faith, Reason and Feeling." *Modern Theology* 27 (2011) 276–97.

————. *The Legend of Death: Two Poetic Sequences.* Eugene, OR: Cascade, 2008.

————. "Man as Creative and Historical Being in the Theology of Nicholas of Cusa." *Downside Review* 97 (1979) 245–57.

————. "Postmodern Critical Augustinianism: A Short *Summa* in Forty-Two Responses to Unasked Questions." In *The Future of Love: Essays in Political Theology,* 337–51. Eugene, OR: Cascade, 2009.

————. "The Poverty of Niebuhrianism." In *The Word Made Strange: Theology, Language, Culture*, 233–45. Oxford: Blackwell, 1997.

————. *Radical Orthodoxy: A New Theology.* London: Routledge, 2002.

————. "Religion, Culture and Anarchy: The Attack on the Arnoldian Vision." In *The Future of Love: Essays in Political Theology,* 25–35. Eugene, OR: Cascade, 2009.

————. *Theology and Social Theory.* 1st ed. Oxford: Blackwell, 1990.

————. *Theology and Social Theory: Beyond Secular Reason.* 2nd ed. Oxford: Blackwell, 2006.

Milbank, John, and Alison Milbank. "A Visit to the Coptic Orthodox Church." *Sobornost* 2.2 (1980) 57–64.

Milbank, John, and Catherine Pickstock. *Truth in Aquinas.* London: Routledge, 2001.

Moody, Andrew. "The Hidden Center: Trinity and Incarnation in the Negative (and Positive) Theology of Rowan Williams." In *On Rowan Williams*, edited by Matheson Russell, 25–46. Eugene, OR: Cascade, 2009.

Moorhead, James H. "The American Israel: Protestant Tribalism and Universal Mission." In *Many Are Chosen: Divine Election and Western Nationalism*, edited by William R. Hutchison and Hartmut Lehmann, 145–66. Minneapolis: Fortress, 1994.

Morgan, Catherine. *Early Greek States beyond the Polis.* London: Routledge, 2003.

————. "Ethnicity" in *The Oxford Classical Dictionary.* 3rd ed. Edited by Simon Hornblower and Antony Spawforth, 558–59. Oxford: Oxford University Press, 2003.

Morgan, D. Densil. *The Span of the Cross: Christian Religion and Society in Wales 1914–2000.* Cardiff: University of Wales Press, 1999.

————. *Wales and the Word: Historical Perspectives on Religion and Welsh Identity.* Cardiff: University of Wales Press, 2008.

Morris, Benny. *The Birth of the Palestinian Refugee Problem.* Cambridge: Cambridge University Press, 2004.

Moseley, Carys. *Nations and Nationalism in the Theology of Karl Barth*. Oxford: Oxford University Press, 2013.

Murphy, Francesca Aran. *God Is Not a Story: Realism Revisited*. Oxford: Oxford University Press, 2007.

"Natio." In *The Oxford Latin Dictionary*, edited by P. W. Glare, 1158. Oxford: Clarendon, 1976–82.

Naveh, Eyal. "The Hebraic Foundation of Christian Faith according to Reinhold Niebuhr." *Judaism* 41 (1992) 37–56.

———. *Reinhold Niebuhr and Non-Utopian Liberalism: Beyond Illusion and Despair*. Brighton, England: Sussex Academic Press, 2002.

Nelson, Eric. *The Hebrew Republic: Jewish Sources and the Transformation of European Political Thought*. Cambridge: Harvard University Press, 2010.

Nicholls, David. *Deity and Domination*. London: Routledge, 1989.

———. *God and Government in an "Age of Reason."* London: Routledge, 1995.

Niebuhr, Reinhold. "America and Europe." [1923] In *Young Reinhold Niebuhr: His Early Writings, 1911–1931*, edited by William G. Chrystal, 141–44. New York: Pilgrim, 1977.

———. *The Children of Light and the Children of Darkness: A Vindication of Democracy and a Critique of Its Traditional Defence*. New York: Scribner's Sons, 1944.

———. *Christian Realism and Political Problems*. London: Faber & Faber, 1956.

———. "Christians and the State of Israel." *Christianity and Society* 14.3 (1949) 3.

———. "David and Goliath." *Christianity and Crisis* 27 (26 June 1967) 141.

———. *Discerning the Signs of the Times: Sermons for Today and Tomorrow*. New York, 1946.

———. Editorial note. *Christianity and Crisis* 8 (15 March 1948) 30.

———. *Faith and History: A Comparison of Christian and Modern Views of History*. New York: Scribner's Sons, 1949.

———. "The Future of Israel." *Messenger* 13 (8 June 1948) 12.

———. "The Hazards and the Difficulties of the Christian Ministry." In *Justice and Mercy*, edited by Reinhold Niebuhr and Ursula M. Niebuhr, 129–30. New York: Harper & Row, 1974.

———. *An Interpretation of Christian Ethics*. New York: Harper & Brothers, 1935.

———. "Jews after the War: Parts I and II." In *Love and Justice: Selections from the Shorter Writings of Reinhold Niebuhr*, edited by D. Robertson, 132–41. Louisville: Westminster John Knox, 1992.

———. "Judah Magnes and the Zionists." *Detroit Times* (28 December 1929) 16.

———. *Moral Man and Immoral Society*. New York: Scribner's Sons, 1932.

———. "My Sense of Shame." *Hadassah Newsletter* 19 (December 1938) 59–60.

———. *A Nation So Conceived: Reflections on the History of America from Its Early Vision to Its Present Power*. London: Faber & Faber, 1963.

———. *The Nature and Destiny of Man: A Christian Interpretation*. New York: Scribner's Sons, 1941.

———. "Our Stake in the State of Israel." *New Republic* 136 (4 February 1957) 9–12.

———. "Palestine." *Christianity and Society* 13 (Winter 1948) 5.

———. "The Partition of Palestine." *Christianity and Society* 13 (Winter 1948) 3–4.

———. "Providence and Human Decisions." *Christianity and Crisis* (24 January 1949) 185–86.

———. "The Return of Primitive Religion." *Christendom* 3 (Winter 1938) 1, 6.

————. *The Self and the Drama of History*. New York: Schribner, 1955.

————. "Seven Great Errors of US Foreign Policy." *The New Leader* 24–31 (December 1956) 3–5.

————. "Statement to Anglo-American Committee of Inquiry." Reinhold Niebuhr Papers, Library of Congress; also, Central Zionist Archives/box F40/file no. 59.

————. *The Structure of Nations and Empires*. New York: Scribner, 1959.

Noll, Mark A. *Between Faith and Scholarship: Evangelicals, Scholarship and the Bible in America*. Grand Rapids: Baker Academic, 1991.

O'Regan, Cyril. *The Heterodox Hegel*. Albany, NY: SUNY, 1994.

Ottelenghi, Emmanuele. "Making Sense of European Anti-Semitism." *Human Rights Review* 8 (2007) 104–26.

Parkes, James. *Judaism and Christianity*. Chicago: University of Chicago Press, 1948.

Parrinder, Geoffrey. *Jesus in the Quran*. Oxford: Oneworld, 1995.

Partridge, Christopher. *The Re-Enchantment of the West: Alternative Spiritualities, Sacralisation, Popular Culture and Occulture*. 2 vols. London: T. & T. Clark, 2004–5.

Pearson, Joanne. *Wicca and the Christian Heritage: Ritual, Sex and Magic*. London: Routledge, 2007.

Peters, Rudolph. *Crime and Punishment in Islamic Law: Theory and Practice from the Sixteenth to the Twenty-First Century*. Cambridge: Cambridge University Press, 2005.

Pinker, Steven. *The Better Angels of Our Nature: The Decline of Violence in History and its Causes*. London: Lane, 2011.

Poimandres. In *Hermetica: The Greek* Corpus Hermeticum *and the Latin* Asclepius *in a New English Translation*, edited and translated by Brian P. Copenhaver, 1–7. Cambridge: Cambridge University Press, 1995.

Pope Clement XII. *In eminenti*. 1738. No pages. Online http://www.papalencyclicals. net/Clem12/c12inemengl.htm.

Pope, Robert. *Seeking God's Kingdom: The Nonconformist Social Gospel in Wales, 1906–1939*. Cardiff: University of Wales Press, 1999.

Raaflaub, Kurt A. "Poets, Lawgivers, and the Beginnings of Political Reflection in Archaic Greece." In *The Cambridge History of Greek and Roman Political Thought*, edited by Christopher Rowe and Malcolm Schofield, 24–25. Cambridge: Cambridge University Press, 2000.

Radcliffe, Timothy. "The Old Testament as Word of God: Canon and Identity." *New Blackfriars*, 61.721 (1980) 266–75.

Ramsey, Paul. *Speak Up for Just War or Pacifism: A Critique of the United Methodist Bishops' Pastoral Letter "In Defence of Creation."* University Park, PA: Pennsylvania State University Press, 1988.

Reeves, John C., editor. *Bible and Qur'ān: Essays in Scriptural Intertextuality*. Atlanta: Society for Biblical Literature, 2003.

Rice, Daniel F. "Felix Frankfurter and Reinhold Niebuhr, 1940–1964." *Journal of Law and Religion* 1.2 (1983) 325–426.

————. "Reinhold Niebuhr and Hans Morgenthau: A Friendship with Contrasting Shades of Realism." *Journal of American Studies* 42 (2008) 255–91.

Richards, Jeffrey, et al., editors, *Diana: The Making of a Media Saint*. London: I. B. Tauris, 1999.

Ridley, Jasper. *The Freemasons*. London: Constable, 2004.

Riggans, Walter. *Israel and Zionism.* Edinburgh: Handsel, 1988.

Roberts, Peter. "The Union with England and the Identity of 'Anglican' Wales." *Transactions of the Royal Historical Society,* 5th series, 22 (1972) 49–70.

Roberts, Richard H. "Transcendental Sociology? A Critique of John Milbank's *Theology and Social Theory: Beyond Secular Reason.*" *Scottish Journal of Theology* 46 (1993) 527–35.

Roberts, W. Arvon. *150 Welsh Americans.* Llanrwst, Wales: Gwasg Carreg Gwalch, 2007.

Robinson, John A. T. *Honest to God.* London: SCM, 1963.

Robison, John. *Proofs of a Conspiracy against All the Religions and Governments of Europe: Carried on in the Secret Meetings of Freemasons, Illuminati and Reading Societies.* Boston: Bloomfield, 1967.

Rose, Gillian. *The Broken Middle: Out of Our Ancient Society.* Oxford: Blackwell, 1992.

———. *Dialectic of Nihilism: Post-Structuralism and Law.* Oxford: Blackwell, 1984.

———. *Hegel contra Sociology.* London: Athlone, 1985.

———. *Judaism and Modernity: Philosophical Essays.* Oxford: Blackwell, 1993.

———. *Love's Work: A Reckoning With Life.* London: Chatto and Windus, 1995.

———. *Mourning Becomes the Law.* Cambridge University Press, 1995.

———. *Paradiso.* London: Menard, 1999.

Rosenblatt, Helena. *Rousseau and Geneva: from the First Discourse to the Social Contract, 1749-1762.* Cambridge: Cambridge University Press, 1997.

Rosenzweig, Franz. *The Star of Redemption.* Notre Dame, IN: Notre Dame University Press, 1985.

Routledge, Bruce. "The Antiquity of the Nation? Critical Reflections from the Ancient Near East." *Nations and Nationalism* 9.2 (2003) 213–34.

Ruether, Rosemary Radford. *Sexism and God-Talk: Towards a Feminist Theology.* Boston: Beacon, 1983.

Russell, Matheson. "Dispossession and Negotiation: Rowan Williams on Hegel and Political Theology." In *On Rowan Williams: Critical Essays,* edited by Matheson Russell, 85–114. Eugene, OR: Cascade, 2009.

Ruston, Roger. *Human Rights and the Image of God.* London: SCM, 2004.

Sagorin, Perez. "Cudworth and Hobbes on Is and Ought." In *Philosophy, Science, and Religion in England 1640-1700,* edited by Richard Kroll et al., 128–48. Cambridge: Cambridge University Press, 1992.

Scheil, Andrew P. *The Footsteps of Israel: Understanding Jews in Anglo-Saxon England.* Ann Arbor, MI: University of Michigan Press, 2004.

Scholem, Gershom. *Origins of the Kabbalah.* New York: Jewish Publication Society, 1987.

Schwartz, Howard, editor. *Tree of Souls: The Mythology of Judaism.* Oxford: Oxford University Press, 2007.

Scofield, Cyrus I. *The Scofield Reference Bible.* [1909]. Reprinted as Cyrus Scofield, *The Scofield Study Bible.* New York: Oxford University Press, 1945.

Scruton, Roger. *England: An Elegy.* London: Chatto & Windus, 2000.

Segal, Robert A. Review of *From Faith to Fun: The Secularisation of Humour* by Russell Heddendorf. *Times Higher Education,* 8 April, 2010.

Seitz, Christopher R. "Scripture Becomes Religion(s): The Theological Crisis of Serious Biblical Interpretation in the Twentieth Century." In *Renewing Biblical Interpretation,* edited by Craig Bartholomew et al., 40–65. Carlisle, England: Paternoster, 2000.

Sell, Alan P. F. *Defending and Declaring the Faith: Some Scottish Examples 1860–1920.* Exeter, England: Paternoster, 1987.

———. *Nonconformist Theology in the Twentieth Century.* Milton Keynes, England: Paternoster, 2006.

———. *Philosophical Idealism and Christian Belief.* Cardiff: University of Wales Press, 1995.

Senior, Michael. *Did Prince Madog Discover America? An Investigation.* Llanrwst, Wales: Gwasg Carreg Gwalch, 2004.

Sennett, Richard. *The Craftsman.* London: Penguin, 2009.

Seward, Desmond. *The Monks of War: The Military Religious Orders.* London: Penguin, 1995.

Shanks, Andrew. *Against Innocence: Gillian Rose's Reception and Gift of Faith,* with a foreword by Giles Fraser. London: SCM, 2008.

———. *Civil Society, Civil Religion.* Oxford: Blackwell, 1995.

———. *Hegel's Political Theology.* Cambridge: Cambridge University Press, 1991.

———. *The Other Calling: Theology, Intellectual Vocation and Truth.* Aldershot, England: Ashgate, 2007.

Shepherd, Robin. *A State Beyond the Pale: Europe's Problem With Israel.* London: Weidenfeld & Nicolson, 2009.

Shils, Edward. "Nation, Nationality, Nationalism and Civil Society." *Nations and Nationalism* 1 (1995) 93–118.

———. "Primordial, Personal, Sacred and Civil Ties." *British Journal of Sociology* 7 (1957) 13–45.

Shortt, Rupert, editor. *God's Advocates: Christian Thinkers in Conversation.* London: Darton, Longman, and Todd, 2005.

———. *Rowan's Rule: The Biography of the Archbishop.* London: Hodder & Stoughton, 2008.

Siker, Jeffrey S. *Scripture and Ethics: Twentieth-Century Portraits.* New York: Oxford University Press, 1997.

Silver, Abba Hillel. *A History of Messianic Speculation in Israel: From the First through the Seventeenth Century.* New York: Macmillan, 1927.

Smalley, Beryl W. *Historians in the Middle Ages.* London: Thames and Hudson, 1974.

Smith, Anthony D. "Adrian Hastings on Nations and Nationalism." *Nations and Nationalism* 9 (2003) 25–28.

———. *Chosen Peoples: Sacred Sources of National Identity.* Oxford: Oxford University Press, 2003.

———. *The Cultural Foundations of Nations: Hierarchy, Covenant, and Republic.* Oxford: Blackwell, 2008.

———. *The Ethnic Origins of Nations.* Oxford: Blackwell, 1986.

———. *Myths and Memories of the Nation.* New York: Oxford University Press, 1999.

———. "Nationalism and Classical Social Theory." *British Journal of Sociology* 34 (1983) 19–38.

———. "Nations and History." In *Understanding Nationalism,* edited by Monsterrat Guibernau and John Hutchinson, 9–31. Cambridge: Polity, 2005.

———. *Nationalism and Modernism.* London: Routledge, 1998.

Solomon, Norman et al., editors. *Abraham's Children: Jews, Christians and Muslims in Conversation.* New York: Continuum, 2005.

Song, Robert. *Christianity and Liberal Society.* Oxford: Oxford University Press, 1997.

Spector, Stephen. *Evangelicals and Israel: The Story of American Christian Zionism.* Oxford: Oxford University Press, 2009.

Stein, Jock. "Scots wha hae . . . !" *Prophecy Today* 13.2 (1997) 19–20.

Steiner, George. *Real Presences: Is There Anything In What We Say?* London: Faber & Faber, 1989.

Stone, Ronald H. *Professor Reinhold Niebuhr: A Mentor to the Twentieth Century.* Louisville: Westminster John Knox, 1992.

————. *Prophetic Realism: Beyond Militarism and Pacifism in an Age of Terror.* London: T. & T. Clark, 2005.

————. *Reinhold Niebuhr: Prophet to Politicians.* Washington, DC: University Press of America, 1981.

Stout, Jeffrey. *Ethics After Babel: The Language of Morals and their Discontent.* Rev. ed. Princeton, NJ: Princeton University Press, 2001.

Strathmann, H. "*Laos.*" In *Theological Dictionary of the New Testament*, edited by Gerhard Kittel and Gerhard Friedrich, 499–505. Grand Rapids: Eerdmans, 1985.

Strauss, Leo. *Natural Right and History.* Chicago: Chicago University Press, 1953.

Stroumsa, Gedaliahu. *Another Seed: Studies in Gnostic Myth.* Leiden: Brill, 1984.

Sturlusonar, Snorri. *The Prose Edda: Tales from Norse Mythology.* Translated by Jesse L. Byock. New York: Penquin, 2005.

Swerdlow, N. M., editor. *Ancient Astronomy and Celestial Divination.* Cambridge: MIT, 1999.

Sykes, Stephen. *Power and Christian Theology.* London: Continuum, 2008.

Taylor, Charles. *The Ethics of Authenticity.* Cambridge, MA. Harvard University Press, 1992.

————. "Nationalism and Modernity." In *Dilemmas and Connections: Selected Essays*, 81–104. Cambridge: Belknap Press of Harvard University Press, 2011.

————. "The Politics of Recognition." In *Multiculturalism: Examining the "Politics of Recognition,"* edited by Amy Guttman, 25–74. Princeton, NJ: Princeton University Press, 1994.

————. *A Secular Age.* Cambridge: Belknap Press of Harvard University Press, 2007.

————. *Sources of the Self: The Making of Modern Identity.* Cambridge: Cambridge University Press, 1989.

Temple Church History Timeline. Online: http://www.templechurch.com/TC_History/timeline2.html.

Thiemann, Ronald. "The Promising God: The Gospel as Narrated Promise." In *Why Narrative? Readings on Narrative Theology*, edited by Stanley Hauerwas and L. Gregory Jones, 320–47. Grand Rapids: Eerdmans, 1989.

Thomas, Keith. *Religion and the Decline of Magic: Studies in Popular Beliefs in Sixteenth and Seventeenth Century England.* New York: Oxford University Press, 1997.

Thomas, George (Viscount Tonypandy). "Defense of the British Parliament." *Prophecy Today* 13.3 (1997) 17–18.

Thomas, Keith. *Religion and the Decline of Magic.* Harmondsworth, England: Penguin, 1974.

Tierney, Brian. *The Origins of Papal Infallibility, 1150–1350: A Study of the Concept of Infallibility, Sovereignty and Tradition in the Middle Ages.* Leiden: Brill, 1988.

Tomasoni, Francesco. *Modernity and the Final Aim of History: The Debate over Judaism from Kant to the Young Hegelians.* Dordrecht: Kluwer Academic, 2003.

Torrance, David, and George W. Taylor. *Israel God's Servant: God's Key to the Redemption of the World*. Milton Keynes, England: Paternoster, 2007.

Touraine, Alain. *Un désir d'histoire*. Paris: Stock, 1977.

Troeltsch, Ernst. *The Social Teaching of the Christian Churches*. Translated by Olive Wyon. Chicago, IL: University of Chicago Press, 1981.

Tsimhoni, Daphne. "Continuity and Change in Communal Autonomy: The Christian Communal Organizations in Jerusalem, 1948–1980." *Middle Eastern Studies* 22 (July 1986) 398.

Van Bladel, Kevin. *The Arabic Hermes: From Pagan Sage to Prophet of Science*. Oxford: Oxford University Press, 2009.

Van Buren, Paul M. *Discerning the Way*. New York: Seabury, 1980.

———. *The Edges of Language*. New York: Macmillan, 1972.

———. *The Secular Meaning of the Gospel*. New York: Macmillan, 1963.

———. *Theological Explorations*. London: SCM, 1968.

———. *A Theology of the Jewish-Christian Reality*. 3 vols. San Francisco: Harper & Row, 1980–1988.

Van Der Berghe, Pierre. *The Ethnic Phenomenon*. New York: Elsiever, 1979.

Van Driel, Edwin Chr. *Incarnation Anyway: Arguments for Supralapsarian Christology*. New York: Oxford University Press, 2008.

Vidu, Adonis. *Postliberal Theological Method: A Critical Study*. Milton Keynes, England: Paternoster, 2005.

Voegelin, Eric. "On Hegel: A Study in Sorcery." In *Published Essays 1966–1985. The Collected Works of Eric Voegelin*, vol. 12, edited by Ellis Sandoz, 213–55. Baton Rouge, LA: Louisiana State University Press, 1990.

Wachter, Johann Georg. *De primordiis Christianae religionis*. Freidenker der europäischen Aufklärung vol. 1. Stuttgart-Bad Cannstatt: Frommann-Holzboog, 1995.

Wallace, Robert M. *Hegel's Philosophy of Reality, Freedom and God*. Cambridge: Cambridge University Press, 2005.

Wallis, James H. *Post-Holocaust Christianity: Paul van Buren's Theology of the Jewish-Christian Reality*. Lanham, MD: University Press of America, 1997.

Ward, Benedicta. *The Venerable Bede*. New York: Continuum, 2002.

Ward, Michael. *Planet Narnia*. Oxford: Oxford University Press, 2008.

Webb, James. *The Harmonious Circle: The Lives of G. I. Gurdjeff, P. D. Ouspensky, and Their Followers*. New York: Putnam, 1980.

Weber, Max. *The Sociology of Religion*. Translated by Ephraim Fischoff. London: Methuen, 1971.

Weber, Timothy P. *On the Road to Armageddon: How Evangelicals Became Israel's Best Friend*. Grand Rapids: Baker Academic, 2004.

Webster, John. "Rowan Williams on Scripture." In *Scripture's Doctrine and Theology's Bible*, edited by Markus Bockmuehl and Alan J. Torrance, 105–24. Grand Rapids: Baker Academic, 2008.

Whalen, Brett Edward. *Dominion of God: Christendom and Apocalypse in the Middle Ages*. Cambridge: Harvard University Press, 2009.

Williams, Diane M., and John R. Kenyon, editors. *The Impact of the Edwardian Castles in Wales: The Proceedings of a Conference Held at Bangor University, 7–9 September 2007*. Oxford: Oxbow, 2010.

Williams, Gwyn A. *Madoc: The Making of a Myth*. Oxford: Oxford University Press, 1987.

Williams, Rowan. *After Silent Centuries*. Oxford: Perpetua, 1994.

———. "Analysing Atheism: Unbelief and the World of Faiths." In *Bearing the Word: Prophecy in Biblical and Quranic Perspective. A Record of the Third "Building Bridges" Seminar Held at Georgetown University, WA DC, 30 March–1 April 2004*, edited by Michael Ipgrave, 1–10. New York: Church, 2005.

———. "Belief and Theology: Some Core Questions." In *God's Advocates: Christian Thinkers in Conversation*, edited by Rupert Shortt, 1–23. London: Darton, Longman and Todd, 2005.

———. "Between Politics and Metaphysics: Reflections in the Wake of Gillian Rose." [1995]. In *Wrestling With Angels: Conversations in Modern Theology*, edited by Mike Higton, 53–76. London: SCM, 2007.

———. "Beyond Liberalism." *Political Theology* 3 (2001) 64–73.

———. *Christian Imagination in Poetry and Polity: Some Anglican Voices from Temple to Herbert*. Oxford: SLG, 2004.

———. "Christian Resources for the Renewal of Vision." In *Renewal of Social Vision*, edited by Alison J. Elliott and Ian Swanson, 2–7. Edinburgh: Centre for Theology and Public Issues, University of Edinburgh, 1989.

———. "The Discipline of Scripture." [1990/1991]. In *On Christian Theology*, 44–59. Oxford: Blackwell, 2000.

———. "The Ethics of SDI." In *Nuclear Weapons Debate: Theological and Ethical Issues*, edited by Richard J. Bauckham and R. John Elford, 162–67. London: SCM, 1989.

———. "The Finality of Christ." [1990]. In *On Christian Theology*, 93–106. Oxford: Blackwell, 2000.

———, editor. *The Gemini Poets*. Cambridge: Gemini, 1972.

———. *Headwaters*. Oxford: Perpetua, 2008.

———. "Hegel and the Gods of Postmodernity." [1992]. In *Wrestling with Angels: Conversations in Modern Theology*, edited by Mike Higton, 25–34. London: SCM, 2007.

———. "Holy Land, Holy People." 14 April 2004. No Pages. Online http://www.archbishopofcanterbury.org/articles.php/1840/lecture-to-the-5th-international-sabeel-conference-holy-land-and-holy-people-jerusalem.

———. "Incarnation and the Renewal of Community." [1989]. In *On Christian Theology*, 225–38. Oxford: Blackwell, 2000.

———. "The Judgment of the World." [1989]. In *On Christian Theology*, 29–43. Oxford: Blackwell, 2000.

———. "Lossky, the *Via Negativa* and the Foundations of Theology." [1980]. In *Wrestling with Angels*, edited by Mike Higton, 1–24. London: SCM, 2007.

———. *Lost Icons: Reflections on Cultural Bereavement*. London: T. & T. Clark, 2003.

———. "Mankind, Nation, State." In *This Land and This People*, edited by Paul Ballard and Huw Jones, 119–25. Cardiff: Collegiate Centre of Theology, University College, 1979.

———. "The Nature of a Sacrament." [1987]. In *On Christian Theology*, 197–208. Oxford: Blackwell, 2000.

———. "The Necessary Non-Existence of God." In *Simone Weil's Philosophy of Culture: Readings toward a Divine Humanity*, edited by Richard H. Bell, 52–76. Cambridge: Cambridge University Press, 1993.

————. "Nobody Knows Who I Am till the Judgment Morning." [1988]. In *On Christian Theology*, 276–89. Oxford: Oxford University Press, 2000.

————. "On Being Creatures." [1989]. In *On Christian Theology*, 64–78. Oxford: Blackwell, 2000.

————. *Remembering Jerusalem*. Oxford: Perpetua, 2001.

————. "Richard Hooker (1554–1600): Contemplative Pragmatism." In *Anglican Identities*, 24–39. London: Darton, Longman and Todd, 2004.

————. *Sergei Bulgakov: Towards a Russian Political Theology*. Edinburgh: T. & T. Clark, 1999.

————. "The Spirit of the Age to Come." *Sobornost: The Journal of the Fellowship of St. Alban and St. Sergius* 6 (1974) 613–26.

————. *Star Wars: Safeguard or Threat?: A Christian Perspective*. Cana Occasional Papers 1. Worcester, England: Clergy Against Nuclear Arms, 1987.

————. "This Scepter'd Isle: Culture and Power in an Offshore Setting." In *Being British: The Search for the Values that Bind the Nation*, edited by Matthew D'Ancona, 145–53. Edinburgh: Mainstream, 2009.

————. "Trinity and Ontology." [1989]. In *On Christian Theology*, 148–66. Oxford: Blackwell, 2000.

————. "Trinity and Revelation." [1986]. In *On Christian Theology*, 131–47. Oxford: Blackwell, 2000).

————. "Violence and the Gospel in South Africa." *New Blackfriars* 65.774 (1984) 503–13

————. "Violence, Society and the Sacred." Oxford: Oxford Project for Peace Studies, 1989.

————. *The Wound of Knowledge: Christian Spirituality from the New Testament to Saint John of the Cross*. London: Darton, Longman and Todd, 1979.

Williams, Rowan, and Mark Collier. *Peacemaking Theology: A Study Book for Individuals and Groups*. Beginning Now 1. London: Dunamis, 1984.

Williams, W. Llewelyn. *Young Wales Movement: Cymru Fydd: Its Aims and Objects*. Roberts Bros., 1894. Wilson, Bryan. *Religion in Sociological Perspective*. Oxford: Oxford University Press, 1982.

Winn, Christian T. Collins. *"Jesus is Victor!" The Significance of the Blumhardts for the Theology of Karl Barth*. Eugene, OR: Pickwick, 2009.

Witsius, Herman. *The Question, Was Moses the Author of the Pentateuch, Answered in the Affirmative*. Translated by John Donaldson. Edinburgh: Maclaren & Macniven, 1877.

Wolf, Arnold Jacob. "The Tragedy of Gillian Rose." *Judaism* 46 (1997) 481–88.

Wolfson, Eliot. "Messianism in the Christian Kabbalah of Johann Kemper." In *Millenarianism and Messianism in the Early Modern European Culture: Jewish Messianism in the Early Modern World*, edited by M. D. Goldish and R. H. Popkin, 139–87. Dordrecht: Kluwer Academic, 2001.

Wolterstorff, Nicholas. *Justice: Rights and Wrongs*. Princeton, NJ: Princeton University Press, 2008.

Yoder, John Howard. "Reinhold Niebuhr and Christian Pacifism." *Mennonite Quarterly Review* 29 (1955) 101–17.

Yovel, Yirmyahu. *Dark Riddle: Hegel, Nietzsche and the Jews*. Philadelphia: Pennsylvania State University Press, 1998.

Index

13932638R00180

Printed in Poland
by Amazon Fulfillment
Poland Sp. z o.o., Wrocław

The Basic Teachings of Judaism

The tenth and eleventh fundamental beliefs are in God's knowledge of the deeds of humankind and his concern about them; and that the rewards and punishes people for their good or evil ways. This is meant to negate the ideas that God has withdrawn from involvement in the day-to-day running of the world, and that there is no ultimate justice. **The notion of a God who is interested in the doings of both nations and individuals,** and who metes out the deserts of the righteous and the wicked, characterizes the salvation-history of the Bible and is the assumption behind the commandments and laws which presuppose that Jews are free to choose how they behave and are consequently responsible for their choices. Although some radical theologians have questioned these basic assumptions about God, particularly in the light of the killing of millions of Jews by the Nazis, which seems to make a mockery of the idea of a just world and a caring God, they have remained part and parcel of mainstream Jewish thought in the modern world.